IN PURSUIT OF JUSTICE: EXAMINING THE EVIDENCE OF THE HOLOCAUST

IN PURSUIT

EXAMINING THE EVIDENCE OF THE HOLOCAUST

OF JUSTICE

UNITED STATES HOLOCAUST MEMORIAL MUSEUM WASHINGTON, DC

A PROJECT OF THE UNITED STATES HOLOCAUST MEMORIAL COUNCIL

Library of Congress Card Number: 96-061170

ISBN: 0-89604-702-4

Project Director: Stephen Goodell

Editor: Kevin Mahoney
Historians: Patricia Heberer, Sybil Milton
Editorial Assistants: Neal Guthrie, Linda Bixby, Jeremy Leffler
Research Assistants: Carolyn Van Newkirk, Wendy Lower
Photo Research: Anthony Sheehan
Map Research: Dewey Hicks
Copy Editor: Edward Phillips

Design: Marc Zaref Design, Inc.
Printing: Collins Lithographing, Inc.

Cover: The defendants in the dock at the INTERNATIONAL MILITARY TRIBUNAL; ca. 1945. *Front row, left to right:* Göring, Hess, von Ribbentrop, Keitel, Kaltenbrunner, Rosenberg, Frank, Frick, Streicher, Funk, and Schacht; *rear row:* Dönitz, Raeder, von Schirach, Sauckel, Jodl, von Papen, Seyss-Inquart, Speer, von Neurath, and Fritzche. (NARA)

Frontispiece: The headphones worn by Walter Funk, a defendant at the INTERNATIONAL MILITARY TRIBUNAL, that enabled him to hear simultaneous translation of the trial proceedings.
(Documents courtesy Archive, Research Institute, USHMM; headphones gift of IBM Corporation, Collections, USHMM; photograph by Edward Owen)

NOTE TO THE READER

This volume examines ten major aspects of the Holocaust using documents gathered as evidence for the numerous war crimes trials of the past fifty years. These themes provide the reader a framework for studying the events that led to and comprised the Holocaust from the discriminatory laws of 1933 to the murder of millions during World War II. Most of the selected documents served as prosecution exhibits and, having therefore met strict "rules of evidence," their authenticity is beyond doubt. The trial at which each was introduced is noted and cross-referenced to the Trials Appendix. A few additional selections have been included to address facets of the Holocaust that were never subject to a war crimes trial.

The following notes briefly explain the editorial conventions used in this volume:

Glossary entries: Names and terms highlighted in SMALL CAPITALS in the introductions, essays, and back matter are more fully explained in the Glossary.

Trial appendix entries: Names of trials highlighted in UNDERLINED SMALL CAPITALS in the introductions, essays, and back matter are more fully explained in the Trials Appendix.

Spelling: All sections contain the originally published spellings except where noted. As a result, German language terminology may vary, and German vowels with an umlaut are often transliterated by the addition of an "e": for example, Führer becomes Fuehrer.

Photographs: Photo credit abbreviations are

    USHMM: Photo Archives, United States Holocaust Memorial Museum, Washington, D.C.

    NARA: Still Picture Branch, National Archives and Records Administration, College Park, Maryland.

Prints of all the photographs used in this volume may be found in the Photo Archives, Research Institute, United States Holocaust Memorial Museum.

CONTENTS

MESSAGE FROM THE COUNCIL

The United States Holocaust Memorial Museum serves as this country's memorial to the millions of people murdered during the Holocaust, the state-sponsored, systematic persecution and annihilation of European Jews by Nazi Germany and its collaborators between 1933 and 1945. Jews were the primary victims—six million were murdered; Gypsies, the handicapped, and Poles were also targeted for destruction or decimation for racial, ethnic, or national reasons. Millions more, including homosexuals, Jehovah's Witnesses, Soviet prisoners of war, and political dissidents, also suffered grievous oppression and death under Nazi tyranny.

Chartered by a unanimous Act of Congress and situated adjacent to the national Mall in Washington, D.C., the Museum strives to broaden public understanding of the history of the Holocaust and related issues, including those of contemporary significance, through exhibitions; research and publications; the collection and preservation of material evidence, art, and artifacts relating to the Holocaust; the distribution of educational materials and teacher resources; and a variety of public programming.

This year marks the 50th anniversary of the verdict from the International Military Tribunal that passed judgment on the Holocaust's major perpetrators. What made these trials so significant is the fact that after victory the Allied forces did not pursue vengeance. Instead, they chose to implement a due process of law to hold Germany's political and military leaders personally accountable for the heinous crimes they committed. This volume examines the events of the Holocaust using evidence presented at this tribunal and at some of the many war crimes trials that have taken place since 1945. Together the trials accomplished two ancilliary objectives—the establishment of complicity by all layers of the society that perpetrated the crimes and the thorough documentation of these unprecedented atrocities.

United States Holocaust Memorial Council

Miles Lerman, Chairman
Ruth B. Mandel, Vice Chair

Days of Remembrance Committee

Benjamin Meed, Chair

ACKNOWLEDGMENTS

Compilation of materials for a book of this nature requires a wide range of expert skills and many institutional resources.

We thank Professor Benjamin Ferencz, chief prosecutor for the United States at the *Einsatzgruppen* Trial of the Nuremberg war crimes trials and professor of international law at Pace University School of Law, whose comprehensive introductory essay provides understanding of the development of war crimes trials to the present day and for the future.

We express our appreciation to the academic reviewers: Professor Henry Friedlander, Brooklyn College of the City University of New York; Counsellor Alan A. Ryan, Jr., University Attorney, Harvard University; and Professor James J. Weingartner, Southern Illinois University at Edwardsville.

We thank Michael Berenbaum, Director, Research Institute, United States Holocaust Memorial Museum, and the personnel of the Research Institute's departments: Genya Markon, Director, Leslie Swift, Archivist, and the staff of the Photo Archives; the staff of the Library; Brewster Chamberlin, Director, Jerzy Halberstadt, Project Director —Poland, and the staff of the Archives; and William Meinecke, Historian, of the Wexner Learning Center.

We appreciate the contribution of Robin Cookson of the Textual Reference Branch of the National Archives and Records Administration, College Park, Maryland.

We graciously thank the authors, publishers, archives, and photographers who have granted permission to use their materials. Any requests for reproduction of these materials should be directed to the publishers or archives.

AXIS CONTROL IN EUROPE, 1942

● Cities   —— Europe 1937 Boundaries   **——** Front Line, Fall 1942   ▓▓ Furthest Extent of Axis Control in Europe, Fall 1942

Benjamin Ferencz (behind microphone), chief prosecutor at the
<u>EINSATZGRUPPEN TRIAL</u> (and author of the introductory essay in this
volume), presents evidence during the trial; ca. 1947. (USHMM)

WAR CRIMES TRIALS
THE HOLOCAUST AND THE RULE OF LAW

by Benjamin B. Ferencz

Background

From the ashes of the Holocaust there arose the universal determination that such crimes against humanity would never again be allowed to occur. The agonizing memories of millions slaughtered cried out for justice or revenge. The German leaders had been clearly and repeatedly warned that they would be held accountable for violating standards long proclaimed by civilized nations. Great Britain's Prime Minister Winston Churchill favored summary execution of the top Nazi officials, but the United States insisted upon punishment of only the guilty after conviction in a fair trial.

At the International Military Tribunal established just after World War II to try the major criminals of the German regime, the chief prosecutor for the United States, Supreme Court Justice Robert H. Jackson, explained that this unprecedented trial was not a case of victors' revenge: "That four great nations flushed with victory and stung with injury stay the hand of vengeance and voluntarily submit their captive enemies to the judgment of the law is one of the most significant tributes that Power ever has paid to Reason. . . . We must never forget that the record on which we judge these defendants today is the record on which history will judge us tomorrow."[1] Thus began a historical process whereby the rule of law became a leading instrumentality for articulating, vindicating, and protecting the fundamental human rights of people everywhere—regardless of their race or creed.

The movement away from barbarism toward a new humanity had been a slow, evolutionary development. In ancient times it was considered legitimate to kill one's enemies as well as their suckling babes. Taking one's foes as slaves was a step forward compared to outright slaughter. Though the modern concept of human rights was then unknown, medieval theologians who advocated the divine right to subjugate and slaughter infidels as "barbarians" faced dissent. In revulsion against the cruelties of man's most inhumane activity—warfare—humanitarian obligations began to be asserted. The old ecclesiastical idea of a "just war" was clarified: wars had to be a last resort, justly caused and justly fought and proportional to the injuries sought to be corrected. Specific rules were agreed upon that defined the limits of permissible conduct even in warfare.

Among the modern milestones in the trend toward international agreements about the conduct of war and international arbitration were the Hague Conventions of

The Palace at the Hague, Netherlands. (NARA)

1899 and 1907. Signed by representatives of twenty-six countries, the Convention of 1899 introduced a "Permanent Court of Arbitration" for the "pacific settlement of international disputes" as well as declarations prohibiting gas warfare and certain types of explosives. The Convention of 1907, proposed by U.S. President Theodore Roosevelt and ratified by forty-four nations, asserted that international conflicts could best be resolved through a series of international conferences and arbitration.

These conventions demonstrated positive steps toward peace and humane conduct. There remained a substantial gap, however, between the agreements on humanitarian conduct and the actual practices of nations still insisting that sovereign states were above the law. During World War I—as in later wars—"military necessity" became the excuse to subordinate humanitarian considerations to the drive for victory. After Germany's defeat in World War I, an Allied commission concluded in 1919 that those who had violated the laws of war and humanity, by aggression and atrocities such as the use of poison gas and the bombing of civilians, should stand trial, "however high their position."[2] The former kaiser of Germany, Wilhelm II, was to face an international tribunal for "a supreme offense against international morality and the sanctity of treaties";[3] the Netherlands, however, refused to extradite him.

German officers who were eventually put before a German court for atrocities and war crimes got off with a slap on the wrist. The victors, recognizing that a head of state had never before been charged with aggression or "war crimes," did not try to enforce the trial obligations set down by the Treaty of Versailles (1918). They expressed their clear intention, however, that henceforth the prohibitions and responsibilities would be clarified in order to counter any future argument that punishment was based on *ex post facto* law. The world was put on notice that aggressive war was illegal and the initiation of war would be considered a punishable individual crime in the future. This intention was reinforced by the internationally ratified Kellogg-Briand Pact of 1928 that outlawed war as an instrument of national policy.

The League of Nations, the forerunner to the United Nations, appointed a Committee for the Progressive Codification of International Law. This Committee sought to reach agreements on international pacts of peace during the interwar era. But such agreements were normally vague or evasive, and sovereign nations were very reluctant to be bound by legal restraints that might affect their vital interests. The absence of a clear code of permissible or prohibited behavior that would bind all countries as well as the unwillingness of sovereign states to accept the compulsory jurisdiction of any international tribunal—civil or criminal—left international law severely impaired. Ironically, the United States was unable to join the League because President Woodrow Wilson, despite approval by a majority of senators, was unable to muster the required consent by two-thirds of the full U.S. Senate. With its principal sponsor and most powerful supporter absent, the League turned out to be a paper tiger.

The League proved impotent when Japan assaulted Manchuria in 1931–32, Italy committed clear aggression against Ethiopia in 1935, and Germany reoccupied the Rhineland in 1936—all violations of international law. France and Great Britain were unwilling to act collectively and decisively to maintain peace. The world community lacked any effective enforcement agency to punish international criminals. Under such circumstances of inadequate international organization, the belligerent drives of Japan, Italy, and Germany spiraled into a worldwide calamity—World War II.

With Adolf Hitler's rise to power in Germany in 1933, the world was soon to witness massive persecutions on a scale never before seen in human history. In his book *Mein Kampf* (My Struggle), Hitler made plain his perception that the "Aryan" German people were the highest species of humanity on earth, stating that "in a bastardized and niggerized world all concepts of the humanly beautiful and sublime . . . would be lost forever."[4] Without any rational basis in fact, those of Jewish descent were demonized as parasitic criminals, the cause of Germany's ills, and the main threat to the German future. Political or racial opponents of the National Socialist (Nazi) Party were beaten by Nazi thugs and thrown into concentration camps. Discriminatory laws drove the Jews from the civil service and curtailed their freedoms; they were eventually denied their German citizenship. Hundreds of German decrees imposed restraints on property owned by Jews. Special taxes and fines, boycotts, and a host of prohibitions were designed to make life miserable or intolerable for Jews in Germany, de-

The signing of the Kellogg-Briand Pact in Paris, France; August 27, 1928. (NARA)

Polish hostages rounded up by the Germans, including several Roman Catholic priests, await their fate in the town square in Bydgoszcz, Poland; September 1939.
(Main Commission for the Investigation of Nazi Crimes, Warsaw, Poland)

fined as an inferior "stateless" race. All of this was public knowledge and generally accepted by the German population. It was a portent of things to come, what Nazi leaders would call "The Final Solution to the Jewish Question."

In 1938, the British and French accepted Hitler's *Anschluss* (annexation) of Austria into Germany and his forcible absorption of the Sudetenland of Czechoslovakia into the Greater Reich. On September 1, 1939, Germany attacked its neighbor, Poland, in a blatant act of calculated aggression. England and France, whose self-deluded leaders had vainly hoped for peace through appeasement, went to war within forty-eight hours to defend their Polish ally. World War II had begun. By June 1940 the Low Countries and France were overrun, and Germany attacked Greece and Yugoslavia the following spring before launching its attack against the Soviet Union on June 22, 1941.

In war, as in peace, the elimination of the Jews was an integral part of the diabolical Nazi design to create a new "Aryan" order in Europe. Millions of Jews came under German control and were systematically exterminated in the killing centers of German-occupied Poland. Though several state and private agencies contributed to the "Final Solution of the Jewish Question," the leading organizations behind its implementation were the Central Office for Reich Security and the Nazi Party's black-uniformed SS *(Schutzstaffel)* police commanded by the feared Heinrich Himmler. Besides the Jews, the Nazis and their collaborators eliminated other "undesirables" from the new "Aryan" order such as Gypsies, Polish intellectuals, the handicapped, and Soviet prisoners of war. Eastern Europe, occupied by the German army, was to become their graveyard.

As word of growing German atrocities began to leak out of occupied Europe, many warnings were sent to the Germans to cease and desist their illegal acts. Winston Churchill, Britain's prime minister, joined President Franklin

D. Roosevelt in such a warning as early as October 25, 1941, when Churchill announced that punishment of war crimes should be "counted among the major goals of the war" and Roosevelt warned that German acts (referring specifically to execution of hostages) would "bring fearful retribution."[5] Representatives of the nations that Germany had overrun met at St. James Palace in London for an Inter-Allied Conference on the Punishment of War Crimes. They issued a joint declaration on January 13, 1942, that referred explicitly to the Hague Conventions being violated by Germany and again warned those responsible that one of the principal aims of the war would be "the punishment through the channel of organized justice, of those guilty or responsible for these crimes."[6] German leaders disregarded these threats and continued to direct Reich policies of torturing, starving, and executing civilians and prisoners of war.

On December 7, 1941, Japan launched its sneak attack on the United States at Pearl Harbor. Four days later, Germany declared war on the United States. The fortunes of Hitler's Third Reich began to ebb by the end of 1942. Nazi crimes increased even as the German military position became more desperate. Convincing evidence of massive war crimes received from underground sources in the German-occupied territories of Europe induced Allied leaders to denounce these acts as crimes and contributed to the legal definition of war crimes. Leading personalities who had been driven by the Nazis from their homes in Europe and found refuge in England organized an unofficial body of prominent jurists called the London International Assembly. It was the forerunner to the official United Nations Commission for the Investigation of War Crimes announced by the Americans and the British in 1942. On October 7, 1942, President Roosevelt issued a press release declaring: "The commission of these crimes continues. . . . [It is] the intention of this Government that the successful close of the

The "Big Three"—Soviet Premier Joseph STALIN, American President Franklin D. ROOSEVELT, and British Prime Minister Winston CHURCHILL—at the Teheran Conference, Teheran, Iran, soon after the signing of the Moscow Declaration; December 1943. (USHMM)

war shall include provision for the surrender to the United Nations of war criminals."[7] The Soviet government refused to join the UN commission and established instead its own war crimes agency, the Soviet Extraordinary Commission to Investigate War Crimes.

On December 17, 1942, a U.S. State Department press release confirmed that the Germans were carrying out their intention to "exterminate the Jewish people in Europe."[8] By the end of 1942, Allied legal experts, after difficult deliberations, had outlined the main principles of existing international law relating to war crimes: that aggression and crimes against humanity would be punishable, that even a head of state would be liable, and that superior orders would be no defense.[9] The term "crimes against humanity" originated with a 1915 declaration by France, Great Britain, and Russia that the massacre of Armenians by the Ottoman Turkish government constituted "crimes against civilization and humanity."[10] However, it was in the context of Nazi brutalities and the Holocaust that Allied jurists and leaders further defined this crime.

In the Moscow Declaration of November 1, 1943, a joint statement issued by President Roosevelt, Prime Minister Churchill, and Premier Stalin warned again, "Let those who have hitherto not imbued their hands with innocent blood beware lest they join the ranks of the guilty, for most assuredly, the Three Allied Powers will pursue them to the uttermost ends of the earth and deliver them to their accusers in order that justice may be done."[11] On March 24, 1944, Roosevelt issued another appeal to the German people to disassociate themselves from the terrible crimes against humanity that were being committed in their name.[12]

Never let it be said that the German leadership did not know that their evil deeds were crimes that would be punished. It is true that the world—and surely many Germans —did not know the details of the atrocities, nor could they imagine the magnitude and scale of the genocide. The complete picture only became apparent when the perpetrators were called to account before newly created courts of law that were determined to vindicate the established standards of civilized nations.

The International Military Tribunal at Nuremberg

The most famous of the many proceedings that sought to bring war criminals to book was the trial conducted shortly after the war by the four victorious powers in the Palace of Justice in Nuremberg, a city noted for the Nazis' flamboyant party rallies. Since Germany had been required to surrender unconditionally, the conquerors were thereby vested with lawful authority to serve as the new government of the defeated Reich. The British government initially proposed that Hitler and similar arch-criminals be executed without trial. The Americans argued that a judicial proceeding would be more just and effective. After some difficult diplomatic negotiations, the U.S. view prevailed. The legal basis for the International Military Tribunal (IMT), which tried the major Nazi war criminals, was a charter carefully worked out after only six weeks of final negotiation by outstanding lawyers from the United States, France, Great Britain, and the Soviet Union. The IMT charter, annexed to what became known as the London Agreement of August 8, 1945, set forth the laws and procedures that would govern the new tribunal for "the trial and punishment of the major war criminals of the European Axis countries."[13]

According to its Charter, the International Military Tribunal had legal jurisdiction to try individuals accused of

(a) *crimes against peace*: the planning, preparation, initiation, or waging of a war of aggression or in violation of international treaties or assurances; (b) *war crimes*: violations of established laws and customs of war, such as those prohibiting ill-treatment of prisoners, killing of hostages, using civilians as slave labor, and wanton destruction not justified by military necessity; (c) *crimes against humanity*: atrocities such as murder, extermination, deportation of civilian populations, and persecutions on political, racial, or religious grounds; (d) *conspiracy to commit these crimes*. Leaders, organizers, instigators, and accomplices would be as accountable as direct perpetrators, and the official position of a defendant—no matter how high his rank—would not free him from full responsibility. Superior orders from the Nazi administrative hierarchy would be no excuse, but it could ameliorate punishment if justice so required.

Each of the four signatories was to appoint a chief prosecutor to help with the investigations and prosecution. Procedures to guarantee a fair trial for the defendants were written into the Charter, and detailed rules were worked out shortly thereafter.[14] Those accused of the most atrocious crimes in history were to be given "the kind of a trial which they in the days of their pomp and power, never gave to any man."[15] Chief U.S. Prosecutor Jackson—the driving force behind the trial—gave clear assurances that the objective was to advance the rule of law. "We must summon such detachment and intellectual integrity to our task that this trial will commend itself to posterity as fulfilling humanity's aspirations to do justice."[16]

On October 18, 1945, less than half a year after the war ended, twenty-four major Nazi war criminals were indicted for their crimes. Hitler and some of his leading henchmen, such as Reich Leader of the SS and Chief of the German Police Heinrich Himmler and Propaganda Minister Joseph Goebbels, were absent—they had all committed suicide when they saw the war was lost. The head of Hitler's Nazi Party Chancellery and his private secretary, Martin Bormann, had disappeared and was to be tried *in absentia*. Leader of the German Labor Front Robert Ley took his own life after the indictment was served upon him. Hermann Göring, Hitler's second in command and a major planner of the Nazi policies of persecution and extermination, sat morosely at the head of the dock. The evidence against him was overwhelming, but he too was to cheat the hangman by swallowing a cyanide capsule after being convicted on all counts on October 1, 1946.

Another defendant who evaded trial was the aged and infirm Gustav Krupp, a leading German industrialist, as well as Hitler's strong supporter and largest armaments supplier. When it was recognized that he was completely senile and had turned full responsibility over to his son Alfried during the last years of the war, all charges against the old man were dropped. Rudolf Hess, one of Hitler's earliest confidants, the deputy leader of the Nazi Party, and third in command, refused to testify but admitted that he had only feigned insanity. He would, after conviction, spend the rest of his life in Spandau prison in Berlin, the question of his sanity remaining in doubt.

At the trial, the defendants were confronted primarily with thousands of their own documents, official reports, and records that chronicled their crimes in signed orders, letters, diaries, films, and photographs. Dozens of witnesses and

Delegates to the United Nations War Crimes Conference during the negotiations that led to the signing of the London Agreement; August 1945.

(Imperial War Museum, London, United Kingdom)

Four judges of the INTERNATIONAL MILITARY TRIBUNAL sit at the bench during the trial. *Left to right:* Major General I.T. Nikitchenko, Soviet Union; Justices Norman Birkett and Lord Justice Lawrence, Great Britain; and Francis Biddle, United States; ca. 1945
(Harry S Truman Library, Independence, Missouri)

many of the defendants themselves confirmed the authenticity of the official evidence. It was an undeniable and irrefutable historical record of unmitigated barbarism, spawned by a distorted ideology of racial hatred and arrogance.

After a trial that lasted nearly a year, the verdicts were mixed. Many defendants were found guilty of one or more of the charges against them but not on all of the counts of the indictment. The sentences were based solely on the charges clearly proven. Where the evidence was insufficient to establish guilt beyond a reasonable doubt, or the judges were evenly divided on the question, the defendants were acquitted and released. Financier Hjalmar Schacht, an early supporter who had broken with Hitler, was set free, as was diplomat Franz von Papen and propagandist Hans Fritzsche —admittedly much to the latter's surprise.[17]

Ten of the Nazi killers were found guilty of the most serious charges and hanged: Ernst Kaltenbrunner, chief of the Central Office for Reich Security was held responsible for the murder of millions of innocent people; Hans Frank, the Nazi Party's leading jurist and governor-general of Poland during the war, whose own diary detailed incredible massacres; Fritz Sauckel, plenipotentiary-general for labor mobilization, for mistreatment of millions of slave laborers; Foreign Minister Joachim von Ribbentrop, who helped plot Germany's aggressions; Field Marshal Wilhelm Keitel, chief of the *Wehrmacht* high command, whose own orders for the commission of atrocities condemned him; General Alfred Jodl, chief of the *Wehrmacht* operations staff, for illegal killings on the Russian front; Alfred Rosenberg, head of the Nazi Party's foreign affairs department, who looted art treasures and assisted mass killings; Wilhelm Frick, Reich minister of interior, who enforced the discriminatory "Nuremberg Laws" and the euthanasia programs to kill the mentally ill and mentally retarded; Julius Streicher, whose notorious antisemitic newspaper *Der Stürmer* incited racial hatred and murder; Arthur Seyss-Inquart, Reich governor of Austria, for deportations and concentration camp deaths. All of the guilty verdicts were reviewed and confirmed by the Allied Control Council for Germany before the convicted defendants were executed and their ashes dumped in the Isar River near Munich.

Others received lesser sentences. Albert Speer, Hitler's general architectural inspector of the Reich and Reich minister for armaments and war production, was acquitted of conspiracy to commit aggression but convicted for his responsibility in the employment of millions of abused slave laborers. Whereas practically none of the other defendants had shown any real sign of regret or remorse, Speer openly acknowledged a sense of shame and responsibility for having contributed to programs that for many ended in the extermination camp of Auschwitz. Some saw his confessed contrition as a clever ploy to save his own skin. In contrast to Sauckel, who was hanged for similar crimes, Speer was sentenced to confinement in Spandau prison for twenty years, where he became a bestselling author before he was released and retired to comfort in Heidelberg.

Some critics have claimed that the IMT was nothing more than "victors' vengeance" that imposed *ex post facto* laws on soldiers and civilians who had no choice but to obey. It was noted, not without cause, that some of the judges came from countries that had committed similar crimes and, therefore, the Nuremberg trial was inherently unfair. These allegations are understandable but are unfounded as an excuse or justification. The fact that some of the prosecuting nations may not have had completely clean hands themselves may have affected their moral standing in bringing the complaints, but it did not diminish the guilt of those who were accused and convicted at Nuremberg.

Had the IMT trial been nothing more than a mask of justice hiding the face of vengeance, there would have been no acquittals. In fact, when the Soviet judge voted to condemn all of the accused, he was voted down by the others. Individual offenders placed on trial are no more "vanquished" than an ordinary criminal placed on trial by police representing law-abiding society. The British, once having given up their early thought of a "political solution" (just shooting top Nazi leaders), treated the defendants with courtesy and consideration. The president of the Tribunal was Lord Justice Sir Geoffrey Lawrence of the British Court of Appeal, whose objectivity was widely recognized. All of the proceedings were open to the public and carefully recorded in English, French, Russian, and German. Defense counsel, selected by the defendants themselves and paid for generously by the Allies, were granted much latitude despite their own Nazi backgrounds. The German population itself generally recognized the fairness of the court. It was unthinkable that any of the judges or prosecutors—pledged to uphold the rule of law and bound by the published rules guaranteeing fairness to the accused—would lend themselves to a mock trial that would soil their names and honor forever.

After careful deliberation, the judgment of the Tribunal declared that the defendants must have known from the historical evolution of the relevant law that the crimes of which they were accused were illegal deeds at the time they were committed and were not *ex post facto* innovations designed unfairly to punish unsuspecting innocents. The frequently argued defense that criminal acts were done only in response to "superior orders" was really a sham. It was a myth that German soldiers would face execution for failure to obey an order that clearly violated the law. Every German soldier carried a statement in his pay book indi-

cating that it was, in fact, a crime to follow illegal orders. There could be no doubt that slaughtering helpless women and children was murder pure and simple. The crimes committed by these defendants, and others, were committed by persons who were not being coerced to act against their will but who, in almost all cases, carried out their persecutions and executions with enthusiasm and conviction that they were performing a patriotic deed.[18]

Nuremberg was an important stepping-stone in the effort to replace inhumanity by humanity and to replace the law of force by the force of law. Its significance can only be judged in the light of a much broader panorama that includes other war crimes trials that took place after World War II. Its enduring value can be measured by its impact on subsequent efforts to use law as an instrumentality for the protection of the human rights of people everywhere.

Other War Crimes Proceedings

Despite the wide publicity it received, the trial of major war criminals before the International Military Tribunal at Nuremberg represented only one facet in the wider scope of postwar war crimes prosecutions. The overwhelming number of war crimes trials adjudicated in Allied-occupied Central Europe tried relatively "minor" war criminals—civilians or members of the Axis military forces whose alleged crimes were confined to a specific locale, such as a governmental district, city, or concentration camp. At the Moscow Conference in October 1943, the Allied foreign ministers had resolved that, at the time of an armistice, those individuals suspected of war crimes that could be pinpointed to a specific geographical location would be

American soldiers attempt to identify one of their comrades who had been executed after their surrender to German troops at Malmedy, Belgium, during the December 1944 "Battle of the Bulge"; January 1945. (UPI/Corbis-Bettmann)

returned to the countries in which those crimes had been committed and prosecuted according to the laws of the nation concerned. Hundreds of war crimes proceedings were held before national or military tribunals in Belgium, Czechoslovakia, Greece, Holland, Poland, Yugoslavia, and other lands previously occupied by the Germans. Thus, SS General Jürgen Stroop, commander of those German forces that brutally suppressed the Warsaw Ghetto uprising, and Amon Goeth, notorious commander of Plaszow concentration camp, were both returned to Poland to be tried and hanged—as was Auschwitz commandant Rudolf Höss, who was sentenced to death by the Polish supreme court in Warsaw in 1947. Impromptu trials undoubtedly also took place when the Soviet Army caught up with those who had mercilessly devastated its country. During World War II, trials before Soviet military tribunals at Kharkov and Krasnodar served both as vengeful warning and deterrent by meting out quick justice to those who had committed indescribable atrocities against Soviet citizens. Relatively little is known in the West concerning such wartime or immediate postwar trials in the Soviet Union and in Soviet-occupied Eastern Europe.

Long before the war was over, and even while German armies were sweeping across Europe, the Allied governments—confident that there would be a day of reckoning —had warned the Germans to cease their criminal activities or face trial for their actions. When the tide turned and the German army was forced into retreat, Allied troops began to uncover shocking evidence of atrocities committed by German soldiers. The massacre of American prisoners of war captured by a *Waffen SS* unit at Malmedy in Belgium

Prisoners carry stones up the infamous "stairway of death" in the quarry at the MAUTHAUSEN concentration camp; spring 1942.
(Rijksinstituut voor Oorlogsdocumentatie, Amsterdam, Netherlands)

Former CONCENTRATION CAMP prisoners are interviewed by French military officials gathering evidence of WAR CRIMES; spring 1945.
(Main Commission for the Investigation of Nazi Crimes, Warsaw, Poland)

was widely reported in the American press. Allied airmen shot down over German territory were frequently murdered by angry German civilians. In these cases of traditional war crimes, Allied investigators collected evidence of the crimes and names of the perpetrators. Yet it was the discovery of the Nazi concentration camps such as Bergen-Belsen, freed by the British, and Buchenwald, Dachau, and Mauthausen, freed by the Americans, that most steeled the liberators in their determination to bring captured Nazi war criminals to justice.

In general, the efforts of Western military authorities in Germany to try war criminals within their zones of occupation in Germany and Austria went hand in hand with their commitment to denazification and "democratization." On December 20, 1945, the Allied Control Council for Germany promulgated Control Council Law No. 10, which authorized each of the four occupying powers to bring war criminals to trial within its own zone before such tribunals as it might see fit. At the same time, the occupying nations reconfirmed the validity of the four criminal charges originally spelled out in the London Charter, with the added proviso that the charge "crimes against humanity" might be leveled even if the crime in question was committed against German citizens before Germany was at war—an important clarification and an affirmation that gross abuse of one's own citizens in peacetime was also a punishable offense under international law. Hundreds of proceedings were held by military commissions or tribunals in the British, French, Soviet, and American zones of Germany and Austria from 1945 to 1948. In the British-occupied zones, trials were held under the provisions of the Royal Warrant of June 19, 1945, which provided British courts the basis for trying German and Japanese war criminals; the most notable of these proceedings were the trials against captured SS officers responsible for atrocities in the concentration camp at Bergen-Belsen. The French conducted some trials at Rastatt in the French zone. The Soviets reported very little about the fate of Nazis captured in their zone of Germany; the Communist government established by the Soviets in eastern Germany soon bragged that all known Nazis in its area had been purged. The trial of SS men who ran the concentration camp at Sachsenhausen, in the Soviet zone, however, was widely reported.

Facing tremendous pressure from the home front to purge Germany thoroughly of its Nazi elements, the Americans carried out an aggressive denazification program by means of a rigorous series of trial proceedings against Nazi offenders great and small. American adjudication of war criminals began in July 1945 with the so-called Darmstadt Trial of eleven German civilian defendants charged with the beating deaths of six downed American airmen. In October 1945, officials of the U.S. Judge Advocate General's Office (JAG) won convictions against seven staff members of the euthanasia facility at Hadamar in connection with the murder of 476 Russian and Polish forced laborers imprisoned there. Symbolically, it was in the liberated concentration

Brigadier General Telford Taylor speaks during the DOCTORS TRIAL; ca. 1946. (USHMM)

camp at Dachau, near Munich, that the United States Army established a number of war crimes tribunals to try those captured SS officers and guards who had held leading positions in camps liberated by the United States or who had committed crimes against American nationals. The prosecutions conducted at Dachau and elsewhere in the American zone were trials by military commissions, organized in accordance with U.S. Army Articles of War, where judges, prosecutors, and counsel for the defendants were primarily American Judge Advocate General officers. The accused were charged with crimes that violated established rules for the conduct of warfare. These war crimes trials resembled courts-martial proceedings and bore very little relationship to the elaborate development of international law regarding aggression or crimes against humanity that were espoused by the IMT and subsequent proceedings at Nuremberg.

The IMT had dealt with only a small number of defendants and, despite the impressive volume of documentation, had merely scratched the surface of German criminality. If the world was to be protected from future depravities, there was need for a more comprehensive picture showing how crimes of such enormous magnitude and range could be organized and who should be held accountable. The London Charter envisaged more than one international trial by the four Allies, but apart from the IMT, such proceedings did not materialize. The United States decided to proceed on its own and to use the repaired Nuremberg courthouse, in the American zone, for further prosecutions of other major war criminals. Following in the footsteps of the IMT, a dozen additional trials were held at Nuremberg. General Telford Taylor, a distinguished IMT lawyer (later to become a professor at Columbia University School of Law and Cardozo law school at Yeshiva University), was designated to succeed Justice Jackson. Under Taylor's able supervision, 185 leading officials who played key roles in the criminal programs of the Reich were called to account between 1946 and 1949: physicians who had performed illegal medical experiments; judges and lawyers who perverted law and justice

The Japanese defendants at the International Military Tribunal for the Far East stand in the dock; Tokyo, Japan, May 1946. (NARA)

and committed judicial murder of political opponents; SS officers and commanders of murderous *Einsatzgruppen* (extermination squads) responsible for genocidal extermination of more than a million helpless people (including 33,771 Jews slaughtered in 1941 in Babi Yar near Kiev); Nazi officials engaged in racial "resettlement"; government ministers who planned aggression and other crimes; military leaders who defied the laws of war; and major industrialists who worked camp inmates to death and supplied Zyklon B poison gas to eliminate those who could not work.[19]

Although the judges for these twelve "Subsequent Proceedings" at Nuremberg were recruited from the United States, the fact that the trials were conducted pursuant to the London Charter and a quadripartite Control Council law and were obliged to enforce international law gave their decisions the same legal standing as the IMT. Their judgments shed further light on which acts could properly be punishable as "aggressive war" and how far responsibility could descend down the government's bureaucratic ladder. The limits of "military necessity" as a defense were also clari-

fied. It was repeatedly confirmed that the massive abuse by a state of its own citizens, even in time of peace, can be a violation of international law. If the magnitude of abuse shocks the conscience of humanity, such persecution becomes a crime against humanity that justifies international intervention and prosecution wherever the accused state, owing to indifference, impotence, or complicity, is unable or unwilling to halt the crimes and punish the criminals.[20] The IMT and the subsequent trials at Nuremberg, in the words of Telford Taylor, "added enormously to the body and the living reality of international penal law. No principle deserves to be called such unless men are willing to stake their consciences on its enforcement. That is the way law comes into being, and that is what was done at Nuremberg."[21]

While the Nuremberg trials were still in progress, on the other side of the world other war crimes trials were also begun. In late 1945, Japanese General Tomoyuki Yamashita, commander of the Philippines at the time of their liberation by American forces, was sentenced to death by an American military court in Manila for having failed to prevent the commission of widespread war crimes by troops under his command. The U.S. Supreme Court refused to reverse the decision, which many American officials felt went too far.[22] In spring 1946, the victorious supreme commander for Allied forces in the Pacific, General Douglas MacArthur, established the International Military Tribunal for the Far East for the trial in Tokyo of major Japanese war crimes suspects. Following principles similar to those in the London Charter for the IMT, the Tokyo proceedings turned out to be the biggest trial in recorded history. It lasted from May 1946 to November 1948, during which time more than 400 witnesses were heard, 4,000 documents were received in evidence, and 50,000 pages of transcript were recorded. Eleven judges from countries that had been at war with Japan heard the indictment against twenty-eight high-ranking defendants, all of whom were convicted. Seven were sentenced to death by hanging and most of the others to imprisonment for life.

Not all of the judges concurred with the findings of the majority. Justice Bert V. A. Röling, a distinguished jurist from the Netherlands, called for further clarification of international law to meet the needs for peace in the future. In a 500-page dissenting opinion, the learned Judge Pal of India, finding all defendants not guilty on all counts, expressed similar views and emphasized the need to form an international community under the reign of law "in which nationality or race should find no place."[23] These farseeing jurists were reaching out for a more humane world under clear and binding international law.

The criminals tried at Tokyo and Nuremberg were only a small sampling. The Allies never intended to put all war crimes suspects or their accessories on trial; that would have been a political, financial, and logistical impossibility. Eight-and-a-half million Germans were registered members of the Nazi Party; many belonged to the SS and other Nazi organizations branded by the London Charter as criminal enterprises. All that could be done was to urge the new German authorities to classify their citizens into various categories of responsibility and to impose small fines or disqualification from office, depending on the outcome of a brief administrative hearing. The "denazification" process, begun with such fervor in the American zone, had very little if any significance in advancing the rule of humanitarian law.

When the subsequent Nuremberg trials ended in the American zone, there remained on hand large masses of incriminating evidence against persons who had committed various crimes but could not be found or who were lucky enough—for purely administrative reasons—not to have been selected for trial. After all, six million and more innocent people could not have been slaughtered without the help of hundreds of thousands of executioners and accomplices. In the hope that greater justice would be done and that fewer criminals would escape, the incriminating evidence was turned over to the Departments of Justice of the various west German regional state governments. Empowered by Allied Control Council Laws Nos. 4 and 10, reconstituted German courts were authorized to try certain Nazi crimes that had been committed by Germans against Germans or against stateless persons. In 1950, after the establishment of the Federal Republic of Germany, Allied restrictions on such German courts were lifted, and German prosecutors were free to embark on their own systematic investigation and prosecution of Nazi war crimes. At that time, however, German citizens were more concerned with their own economic recovery than with pursuing Nazi colleagues or advancing international law.

It was the investigation and trial of German *Einsatzgruppen* members in Ulm in the late 1950s that signalled a profound change in the course of prosecuting Nazi crimes. The wealth of newly uncovered evidence collected for this trial convinced German justice officials that many of the most heinous Nazi crimes—especially those committed in the East—had yet to be investigated and prosecuted. In October 1958, justice ministers representing all German federal states agreed to establish a Central Office of State Administrations of Justice. This office, staffed in Ludwigsburg by dedicated democrats, opened dossiers on many thousands of war crimes suspects. In its first year, the Central Office launched 400 judicial inquiries; major cases concerned the crimes committed by *Einsatzgruppen*, units of the Security Police and Security Service (SD), and in the killing centers of Auschwitz, Belzec, Chelmno, Sobibor, and Treblinka.[24] From its inception in December 1958 until summer 1986, it initiated investigations of over 5,000 cases, which led to 4,853 official criminal proceedings.

Throughout the 1960s and 1970s, the Federal Republic of Germany embarked on a number of major war crimes

British troops arrest Josef Kramer, former commandant of the AUSCHWITZ-BIRKENAU and BERGEN-BELSEN concentration camps; April 1945. (Imperial War Museum, London, United Kingdom)

trials. Between 1963 and 1966, three separate trials of former Auschwitz personnel took place in Frankfurt am Main. In 1964, a trial of Treblinka guards ended in the conviction of nine of its ten defendants. In 1967, Wilhelm Harster and two others were convicted in Munich of aiding and abetting the deportation of Dutch Jews; in 1970, Austrian Franz Stangl, former commandant at Sobibor and Treblinka, was sentenced to life imprisonment before a state court in Düsseldorf for his role in the deaths of at least 400,000 persons at Treblinka. Officers of the Nazi extermination squads that murdered more than a million innocent men, women, and children were tried in various *Einsatzgruppen* cases at Darmstadt. Since fair trial and due process of law was the rule in the new Germany, and the statute of limitations for all but the most heinous crimes enabled lesser offenders to avoid trial, even diligent prosecutors had a difficult time in obtaining convictions. At least the ordinary Germans could see for themselves, in an open *German* court, the true nature of the Nazi regime that so many of them had hailed so enthusiastically.

By the late 1970s, trials of Nazi war criminals were relatively limited, and at this late date the number of convictions minimal. In view of the fact that we have relatively little knowledge of persons sentenced in the Soviet Union, Czechoslovakia, Yugoslavia, and other Eastern European countries, it is difficult to estimate the total number or German nationals tried at home and abroad since May 1945. According to statistics by the Federal Ministry of Justice, German public prosecutors had opened some 85,802 proceedings between May 1945 and December 31, 1978, against individuals suspected of committing Nazi crimes; of these 6,440 persons were convicted and received non-appealable sentences.[25]

Fugitive Nazi criminals have been found hiding throughout the world. The most notorious was Adolf Eichmann, the SS officer in charge of deporting the Jews of occupied Europe to their death in Auschwitz. Unable to obtain his extradition from Argentina, the government of Israel abducted him illegally and put him on public trial in 1960 in Jerusalem, where he was duly convicted and, after confirmation on appeal, hanged. In 1973, Hermine Braunsteiner, known as "The Mare of Majdanek," was extradited to face trial and conviction in Germany. In 1979, the United States Department of Justice created an Office of Special Investigations to deal with war crimes suspects who had entered the United States illegally by falsifying their real identity or background. One such suspect, John Demjanjuk, believed to be the murderous guard "Ivan the Terrible" from the killing center at Treblinka, was extradited to Israel to stand trial for atrocities. After long proceedings, it turned out that it was probably a case of mistaken identity. Although there was evidence that Demjanjuk had been a guard in another killing center, he was released and returned to the United States as a free man.

War crimes proceedings against a limited number of fugitive Nazis continued in the United States and in Canada for many years. In France a famous trial was conducted in 1987 against Gestapo officer Klaus Barbie, known as the "Butcher of Lyon," for having deported many French Jews to their death. As the years pass, however, the number of such prosecutions and the possibility of obtaining convictions diminishes. Italy opened what could be the last such proceeding on December 7, 1995: after obtaining extradition from Argentina, SS Captain Erich Priebke was put on trial for the 1944 massacre of 335 men and boys in the Ardeatine Caves south of Rome.[26]

As of 1996, many criminals remain in hiding abroad, supported by their ill-gotten plunder or former Nazi friends. The identity of some—like the notorious Auschwitz physician Josef Mengele, noted for his selection of

Adolf EICHMANN sits in the glass booth erected for his protection during the EICHMANN TRIAL; 1961.
(Government Press Office, Jerusalem, Israel)

The General Assembly of the United Nations as it appeared during the first session of the Security Council; March 1946. (NARA)

twin inmates for medical experiments and death—were revealed only after their demise in some foreign land where they had found asylum. The survivors of persecution and their sympathizers as well as those who seek a more humane world continue the search, determined that their tormentors find no rest and that the Holocaust and similar crimes against humanity happen *"never again!"*

The Legacy of the Postwar Trials

Perhaps the most hopeful product of the Allied cooperation in World War II was the formation of the United Nations. Within only a few days of the opening of the IMT, the new organization's charter went into force. It reaffirmed faith in fundamental human rights and respect for international law and justice in order to "save succeeding generations from the scourge of war." When the General Assembly of the new United Nations Organization convened toward the end of 1946, the impact of the atrocities revealed at the IMT trial in Nuremberg was fresh in everyone's mind. The Nuremberg doctrines of international justice attracted great public support, and the world looked to the UN to take whatever action was required to prevent the recurrence of such crimes.

The first session of the General Assembly unanimously affirmed the principles of international law recognized by the London Charter and the judgment of the Nuremberg Tribunal. A committee was appointed to start work on a criminal code and court to implement those principles. At the same time it was confirmed that genocide—the denial of the right to existence of entire human groups—was a punishable crime under international law.[27] Various UN committees began drafting the required criminal code to protect the peace and security of humankind, a convention outlawing genocide, and statutes for the proposed international criminal court.

For many years, no agreement could be reached on a definition of aggression, which Nuremberg had correctly condemned as the greatest of all crimes because it encompassed all the other crimes. Those who were hesitant or unwilling to be bound by universal rules argued that, without an agreed definition of aggression, there was no need to proceed further with drafting an international criminal code. It was then argued that without a code, an international criminal court could not function; hence, there was no need for such a court. Everything was thus linked, and for a quarter century the package intended to expand on the work at Nuremberg was put into a deep freeze by the Cold War.

It was not until 1974 that a consensus agreement could be reached on a definition of aggression.[28] That hurdle having been overcome and the excuse for inaction removed, the door was soon opened for further work on the criminal code and court. But nations remained reluctant to accept the jurisdiction of any new international tribunal. Even the existing International Court of Justice in The Hague that had been created under the League of Nations was authorized only to deal with disputes voluntarily submitted by consenting states. It had no jurisdiction whatsoever over individuals or criminals, and it had no independent means to enforce its decisions. The absence of courts with

A poster for
American soldiers
explaining the
indictment of the
International
Military
Tribunal; 1945.
(Archive, USHMM)

DISPLACED PERSONS

THE JUDGES

THE BERLIN INDICTMENT

- DEFENDANTS: 24 NAZI WAR LEADERS
- CHARGE: A PLOT AGAINST HUMANITY

STALINGRAD RUINS

Twenty-four of Germany's leaders (whose pictures make up the swastika) were indicted as war criminals on 18 October. The indictment was returned in Berlin before the International Military Tribunal, representing the United States, Russia, Britain and France. Trial of the cases is scheduled to start in Nuremberg on 20 November. Conviction might mean the death penalty.

There are four counts in the indictment. All the defendants were accused under the first count, charging conspiracy. Some of them were indicted under all four counts. The counts:

I. THE COMMON PLAN OR CONSPIRACY: The defendants were accused of participating in a plan to commit "crimes against peace, war crimes and crimes against humanity, as defined in the Charter of this Tribunal" and were held "individually responsible for their own acts and for all acts committed by any person in the execution of such plan or conspiracy."

II. CRIMES AGAINST PEACE: "Planning, preparation, initiation or waging of a war of aggression, or war in violation of international treaties, agreements or assurances."

III. WAR CRIMES: "Violation of the laws or customs of war including murder, ill treatment or deportation to slave labor or for any other purpose of civilian population * * * murder of prisoners of war * * * killing of hostages * * * plunder of public or private property, wanton destruction of cities, towns or villages or devastation not justified by military necessity."

IV. CRIMES AGAINST HUMANITY: "Murder, extermination, enslavement, deportation and other inhumane acts against any civilian population before or during the war; or persecutions on political, racial or religious grounds in execution of any * * * crime within the jurisdiction of the Tribunal."

NEWSMAP
OVERSEAS EDITION
FOR THE ARMED FORCES

compulsory jurisdiction and binding authority remained a fatal gap in the international legal order.

While work at the UN has at times seemed to be going nowhere, terrorism, apartheid, and genocidal acts spawned by racial hatred have continued unabated throughout the world. The tragic fact is that crimes against humanity have been committed again and again, and yet—despite the promise of Nuremberg—the world community has not seen fit to establish a permanent international criminal tribunal to bring the wrongdoers to justice.

In 1991, when the multiethnic Socialist Federal Republic of Yugoslavia came apart, the newly independent Republic of Bosnia and Herzegovina, populated by Muslims, Orthodox Christian Serbs, and Roman Catholic Croats, erupted into a ferocious racial and ethnic duel. The Serbs, assisted by the Yugoslav army, were accused of massive and systematic human rights violations designed to drive the Moslem inhabitants from their homes. "Ethnic cleansing" was the euphemistic description given to the harassment, discrimination, beatings, torture, rape, summary executions, shelling of civilian populations, forcible relocation, and destruction of places of worship designed to rid the territory of an unwanted and feared minority. An investigative commission appointed by the United Nations confirmed the atrocities that were committed in varying degrees by all sides.[29]

A host of UN Security Council resolutions warned all the parties to the conflict that the 1949 Geneva Convention requiring humanitarian conduct was legally binding, and violators would be held individually responsible. On February 22, 1993, the Security Council—relying on the Nuremberg precedent and earlier UN studies—decided that a new international tribunal should be established quickly to prosecute persons responsible for serious violations of international humanitarian law committed in the territory of the former Yugoslavia since 1991.[30] Within sixty days of the Security Council's decision, the statute for an ad hoc International Criminal Tribunal for Yugoslavia was drafted. By November 1993, eleven international judges, elected by the Assembly, took office. Empowered to punish war crimes, genocide, and crimes against humanity, the creation of the tribunal by the Security Council acting within its power under the UN Charter was the most significant advance toward the rule of law since the Nuremberg courts were adjourned nearly a half-century before.

In 1994, Rwanda was wracked by acts of genocide as part of a civil war that had erupted earlier. Humanitarian assistance and military observers from the United Nations were unable to prevent or curb the commission of massive crimes against humanity. The dominant Hutu tribal group was reported to be committing genocide against the minority Tutsi group. It was estimated that more than a half-million Tutsis were slaughtered, and that 100,000 Rwandans were involved in massacres carried out mostly with machetes and automatic weapons.

Again, the UN appointed an investigative commission to confirm the carnage. On November 8, 1994, the Security Council, drawing on its experience in setting up the tribunal for the former Yugoslavia, quickly created another ad hoc international criminal tribunal to prosecute persons responsible for genocide and other crimes against humanity in Rwanda during 1994.[31] Rwandan jails were jammed with suspects as they awaited justice from the second international tribunal established by the United Nations.

To be sure, the creation of ad hoc tribunals with limited and specialized jurisdiction every time massive atrocities are committed anywhere in the world is a rather ineffective, if not absurd, way to affirm the rule of law. What is needed, of course, is a permanent international criminal court to hold accountable those persons who violate the approved standards of behavior whenever and wherever they occur. The innocent have nothing to fear from the rule of law. All who imperil humanity must know that they will be held to personal account, regardless of rank, station, or nationality. That is what Nuremberg was all about, and that is what law is all about.

These rather obvious truths have not escaped members of the United Nations. Various UN committees have continued to work on the creation of a permanent international criminal court—so far without success. The truth is that the necessary political will is still lacking. Many sovereign states remain unwilling to recognize that a peaceful world requires changes in the way international society is organized and run. The Covenant of the League of Nations, drawn up after twenty million people were killed in World War I, and the Charter of the United Nations, drawn up after another forty million perished in World War II—including over six million Jews murdered in the Holocaust—set out guidelines that might save civilization from destruction. Yet twenty million more have died in wars since the UN Charter was signed in 1945, and massive crimes continue to be committed against innocent people to this day.

Without law and order in international affairs there will be continuing chaos. But there is no cause for despair. The Nuremberg tribunals and the subsequent trials elsewhere demonstrated a persistent determination that those who commit genocidal acts will be brought to justice. In the last quarter century more progress can be detected than can be found in all of the preceding history of man on earth. The international community has been slowly inching toward a more democratic system where the absolute sovereignty of the state will yield to the human rights of the individual.

Hope is nurtured by such advances as the decline of totalitarianism, the acceptance of universal human rights declarations, the functioning courts of human rights in the European Community and Latin America, the adoption of the Genocide Convention by most nations, the recognition by Germany and others that victims of persecution are legally entitled to compensation and rehabilitation, the awakening of the social conscience, and the increased capacity of mass media to inform and educate the public.

The recent Security Council actions creating ad hoc war crimes tribunals can be forerunners of a permanent international criminal court to protect the most fundamental human right—the right of everyone everywhere to live in peace and human dignity protected by the rule of law. This is the enduring legacy of Nuremberg.

Benjamin B. Ferencz was the chief prosecutor for the United States in the Nuremberg war crimes trial against the SS Einsatzgruppen. *He is a professor of international law and the author of many books and articles on world peace.*

Notes

1. Robert H. Jackson, *The Case against the Nazi War Criminals* (New York, 1946), 3, 7.

2. Department of State, *The Treaty of Versailles and After. Annotations of the Text of the Treaty* (Washington, 1947), 371.

3. Ibid., 227.

4. Adolf Hitler, *Mein Kampf* (Boston, 1971), 383.

5. Whitney Harris, *Tyranny on Trial: The Evidence at Nuremberg* (Dallas, 1954), 3.

6. *Inter-Allied Declaration Signed at St. James Palace, London on January 13, 1942* (London, 1942), 15.

7. Benjamin B. Ferencz, *An International Criminal Court*, 2 vols. (New York, 1980), 1: 441.

8. Ibid., 442.

9. *United Nations War Crimes Commission History* (London, 1948), 99, 441.

10. M. Cherif Bassiouni, *Crimes against Humanity in International Criminal Law* (Dordrecht and Boston, 1992), 168–69.

11. Ferencz, *International Criminal Court*, 1: 443–44.

12. Ibid., 444–45.

13. Ibid., 456–64.

14. Ibid., 464–68.

15. Closing statement of Justice Jackson, IMT Transcript, p. 4333; see Benjamin B. Ferencz, "Nuremberg Trial Procedure," *Journal of Criminal Law and Criminology* 39 (July–August 1948): 144.

16. Jackson, *Case against the Nazi War Criminals*, 3–7.

17. See Telford Taylor, *The Anatomy of the Nuremberg Trials* (New York, 1992), 598.

18. See Daniel J. Goldhagen, *Hitler's Willing Executioners* (New York, 1996), passim.

19. The dozen trials, as well as the trial procedures, are reported in *Trials of War Criminals before the Nuernberg Military Tribunals under Control Council Law No. 10*, 15 vols. (Washington, D.C., 1949–53). For the attitude of German industrialists see Benjamin B. Ferencz, *Less Than Slaves* (Harvard, 1979).

20. See "United States of America v. Otto Ohlendorf, et al. (Case 9: Einsatzgruppen Case)," *Trials of War Criminals* 4: 498; and "United States of America v. Josef Alstoetter, et al. (Case 3: Justice Case)," *Trials of War Criminals* 3: 979.

21. Office of Military Government, Office of the Chief Counsel for War Crimes, *Final Report to the Secretary of the Army of Nuernberg War Crimes Trials under Control Council Law No. 10*, (Washington, D.C., 1949), 112.

22. In re *Yamashita*, 327 U.S. 1 (1946).

23. Extracts reproduced in Ferencz, *Criminal Court*, Doc. 16, 502–38.

24. Adalbert Rückerl, *The Investigation of Nazi Crimes, 1945–1978: A Documentation*, trans. Derek Rutter (Hamden, CT, 1980), 52.

25. Ibid., 117. This figure includes 12 death sentences (promulgated before the enforcement of the German constitution, which prohibited capital punishment); 156 life sentences, and 114 fines. One individual was sentenced under the provisions of the Juvenile Court system.

26. *New York Times*, 8 December 1995.

27. UN, General Assembly, Official Records, General Assembly Resolution 95 (I), 96 (I), 11 December 1946.

28. UN General Assembly, Official Records, General Assembly Resolution 3314 (XXIX), 14 December 1975; see Benjamin B. Ferencz, "The United Nations Consensus Definition of Aggression: Sieve or Substance?" *Journal of International Law and Economics* 10 (December 1975): 701.

29. UN, Security Council, Official Records, Report of the Commission headed by Professor Cherif Bassiouni, Security Council Document S/1994/674, 27 May 1994.

30. UN Security Council, Official Records, Security Council Resolution 808, 22 February 1993.

31. UN Security Council, Official Records, Security Council Resolution 955 (194), 8 November 1994.

Some of the thousands of German documents that were collected from the former THIRD REICH and the areas it occupied in 1945 as evidence for the INTERNATIONAL MILITARY TRIBUNAL; ca. 1945. These documents were also used in the NUREMBERG MILITARY TRIBUNALS and other later war crimes trials. (NARA)

WAR CRIMES DOCUMENTS

As World War II drew to a close, the ALLIES developed a plan to gather all German documents that could be located. Military commanders instructed their forces to secure any records found in liberated concentration camps and to collect all documents possible from German archives and libraries. No judgment about the significance of records was to be made; they were to be held until teams devoted to the gathering of documents could be dispatched to collect them. Records from the BUCHENWALD and NATZWEILER concentration camps were secured in this manner. Masses of other German documents were uncovered in various hidden storage areas. A salt mine near Merkers, Germany, yielded tons of documents including German Army High Command records, library holdings and city archives, and files from the Krupp and other German industrial concerns.

Hidden stocks of German documents, including those of Alfred ROSENBERG, Heinrich HIMMLER, and the Foreign Ministry, continued to be uncovered throughout 1945. When central files had been destroyed by the Germans, it was often possible to reconstruct them from other sources. For example, the records of the CENTRAL OFFICE FOR REICH SECURITY were burned in the basement of its Prague headquarters as the war ended; copies of many documents, however, were found among the files of local GESTAPO offices across Germany.

Once in the Allies' possession, intelligence services and war crimes investigation teams, whose job it was to identify and apprehend suspected war criminals, worked together at the monumental task of cataloging and indexing the millions of captured documents. By September 1945, thirteen Allied document collection centers operated in Germany and Austria. The holdings of these centers soon reached immense proportions: the collection center at Kassel, Germany, held 1,700 tons of documents by early autumn 1945. Documents related to possible war crimes and hence of value to the American prosecution staff at the INTERNATIONAL MILITARY TRIBUNAL were assembled by a military unit headed by Colonel Robert Storey. Eventually some 2,500 documents were gathered at Nuremberg. Each was cataloged, photographed, translated into English, and given a unique document number; a record of the circumstances of each document's discovery and authenticity was also made to provide legal provenance. Thousands of these documents were introduced as evidence at the International Military Tribunal during 1945 and 1946; others were used at the subsequent NUREMBERG MILITARY TRIBUNALS from 1946 to 1948. Examples are reproduced throughout this book and can be readily identified by the citation "The National Archives and Records Administration, National Archives Collection of World War II War Crimes Records, Record Group 238, Office of the U.S. Chief of Counsel for War Crimes," with its individual document number.

The discovery of previously unknown documents related to the Holocaust continues today; some have been used as evidence at the war crimes trials over the past fifty years. In many cases, perpetrators have been convicted, in no small part, by such documents bearing their own signatures.

Viennese residents examine posters displayed outside of the
Gausippenamt (District Office for Racial Genealogy) in June 1938.
The posters offer a National Socialist interpretation of "Aryan" and
Jewish genealogy. The tables on the wall define, left, *Mischling I* grade
(Half-Jews), and right, *Jude* (Jew), as proclaimed in an ancillary decree
to the Nuremberg Laws. (Austrian National Library, Vienna, Austria)

DISCRIMINATORY LAWS

Antisemitism, and with it the persecution of Jews, represented a central tenet of NAZI ideology. In their 25-point Party Program, published in February 1920, NAZI PARTY members publicly declared their intention to segregate Jews from "ARYAN" society and to abrogate the Jews' legal and political rights. Soon after their seizure of power, Nazi leaders began to make good on their pledge to persecute German Jews. The first law to curtail the rights of Jewish citizens was the "Law for the Restoration of the Professional Civil Service" of April 7, 1933, according to which Jewish and "politically unreliable" civil servants and employees were to be excluded from state service. At this early point in his chancellorship, however, Hitler was still constrained to make political compromises with non-Nazi members of his government; thus, he reluctantly conceded to REICH President Paul von Hindenburg's demand in this case to exempt from dismissal those civil servants who were veterans of the First World War or whose fathers or sons had fallen in that conflict.

The Civil Service Law represented the NATIONAL SOCIALISTS' first formulation of the so-called Aryan Clause —a regulation to exclude Jews and other non-Aryans from organizations, professions, and other aspects of public life. On April 25, 1933, the clause was extended to the educational sphere with the "Law against the Over-crowding of German Schools and Universities," which restricted the number of Jews to a maximum 1.5 percent of the total student body attending German institutions of learning. In the same month, participation in the medical and legal professions was severely restricted. Jewish physicians, dentists, and medical technicians were forbidden to work under the public insurance system; many non-Aryan lawyers were forbidden to practice, and Jews were no longer issued pharmacy licenses. By summer 1933, the Aryan clause was broadened so that even marriage to a non-Aryan excluded German citizens from civil service careers and from many other public service professions.

In the first two years of Nazi rule, German discriminatory laws were limited primarily to excluding Jews from specific professions. This effort was paralleled by measures to exclude them from German cultural life as well. The Reich Culture Chamber, which encompassed and effectively regulated all cultural professions (including radio, theater, music, writing, and the fine arts), was established in September 1933; its mandate specifically excluded non-Aryans from the organization. Further discriminatory legislation was promulgated on a state-by-state basis; local decrees and ordinances, for example, denied Jews the use of public pools, parks, inns, and recreational establishments. From 1933 to 1935, legal discrimination worked in tandem with a decentralized but universal boycott effort against Jewish businesses in gradually isolating Jews both socially and economically.

The two racial laws that comprised the so-called NUREMBERG LAWS of September 15, 1935, were the first legislative acts that radically affected all German Jews. The "Reich Citizenship Law" excluded Jews and other non-Aryans from Reich citizenship (Reichsbürgerschaft), although they remained "citizens of the German state" (Staatsangehörige). Ancillary ordinances to the citizenship law disenfranchised Jews and deprived them of other political rights, such as that of holding public office. Within this framework, all Jewish civil servants previously exempted by the Civil Service Law were dismissed. Likewise, a second ordinance to the citizenship law banned Jewish physicians, professors, teachers, and notaries from state service. In subsequent years, the number of restrictions placed on Jews in professional life increased until, in 1938, in conjunction with the ARYANIZATION effort, an outright ban prohibited Jews from practicing a wide number of professions, including those that required academic training.

The second of the anti-Jewish Nuremberg Laws promulgated in September 1935 was the "Law for the Protection of German Blood and German Honor," which institutionalized many of the racial theories prevalent in Nazi ideology. As the law's preamble explains, the Nazis believed "that the purity of German blood [is] the essential condition for the continued existence of the German people." In an attempt to ensure that "German blood" would remain untainted by the blood of "inferior races," the law prohibited marriage and extramarital sexual relations between Germans and Jews. The law sought further to curtail the possibility of German-Jewish sexual liaisons by forbidding Jews to employ as household servants any Aryan woman younger than 45 years of age. Although Gentile-Jewish marriages contracted before the publication of the Nuremberg Laws were exempted from the decree, harsh punishments were meted out to those convicted of miscegenation or "race defilement" (Rassenschande). Ancillary legislation extended the ban to include interracial marriage with Blacks and GYPSIES and introduced elaborate procedures to protect the nation's genetic pool from other racial influences. A "Certificate of Marital Fitness" was required before German couples could be married. Along the same lines, Nazis intensified their persecution of German male homosexuals, who, according to Nazi ideology, represented a negative factor in the Germans' effort to increase their dwindling birth rate.

The Nuremberg Laws initiated the systematic exclusion of Jews from political and social spheres and successfully effected their separation from non-Jews in German society. Still, a comprehensive and uniform exclusion of Jews from all facets of German life was not attained before 1938. During 1936 and 1937, there was a certain deceleration in discriminatory policy, even as, behind the scenes, the consolidation of Section II 112 (Jewish Affairs) of the Security Service under Adolf EICHMANN in late 1936 initiated the centralization of anti-Jewish policy in the hands of the GESTAPO and the SS. It was on June 14, 1938, that Nazi leaders decided to eliminate Jews from the economic life of the nation. Aryanization, or the forced transfer of

An identity card issued to Ellen Sara Wertheimer, a German Jewish woman living in Frankfurt am Main. All German citizens carried such identity cards; those for Jews had the gothic letter "J" imprinted, as in this example. The middle name Sara was required on all documents for Jewish women (or Israel for men) with non-Jewish first names by a German government order in August 1938; effective January 1939. At bottom left, the phrase "evacuated September 15, 1942" has been stamped on the card, indicating that this woman was deported. Ms. Wertheimer was deported to THERESIENSTADT, where she remained for the duration of the war. (USHMM, Collection of Ellen Wall)

Jewish stores and businesses into Aryan hands, began in earnest in the second half of 1938 and worked in tandem with the discriminatory laws that restricted Jews from various professional groups. These measures aimed at encouraging Jewish emigration.

The POGROM of November 9–10, 1938, however, was the pivotal event in Nazi anti-Jewish policy. Following KRISTALLNACHT, anti-Jewish measures intensified; the confiscation of Jewish property and assets accelerated with the November 12 "Decree for the Exclusion of Jews from German Economic Life," while a new tide of laws and ordinances deprived Jews of most of their remaining rights. Jews were deprived of their radios, their driver's licenses, and of any jewelry containing precious or semiprecious stones or metals. Jewish parents were required to give their children only "Jewish" names prescribed by law (as if ordinary "German" names like Elisabeth, Michael, or Maria were not of Hebrew derivation). By January 1939, Jewish men and women bearing names of "non-Jewish" origin had to add Israel or Sara, respectively, to their given names. All Jews were now obliged to carry identity cards that indicated their Jewish heritage, and by October 1939, all Jewish passports were stamped with the letter "J." It should be pointed out that these discriminatory laws and decrees applied to Austrian Jews as well. With the ANSCHLUSS of March 1938, at which time Austria was incorporated into the German Reich, all discriminatory legislation, including that which had initially affected only German Jews, was extended to Austrian Jewry as well.

In addition to those measures that deprived Jews of

their possessions, their political freedoms, and their livelihoods, many discriminatory laws following Kristallnacht succeeded increasingly in physically isolating and segregating Jews from their fellow Germans. In April 1939, laws set up for the protection of tenants in housing complexes were lifted for Jewish residents; many Jews were forced to move from their dwellings or to accept new Jewish subtenants into their homes, according to the whims of local officials. Jewish students were now formally banned from Aryan public schools and from all German universities, and Jews were henceforth totally excluded from cinemas, theaters, and sports facilities. In many cities, Jews were forbidden to enter designated Aryan zones; this kind of legislation was vigorously enforced by local Nazi zealots, so that by the outbreak of war in September 1939, Jews increasingly became socially isolated within the very towns and city neighborhoods where many had lived their entire lives. The advent of war was an excuse for further discrimination and isolation. On September 1, 1939, the day of the Polish invasion that began World War II, Nazi officials imposed an evening curfew for German Jews. Likewise, in a nation soon threatened by aerial bombardment, Jews were restricted from Aryan bomb shelters and from taking part in air raid evacuation exercises. The outbreak of war with the Soviet Union in summer 1941 brought even more repressive measures. Jews were forbidden the use of most public transportation. The most ominous decree to date came in September 1941: a new ordinance required German Jews to wear the JEWISH BADGE as a manner of conspicuous identification. (Jewish Poles had been forced to wear identifying badges, usually bearing the Star of David, since October 1939.)

The first DEPORTATIONS of Jews from the German Reich to the East began in October 1941. Those discriminatory laws that had aimed at separating and isolating Jews from their Aryan neighbors had perhaps accomplished what years of propaganda had often failed to do. Depersonalization—the physical and emotional distancing between Germans and German Jews—at last succeeded in making Jews pariahs within German society and formed a vital link between the period of discriminatory legislation and the "FINAL SOLUTION."

BUYER BEWARE

A centralized, nationwide boycott of Jewish shops and businesses began in Germany on April 1, 1933. The action, ordered by the leadership of the NAZI PARTY, was led by a "Central Committee" headed by anti-Jewish propagandist Julius STREICHER. All over Germany, the NSDAP established local action committees to organize the boycott. At 10:00 A.M. on April 1, uniformed SA and SS sentries posted themselves before the doors of Jewish businesses, harassing customers and distributing antisemitic propaganda. The official boycott, which excited public outrage both at home and abroad, was discontinued after a single day, but "wild" boycotts carried out on local initiative were encouraged by the party and continued in Germany throughout the 1930s.

The official justification for the boycott was the international boycott of German goods imposed by many Jewish organizations worldwide. The centralized action also aimed to harness the momentum of widespread local boycott efforts which had been proliferating throughout Germany in the previous weeks. One such "wild" boycott, described in the news article below, occurred in the city of Münster on March 28, four days before the official boycott.

THE DEFENSIVE MEASURES AGAINST JEWISH STORES IN MÜNSTER

Münster, 28 March [1933]

In the course of the defensive measures against the atrocious propaganda outside of Germany, SA and SS posts were set up in front of Jewish-owned stores in Münster on Wednesday morning at opening time. The action was uniformly carried out during the morning hours after some of the still questionable stores had been omitted. Two to three SA or SS members stood in front of the main and other entrances of the stores and informed the shoppers of the purpose of the action. Later the posts were informed by the party and regiment leadership that they should remain in front of the entrances but should not prohibit customers

from entering. This measure is probably due to the fact that, as stated, a concerted close-down for the present will not take place and that, in accord with the directives of the Reich Party Leader of the NSDAP, the full action against Jewish stores will not take place until Saturday morning. Nowhere in Münster did it come to unforeseen incidents. The actions were initiated and performed everywhere in a very quiet and disciplined manner. Of course the streets were very lively, since the weekly market was taking place at the same time, and one could see a large number of uniformed people in the streets of the city.

Numerous curious onlookers, who had already been informed by the press of the action against Jewish stores, also gathered in front of the affected stores everywhere.

On Salz Street the Woolworth store hung a large poster in the front window shortly after the start of the action that stated that Woolworth is not a Jewish store, and that the firm did not work with Jewish capital. This store was allowed to serve its customers undisturbed.

In the afternoon hours, most of the Jewish stores had sent their personnel home and closed their stores.

An SA troop appeared this morning at the city slaughterhouse and confiscated the butchers' tools.

In the course of the morning, even Jewish professors were prevented from entering the Westphalian State University.

An action in Münster was planned for the afternoon against Jewish lawyers and doctors.

SA in front of the Courthouse

On Wednesday morning an SA troop stood in front of the courthouse to prevent lawyers of Jewish descent and others with Marxist views from further practicing their profession and from entering the courthouse.

The activities of the SA in front of the courthouse proceeded without attracting attention, very calmly and without disruptive crowds.

Jewish judges will not engage in criminal cases in the state court in Münster; there is only one attorney of Jewish heritage working for the Office of the District Attorney; however, he is of Protestant faith.

— Reprinted from Münstersche Zeitung, *March 30, 1933. Translated from the German by Neal Guthrie.*

JEHOVAH'S WITNESSES: SEIZURE AND CONFISCATION

Among the groups persecuted by the NAZIS were the JEHOVAH'S WITNESSES, a small religious community. Known in Germany as Bible Students (Bibelforscher), the Witnesses' cohesive international organization, eschatological doctrine, and vigorous proselytizing soon brought them into conflict with the Nazi regime and the Roman Catholic Church in Germany; the community was officially banned in 1933. Their refusal, on religious grounds, to take the oath of loyalty to Adolf HITLER, to return the Hitler Greeting ("Heil Hitler"), and by 1935, their adamant refusal to serve in the German army and its auxiliary organizations ensured their persecution. By 1936, thousands of Jehovah's Witnesses were arrested, interrogated, and incarcerated in Nazi CONCENTRATION CAMPS.

The following law, promulgated in 1933, was designed to outlaw Jehovah's Witnesses in the German state of Prussia, to confiscate Witness property, and to spread Nazi propaganda about the Witnesses' international organization. Despite these measures, Witnesses withstood Nazi persecution and gained new converts throughout the Nazi reign.

PRUSSIAN MINISTRY
of the Interior

II 1316a/23.6.33   Berlin, June 24, 1933.

By virtue of the Art. 1 of the Decree of the President of the Reich for the Defense of People and State, dated February 28, 1933 (Reichsgesetzblatt I S.83), in connection with Art. 14 of the Police Administration Code, the International Bible Students Association (I.B.V.) and all its organizations (Watchtower Society at Lünen-Magdeburg, the New Apostolic Sect . . .) are herewith dissolved and prohibited [from] the territory of the Free State of Prussia. Their property is seized and confiscated.

Non compliance with this order will be punished by virtue of Art. 4 of the Decree of February 28, 1933.

<u>Reasons.</u>

The I.B.V. and sub-organizations attached to it, under the cloak of supposedly scientific Bible research, carry on in their preachings and writings [in] what is unmistakably incitement of hatred against the institutions of State and Church. By calling both State and Church executives of Satan they undermine the principal pillars of national society. In their many publications (compare the tract Mill. etc., page 18 ff. kf, ws, pv, vu, hf, kr, and other publications), they ridicule the institutions of State and Church by malevolently distorting and misrepresenting Biblical episodes.

Their methods of attack are characterized by a fanatical influencing of their followers; by the employment of considerable funds their bolshevistic and seditionary work gains impetus. The influence they hold over a great number of people is in part due to their strange ceremonies which make fanatics of their adherents and cause direct disturbances of the spiritual equilibrium of the people concerned. According to the aforesaid the above societies are quite obviously antagonistic to the present State and its cultural and ethical structure. Therefore the members of the International Bible Students Association, in accordance with their aims, look upon the Christian and National State which was the result of the national resurgence, as a specially dangerous enemy against whom they have radically aggravated their methods of attack. This is proven by different malicious attacks of leading functionaries of the I.B.V. which have been most recently undertaken both in speech and in writing against National Socialism and its important leaders (compare report of the President of Police of Wuppertal, dated May 31, 1933, I Ad. I 60001). These facts refute the contention that a purely religious and philosophical work is involved.

The danger of the activities of the aforementioned societies to the present State is increased by the fact that of late members of the former communistic and socialistic parties have joined these organizations in suspiciously large numbers hoping to find a secure refuge in this alleged purely religious society, where they could under camouflage continue their fight against the present governmental system. The I.B.V. and the organizations closely connected with it have in the field of pure politics assisted Communism and are just about to develop into a disguised organization for the rallying of various elements dangerous to the State. A systematic and organized communistic activity is being performed by the communist adherents of the movement.

The dissolution of these organizations as [a] defensive measure against communist plots and in order to maintain public order is necessary for the protection of people and State.

In Charge:
(sgd.) **Grauert.**

— *Reprinted from National Archives and Records Administration, Records of Foreign Service Posts, Record Group 84, American Legation Berlin, General Records 1930–40, Decimal 362.1163, Box 1675.*

NUREMBERG LAWS

Following the promulgation of the infamous 1935 NUREMBERG LAWS, a complex series of decrees followed, redefining German society along racial lines. One of these Nuremberg Laws, the Reich Citizenship Law, created for "ARYANS" a new status, that of "REICH citizen," (Reichsbürger) to whom in the future all political rights as citizens would be accorded. Ancillary legislation to the Nuremberg Laws denied Jews, as "state citizens" (Staatsangehörige), these political rights.

Shortly after the proclamation of the Nuremberg Laws, a controversy developed between the NSDAP and Germany's ministerial bureaucracy concerning who precisely was a Jew. The government wanted to define as Jews only those with four Jewish grandparents; party officials countered that an individual was a non-Aryan whether "full," "half," or "quarter" Jewish. The First Ordinance to the Reich Citizenship Law, which provided a legal definition of Jewish status, represented a compromise between the two positions. This ordinance was introduced as evidence at the <u>INTERNATIONAL MILITARY TRIBUNAL</u>. The first page is reproduced at right.

A Viennese family examines a sign plastered at the entrance of a restaurant; 1938. The sign warns, "Jews are not wanted." (NARA)

[Page] 1333

Reich Law Gazette
Part I

1935   Issued in Berlin, 14 November 1935   No. 125

Day	Contents	Page
14 November 1935	First Regulation to the Reich Citizenship Law	1333
14 November 1935	First Regulation of the Law for the Protection of German Blood and German Honor	1334

First Regulation to the Reich Citizenship Law of 14 November 1935

On the basis of §3, Reich Citizenship Law of 15 September 1935 (Reich Law Gazette I, p. 1146) the following is ordered:

§ 1

(1) Until further issuance of regulations regarding Reich citizenship, the following shall for the time being be considered as Reich citizens: all subjects of German or kindred

blood who, at the time the Reich Citizen Law came into effect, possessed the right to vote in the Reichstag elections or those on whom the Reich Minister of the Interior, in agreement with the Deputy to the Führer, has bestowed provisional citizenship.

(2) The Reich Minister of the Interior, in agreement with the Deputy to the Führer, can revoke the provisional Reich citizenship.

§ 2

(1) The regulations of § 1 are also valid for Reich subjects who are Jewish *Mischlinge* [crossbreeds].

(2) A Jewish crossbreed is one who is descended from one or two grandparents who were racially full Jews, insofar as he does not count as a Jew according to § 5, para. 2. A grandparent shall be considered a full-blooded Jew without further ado if he was a member of the Jewish religious community.

§ 3

Only a Reich citizen, as bearer of full political rights, can exercise the right to vote in political matters and hold public office. The Reich Minister of the Interior, or the agency he designates, can make exceptions with regard to occupying public offices during the transition period. The affairs of religious organizations will not be affected.

§ 4

(1) A Jew cannot be a citizen of the Reich. He has no right to vote in political matters; he cannot occupy a public office.

(2) Jewish officials shall be retired as of 31 December 1935. If these officials fought at the front in the World War, either for Germany or its allies, they shall receive the full pension to which they are entitled on the basis of their last pensionable wages until they reach the retirement age limit; they shall not, however, advance in seniority. After reaching the retirement age limit, their pension shall be recalculated according to the last received pensionable salary.

(3) The affairs of religious organizations shall not be affected.

(4) The conditions of service for teachers in Jewish public schools remain unchanged until new regulations of the Jewish school systems are issued.

§ 5

(1) A Jew is anyone who is descended from at least three grandparents who were racially full Jews. § 2, para. 2, sentence 2 applies.

(2) A national who is a Jewish crossbreed descended from two full-Jewish parents shall be considered a Jew if:
(a) he belonged to the Jewish religious community at the time this law was promulgated, or who becomes a member thereafter;
(b) he was married to a Jew at the time the law was promulgated or marries one thereafter;
(c) he is the offspring from a marriage with a Jew, in the sense of para. 1, which was contracted after the Law for the Protection of German Blood and German Honor of 15 September 1935 became effective (Reich Law Gazette I, p. 1146);
(d) he is the offspring of an extramarital relationship with a Jew, according to para. 1, and will be born out of wedlock after 31 July 1936.

§ 6

(1) Insofar as the laws or the regulations of the National Socialist German Workers' Party [NAZI PARTY] and its organizations make requirements in regard to the pureness of blood that exceed those of § 5, they will not be affected.

(2) Any other demands in regard to pureness of blood that exceed § 5 can only be made with permission of the Reich Minister of the Interior and the Deputy to the Führer. In the event any such demands have already been requested, they will be void as of 1 January 1936 if they have not been approved by the Reich Minister of the Interior in agreement with the Deputy to the Führer. The request for approval must be addressed to the Reich Minister of the Interior.

§ 7

The Führer and Reich Chancellor can grant exemptions from the regulations of the implementing ordinance.

Berlin, 14 November 1935
The Führer and Reich Chancellor
Adolf Hitler

The Reich Minister of the Interior
Frick

The Deputy to the Führer
R. Hess
Reich Minister without Portfolio

— *Reproduced from the National Archives and Records Administration, National Archives Collection of World War II War Crimes Records, Record Group 238, Office of the U.S. Chief of Counsel for War Crimes, Document 1417-PS. Translated from the German by Gerald Schwab.*

NEW MARRIAGE REGULATIONS

At the end of the nineteenth century, doctors commonly believed that interracial marriage produced infertility, birth defects, retardation, or other forms of racial degeneration in children. This belief, held by many American and European geneticists, fed NAZI fears for the stagnation and decline of the "ARYAN race" and spurred Nazi legislation designed to protect the German genetic pool from this impending "danger." Based on the NUREMBERG LAW for the Protection of German Blood and Honor, these decrees required evidence of "racial purity" before allowing individuals to marry. Demonstrated by a Certificate of Marital Fitness, evidence of "racial purity" could be obtained only after thorough medical examinations including blood tests, lung x-rays, neurological tests, and genealogical research. Failure to comply with the law resulted in stiff fines or jail terms.

The following instructions to marriage registry officials and public health offices clarify requirements for German racial purity.

The Reich and Prussian
Minister of the Interior
No. 1 B (1 B3 429)
[. . .]

Berlin RW 40, 3 January 1936
Königsplatz 6
[. . .]

Confidential!

To the Provincial Governments
In Prussia: To the Marriage Registry Officials and
                    their supervisors
CC: To the Public Health Offices

(1) According to §6 of the First Implementation Ordinance to the Law for the Protection of German Blood, a marriage may not be performed when the issue of such a union may be suspected of endangering the maintenance of the purity of German blood. This regulation prevents marriage between persons of German blood and such persons who certainly possess no Jewish blood strain, but are of another type of alien blood. Jewish crossbreeds [*Mischlinge*] with one grandparent of full-Jewish ancestry, (crossbreeds second degree) are to be placed on the same level as persons of German blood in this respect.

(2) By the application of this ordinance, the following points are especially to be considered:

a) The German people is composed of members of different races (Nordic, Palatine, Dinaric, Alpine, Mediterranean, East Baltic) and the results of their mixing together among themselves. Accordingly, the blood present in the German people is the German blood.

b) German blood is of a type related to the blood of those peoples whose racial composition is related to the German. This is always the case with peoples whose settlement has been confined to Europe and with those of their descendants in other parts of the world who have not mixed with alien races.

c) To the alien races belong all other races; besides the Jews, this is true in Europe generally only of the Gypsies.

(3) In the interest of the necessary maintenance of pure German blood, marriages that introduce alien blood to German blood cannot be tolerated in any manner when it concerns a significant influx of alien blood in an individual case. This conclusion springs not from the understanding that the German blood is of greater worth than the alien blood, but rather from the realization that they are of different types, so that a mixing is disadvantageous to the alien blood as well as to the German blood. Basically, one must adhere to the principle that every marriage between a person of German blood and a person of pure extraction of alien blood represents a danger to the German blood. The same must also hold true when a person of German blood wishes to marry a crossbreed who possesses a half-portion of alien blood. On the contrary, no reservations will be raised against the marriage of a crossbreed with a quarter or lesser portion of alien blood to a person of German blood. This is not true, however, if the crossbreed in question has an admixture of Negro blood. The Negro blood has such a powerful effect that often in the seventh and eighth generation, it still manifests itself in one's outward appearance. In instances involving an admixture of Negro blood, each individual case is to be put to a particularly thorough examination and, according to its results, be decided whether the marriage is permissible or not. In cases of doubt, the case is to be reported to me through official channels before the decision is to be reached.

(4) If both of the parties to be married are of foreign citizenship, then §6 of the First Implementation Ordinance to the Law for the Protection of German Blood presents no obstacle to the marriage. The same is true when the male to be married is of foreign citizenship, since in this case children proceeding from the union are not eligible for German citizenship, so that an endangering of German blood does not come into question.

(5) Stateless persons who have their residence or regular domicile in the country are to be treated as indigenous persons regarding the application of §6 of the First Implementation Ordinance to the Law for the Protection of German Blood. For stateless persons living abroad, on the other hand, the same is true only if they have formerly possessed German Reich citizenship.

(6) Evidence that no encumbrances to marriage exist according to §6 of the First Implementation Ordinance to

the Law for the Protection of German Blood shall be adduced by a Certificate of Marriage Fitness provided by the Office of Public Health. This [certificate] shall indicate at the same time that no impediment to marriage exists under §1 of the Marital Health Law. Regarding the procedure for the provision [of a certificate], the circular decree of 12 December= 1935 (MBliB, p. 1489) will be referred to.

(7) Up to a certain time, still to be determined by me, the marriage registry official may only demand a Marital Fitness Certificate when, during examination of the lineage of the intended parties, he ascertains knowledge that one of their pure-blooded direct relations is of an alien race or is related to one of half-alien blood, or possesses an admixture of Negro blood. The marriage registry official's obligation to require a Certificate of Marital Fitness when he has reasonable grounds to believe that an impediment to marriage exists according to §1 of the Marital Health Law remains unchanged.

(8) If the Certificate of Marital Fitness is denied, only a written complaint concerning the official involved will be permissible.

(9) If the female party to be wed is a citizen of a foreign country, then the Office of Public Health, when it wishes to deny a Certificate of Marital Fitness, must pursue official channels to obtain my decision, which is binding for all participants. Moreover, the Office of Public Health shall obtain my decision before refusal of the Certificate of Marital Fitness can be given, even if both parties are Reich citizens, when the foreign admixture of blood traces back to a member of the Japanese, Chinese, Indian, or one of the Central American or South American peoples. The same is true when the Office of Public Health, based on the results of the racial-biological examinations, wishes to grant or deny the Certificate of Marital Fitness in other cases, contrary to those rules listed in para. (3).

(10) The marriage registry officials may only provide a Certificate of Marital Eligibility for a marriage performed abroad following the date named in para. (7) if a Certificate of Martial Fitness is presented to him. Up until that time, the marriage registry official may not make the provision of the Certificate of Marital Eligibility dependent upon the presentation of a Certificate of Marital Fitness.

(11) This decree is meant only for official usage; it may not be published.

signed Frick
[seal of the Reich Ministry of Interior]

— *Reprinted from Rose Romani, ed.,* Der nationalistische Völkermord an den Sinti und Roma *(Heidelberg, 1995), 25–26. Recently published in English as* The Nazi Genocide of the Sinti and Roma. *Translated from the German by Patricia Heberer.*

"RESPONSIBLE" OFFICIALS REJECT JEWISH PHYSICIANS

Discriminatory laws designed to remove Jews from specific professions began as early as April 1933 with the Civil Service Law that removed Jews and politically unreliable civil servants and employees from state service. By 1935, Jewish physicians were also being targeted by discriminatory legislation. In December of that year, the Reich Physicians' Ordinance prohibited the further licensing of Jewish doctors. At the same time, all Jewish medical school professors were dismissed from their posts. Instigated in part by German health care professionals, who could only gain by the exclusion of Jews from their profession, legislation soon forbade Germany's vast pool of civil servants from obtaining care from "non-ARYAN" physicians. Such regulations, combined with the refusal of health insurance providers to reimburse medical practices employing non-Aryans and the public harassment of patients still willing to visit Jewish doctors, drove many Jewish physicians from their profession.

When the following decertification regulation was enacted in July 1938, the few remaining Jewish doctors were demoted to the rank of Krankenbehändler *(medics), charged to treat only Jewish patients. The last page of the decree is reproduced in facsimile.*

Fourth Regulation to the Reich's Citizenship Law of 25 July 1938

On the basis of §3 of the Reich's Citizenship Law of 15 September 1935 (Reich Law Gazette I, p. 1146) the following is decreed:

§ 1

Appointments (licenses) of Jewish physicians expire on 30 September 1938.

§ 2

The Reich Minister of the Interior or the office designated by him can, at the recommendation of the Reich Medical Council, grant revocable appointments to physicians whose licenses have expired as a result of §1. The approval can be granted by a judge's order.

§ 3

(1) Jews whose appointment (license) has expired and who subsequently have not received approval under §2 are prohibited from practicing medicine.

(2) A Jew who is granted permission under §2 may, other than his wife and his own children, treat only Jews.

(3) Whosoever purposely or through carelessness violates the regulations under (1) or (2) is subject to a jail sentence of up to one year, a fine, or both of these punishments.

§ 4

The appointment as physician cannot be granted to a Jew.

§ 5

(1) Physicians whose appointment (license) has expired as a result of these regulations and who were front line soldiers can, in the event of need and if deserving, be granted a subsistence allowance by the Reich Medical Council that can be revoked at any time.

(2) Details are to be determined by the Reich Medical Council with the agreement of the Reich Minister of the Interior and the Reich Minister of Finance.

§ 6

Employment contracts calling for the employment of a Jewish physician affected by §1 can be terminated by both parties with six weeks' notice effective 31 December 1938, even if legal or contractual regulations only permit the termination of the employment service at a later date. Legal or contractual regulations which permit the termination of the service contract already at an earlier time are not affected.

§ 7

(1) In regard to the termination of a lease covering rooms that a Jewish physician has rented for himself, his family, or his professional office, the regulations of the law regarding lease termination rights of persons affected by

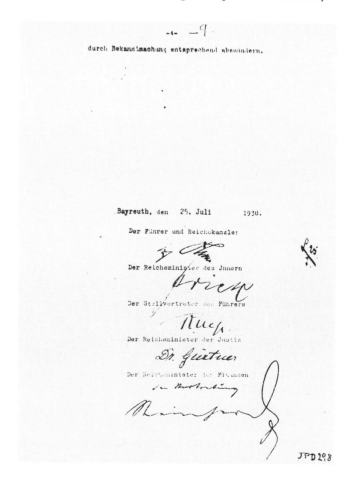

A sign on the gate of an Austrian Jewish doctor's office in Vienna; ca. 1938. The sign reads, "Dr. Herbert Neuwalder: Reception 15–16: medical treatment authorized for Jews only." (Österreichische Gesellschaft für Zeitgeschichte, Vienna, Austria)

the Reorganization of the Civil Service of 7 April 1933 (Reich Law Gazette I, p. 187) apply. In Austria the regulations of §13 of the Regulation for the Reorganization of the Austrian Civil Service of 31 May 1938 (Reich Law Gazette I, p. 607) are applicable. The notice of termination must be effective on 30 September 1938 and must reach the landlord no later than 31 August 1938. Opposition by the landlord to the termination of the lease is not permitted if the landlord is assigned another medical tenant by the Reich Medical Council or by an office designated by it.

(2) The landlord can terminate the rental agreement under the same conditions within the same period. The tenant has no right of appeal.

(3) The regulations of para. 1, sentence 1, are applicable to the employees of Jewish physicians if, as a result of the termination of the appointments (license) they become unemployed.

(4) The Reich Minister of Interior is empowered, in agreement with the Reich Minister of Justice, to issue regulations concerning the termination of rental agreements of the named quarters in para. 1.

§ 8

The Reich Minister of Interior is authorized to amend the Reich Physician Order of 13 December 1935 (Reich Law Gazette I, p. 1433) through appropriate regulations.

Bayreuth, 25 July 1938

The Führer and Chancellor
[signature] A. Hitler

The Reich Minister of Interior
[signature] Frick

The Deputy Führer
[signature] R. Hess

The Reich Minister of Justice
[signature] Dr. Gürtner

The Reich Minister of Finance
[signature] [illegible]
acting for
Steinhardt

— *Reproduced from the National Archives and Records Administration, National Archives Collection of World War II War Crimes Records, Record Group 238, Office of the U.S. Chief of Counsel for War Crimes, Document NG-2612. Translated from the German by Gerald Schwab.*

JEWISH BUSINESSMEN—OUT OF BUSINESS

On November 12, 1938, two days after KRISTALLNACHT, *Hermann* GÖRING, *plenipotentiary for the* FOUR-YEAR PLAN, *chaired an important meeting of* NAZI *economic officials to discuss the ramifications of the* POGROM. *The meeting's participants agreed to the imposition of a fine of 1 billion Reichsmarks on the German Jewish community as a "penalty" for the murder of Ernst vom Rath, legation secretary of the German embassy in Paris, and ruled to seize insurance indemnities awarded to Jewish owners of destroyed property. More importantly, however, they issued several important edicts aimed at the complete expulsion of Jews from the German economy. One of the* ARYANIZATION *decrees resulting from the November meeting, reproduced below, was used as evidence at the* INTERNATIONAL MILITARY TRIBUNAL *at Nuremberg.*

Reich Law Gazette, Year of Issue 1938, Part I

**Decree
on the Exclusion of Jews from German Economic Life
of 12 November 1938**

On the basis of the Decree for the Implementation of the Four-Year Plan of 18 October 1938 (Reich Law Gazette I, p. 887) the following is decreed:

§ 1

(1) Jews (§5 of the First Decree on the Reich Citizen Law of 14 November 1935—Reich Law Gazette I, p. 1333) are as of 1 January 1939 prohibited from operating retail businesses, mail-order businesses, or trading posts, as well as from independently operating crafts businesses.

(2) Further, effective the same day, they are prohibited from offering goods, advertising for them, or taking orders in all types of markets, fairs, and exhibitions.

(3) Jewish commercial businesses (Third Decree of the

Reich Citizen Law—Reich Law Gazette of 14 June 1938, p. 627) that are being operated against this prohibition are to be closed down by the police.

§ 2

(1) As of 1 January 1939 a Jew can no longer be a business manager as defined by the Law for the Regulation of National Labor of 20 January 1934 (Reich Law Gazette I, p. 45).

(2) If a Jew is an executive in a business enterprise, he can be given a six-week termination notice. When this period of notice has expired, all claims from the employee's terminated contract become null and void, especially all claims of compensation and severance pay.

§ 3

(1) A Jew cannot be a member of a cooperative.

(2) Jewish members of a cooperative are expelled as of 31 December 1938. A special termination notice is not required.

§ 4

The Reich Minister of Economics has the authority to issue the necessary implementing regulations in agreement with the participating Reich ministers. He can approve exceptions insofar as this is required for the transfer of a Jewish business into non-Jewish ownership, for the liquidation of Jewish businesses, or in special cases for securing necessary conditions.

Berlin, 12 November 1938

The Commissioner for the Four-Year Plan
Göring
General Field Marshall

— *Reproduced from the National Archives and Records Administration, National Archives Collection of World War II War Crimes Records, Record Group 238, Office of the U.S. Chief of Counsel for War Crimes, Document 1662-PS. Translated from the German by Wendy Lower and Linda Bixby.*

YELLOW STARS

One method of NAZI discrimination against Jews was the enforced identification of Jewish individuals with JEWISH BADGES or arm bands, most often marked with the yellow Star of David. Introduced in occupied Poland in November 1939 and in the German Reich in September 1941, the badges aimed to segregate Jews from the rest of society and make them targets of public humiliation, ridicule, and violence. The following document, used as evidence in the ASCHE TRIAL, describes the preparations for the promulgation of badge regulations in western Europe. Although scheduled for release on April 15, 1942, ministerial opposition, principally from the VICHY government, delayed the implementation of these regulations in France until early June 1942.

IV J   Paris, 15 March 1942
SA.221 b.

<u>Re:</u> Marking of Jews

1. Note:

The official in charge of Jewish affairs from the Brussels office, *SS-Obersturmführer* [SS 1st Lieutenant] **Asche**, participated in the scheduled conference on 14 March 1942. *SS-Sturmbannführer* [SS Major] Lages from the Amsterdam branch office had declined since he could not leave Amsterdam due to his deputy's absence.

Regarding marking of Jews, the following was agreed:

a) In the regulations to be issued for Holland as well as for the occupied Belgian and French territories, there shall be basically no exceptions to speak of. Reference will only be made exclusively to "Jews," as was the case in previous regulations.

b) The yellow Jewish star used in Germany (approx. 10 cm² in size [4 square inches]) will be adapted with the inscription in the country's language or bilingually in Belgium.

A German Jewish boy wearing the Star of David in the Riga GHETTO; 1942.
(Bildarchiv Preussischer Kulturbesitz, Berlin, Germany)

c) The German Embassy Paris related that, as far as they are concerned, they have no objections if the regulations refer exclusively to Jews not excluding certain nationalities. If in an isolated case in other countries a special agreement cannot be avoided, then a decree can be made through inner office channels.

d) For mixed marriages, no allowances will be made. The Jewish mate has to wear the star.

The Amsterdam office from this point on is informed and requested to state its position to the departments of Jewish affairs in the Brussels and Paris offices.

A tentative date of 15 April 1942 has been determined. Final agreements will be made after concluding talks among the three participating offices.

In summary it should be maintained that the marking of Jews in the designated western territories must reach a point of consensus in the context of the Final Solution of the European Jewish question. A reason—for example in the form of a preamble to the regulations—is therefore redundant.

This does not exclude, of course, the propagandistic preparation.

In regard to the penal provisions, one must adhere to the principle of formal conviction to a prison sentence or fines. In each case, however, the assignment to a Jewish concentration camp must be possible.

The penal provisions are therefore to be formulated as follows:

"Offenses against regulations will be punished by imprisonment and fine, or by one of these penalties. The assignment to a Jewish concentration camp is permissible."

In practice one will refrain from dealing with German courts in such cases, and in the interest of the intimidating effect in principle, the assignment to a concentration camp is to be ordered. We need to work toward the establishment of women's concentration camps for convicted Jewesses.

The three officials will mutually inform one another about possible upcoming new factors or unbridgeable difficulties.

[signature] Asche   [signature, illegible]
SS-Obersturmführer   *SS-Hauptsturmführer*
[SS 1st Lieutenant]   [SS Captain]

2. [copy] To remain in the Paris office.

— *Reprinted from Eckhard Colmorgen, Maren Wulf, and the Working Group for the Asche Trial,* Dokumente der Asche-Prozess *(Kiel, 1985), 66–67. Translated from the German by Wendy Lower and Linda Bixby.*

Cases of jewelry confiscated from Jews in the Lodz GHETTO and prepared for shipment to the REICH. All items of potential value to the REICH were taken from Jews. (Yad Vashem, Jerusalem, Israel)

CONFISCATION OF PROPERTY

Soon after Adolf Hitler became chancellor of Germany, National Socialist leaders began to enact a series of laws and programs designed to isolate Jews, political opponents, Gypsies, Jehovah's Witnesses, and other groups in both social and economic spheres. Among the most effective measures of excluding German Jews from the economic life of the nation was Aryanization, the effort to transfer Jewish-owned economic enterprises to "Aryan" German ownership. Aryanization proceeded in two distinct phases. From 1933 through summer 1938, "voluntary Aryanization" encouraged Jewish businessmen, in the face of increasing economic and social discrimination, to sell their businesses and enterprises at radically reduced prices. In early 1933, there were some one hundred thousand Jewish-owned businesses in Germany. By 1938, however, the combination of Nazi terror, propaganda, boycott, and legislation was so effective that some two-thirds of all Jewish-owned or operated businesses within Germany had been liquidated or sold. Jewish owners, often desperate to emigrate or to sell a failing business, accepted a selling price that was only twenty to thirty percent of the enterprise's actual value. Following the Anschluss of Austria in March 1938, the pauperization of Jews and the exploitation of Jewish-owned capital proceeded at a far more rapid rate in Austria than it had in Germany.

Immediately following the violent Kristallnacht pogrom of November 9–10, 1938, Aryanization entered its second stage: the obligatory transfer of all Jewish enterprises to non-Jewish ownership. Every remaining Jewish business was assigned a trustee to oversee its immediate, forced sale. The trustee's fee for this required service was often only slightly less than the sale price and was paid by the former Jewish owner. A further percentage of sale profits funded the Office of the Four-Year Plan headed by Hermann Göring, later a defendant at the International Military Tribunal.

Developed in August 1938, the Four-Year Plan rapidly prepared the German economy for war. The massive funds needed to initiate large-scale armament production were raised in part through the confiscation of property and valuables. German Jews who wished to emigrate were forced to forfeit much of their property. A portion of these assets went directly to the Reich government in the form of a special emigration "escape tax" (Reichsfluchtsteuer), while the rest was deposited as liquid assets into special non-transferable bank accounts whose access was severely restricted. The assets of those Jews who remained in Germany were likewise placed in blocked accounts beginning in early 1939; their owners were allowed to withdraw from them only a fixed monthly sum, the bare minimum needed for meeting their expenses. In addition, after Kristallnacht, German Jews were required to pay one billion Reichsmarks as a penalty; the state confiscated all the insurance payments that should have been paid to Jewish property

A closed Jewish storefront was defaced with a taunting inscription: "[Store owner Hermann Tuchner] is in Dachau," the concentration camp; late 1938.
(Yivo Institute for Jewish Research, New York)

owners. The latter were responsible for all property repairs themselves.

Jews were not the only victims of Nazi property confiscation. Any group or organization considered detrimental to the National Socialist cause was discouraged, disbanded, or destroyed. In the process, valuables that could be used to enrich individual Nazis or the coffers of the THIRD REICH were confiscated. In order to raise revenue, property belonging to convents and monasteries throughout the Reich was seized, as were the libraries and holdings of Masonic lodges in Germany and Austria.

The Nazis also looted European art treasures for profit. Before the outbreak of World War II, the German government had encouraged museums throughout Germany, Austria, and the Sudetenland to purge their collections of "dangerous" works. Referred to as "degenerate art" by National Socialist propaganda, the works of renowned masters such as Chagall, Gauguin, Van Gogh, Klee, Kandinsky, Braque, Picasso, Modigliani, Matisse, Marc, Kokoschka, and others were considered as decadent or inferior because of their subject matter, method of expression, or because of the personal convictions of the artist. Many of these works were subsequently auctioned on the world market in exchange for foreign currency with which to bolster the German economy.

Once World War II had begun, Nazi leaders sought to exploit fully those territories they occupied through the confiscation of all valuable property. German officials sold a wide variety of confiscated materials, including priceless objets d'art, to private investors and collectors through the black market. The sale of seized treasures became so lucrative that, in September 1940, Hitler established the Special Staff for the Fine Arts *(Sonderstab Bildende Kunst)*. Headed by Alfred ROSENBERG, later a defendant in the International Military Tribunal, the Special Staff systematically searched museums, libraries, universities, castles, warehouses, and homes throughout German-occupied territory in search of valuable art, furniture, manuscripts, and jewels. In France alone, an estimated 22,000 paintings, sculptures, and objects from all historical periods were stolen from public and private museums. Famous masterpieces by da Vinci, Rembrandt, Dürer, Raphael, and Michelangelo vanished after the war; many of these reappeared in private collections and auction houses around the world.

One of the most notorious sources of plundered revenue for the Nazis was the seizure of personal effects from the victims of GENOCIDE. Nazi officials seized the property and assets of Jews at the time of their deportation. Arriving at KILLING CENTERS such as BELZEC, SOBIBOR, TREBLINKA, and AUSCHWITZ, prisoners were systematically stripped of all those possessions that they had carried with them from their homes, whether valuable or humble. SLAVE LABORERS were forced to shave prisoners' hair; the hair was then processed into felt designated for the war effort. On the way to the GAS CHAMBERS, victims were forced to undress; their clothing was sold or redistributed. After gassing, the

A moving van of the Dutch company A. Puls, which moved much of the property confiscated from deported Dutch Jews. Vans like these became so common in Amsterdam's Jewish quarter during 1942–43 that the word "pulsen" was coined to denote stealing.
(Rijksinstituut voor Oorlogsdocumentatie, Amsterdam, Netherlands)

bodies of the dead were searched for hidden valuables and gold teeth. Finally, the cremated remains of the victims were sometimes utilized as fertilizer.

Evidence documenting the extent of Nazi theft, plunder, and exploitation did not appear in the earliest war crimes trials. Later, at the International Military Tribunal, crimes involving property paled in comparison to other Nazi atrocities. In ten of the twelve subsequent NUREMBERG MILITARY TRIBUNAL trials, however, property crimes became a major component in each indictment. In the JURISTS', FLICK, and MINISTRIES TRIALS, Nazi confiscation of property played a central role in the charges. Aryanization and the seizure of property from Freemasons, churches, and political opponents of National Socialism before 1939 were considered CRIMES AGAINST HUMANITY. This established the jurisdiction of the American tribunals to try crimes committed against German civilians prior to the outbreak of war in Europe. The I.G. FARBEN and KRUPP TRIALS further charged that participation in the development of the Four-Year Plan constituted intent to wage aggressive war. Occupation policies that robbed civilian populations stood in clear violation of the HAGUE CONVENTION of 1907 and formed the basis for further charges of WAR CRIMES not justified by military necessity in all ten of the cases involving property crimes. Later war crimes trials, however, did not often charge defendants with crimes of this nature because of the complexity of the evidence and the short statute of limitations for property crimes.

Some of the documents in the following chapter were introduced as evidence in various trials, while others serve to illustrate the wide range of Nazi crimes involving the confiscation and exploitation of property.

A FINE AGAINST THE JEWS OF GERMANY

Following the assassination of German diplomat Ernst vom Rath in Paris by a Jewish youth, a wave of antisemitic terror swept throughout Germany and Austria. During the night of November 9–10, 1938, more than 90 people were killed; more than 1,000 synagogues were desecrated and deliberately burned, 7,000 Jewish shops were looted, and countless Jewish homes, schools, hospitals, and cemeteries burned or destroyed. Later called KRISTALLNACHT, *or the "Night of Broken Glass," the mass destruction was portrayed by the* NAZIS *as a spontaneous display of public outrage against vom Rath's assassination. In actuality, the* POGROM *was planned and directed by elements of the German government.*

Confronted with the damages of Kristallnacht, Hermann GÖRING, *in his capacity as plenipotentiary for the* FOUR-YEAR PLAN, *convened a high-level ministerial meeting on November 12. It was decided that the insurance monies due to German Jewish businesses for damage incurred during Kristallnacht would be turned over to the German government. On the same day Göring issued a decree imposing an aggregate fine of one billion Reichsmarks on German Jews as "punishment" for the assassination of vom Rath. The text of this decree, introduced as evidence at the* MINISTRIES TRIAL, *is reproduced below.*

1579

REICH LAW GAZETTE
Part I

1938 Issued from Berlin, 14 November 1938 No. 189 [...]

Decree
Concerning a Penalty Compensation from Jews of German Nationality
of 12 November 1938

The hostile attitude of the Jews against the German people and the Reich does not even shrink from cowardly deeds of murder and demands decisive resistance and harsh penalty.

I therefore order the following on the grounds of the decree for the execution of the Four-Year Plan of 18 October 1936 (Reich Law Gazette Part I, page 887):

§ 1

The payment of 1,000,000,000 Reichsmarks is imposed on the entire population of Jews of German nationality.

§ 2

Regulations are being issued by the Reich Finance Minister in coordination with the participating Reich Ministers.

Berlin, 12 November 1938

The Commissioner for the Four-Year Plan
Göring
General Field Marshal

Reich Law Gazette 1938 I   p. 415

— Reproduced from the National Archives and Records Administration, National Archives Collection of World War II War Crimes Records, Record Group 238, Office of the U.S. Chief of Counsel for War Crimes, Document 1412-PS. Translated from the German by Wendy Lower.

ROOMS FOR RENT

Systematic DEPORTATION *of German Jews began in October 1941. In mid-November,* NAZI *officials informed the Jews of Bremen that they were to be resettled in the East in order to secure new living quarters for their "*ARYAN*" neighbors. Since the early days of the war, northern German port cities like Bremen had been particular targets of* ALLIED *bombings; by 1941, Bremen had suffered heavy damage, and living space was at a premium.*

*The information that the Bremen Jews received was not wholly inaccurate. On November 18, 1941, 440 Jews were deported; on the same day Nazi officials seized their homes and property, which were then distributed to bombing victims. This deportation occurred just days before the promulgation of the eleventh Citizenship Decree, which enabled German officials to strip German Jews of their citizenship and thus legally confiscate their property. Concerning the Jews' "*RESETTLEMENT*," however, the Germans had been more duplicitous. The transport went directly to the Minsk ghetto, where most were murdered within the year. Only six Jews from the transport survived the war.*

Copy
The Ruling Mayor   Bremen, 18 November 1941
   RV 1504/41

To the Reich Defense Commissioner
in the area of Military District 10

Hamburg 13

Harvestehuderweg 12

Re: Apartments and Furniture of Jews Evacuated to the East

According to a decree from the security and main offices [*sic*], the apartments and furnishings of Jews evacuated to the East are to be seized for the benefit of the Reich.

I request the order be given that these apartments and furnishings be made available by the Reich to the local authorities exclusively for the use of our populace that has become homeless because of air raids, as soon as these premises can be placed at their disposal; however, it is the prerogative of these local administrative offices to release such apartments and furnishings not suitable for the homeless for other purposes.

On behalf of
signed Fischer

copy

to the Housing Assignment Office
for information

Bremen, 18 November 1941
The Ruling Mayor
On behalf of
signed Dr. Fischer
as RV-Referent

[handwritten notations]
[stamp]

Housing Assignment Office Bremen
[signature, illegible]

— Reproduced from the Staatsarchiv Bremen, Document 3.W.11 Nr 34[39]. Translated from the German by Johannes Ungar.

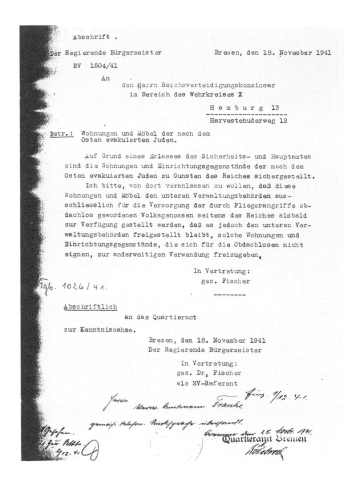

Members of a French commission formed to confiscate Jewish apartments place a seal on the door of the Paris apartment of former French Colonial Minister Georges Mandel; 1941. As a Jew and traditional conservative, Mandel was sharply opposed to French collaboration with NAZI Germany. After internment at the SACHSENHAUSEN and BUCHENWALD concentration camps, Mandel returned to Paris in early July 1944, where he was shot on the orders of Joseph Darnand, head of the *Milice,* the VICHY paramilitary force that aided the Germans in rounding up Jews in France.
(Bundesarchiv Koblenz, Germany)

The former Jewish rubber-goods store Gummi Weil in Hamburg after its ARYANIZATION in 1938. It was renamed Stamm and Bassermann to reflect its new "ARYAN" ownership.
(Bildarchiv Preussischer Kulturbesitz, Berlin, Germany)

THE CONFISCATION OF JEWISH PROPERTY

Before November 1938, NAZI officials used boycotts, harassment, and physical violence to pressure Jewish entrepreneurs into selling their businesses at drastically reduced prices. With the assault on Jewish homes and businesses during KRISTALLNACHT, the Nazi government adopted new tactics to deprive German Jews of their livelihood. Immediately after the POGROM, new regulations prohibited Jews from undertaking most economic activities. By December 1938, legal measures compelled Jews to sell or transfer workshops, factories, and businesses to "ARYANS" or government-appointed trustees. Laws like the one reproduced below from the Reich Law Gazette were designed to exclude Jews from the economic life in Germany and to encourage their emigration; the proceeds from this compulsory ARYANIZATION filled the government coffers. The document reproduced here was used as evidence at the INTERNATIONAL MILITARY TRIBUNAL.

No. 206—Day of Issue: 5 December 1938

Decree Concerning the Utilization of Jewish Property of 3 December 1938

On the basis of §1 of the Second Regulation by the Commissioner of the Four-Year Plan based on the Decree of 24 November 1938 for the Registering of Jewish-Owned Property (Reich Law Gazette I, p. 1668), the following

is decreed in agreement with the participating Reich Ministers:

Article I
Commercial Businesses
§ 1

The owner of a Jewish commercial business (Third Decree on Reich Citizenship Law of 14 June 1938—Reich Law Gazette I, p. 627) can be ordered to sell or liquidate the enterprise within a specified time. Certain conditions may be stipulated in the order.

§ 2

(1) For a Jewish commercial business whose owners according to §1 have been ordered to sell or liquidate, a trustee may be appointed for the temporary continuation of the business and for the completion of the sale or liquidation, especially if the owner of the enterprise has not complied with the order within the specified period and his application for an extension of time has been rejected.

(2) The trustee is empowered to undertake all judicial and extrajudicial actions and legal measures that the business of the said company, its liquidation, or sale require. His authority replaces any legally required power of attorney.

(3) The trustee must exercise the care of a responsible businessman and is subject to state control.

(4) The expenses of the trustee administration are carried by the business owner.

§ 3

(1) The owner of the Jewish commercial business is to be notified of the instructions specified in §§1 and 2.

(2) In case of the owner's absence, notification may take place through publication in the *German Reich Bulletin* and *Prussian State Bulletin*. In these cases, the day of publication stands for the day of notification.

§ 4

Upon notification of the order through which a trustee is appointed in accordance with §2, the owner loses the right to dispose of the property the trustee has been appointed to administer. He regains this right only if the appointment of the trustee is withdrawn.

§ 5

Consent for the sale according to §1 of the Decree, based on the Decree of 26 April 1938 for the Reporting of Jewish-Owned Property (Reich Law Gazette, p. 415), is necessary also in such cases in which the sale has been ordered; this also applies to the sale by a trustee. . . .

Article IV
Jewels, Gems, and Objects of Art
§ 14

(1) Jews are forbidden to acquire, pawn, or sell objects of gold, platinum, or silver, as well as precious stones and pearls. Except when attachments exist on behalf of a non-Jewish creditor at the time this decree goes into effect, such objects may only be acquired by public purchasing offices

established by the Reich. The same applies to other jewels and objects of art insofar as the price of the individual objects exceeds one thousand Reichsmarks.

(2) The provisions of para. 1 does not apply to Jews of foreign citizenship.

Article V
General Regulations
§ 15

(1) Authorization for the sale of Jewish commercial businesses, real estate, or other Jewish property can be granted under conditions that may consist of the payment of money by the buyer to benefit the Reich.

(2) Authorizations of the kind mentioned in para. 1 may also be granted with the proviso that the Jewish seller is to receive obligations of the German Reich or registered titles against the German Reich instead of the total or partial consideration as provided for in the sales contract.

§ 16

The regulations specified for Jews in Article II also apply to commercial businesses as well as organizations, foundations, institutions, and other non-commercial businesses which are not industrial, insofar as they are to be considered Jewish according to the Third Regulation under the Reich Citizenship Law of 14 June 1938 (Reich Law Gazette I, p. 627).

§ 17

(1) The higher administrative authorities are responsible for issuing instructions based on the regulations of Article I and II insofar as the special provisions of paras. 3 and 4 ["and 4" crossed out in original] do not apply. The higher administrative authorities are also to supervise the appointed trustees.

(2) §6 of the Decree of 26 April 1938 determines which authorities are higher administrative authorities within the meaning of this Decree on the Registration of Jewish Property (Reich Law Gazette I, p. 414), with the provision that the following authorities are qualified:

In Anhalt
    the Anhalt State Ministry, Department of Economics;
In Baden
    the Baden minister of finance and economics;
In Württemberg
    the Württemberg minister of economics;
In Austria
    the Reich commissar for the reunification of Austria with the German Reich or the authorities named by him;
In the Sudeten German Territories
    the government presidents.

(3) Insofar as it is a question of agricultural property, the senior president in Prussia (Agricultural Department) and the higher settlement authorities in the non-Prussian states take the place of the higher administrative authorities. Insofar as it is a question of forest property, the higher forest authorities take the place of the higher administrative authorities. . . .

§ 24
This decree goes into effect on the day of publication.

Berlin, 3 December 1938

Reich Minister of Economic Affairs
Walter Funk
Reich Minister of the Interior
Frick

— *Reproduced from the National Archives and Records Administration, National Archives Collection of World War II War Crimes Records, Record Group 238, Office of the U.S. Chief of Counsel for War Crimes, Document 1409-PS. Translated from the German by Wendy Lower.*

THE PLUNDER OF POLAND

NAZI leaders sought to exploit occupied territories through the confiscation of all valuable property. To this end, money, priceless art treasures, and rare library collections were seized from churches, museums, and private collections from all parts of conquered Europe. Fine furniture and art were sent back to Germany or used to decorate the offices and residences of German occupation authorities, while treasures deemed inferior because of their cultural origins or symbolism were destroyed.

The destruction of the King's Palace in Warsaw underscored the Nazis' policy of plunder. Originally built in the thirteenth century, the King's Palace served as a repository for art. Soon after the German occupation of Warsaw began in September 1939, Governor General Hans FRANK issued orders for the Palace's plunder and demolition. In a deposition introduced as evidence at the INTERNATIONAL MILITARY TRIBUNAL, Dr. Stanislaw Lorentz, a lecturer at Warsaw University and Director of the National Museum, detailed the subsequent devastation of the Palace.

At the time of the capitulation and the entry of the German army into Warsaw [in September 1939], the Palace with the exception of a few damages done during the siege, was on the whole in a satisfactory state.

The municipal administration of Warsaw had immediately taken measures to preserve the building and already in the first days of October, they had begun to rebuild the temporary roof over the wing containing the magnificent reception apartments. In October 1939, Hans Frank, who was then the Governor, arrived in Warsaw.

He stopped at the Warsaw Palace and declared to representatives of [the] Warsaw Municipal Administration that the Palace should be pulled down; furthermore he opposed himself to any work for the restoration or the

American generals Omar Bradley, George Patton, and Dwight D. EISENHOWER examine paintings found in a mine in Germany by ALLIED troops; April 12, 1945. The Germans looted objects d'art throughout occupied Europe. (NARA)

preservation of the building which was only slightly damaged during military operations.

With his own hand, Frank tore off the silver eagles from the royal canopy and put them into his pockets. By this act, he gave [the] signal for the beginning of the general plunder of the Palace installations, which lasted for several weeks. Pictures, upholsteries, wainscotting were torn off the walls and stolen. At the same time, the German miners made holes in the Palace walls for the purpose of laying mines. The soldiers did not keep secret the object of the preparations: the Palace was doomed to destruction by explosion. The disclosures made by the soldiers were confirmed by the arrival of architects and German building contractors under the personal direction of Architect Heidelberg, Director of [the] Architecture Department of Warsaw District. These people, with the help of hundreds of Jews brought daily to the spot, began taking down the building. With electric boring machines they made two rows of holes, with an interval of 75 [centimeters, 29 in.] between them, and at a height of 1.5 metre [ca. 5 ft.] from the ground. In two months several thousands of these holes had been bored in the outer and the interior walls of the palace. During these demolitions, the Palace changed its aspect from day to day and from month to month whilst at the end it looked a mere heap of ruins.

The principal tools used were picks and axes. Precious wainscotting was torn off the walls, marble mantle pieces and wood parquets with beautiful design were wrenched out. The marble, wood and stone staircases were broken up. Roofs and ceilings were also torn off, as well as the iron beams which had been placed in 1918–1939, during the preservation works. The ruins of the Palace remained in this state for nearly five years and were still in the same state after the insurrection [of the Polish Home Army in August 1944].

All the furniture of the Palace had been stolen: hundreds of pictures, sculptures including antique pieces as well as sculptures by artists of the XVIIIth century: Houdon, Le Brun, Monaldie; upholsteries, Renaissance, Baroque, Rococo, classical and empire furniture, clocks, especially those of the XVIII century, chandeliers, candelabras, six of which—the large ones—were in bronze of Gaffieri, vases by Thomin and numerous other objects of art; especially those of the XIIIth century. In addition to the objects of art which belonged to the Palace itself and were included in its inventory, there were fine collections of art treasures and souvenirs in the depository of the State Department of Art Collections. These comprised the collections which had been claimed from Russia after 1920, the collections from the Rappersville Museum in Switzerland which had been transferred to Poland, collections brought and given. The depository contained about 1,000 pictures, numerous sculptures, various objects of arts, graphic collections, archives and incunabula. The transport and the packing of the stolen objects were very primitive. Wooden beams and marble plates were thrown out through the windows of the Palace, or were left under [the] open sky in November and December under rain and snow, during great frosts, they lay about in great confusion, mixed up with hot-water piping, central heating boilers, wainscotting, modern kitchen appliances and blocks of ancient wooden floors.

The objects stolen from the Palace were sent either to destinations which are unfortunately unknown to us, or to the four large storehouses in Warsaw, from where they were later distributed following the applications of various German building contractors.

The material necessary for the transformation of the offices of the Premier Minister into "Deutsche Haus," for the transformation of the Belweder Palace into the residence of the Governor General Frank, for the accommodation of the Warsaw Casino as headquarters of the Gestapo, and for other works of reconstructions came from these store-houses. The collections from the Palace were also transferred to Krakow, where they were temporarily stored, in view of their ultimate transfer to Germany. The material from these store-houses was also used for the decoration of the offices and private apartments of German officials, for the exchange of presents between the members of civil administration, Gestapo and the army. Furthermore, Governor Fischer and President Dengel gave the authorization to various offices and to employees to chose any objects they liked from those included in the Palace inventory. The ambition of President Dengel was to send the greatest possible quantity of collections to Wuerzbourg [Würzburg], his native city. Amongst the offices which were not in Warsaw, it was the Gestapo in Lublin and in Radom who had shown the greatest zeal. There was also one more method: that was the ordinary plunder practised by the Feldgendarmerie [German military police] of Potsdam as from the beginning of October 1939, and later by all kinds of German officials. The objects stolen were sent either to Germany or to Warsaw market where they could be bought for a low price. At the beginning of December 1944, two months after the capitulation of Warsaw [after the Warsaw Uprising], some German military units placed cartridges with dynamite in the holes made in 1939 and blew up the Palace. The cellars and the foundation are all that remained.

In conclusion, I emphasize that the Germans—on the order of the ex-Governor-General Frank, had closed—immediately after their entry into Poland—all the museums, cultural Polish institutions and societies, whilst the property of all these institutions was confiscated and subsequently most of it was plundered.

— *Reprinted from the National Archives and Records Administration, National Archives Collection of World War II War Crimes Records, Record Group 238, Office of the U.S. Chief of Counsel for War Crimes, Document 954-D, 2–5.*

"SECONDHAND CLOTHING"

Those condemned to die in the KILLING CENTERS were forced to undress before entering the GAS CHAMBERS. Ever efficient, the Germans reutilized their clothing. Teams of prisoners, called SONDERKOMMANDOS, carefully searched the clothing for hidden valuables, removed all traces of the previous owners, and sorted the apparel by quality and type. Clothing of high quality was reserved for German soldiers or sold to those Germans who had resettled in annexed German territories. Goods of lesser quality went to ETHNIC GERMANS slated for Germanization. Household goods and luggage collected at the DEPORTATION sites and CONCENTRATION CAMPS was also distributed in the same manner.

The letter reproduced below, introduced as evidence at the RuSHA TRIAL, conveys Heinrich HIMMLER's orders for a special clothing shipment to be made in time for Christmas.

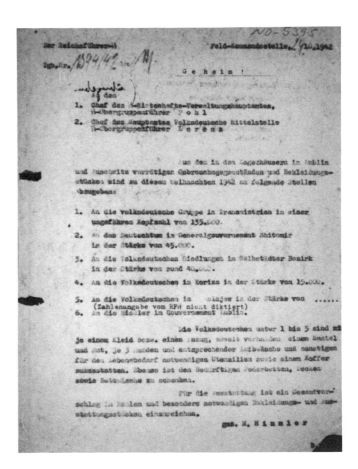

The *Reichsführer-SS*
                  Field Command Post 24 October 1942
Journal No. B 94/42-Top Secret
                  Secret!

To the
1. Chief of the SS Central Office for Economy and
   Administration
   SS-Obergruppenführer [SS Lieutenant General] **Pohl**
2. Chief of the Central Office for Ethnic Germans
   SS-Obergruppenführer **Lorenz**

From the warehouses in Lublin and Auschwitz, available household items and articles of clothing are to be delivered this Christmas 1942 to the following places:

1. To the ethnic German group in Transnistria of about 135,000 persons.
2. To the ethnic German community of 45,000 in General Commissariat Zhytomyr.
3. To the ethnic German settlements in the Halbstadt district, of approximately 40,000.
4. To the ethnic Germans in Koriza of about 15,000 persons.
5. To the ethnic Germans in Nicolajew, approximately . . . (Number not dictated by the *Reichsführer-SS* [Himmler].)
6. To the settlers in the Lublin government.

The ethnic Germans under ages one to five are to be provided each with a dress or suit and, as far as available, with a coat and hat, three shirts, appropriate underclothing, and other items of daily use as well as a suitcase. Needy persons are also to be given feather beds, blankets, as well as bed linen.

A total estimate broken down in figures for the required supplies, and especially for necessary articles of clothing and equipment, is to be submitted.

                                    signed H. Himmler

2.) *SS-Obergruppenführer* Prützmann
3.) *SS-Oberführer* [SS Colonel] Hofmeyer
                                    [handwritten, illegible]
Carbon copied and sent with the request for acknowledgement.

                                    1. [initial] B.S.
          SS-Obersturmbannführer [SS Lieutenant Colonel]

— *Reproduced from the National Archives and Records Administration, National Archives Collection of World War II War Crimes Records, Record Group 238, Office of the U.S. Chief of Counsel for War Crimes, Document NO-5395. Translated from the German by Wendy Lower.*

Property expropriated from German Jews before the war is sold to "ARYAN" Germans. (Yivo Institute for Jewish Research, New York)

"REALLOCATING" THE POSSESSIONS OF THE MURDERED

Many valuables and possessions that the Germans obtained through confiscation, DEPORTATION, *and murder were sold or reused to fund German government programs.* NAZI *officials used euphemistic language to describe the seizure of these goods. Thus, Nazi bureaucrats could justify the plunder as "confiscation of stolen property," "impounding hoarded goods," and "seizure of property originating from theft."*

The SS CENTRAL OFFICE FOR ECONOMY AND ADMINISTRATION *(WVHA), used the revenue from sales of confiscated valuables to pay for the operation of the* CONCENTRATION CAMP *system. Prisoners' clothing and household possessions were sold by the WVHA to the* CENTRAL OFFICE FOR ETHNIC GERMANS *(VoMi). In turn, VoMi resold or redistributed these goods to German soldiers or ethnic Germans in order to defray the costs of the* GERMANIZATION *program.*

SS-Brigadeführer (SS Brigadier General) August Frank, employed in the WVHA, sent the following letter

Copy   26 September 1942

Secret Commando Matter!

Chief A/Pr./B.   6 copies
Journal No. 050/42 secret   4th copy
V S 96/42

Re: Utilization of the Property Occasioned by the
Deportation and Resettlement of Jews

To the
Director of the SS Administration **Lublin**
Director of the Administration of Concentration Camp
Auschwitz

Regardless of the general order that is to be expected in the course of October regarding the utilization of the moveable and non-moveable property of the deported Jews, the following directions are now issued with regard to the property, which will be referred to in all future orders as stolen, fenced, and hoarded goods:

1. a) All cash in German Reichsbank notes is to be paid to the account of the SS Central Office for Economy and Administration 158 1488 at the Reichsbank Berlin-Schöneberg.

    b) Foreign currency (coins or bills), precious metals, jewelry, precious or semi-precious stones, pearls, gold teeth, and gold fragments are to be delivered to the SS Central Office for Economy and Administration. This Office is responsible for the immediate forwarding to the German Reichsbank.

    c) Watches of all kinds, alarm clocks, fountain pens, mechanical pencils, manual and electric razors, pocket knives, scissors, flashlights, wallets, and purses will be repaired, cleaned, and valued by the SS Central Office for Economy and Administration in special workshops in order that they be sent as soon as possible to the front troops. Delivery to the troops follows payment through the supply depot. There are three to four price categories to fix and guarantee that every leader or soldier can at the most buy a watch. Excepted from sale are gold watches; their utilization will be at my discretion. The total proceeds will go to the Reich.

    d) Men's underwear, men's clothing, including footwear, are to be sorted and valued. After covering

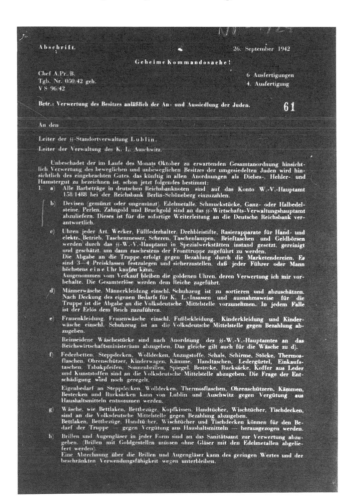

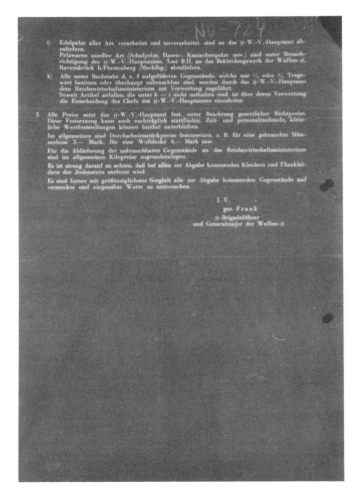

one's own needs for the concentration camp inmates and in exceptional cases for the troops, the goods are to be delivered to the Office for the Repatriation of Ethnic Germans. In any case, the proceeds will go to the Reich.

e) Women's clothing, women's underwear, including footwear, children's clothing, children's underwear, including footwear, are to be delivered against payment to the Office for the Repatriation of Ethnic Germans. Pure silk underwear is to be delivered according to an order of the SS Central Office for Economy and Administration to the Reich Ministry of Economics. The same pertains to the underwear in (d).

f) Feather beds, quilts, wool blankets, suiting material, scarves, umbrellas, canes, thermos flasks, earmuffs, baby carriages, combs, handbags, leather belts, shopping bags, tobacco pipes, sunglasses, mirrors, cutlery, knapsacks, suitcases made of leather and synthetic material are to be delivered to the Central Office for Ethnic Germans. The question of compensation will be settled later. According to their own needs, quilts, wool blankets, thermos flasks, earmuffs, combs, cutlery, and knapsacks can be obtained by Lublin and Auschwitz against payment from budgetary funds.

g) Linen, such as sheets, quilt covers, pillowcases, towels, dishcloths, tablecloths are to be delivered against payment to the Central Office for Ethnic Germans. Sheets, quilt covers, towels, dishcloths, and tablecloths needed by the troops can be obtained against payment from budgetary funds.

h) Spectacles and eyeglasses of every kind are to be delivered to the Medical Department for utilization. (Glasses with gold frames must be handed in without glass but with the precious metal). A settlement of the spectacles and eyeglasses can remain outstanding because of their small value and limited usage.

i) Valuable furs of all kinds, finished or rough, are to be delivered to the SS Central Office for Economy and Administration. Fur items of lesser value (sheep, hare, rabbit, etc.) are to be delivered with notification to the SS Central Office for Economy and Administration, Department B II; to the Clothing Factory of the *Waffen-SS*, Ravensbrück near Fürstenberg (Mecklenburg).

k) All items mentioned under (d), (e), and (f) which are not more than one-fifth or two-fifths fit for wear or which are completely useless are to be delivered by the SS Central Office for Economy and Administration to the Reich Economic Ministry for utilization. With regard to the delivery of goods which are not mentioned under (b)–(i), the decision about their utilization is left to the chief of the SS Central Office for Economy and Administration.

2. All prices are fixed by the SS Central Office for Economy and Administration in accordance with legal standard prices. This determination can take place subsequently. Petty valuations which take too much time and personnel need not be made.

In general, average prices are to be fixed for every piece, e.g., 3 Reichsmarks for a secondhand pair of trousers, 6 Reichsmarks for a blanket, etc.

The delivery of goods that are of no further use to the Reich Economic Ministry will generally be made on the basis of prices per kilogram.

Special attention is to be paid that the Jewish star is removed from all clothing and outer garments that are being handed in.

Furthermore, all things to be handed in are to be examined with the utmost care for hidden valuables sewn into the clothing.

On behalf of

signed Frank
SS-Brigadeführer and *Generalmajor* of the *Waffen-SS*
[SS Brigadier General]

— *Reproduced from the National Archives and Records Administration, National Archives Collection of World War II War Crimes Records, Record Group 238, Office of the U.S. Chief of Counsel for War Crimes, Document NO-724. Translated from the German by Wendy Lower and Linda Bixby.*

Torahs looted by the Germans from the Lodz GHETTO in Poland. The Germans stole many religious items and objects of art from nations they occupied during the war. (Yad Vashem, Jerusalem, Israel)

GOLD TEETH FOR THE REICHSBANK

The Germans ensured that nothing of value belonging to their victims was wasted or discarded. After they had been murdered in the GAS CHAMBERS, *the prisoners' bodies were examined for hidden valuables, and their artificial teeth were extracted to yield precious metals. These gold teeth and fillings were shipped to a special account, labeled "Max Heiliger," at the Reichsbank, the German central bank. These precious metals were then transferred to the state mint and melted down, making the dental gold, silver, and platinum untraceable.*

The following document is a draft list, prepared by the Reichsbank, of the forty-sixth shipment of gold from human teeth to the Prussian State Mint. It was used by the prosecution at the MINISTRIES TRIAL.

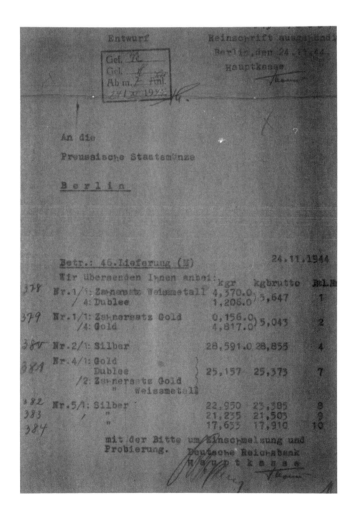

Ka.
Draft
  [stamp]
  Processed: *R*
  Read: *H*
  Enclosures: 7
  24/XI 1944
  [handwritten] H

Final Copy distributed
Berlin, 24 November 1944
Main Cash Desk
[signature] Thoms

To the
Prussian State Mint

Berlin

<u>Re: 46th Delivery (M)</u>   24 November 1944

Enclosed are:	kg	kg gross	bag#
378 No. 1/1: artificial teeth, white metal	4,370.0		
/4: gold-plated	1,206.0	5,647	1
379 No. 1/1: artificial teeth, gold	0,156.0		
/4: gold	4,817.0	5,043	2
380 No. 2/1: silver	28,591.0	28,855	4
381 No. 4/1: gold gold-plated			
/2: artificial teeth, white gold	25,157	25,373	7
382 no. 5/1: silver	22,950	23,385	8
383 / "	21,235	21,503	9
384 / "	17,633	17,910	10

Please melt down and examine.

German Reich Bank
Main Cash Desk
[signature, illegible] [signature] Thoms
[handwritten] M

— *Reproduced from the National Archives and Records Administration, National Archives Collection of World War II War Crimes Records, Record Group 238, Office of the U.S. Chief of Counsel for War Crimes, Document NI(D) 15534. Translated from the German by Wendy Lower.*

Poles claiming German ancestry being registered by officers of the
CENTRAL OFFICE FOR REICH SECURITY on their arrival at a collection
center in Lodz; 1941. They would be held there until their claims
of German heritage were investigated.
(Main Commission for the Investigation of Nazi War Crimes, Warsaw, Poland)

GERMANIZATION

A cornerstone of NAZI ideology was the belief that society was threatened by a constant struggle between racial groups. According to this world view, the biologically superior "ARYAN" race faced threatening competition from inferior races. The Nazis believed that a declining birth rate, a tendency for Germans to marry at an older age, and increasing numbers of cross-cultural marriages further endangered the integrity of the Germanic race. To reverse these trends, the Nazis enacted measures that prohibited interracial marriage and established economic incentives for early marriage and multi-child families. Nazi doctrine also dictated that inferior ethnic groups who might taint "German blood" must be segregated from the German race.

To accommodate the growing German population, Adolf HITLER claimed that the German nation required more *Lebensraum*, "living space" free of harmful racial elements. The "need" for *Lebensraum* provided a pretext for German military expansion. It also promoted large-scale demographic engineering, including the expulsion of "inferior" indigenous populations (such as Jews, GYPSIES, and Slavs), and the systematic DEPORTATION or killing of all supposed "biologically harmful" groups (homosexuals, criminals, and the institutionalized disabled and mentally ill). The Nazi leaders then hoped to "GERMANIZE" the annexed territory with German colonization.

ETHNIC GERMANS, or *Volksdeutsche*, living outside the THIRD REICH, were encouraged to resettle within German-occupied territory. Although resettlement was initially voluntary, government efforts to consolidate all "German blood" within the Reich increased during the war. Before the war was over, several thousand unwilling *Volksdeutsche* were forcibly deported from their homelands for resettlement.

Many ethnic Germans, descendants of medieval German colonists to eastern Europe, were not citizens of the Reich. Instead, they often formed cultural minorities within the nations where they resided. In many cases, such as that of the Transylvanian Saxons of Romania and Hungary, these minorities clearly retained their German ethnic character, language, and cultural identity. In other areas, fully assimilated peoples whose customs indicated possible German ancestry were forcibly deported as ethnic German settlers. Still others were identified as *Volksdeutsche* solely by their "Germanic" physiological features. Marriage to a member of the SS or to a German soldier during the war could also qualify one as an ethnic German if one's heritage was considered to be racially acceptable.

Four separate but related organizations were established to oversee the complex process of Germanization: The REICH COMMISSION FOR STRENGTHENING GERMANISM (RKFDV), the CENTRAL OFFICE FOR ETHNIC GERMANS (*Volksdeutsche Mittelstelle* or VOMI), the SS CENTRAL OFFICE FOR RACE AND SETTLEMENT (RuSHA), and the Well of Life Society (*LEBENSBORN*). The RKFDV acted as a coordinating center for organizations participating in the resettlement of ethnic Germans in annexed Polish territory. Here, the twin processes of depolonization—the eradication of Polish culture—and Germanization were especially thorough. Laws forbade the use of the Polish language, ordered the destruction of Polish monuments, sharply curtailed the education of Polish children, and disbanded Polish social, religious, and cultural organizations. The region's intellectuals, political leaders, and social elite as well as the Polish Jews were expelled and murdered. Polish children were kidnapped and either selected for adoptive homes in Germany or, if rejected, used as SLAVE LABOR or even killed. The RKFDV eventually resettled over 225,000 ethnic Germans in former Polish lands.

The RKFDV also oversaw the compilation of the GERMAN PEOPLES' LIST, which identified ethnic Germans living within German-occupied territory. This list grouped ethnic Germans into four categories: those actively pro-German, those culturally German, those who could be easily Germanized, and those actively anti-German. Individuals in the first two categories were eligible for immediate resettlement and given full German citizenship. Members of the latter two groups were granted provisional citizenship and "encouraged," through terror tactics and discriminatory regulations, to Germanize. Recalcitrants had their homesteads confiscated, and were threatened with incarceration in CONCENTRATION CAMPS and the kidnapping of their children to coerce them to Germanize.

RuSHA, another organization that classified ethnic Germans, employed "racial examiners" to study genealogical backgrounds and physical attributes to determine "racial value." This process classified children conceived by a German and a member of an "undesirable" ethnic group, such as an eastern worker or some prisoners of war, though such liaisons were generally illegal during the REICH. Negative findings resulted in forced abortions and possible incarceration or death for the non-German parent and child; racially valuable children were placed in "reliable" German foster care. Such examinations could also be used,

ETHNIC GERMAN colonists and their families arrive in Jelesnia, Poland; September 1940.
(Main Commission for the Investigation of Nazi War Crimes, Warsaw, Poland)

if necessary, to obtain the official permission to marry required of all German citizens.

The Central Office for Ethnic Germans, or *VoMi*, oversaw the evacuation, transportation, and resettlement of those classified as ethnic Germans. *VoMi* administered transit camps used to temporarily house potential settlers and provided potential resettlers with ideological and cultural indoctrination. The office distributed personal effects confiscated from concentration camp and KILLING CENTER victims to the resettlers for their use. Highly ranked settlers were placed in jobs and housing vacated by deported Jews and Poles. Resettlers with less "Germanic value" were pressed into service in the German army or used as slave labor.

The most notorious organization involved in Germanization was the welfare institution known as *Lebensborn*, whose function was to place "racially valuable" children with adoptive German families. These children were not orphans; they were usually kidnapped from occupied territories. Transported into Germany and compelled to join Nazi youth organizations, *Lebensborn* children were systematically forced to forget their parents and homes and learn German language and customs. *Lebensborn* also cared for and adopted the children of pregnant single women who could prove their child's German paternity. After the war, surviving parents and international tracing services searched for children who were kidnapped and had disappeared through *Lebensborn*, but few were ever found.

Nazi Germanization was a complex policy framework that does not fit the international legal standard for prosecuting only specific criminal acts. Germanization was committed by administrators far removed from the actual terror, kidnapping, theft, and deportation that comprised Germanization. As a result, perpetrators were rarely charged with the offense of Germanization. Based on the precedent set by the INTERNATIONAL MILITARY TRIBUNAL, the RuSHA TRIAL sought first to prosecute Germanization as a WAR CRIME and then to examine the specific individual responsibility of each defendant. Therefore, many perpetrators tried for this crime were only peripherally associated with Germanization. Charges of confiscation of property, deportations, slave labor, and murder often alluded to actions taken by the RKFDV, VoMi, RuSHA, and *Lebensborn*, but these specific organizations themselves were not indicted at the International Military Tribunal.

The RuSHA Trial tried fourteen former officials of the RKFDV and RuSHA for complicity in phases of the Germanization process. In cases before Polish tribunals, such as the STROOP TRIAL (POLISH), defendants were indicted for "crimes against the Polish nation," which included charges of depolonization in regions of Poland annexed by Germany.

Signifying the annexation of the Polish city of Lodz into the Greater German Reich in October 1939, this sign reads: "By order of the Führer this city is now named Litzmannstadt." (Bundesarchiv Koblenz, Germany)

A COLONIZATION DECREE

At the end of the First World War, the Treaty of Versailles created new international borders that truncated the German state and left many former citizens of the German Empire living outside Germany. Once in power Adolf HITLER *sought to abrogate the last vestiges of the treaty and reintegrate Germans into the* REICH *by annexing Polish territory. Eastern Europeans deemed* ETHNIC GERMANS *because of their German ancestry or "ARYAN" features were encouraged to resettle in the annexed territory; other national groups, thought to be racially harmful to Germany, were forcibly removed.*

On October 7, 1939, Hitler appointed Heinrich HIMMLER, *the Reich Leader* SS, *to oversee these population transfers with the following decree. It was used as evidence at the* RuSHA TRIAL *in Nuremberg; the last page is reproduced in facsimile.*

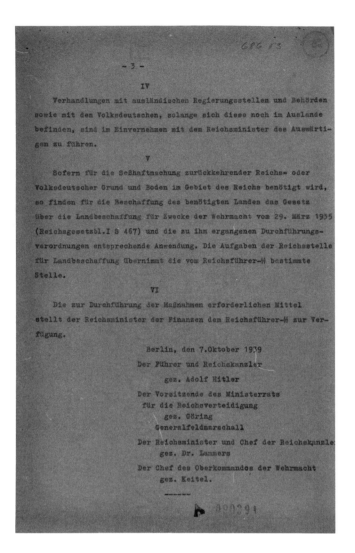

Copy to Rk. 26272 B

Decree
of the Führer and Reich Chancellor for the Strengthening of German National Culture.
7 October 1939

The consequences of the Treaty of Versailles in Europe are eliminated. With that the Greater German Reich has the opportunity to admit into its territory and resettle German persons who until now had to live abroad, and to arrange the settlement of nationality groups within its borders of interest so that better distinctions between them will be attained. I entrust the execution of this task to the *Reichsführer-SS* according to the following regulations:

I.

The *Reichsführer-SS* is obligated according to my directives:

1. to escort suitable Reich and ethnic Germans in foreign lands on the final return home in the Reich;

2. to eliminate the harmful influence of such alien parts of the population that represent a danger to the Reich and ethnic German community;

3. to form new German settlements through resettlement, particularly through the settlement of Reich and ethnic Germans returning home from foreign lands.

The *Reichsführer-SS* is empowered to make all necessary general arrangements and administrative measures to carry out these obligations.

In order to fulfill the tasks appointed to him in Article 1 No. 2, the *Reichsführer-SS* can assign certain living areas to the parts of the population in question.

II.

In the occupied former Polish territories, the Senior Administration Chief East carries out the tasks assigned to the *Reichsführer-SS* according to the latter's general orders. The Senior Administration Chief East and the subordinated administrative chiefs of the military districts are responsible for implementation. Their measures are to conform to the military leadership's needs.

Persons who are provided with special duties for carrying out these tasks do not fall under army jurisdiction.

III.

The tasks assigned to the *Reichsführer-SS*, as far as they concern the restructuring of the German farming system, will be carried out by the Reich Ministry for Nutrition and Agriculture according to the general instructions of the *Reichsführer-SS*.

Otherwise, within the territory of the German Reich, for the execution of this task the *Reichsführer-SS* will make use of the existing agencies and institutions of the Reich, the states, and the communities, as well as other public authorities and the existing settlement associations.

In case an agreement required by law and an administrative organization for this measure is not reached between the *Reichsführer-SS* on the one hand and the highest authority in charge—in the territory of operation the Supreme Commander of the Army—a decision should be obtained through the Reich Minister and the Chief of the Reich Chancellory.

IV.

Negotiations with foreign government agencies and authorities, as well as with ethnic Germans as long as they still reside in foreign lands, are to be conducted in agreement with the Reich Minister of Foreign Affairs.

V.

If land in the territory of the Reich is needed for the settlement of returning Reich or ethnic Germans, then provision for the land will be achieved through the law for the Provision of Land for the Purposes of the Army of 29 March 1935 (Reich Law Gazette I, p. 467) and through the appropriate application of its accompanying implementation decrees. The tasks of the Reich agency for providing land will be taken over by the agency designated by the *Reichsführer-SS*.

In German-occupied Poland, dispirited Poles guarded by members of the *WEHRMACHT* await expulsion from their village; 1940. (Bundesarchiv Koblenz, Germany)

VI.

The Reich Minister for Finance will provide the *Reichsführer-SS* with the necessary means for carrying out the measures.

Berlin, 7 October 1939
The Führer and Reich Chancellor
    signature. Adolf Hitler
The Chairman of the Cabinet Council
for the Defense of the Reich
    signature. Göring
    General Field Marshal
The Reich Minister and Chief of the Reich Chancellery
    signature. Dr. Lammers
The Chief of the High Command of the Armed Forces
    signature. Keitel

> — *Reproduced from the National Archives and Records Administration, National Archives Collection of World War II Crimes Records, Record Group 238, Office of the U.S. Chief of Counsel for War Crimes, Document 686-PS. Translated from the German by Wendy Lower.*

ONE OF A HUNDRED THOUSAND

One component of German occupation policy in conquered lands of Eastern Europe was GERMANIZATION. *To create living space for* VOLKSDEUTSCHE, *who were to be resettled on territories of western Poland annexed by Germany, approximately one million indigenous Poles and Polish Jews were deported to the* GENERAL GOVERNMENT, *the unannexed area of central and eastern Poland; others were sent to Germany as* FORCED LABOR *in the Reich. Deportation became an effective means of plunder and robbery as deportees, ordered to evacuate their homes often at a moment's notice, were forced to leave most of their property and valuables behind. German colonists arrived soon after to take over.*

The following deposition by Mrs. J. K. of Gdynia, Poland, was published by the Polish Ministry of Information in a book chronicling Polish suffering under German occupation. Portions of the volume were introduced as evidence at the <u>INTERNATIONAL MILITARY TRIBUNAL</u>.

"On October 17, 1939, at 8 a.m. I heard someone knocking at the door of my flat. As my maid was afraid to open, I went to the door myself. I found there two German gendarmes, who roughly told me that in a few hours I had to be ready to travel with my children and everybody in the house. When I said that I had small children, that my husband was a prisoner of war, and that I could not get ready to travel in so short a time, the gendarmes answered that not only must I be ready, but that the flat must be swept, the plates and dishes washed and the keys left in the cupboards, so that the Germans who were to live in my house should have no trouble. In so many words, they further declared that I was entitled to take with me only one suitcase of not more than fifty kilograms [110 lbs.] in weight and a small handbag with food for a few days.

"At 12 noon they came again and ordered us to go out in front of the house. Similar groups of people were standing in front of all the houses. After some hours' waiting, military lorries [trucks] drove up, and they packed us in one after another, shouting at us rudely and also striking us. Then they took us to the railway station, but only in the evening did they pack us into filthy goods trucks, the doors of which were then bolted and sealed. In these trucks, most of which were packed with forty people, we spent three days without any possibility of getting out. I hereby affirm that in my truck there were six children of under ten years of age and two old men, and that we were not given any straw, or any drinking utensils, that we had to satisfy our natural needs in the tightly packed truck, and that if there were no deaths in our transport it was only because it was still comparatively warm and we spent only three days on the journey. We were unloaded, half dead, at Czestochowa, where the local population gave us immediate help, but the German soldiers who opened the truck exclaimed 'What! Are these Polish swine still alive?'."

— *Reprinted from Ministry of Information, Poland,* Black Book of Poland *(New York, 1942), 184.*

"RESETTLEMENT"

In order to oversee the huge population transfers necessary for the GERMANIZATION *of western Poland,* HEINRICH HIMMLER *established the* REICH COMMISSION FOR THE STRENGTHENING OF GERMANISM (RKFDV). *This office brought* ETHNIC GERMANS *from eastern Europe (Volhynia, mentioned below, is in present-day Ukraine) to Germany, deported non-Germans from desirable foreign lands, established new settlements of Germans and ethnic Germans in those lands, and redistributed property seized from the deported non-Germans. Most deportees were sent to the* GENERAL GOVERNMENT *to be used as* SLAVE LABOR.

The following decree, issued by Rudolf Creutz, deputy in the Staff Main Office of the RKFDV, details the process of expulsion and resettlement. It was used by the prosecution at the RuSHA TRIAL.

Copy
General Orders and Guidelines of the Reich Commissar
for the Strengthening of German National Culture

I. The first period of our activities must deal with the following things:

1.) The expulsion of some 550,000 Jews as well as leading anti-German Poles and the Polish intelligentsia from Danzig and Poznan over the German border into the Polish General Government. The Jews are to be transferred to the territory east of the Vistula, between the Vistula and Bug rivers.

2.) The confiscation of all landed property of the former Polish State, of the expelled Polish intelligentsia, and of all Poles shot or expelled because of their malevolence. The confiscation is based on the decree of the Führer and Reich Chancellor

ETHNIC GERMAN *(Volksdeutsche)* settlers detrain in Zywiec, Poland, as they prepare to colonize a section of Poland incorporated into the German REICH; October 1940. Resettlement of ethnic Germans in occupied Poland was an integral part of the GERMANIZATION plan for portions of that country.
(Main Commission for the Investigation of Nazi War Crimes, Warsaw, Poland)

A SURVEY

Odilio GLOBOCNIK, *the author of the following "Instructions," was one of Heinrich* HIMMLER's *more ambitious, bloodthirsty* SS *leaders. In 1941, in his capacity as SS and Police Leader for the district of Lublin in occupied Poland, Globocnik formed a team of young, highly educated SS men to assist him in the repopulation of his district. With the creation of his own Research and Planning Office, Globocnik gained Himmler's approval in October 1941 to cluster people of Germanic type with SS garrisons into defense settlements. By March 1944, fifty thousand persons had been classified Germanic types under Globocnik's method of racial screening in Lublin. Those judged to have no trace of German ancestry were marked for* EVACUATION *to make room for German settlers.*

SS and Police Leader
in the Lublin District

[Stamps]	
Dept. of Internal Administration Received 22 May 1941	Chief of the Lublin District Received 22 May 1941

Instructions

In the course of the measures decreed by the *Reichsführer-SS* [Heinrich Himmler] in his capacity as Reich Commissioner for the Strengthening of German National Culture, a statistical survey and a record of all those persons belonging to the declining ethnic German minority among the Polish or Ukrainian nationalities will be carried out in the district of Lublin. This will achieve an overview of those families who come into question for re-Germanization and reunification with the German *Volk* because they possess some portion of German blood.

The units of the SS and German Police should actively muster their forces within the framework of this action. I am making it the duty of all leaders, deputies, and personnel to direct their attention in all administrative dealings and in other contacts with the local population to note the possibility of German derivation in each individual.

All government departments (customs, forestry, labor offices, rural civil administration, etc.) are requested to support this inquiry to the best of their ability. Instructions and reports concerning observations pertaining to the survey are to be forwarded in writing on the enclosed postcards to the office of the SS and German Police in the Lublin District.

For these reports, many criteria should be heeded. In the first case, the reports should serve to locate the more or less missing remnants of the German cultural nation living in this district so that we can secure a basis to reclaim former Germans who are presently a polonized fragment. Those families that come into question for the survey live amid the Polish or Ukrainian population.

[Adolf Hitler] on the Strengthening of German National Culture from 7 October 1939, paragraph 5, in cooperation with the Main Trustee Office East, which had been established by the decree of General Field Marshall Göring on 9 October 1939. The property title is transferred to the German Reich at the disposal of the Reich Commissar for the Strengthening of German National Culture.

3.) A census in the newly acquired territories in the course of December on a certain fixed day.

4.) By spring, the planning of the urban and rural settlements.

5.) The registration and examination of compensation claims by Germans expelled from Poznan and West Prussia.

6.) The temporary sheltering of the migrating ethnic Germans from the Baltic and from Volhynia within the next few weeks.

II. In the subsequent course of affairs, the scheduled settlement of city and land is to take place, which will continue for many years, perhaps decades.

Proofread
[signature illegible]
SS-*Obersturmbannführer.* [SS Lieutenant Colonel]

— *Reproduced from the National Archives and Records Administration, National Archives Collection of World War II War Crimes Records, Record Group 238, Office of the U.S. Chief of Counsel for War Crimes, Document NO-4059. Translated from the German by Wendy Lower.*

Merkblatt

Im Zuge der Maßnahmen, die der Reichsführer-SS in seiner Eigenschaft als Reichskommissar zur Festigung deutschen Volkstums angeordnet hat, wird im Distrikt Lublin eine Erfassung und Aufzeichnung aller ins polnische oder ukrainische Volkstum abgeglittenen deutschen Volkssplitter durchgeführt. Damit soll erreicht werden, dass ein Ueberblick über die Familien gewonnen wird, die auf Grund eines mehr oder minder grossen deutschen Blutanteils für eine Wiedereindeutschung und völkische Rückgewinnung in Frage kommen.

Die Einheiten der SS- und Polizei haben sich im Rahmen dieser Aktion nach Kräften tätig einzusetzen. Ich mache es den Führern, Unterführern und Mannschaften zur Pflicht, bei allen Amtshandlungen und sonstigen Berührungen mit der Bevölkerung ihr Augenmerk auf eine etwaige Deutschblütigkeit der Personen zu richten.

An alle Dienststellen (Zoll, Forst, Arbeitsämter, Kreislandwirte u. s. w.) richte ich das Ersuchen, diese Erhebungen mit besten Kräften zu unterstützen. Hinweise und Meldungen über diesbezügliche Beobachtungen sind schriftlich mit beiliegender Postkarte an die Dienststelle des SS-und Polizeiführers im Distrikt Lublin einzusenden.

Für diese Meldungen sind mannigfache Gesichtspunkte zu beachten. In erster Linie sollen die Meldungen dazu dienen, mehr oder minder verschollene Reste des deutschen Volkstums im hiesigen Distrikt aufzufinden, um die Grundlagen für die Wiedergewinnung ehemals deutscher, heute aber polonisierter Volkssplitter zu erhalten. Die für die Erfassung in Frage kommenden Familien leben inmitten der polnischen oder ukrainischen Bevölkerung.

Am leichtesten sind sie an ihrem Namen kenntlich, wenn diese auch oft stark polonisiert sind. So ist ein Szprynger ein Springer, Presz oder Brucs ein Presch, Gryn ein Grün usw.

Schwieriger ist die Feststellung des Mädchennamens deutschblütiger Frauen, die an Polen verheiratet sind und daher den polnischen Namen des Mannes führen. Selbstverständlich sind auch diese Mischehen zu melden. Deutschstämmige Personen sind auf alle Fälle zu melden, auch wenn sie sich ausdrücklich zum Polentum bekennen.

Neben dem deutschen Namen ist ein weiteres Kennzeichen deutscher Abstammung das rassische Aussehen. Wenn Menschen durch blaue Augen, blondes Haar, Körpergrösse oder durch nordische Kopfform und andere nordische Rassenmerkmale auffallen, dann ist festzustellen, ob eines der Elternpaare oder ihre Grosseltern deutsch waren bzw. deutsche Namen hatten.

Oft weist der Hausbau, die Anlage der Wirtschaftsgebäude, z. B. in einem geschlossenen Hof, oder die besondere Sauberkeit der Leute, auch wenn sie Polen sind, auf einen deutschen Einfluss und auf deutsche Herkunft hin.

Sehr wertvoll sind Meldungen über volkskundliche Gegenstände deutscher Herkunft (Truhen, Spinnräder, Trachten, Urkunden usw.) und alte Aufzeichnungen.

Durch Erfassung dieser deutschen Spuren und Meldung darüber an die Dienststelle des SS und Polizeiführers wird ein wesentlicher Beitrag zur Sammlung verloren gegangenen deutschen Volkstums geleistet.

Der SS- und Polizeiführer
im Distrikt Lublin
gez. *GLOBOCNIK*
SS-Brigadeführer

They are most easily recognizable by their family names, even if these are often heavily polonized. Thus "Szprynger" is "Springer," "Presz" or "Brucs"—"Presch," "Gryn"—"Grün," and so forth.

It is more difficult to determine the maiden names of women of German blood who are married to Poles and thus carry the Polish names of their husbands. Naturally, these "mixed marriages" are also to be reported. Persons of German descent are to be reported in all cases, even if they expressly acknowledge their Polishness.

Besides the German name, a further mark of German heritage is one's racial appearance. When persons are conspicuous on account of their blue eyes, blond hair, body size, or by their Nordic head formation and other features of Nordic racial character, then it is to be determined whether one of the parents or grandparents were German or whether they had German names.

Often the layout of the house, the construction of the farm buildings—for example in a closed courtyard—or the particular cleanliness of the people—even if they are Poles—points to German influence and a German ancestry.

Especially useful are reports concerning traditional objects of German heritage (old chests of drawers, spinning wheels, native costumes, documents, etc.) and old drawings.

Through a survey of these German remnants and reports about them by the Office of the Chief of the SS and German Police, a substantial contribution will be made to gathering the lost remnants of the German cultural nation.

Chief of the SS and German Police
in the Lublin District
signed. GLOBOCNIK
SS-Brigadeführer [SS Brigadier General]

— From Mechtild Roessler, Sabine Schleiermacher et al., eds., Der "Generalplan Ost": Hauptlinien der nationalsozialistischen Planungs und Vernichtungspolitik *(Berlin, 1993), 285. Translated from the German by Patricia Heberer.*

LIDICE

On May 27, 1942, two soldiers of the Czechoslovak Exile Army in England attacked and mortally wounded SS *General Reinhard* HEYDRICH *in a suburb of Prague. In retaliation for his death, the* NAZIS *razed the town of* LIDICE, *near Prague, on June 9. In a single night, all males over the age of 16 were shot for "resistance," the houses were looted and vandalized, and the town burned to the ground. During the following three days, the surviving children of Lidice were forcibly separated from their mothers and tested for "racial value." Of the 105 children held by the* GESTAPO, *eight were deemed suitable for* GERMANIZATION *and sent to a* LEBENSBORN *home, to be reeducated as Germans. The women of Lidice were sent to* RAVENSBRÜCK *concentration camp; the remaining children disappeared.*

The following letter, written by Heinrich HIMMLER *to Max* SOLLMANN, *the director of the* Lebensborn *program, discusses plans for the Lidice children. It was used as evidence at the* RuSHA TRIAL.

The *Reichsführer-SS*
Journal No. 26/31/93 g[secret]
RF[*Reichsführer-SS*]/Rn

> Field Command Post, 21 June 1943
> [stamp]
> Personal Staff of the *Reichsführer-SS*
> Central Archives
> Action no. Order no. 111/1b

Dear **Sollmann**!

I order you to contact immediately *SS-Obergruppenführer* [SS Lieutenant General] **Frank** in Prague. It would be best if you visit him. Certain questions exist about resolving the care, education, and accommodation of Czech children whose fathers or parents had to be executed as members of the resistance movement. The decision must, of course, be a very prudent one. The bad children can be placed in certain children's camps. The racially good children, who could become the most dangerous avengers of their parents

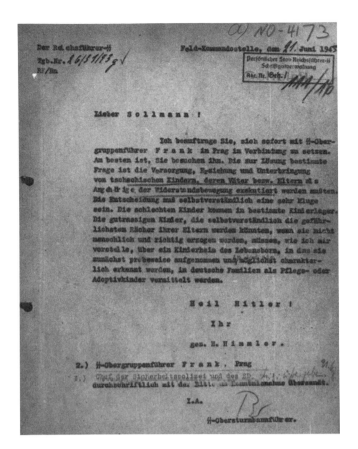

A GRANDMOTHER'S PLEA

Following NAZI racial theory, the Germans sought to reduce the reproductive potential of the "inferior" Slavic races through murder, sterilization, and the abduction of children. Whether violently seized by the German occupation forces, kidnapped from their homes by Nazi "welfare" organizations (such as the German Youth Office, mentioned in the document below), or simply abducted off the street, thousands of children disappeared from their homes in Eastern Europe. After such kidnapppings, relatives searched in vain for their lost children, only rarely discovering a child's eventual fate.

The letter reproduced below, used as evidence at the RuSHA TRIAL, was written by a Polish woman to the head of the German Youth Office in Lodz in search of her eight-year-old grandchild, Halina. There was no response.

if they are not raised in a humane and proper way, I think, must be placed in the charge of the *Lebensborn* orphanage on probation for now, and this would make it possible to observe their character before being placed in German families as foster or adopted children.

Heil Hitler!

Yours,

signed. H. Himmler

2.) *SS-Obergruppenführer* **Frank,** Prague
3.) Chief of the Security Police and Security Service
[handwritten note, "delivered"]
copy transmitted with request for acknowledgement

By Order of

[initialed] Brandt

SS-Obersturmbannführer.
[SS Lieutenant Colonel]

— *Reproduced from the National Archives and Records Administration, National Archives Collection of World War II War Crimes Records, Record Group 238, Office of the U.S. Chief of Counsel for War Crimes, Document NO-4173. Translated from the German by Wendy Lower.*

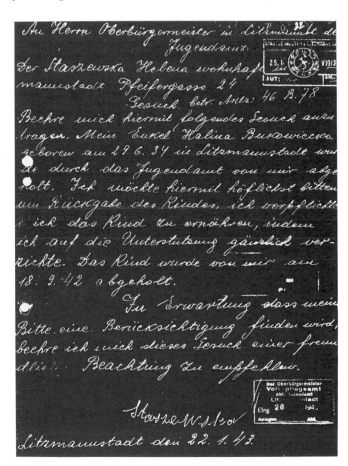

To Lord Mayor of Litzmannstadt[1]
Youth Social Services Office.

[stamp]
Town Administration
Litzmannstadt
25 Jan 1943

Office 460 encl.—

A CONCENTRATION CAMP for Polish juveniles in Lodz, established by the Germans in mid-1942, held approximately 1,000 Polish children who were rejected for GERMANIZATION and forced to work as SLAVE LABOR. Here girls are assembled for a roll call with their commandant, Eugenie Pohl; December 1942. Pohl was tried and convicted of WAR CRIMES by a Polish court after the war. (Main Commission for the Investigation of Nazi War Crimes, Warsaw, Poland)

From Staszewska, Helena, living in Litzmannstadt, Pfeifergasse 24.
Request re: file no. 46 B. 78

Herewith I would like to make the following request. My grandchild, Halina Bukowiecka, born on 29 June 1934 in Litzmannstadt, was taken from me by the Youth Social Services Office. Herewith I would like to ask for the return of the child. I commit myself to support the child by refusing assistance entirely. The child was taken from me on 18 September 1942.

In expectation of consideration of my request, I would be honored if my request received your kind attention.

[signature] Staszewska

[stamp] The Lord Mayor
People's Welfare Office
Dept. Youth Social Services Office
Litzmannstadt
recd: 28   1943

Litzmannstadt, 22 January 1943

1. Litzmannstadt refers to Lodz, Poland, renamed by the Germans in 1939.

— *Reproduced from the National Archives and Records Administration, National Archives Collection of World War II War Crimes Records, Record Group 238, Office of the U.S. Chief of Counsel for War Crimes, Document NO-4899. Translated from the German by Wendy Lower.*

A "FATHER'S" STORY

After being GERMANIZED through the LEBENSBORN program, kidnapped children were placed with German foster families or adopted by German parents. In order to facilitate this process, a child's name, age, birth certificate, and personal history were changed in order to disguise his or her origin. Told that their infant was a "war orphan," prospective German parents rarely questioned the legitimacy of their child's adoption.

After the war, the ALLIES issued orders requiring parents to register all adopted foreign children with the International Tracing Service. Adoptive parents were often reluctant to register their children with the RED CROSS or UNRRA for fear that the children would be returned to the biological parents.

In his testimony at the RuSHA TRIAL, Otto Uebe described the adoption of a Yugoslav orphan from Lebensborn.

Q. When did you first think of adopting a child?
A. In 1942, before my son was killed in combat. He requested me if he were to be killed in the war I was to adopt a child and that I was to bring him up as a monument to him and devote myself again to living with my wife.

[In 1942 Uebe was shown several children at a children's home in Kohren-Salis, but did not succeed in adopting any of them]

Q. Did you continue to correspond with Lebensborn after this?
A. Yes, I repeatedly requested that a child be assigned to me. Later on I asked an acquaintance in Munich to personally speak to Lebensborn and thereupon both he and

Lebensborn informed me that I was again to go to Kohren-Sahlis and there were two children available there, not two years of age yet, one a boy and one a girl. My wife and I, therefore, on the 7th of June [1942] went there because just on this day I was anxious to take over the child, this being my son's birthday, and there together with my wife I took the boy.

Q. Witness, what were you told about those two children and about their parents and what nationality they were?

A. I was told that those children came from South Carniola [current-day Slovenia]. I wasn't interested any further in the girl but I was told about the boy that his parents had probably been murdered by Serbian bands; that this was a full orphan.

Q. Witness, is the child sitting at the prosecution table the child you selected?

A. Yes.

Q. Witness, would you have taken this child if there would have been any doubt in your mind that the parents of this child were living?

A. No. I desired to adopt the child and this could only be done if it was a full orphan.

Q. Witness, did you ask Lebensborn to have the name of the child changed?

A. Yes. I was asked whether I was anxious that the child bear my name immediately. This could be done I was told, and then I replied in the affirmative and in Kohren-Sahlis the child was signed out under the name of Wolfgang Uebe and registered again in that name in Bayreuth.

Q. Did you have any further correspondence with Lebensborn after that?

A. All I did was to request Lebensborn to confirm for me that I was taking care of the child myself so that I could get a tax reduction and furthermore that I would get a child's allowance from the place where I worked. I received another letter thereupon in which it was confirmed that the child Mathias Potucnik, now called Wolfgang Uebe, had been taken into my family and that I alone was responsible for the welfare of the child as there were no other people alive responsible for taking care of it.

Q. After that did Lebensborn ever let you know that anyone else or the parents of this child were living?

A. Yes. At the end of 1944 I was notified that the father had been found and wanted the child returned to him. I was informed about it and asked if and when I was willing to turn over the child to him. On that point I replied that I loved the child, that it was in our family and had become used to us, and would they kindly give me the address of the father so that I could contact him personally. In answer to this I received a letter that I was to do nothing whatsoever; the matter would be submitted to the Reich Leader SS [Heinrich HIMMLER] personally for his decision. Thereupon I heard nothing further from Lebensborn on the subject.

[Immediately after the war, Allied occupation authori-
ties ordered the registration of all foreign children adopted during the war; Uebe complied.]

Q. Did you later hear from Mr. Mathias Potucnik?

A. Yes, I was told by the municipal administration at Oberhausen, where I live, that UNRRA by order of Mr. Potucnik at Klagenfurt, St. Veiterstrasse 77, was inquiring as to the welfare of the child and thereupon knowing that Potucnik was the father, I wrote to him; months passed before a Mr. Fahrenberger notified me that Mr. Potucnik was the father and he demanded that the child should be returned to him; as a matter of fact the letter was very nice. The father himself did not know German well and therefore the gentleman, an uncle and relative was taking up negotiations with me; his father and mother had been in a concentration camp and the mother had died there while the father had come back and now wished to have the child.

Q. Witness, where are you taking the child from here?

A. I am going to take the child to the German-Austrian frontier and there I will hand it over to Mr. Fahrenberger who will turn it over to the father [a Yugoslav].

— *Reprinted from United States of America v. Ulrich Greifelt, et. al. (Case 8: 'RuSHA Case'),* Trials of War Criminals Before the Nurenberg Military Tribunals Under Control Council Law No. 10, 14 vols., *(Washington, D.C, 1950), 4: 1061–62.*

Lfd. Nr.	Kranken Nr.	Familien-Name	Vorname	Stand: led. verh. gesch. verw.	Sterbetag	Alter
1916	2279	Jwanow	Wasil	ledig	15.3.45	
1917	2280	Komonenko	Lena	"	"	
1918	2156	Kusmenko	Nikolay	"	"	
1919	2207	Mornjow	Nikolai	"	"	
1920	2303	Opritschenko	Nadeschda	"	"	
1921	2290	Schlupa	Stefan	verh.	"	
1922	2194	Paralynkin	Wladimir	ledig	"	
1923	2404	Tschumakowa	Maria	"	"	
1924	2276	Biekotow	Jwan	"	16.3.45	
1925	2307	Kachnow	Olga	"	"	
1926	2201	Nimsowa	Maria	"	"	
1927	2286	Pristawka	Alexandra	"	"	
1928	2205	Schrydkun	Jwan	"	"	
1929	2298	Strazulla	Giovanni	"	"	
1930	2292	Styprynski	Kasimir	"	"	
1931	2261	Trofinowa	Antonia	"	"	
1932	2183	Tubinskij	Filip	"	"	
1933	2185	Waschkowa	Marija	"	"	
1934	2474	Baranow	Fedor	"	17.3.45	
1935	2277	Buhanetz	Michail	"	"	
1936	2306	Jakubiak	Franciszek	"	"	
1937	2305	Kadis	Szeslaus	"	"	
1938	2281	Kosenko	Fedor	"	"	
1939	2302	Makarenko	Nina	"	"	
1940	2284	Malnik	Jwan	"	"	
1941	2260	Papunia	Prosina	"	"	
			Michail	"	"	
			Marija	"	"	
			Michael	"	18.3.45	
1945	2275	Basar	Anatolij	"	"	

A page from the death registry at the HADAMAR euthanasia facility, from a photo taken in April 1945. Dr. Adolf Wahlman, the institution's chief physician, confessed at the HADAMAR TRIAL (GERMAN) that the entries under "Cause of Death" were falsified to conceal the murders perpetrated under the "EUTHANASIA" program. (NARA)

Geburtstag:	Geburtsort und Kreis:	Todesursache:	Beerdigu
8.11.31	-	Eitrige tbc. Rippenfellentzündung	Anstalts
9.4.24	-	Tbc. der Lungen u. des Darmes	
20.8.22	-	Tbc. der Lungen	
17.11.23	-	"	
17.11.25	-	Eitrige tbc. Rippenfellentzündung	
13.7.99	-	Tbc. der Lungen	
24.8.24	-	"	
3.6.27	-	"	
23.2.16	-	Eitrige tbc. Rippenfellentzündung	
15.3.22	-	Tbc. der Lungen	
6.11.26	-	"	
27.11.24	Krim	" und der Nieren	
18.9.23	-	"	
12.12.13	̶ ̶ ̶ ̶	" und des Darmes	
25.2.14	-	"	
29.3.21	-	"	
28.8.94	Psarowka	Status epilepticus	
6.4.15	Luschki	Lungenentzündung	
6.5.15	-	Tbc. des Darmes	
14.2.23	-	Offene Tbc. der Lungen	
26.11.27	Sapowa	Tbc. der Lungen	
26.6.26	-	"	
3.3.22	Krasnodar	Tbc. des Darmes	
15.4.26	-	Tbc. der Lungen	
11.9.21	-	"	
9.7.23	-	"	
13.1.13	Kiew	"	
22.6.22	Odesa	Tbc. der Nieren	
12.6.20	-	Offene Tbc. der Lungen	
11.3.21	-	Tbc. der Nieren	
15.11.23	Teramo	Tbc. der Lungen	

The "EUTHANASIA" program implemented in late 1939 represented one of many radical measures by which the NATIONAL SOCIALIST leadership sought to restore the "racial integrity" of the German nation. The National Socialist EUGENICS policy began in 1933 with the mandatory sterilization of Germans suffering from serious hereditary diseases, and ended with the direct extermination of Jews, GYPSIES, and other groups considered racially undesirable. Part and parcel of this eugenics policy was the program to eliminate "life unworthy of life" (*lebensunwertes Leben*): those institutionalized patients, who because of mental retardation, severe physical deformity, or incurable mental illness were regarded as "human ballast," whose institutional care represented a serious financial burden to the state. The NAZI euthanasia program aimed at freeing the nation's economy as well as its genetic resources from the drain of the severely mentally and physically ill. As such, it was clearly in keeping with Nazi racial ideology.

As early as 1935, Adolf HITLER had envisioned euthanasia, or so-called mercy-killing, as a viable solution for eliminating the institutionalized mentally ill. Even at the time, however, Hitler recognized the inherent difficulties in introducing such a program as public policy. Expecting opposition particularly from the German churches, Hitler felt that such a project might be carried out most effectively in time of war, when popular resistance could be most easily countered.

In late 1938, Hitler's private chancellery acknowledged one of several requests for mercy killings that it received from the relatives of newborns and infants with severe physical deformities. Hitler delegated his personal physician, Karl BRANDT, to investigate the incident and to empower the physician to carry out euthanasia as necessary. With this test case successfully concluded, Hitler authorized Brandt and Philipp Bouhler, the head of his private chancellery, to proceed the same way in similar cases. Under the name "Reich Committee for the Scientific Registration of Severe Hereditary and Congenital Diseases," an organization was created to register malformed and retarded children and to select severe cases for elimination. Those children considered "unworthy of life" were sent to so-called pediatric specialty units of selected hospitals and killed through starvation or overdose of medication.

The euthanasia program for mentally ill adults paralleled the killings of mentally and physically handicapped children. At the conclusion of the Polish campaign in fall 1939, Hitler informed Brandt of his intention to "effect a definitive solution to the euthanasia problem." A brief letter of authorization on Hitler's personal stationery to Bouhler and Brandt provided the extra-legal basis for the program. The authorization was back-dated to September 1, 1939— the date of the invasion of Poland, which began the Second World War—in order to give the impression that this measure was related to the war effort. Thus, from the beginning, the adult euthanasia program, like its counterpart for infants and children, was directly linked to Hitler and his chancellery, thereby circumventing standard administrative and legal channels.

On Hitler's authorization, an organized and systematic program of extermination of the institutionalized mentally and physically handicapped was planned under the code name OPERATION T4. T4 stood for Tiergartenstrasse 4, the street address of the villa in Berlin which housed the head offices of the euthanasia program. Under the leadership of Brandt, Bouhler, and high-ranking Führer chancellery administrators Victor Brack and Werner Blankenburg, Nazi Germany's first program of mass murder proceeded in relative secrecy behind the camouflage of three organizations: the REICH ASSOCIATION OF HOSPITAL AND NURSING ESTABLISHMENTS, which selected victims for the program, the Charitable Foundation for Institutional Care, which directed the program's financial arrangements, and the Charitable Patient Transport Corporation (or *Gekrat)*, which transported patients chosen for extermination from their home institutions to the nearest euthanasia facility.

Following a practice developed in the child euthanasia program in October 1939, the Reich Association of Hospital and Nursing Establishments began to distribute carefully formulated questionnaires to all public mental health facilities, private and parochial hospitals, and nursing homes for the chronically ill and aged. The limited space

A 1940 photograph of Tiergartenstrasse 4, Berlin, the address from which the NAZI "EUTHANASIA" program OPERATION T4 took its name. (Landesbildstelle, Berlin, Germany)

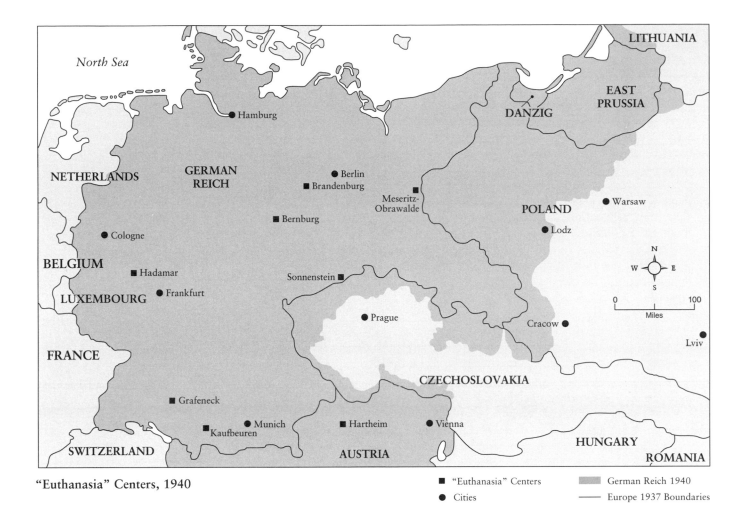

"Euthanasia" Centers, 1940

■ "Euthanasia" Centers   ▨ German Reich 1940
● Cities   — Europe 1937 Boundaries

provided on the forms, as well as the instructions in the accompanying cover letter, suggested that the questionnaires were intended to gather statistics for an administrative or scientific survey. The only clues to the form's sinister purpose was the emphasis the questionnaire placed on the patient's work capacity and on the categories of patients which it required reported to the health authorities: those suffering from schizophrenia, epilepsy, encephalitis, or dementia; the criminally insane; those who were not of "German or kindred blood"; and those who had been housed continually in the institution for more than five years. Completed forms were evaluated by a panel of traveling medical consultants. Following a review of their findings by a central medical commission in Berlin, persons selected for "euthanasia" were transferred to one of six euthanasia facilities throughout Germany and Austria: Grafeneck in Württemberg; Hartheim, near Linz on the Danube; Bernburg and Sonnenstein, both in the German state of Saxony; Brandenburg Prison near Berlin; and Hadamar, near Limburg in central Germany.

Gassing was the preferred method of killing during the initial stages of the T4 program. In a procedure identical to that later employed in the KILLING CENTERS in eastern Europe, the patients selected for extermination were sepa-

rated into groups according to sex and, usually within hours of their arrival at the euthanasia facility, were brought to the GAS CHAMBERS, where they were instructed to undress and given a superficial medical examination. Once in the gas chambers, which had been disguised as tiled shower facilities to avert suspicion, the victims were gassed with carbon monoxide. Following the gassing, staff members extracted the gold teeth and fillings of their victims and dispatched the corpses to the CREMATORIA, whose ever-smoking chimneys quickly became a source of suspicion to inhabitants of the surrounding towns.

Despite elaborate efforts to conceal the lethal nature of the euthanasia program, the killings soon became public knowledge. Public protests—especially from the leadership of the Catholic and Lutheran churches—led Hitler to halt Operation T4 in August 1941. According to the Nazis' own statistics, 70,000 to 80,000 institutionalized mentally and physically handicapped Germans and Austrians were murdered between October 1939 and summer 1941.

Hitler's decision to suspend T4 did not, however, signal an end to the killings. The child euthanasia program continued as before; and beginning in 1941, "OPERATION 14F13" extended Operation T4 to concentration camp prisoners who were deemed mentally ill or incapable of work. In addition, adult euthanasia in hospitals and sanitoria continued, albeit by means of drug overdose and lethal injection rather than gassing. This less centralized killing phase, known as "wild euthanasia," continued in various custodial institutions throughout the REICH until the arrival of ALLIED troops in spring 1945. In all, historians estimate that 200,000 to 250,000 institutionalized mentally and physically handicapped persons were murdered under Operation T4 and other euthanasia programs between 1939 and 1945. This figure does not include the thousands of Polish and Soviet handicapped killed in the German-occupied East, for which mortality figures are not fully recorded.

Many Nazi physicians, administrators, and medical support personnel responsible for euthanasia killings faced prosecution for their crimes before postwar courts and tribunals. Karl Brandt and Viktor Brack figured as major defendants before an American military tribunal in the first subsequent Nuremberg proceeding, the DOCTORS TRIAL, in August 1947 the first of the NUREMBERG MILITARY TRIBUNALS; both were among seven defendants sentenced to death for their roles in medical crimes, including euthanasia. Months before, in the first mass atrocity trial in American-occupied Germany, an American military tribunal convicted seven staff members of the HADAMAR euthanasia facility of WAR CRIMES in connection with the murder of 476 Russian and Polish FORCED LABORERS. American chief prosecutor Leon JAWORSKI had initially aimed to try the seven for the murders of thousands of German mental patients at the facility but discovered the tribunal had jurisdiction to try only war crimes violations against Allied nationals under international law. In 1947, a German tribunal in Frankfurt convicted 25 members of the Hadamar staff for the murders of 15,000 German mental patients between 1941 and 1945. This second HADAMAR TRIAL (GERMAN) was but one of more than twenty euthanasia trials adjudicated by German courts between 1945 and 1966.

THE FÜHRER'S ORDER

In 1935, Adolf HITLER confided to Dr. Gerhard Wagner, then German minister of health, that he had long envisioned "EUTHANASIA" as a viable solution for eliminating Germany's mentally ill. Such a program would have to be carried out under the cover of war, Hitler concluded, since popular opposition, especially from religious circles, was to be expected. At the conclusion of the Polish campaign in the fall of 1939, Hitler announced to Karl BRANDT his decision to "effect a definitive solution to the euthanasia problem." A brief letter from Hitler to the head of his private chancellery provided the legal basis for the euthanasia program. This memorandum, shown below, is especially significant because it is the only known document in which Hitler personally authorized a civilian killing operation. The original authorization, backdated to September 1,

1939—the date of the outbreak of war with Poland—was held in a safe at Hitler's Chancellery and was destroyed along with other copies at the end of the war. This duplicate from the files of Reich Justice Minister Gürnter is the only known surviving copy. It was found by an American officer after the war and introduced as evidence at the INTERNATIONAL MILITARY TRIBUNAL.

[stamp of Hitler's 1939
personal stationery]
ADOLF HITLER   Berlin, 1 September 1939

Reich Leader **Bouhler** and
Dr. of medicine **Brandt**

are charged with the responsibility of extending the authority of certain doctors in such a way that, after a humane assessment of their condition, those suffering from illnesses deemed to be incurable may be granted a mercy death.

[signature] Adolf Hitler

[handwritten]
Given to me by Dr. Bouhler on 27 August 1940
Dr. Guertner

— *Reproduced from the National Archives and Records Administration, National Archives Collection of World War II War Crimes Records, Record Group 238, Office of the U.S. Chief of Counsel for War Crimes, Document 630-PS. Translated from the German by Wendy Lower.*

REPORTING OF DISFIGURED NEWBORN

The NAZI "EUTHANASIA" program began in early 1939 with the murder of malformed and mentally handicapped children. The following instruction circular and subsequent report document the Nazi policy of registering deformed newborns with state health offices connected with the Führer Chancellery. Under the auspices of the newly formed Reich Committee for the Scientific Registration of Severe Hereditary and Congenital Diseases, three central medical experts—Professor Werner Catel, Professor Hans Heinze, and Dr. Ernst Wentzler—determined on the basis of a questionnaire supplied by the Reich Health Ministry which of these registered children should be killed. Wentzler, a pediatric psychiatrist, had treated children of the Nazi party elite and had been invited by Adolph HITLER's personal physician, Karl BRANDT, to serve as an expert consultant for the program. In Wentzler's 1963 trial testimony, he stated, "I had the feeling that my activity was something positive, and that I had made a small contribution to human progress." Such "progress" was demonstrated at the Bavarian facility Eglfing-Haar, where 332 children were starved to death, given overdoses of Luminal or lethal injections of morphine or scopolamine. The Nazi euthanasia program claimed the lives of thousands of children and infants.

Excerpt from the Notice of the Reich Minister of the Interior dated 18 August 1939—IVb 3088/39—1079Mi—concerning the obligation to register deformed, etc., newborn.

1. For the clarification of scientific questions in the area of inborn deformities and mental underdevelopment, a registration of relevant cases is necessary as soon as possible.

2. I therefore order that the midwife who assists in the birth of a child—also in the case when a physician was present during the delivery—must submit a registration to the regional health office for the place of birth on the form available there if the child suffers from any of the following deformations:

    1. Idiotism as well as mongolism (especially cases where the child is blind or deaf);

2. Microcephaly (abnormal smallness of the head, especially the skull);

3. Hydrocephalus (water on the brain), severe or advancing cases;

4. Deformations of any kind, especially the absence of entire limbs, severe clefts of the head and spine, etc.;

5. Paralysis including Little's Disease.

At birthing centers and hospital maternity wards, the obligation to register is only the duty of the midwife when a chief physician (para. 5) is not available or is unable to complete the registration.

3. Furthermore, physicians are to register all children who suffer from any of the conditions listed in para. 2, items 1–5, and who are not older than three years of age if these are discovered by the physicians during regular medical examinations.

4. The midwife will receive two Reichsmarks as compensation for her efforts. Payment of the sum will be through the health office. Payment will be made to her.

5. On the basis of §46, para. 2, items 3 and 4 of the Reich Physician Order of 13 December 1935 (Reich Law Gazette I, p. 1433) through orders of 23 March 1940 (Journal of German Physicians, volume 12), the minister of Reich Health has obligated the chief physicians of birthing houses or maternity wards to file the required registrations for children born in their facilities or ward to their regional health office.

Similar orders from the minister of Reich Health further obligate all physicians to file reports to the regional health office administering the child's place of residence on all children under three years of age who, during medical examination, are found to fall under categories listed in para. 2 of this notice. In cases of an expected long-term stay, the report is to be filed with the regional health office in charge of administering the filing institution.

6. By filing these reports, physicians and midwives fulfill their obligation to report in accordance with article 3, para. 4, of the First Decree for the Fulfillment of the Law for the Prevention of Inherited Diseases dated 5 December 1933 (Reich Health Papers I, p. 1021). Further reporting, especially those in accordance with the Prussian Law for the Care of Invalids dated 6 May 1920 (Ges S., p. 280), still remain in effect.

[stationery]
State Health Office   Tuttlingen, 7 February 1941
Tuttlingen

Entry No. 189
Enclosures: 0   To: The Minister of the Interior
                                         Stuttgart

Pertaining to the Ordinance of 23 April 1940
No. X 1630

Subject: Required Registration for Deformed, etc., Newborn

During the time from 1 October 1939–
31 December 1940, the following two defects in newborn occurred here:

1. Club foot right (Catholic)
2. Flat Feet (non-Catholic)

Public Health Physician

[signature]
Senior Medical Adviser

— *Reprinted from Ernst Klee, ed.,* Dokumente zur "Euthanasie" *(Frankfurt a.M., 1985), 239 and 241. Translated from the German by Neal Guthrie.*

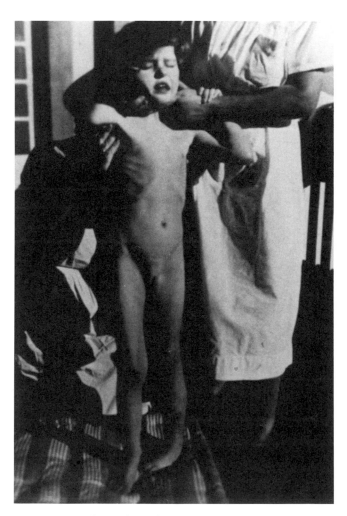

A mentally handicapped girl photographed shortly before she was killed in a "EUTHANASIA" facility in Germany during World War II.
(Karl Bonhoeffer-Nervenklinik, Berlin, Germany)

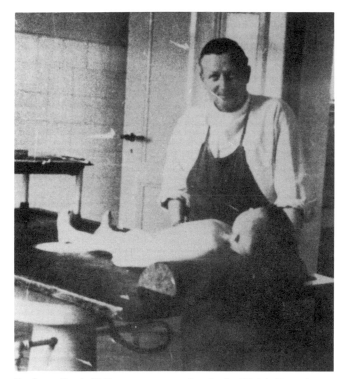

Professor Berthold Ostertag, an associate in the "Reich Committee for the Scientific Registration of Serious Hereditary and Congenital Diseases," i.e., a NAZI euphemism for the child "EUTHANASIA" program. Here, the professor conducts an autopsy on a murdered child.
(Karl Bonhoeffer-Nervenklinik, Berlin, Germany)

A REGISTRATION FORM

One of the first steps in the "EUTHANASIA" program was to devise a means of identifying those individuals to be killed. In October 1939, the REICH ASSOCIATION OF HOSPITALS AND NURSING ESTABLISHMENTS, one of the camouflage euthanasia organizations, distributed a large number of questionnaires, reproduced here, to all state and private mental health facilities, parochial hospitals, and facilities caring for chronically ill and aged patients throughout the THIRD REICH. The patient's work capacity and the presence of certain diseases and disorders (such as schizophrenia, epilepsy, and chronic mental illness) were emphasized with the aim of identifying candidates for euthanasia. Teams of traveling medical consultants reviewed these questionnaires, marking the form with a red "+" sign for those to be killed and "−" for those patients who were not destined for euthanasia. The recommendations of these authorities were forwarded to a central committee of medical experts in Berlin who made the final decision as to who would live and who would die. Instructions forwarded with the questionnaire falsely implied that it was intended to gather statistics for a survey; the impression was further reinforced by a companion questionnaire asking for basic statistics on the staff, size, and budget of each health facility contacted.

Registration Form 1   To be filled out by Typewriter!
Serial No._____

Name of Facility: [stamp] **State Asylum of Haina (Monastery)**
in: [stamp] **Region Kassel**

First and Last Name of Patient: Daniel B——
Maiden Name: n/a

Birth Date: 1 February 1877   Place: Ostha
County: Wolfhagen

Last Residence: Kassel   County: Kassel-City

Single, married, widowed, or divorced: divorced
Religion: Protestant   Race[1]) German blood
Citizenship: German Reich

Address of nearest relative: son: Joh. B—— - Mönchhof,
son: Chr. B—— -   "
daughter: Anna B——, married name
K—— -Nentershausen.

Regular visits and from whom (address): so far none

Guardian or care-giver (Name, address): n/a

Expenses paid by: BFV Kassel
How long in this facility: 30 April 1941

In other institutions, where and for how long:
<u>Karlshospital Kassel; Nerve Clinic Marburg (about 1929)</u>

How long ill: <u>for a few years</u> From where and when admitted: <u>30 April 1941 from Kassel</u>

Twin yes/no <u>No</u> mentally ill blood relation: <u>not known</u>

Diagnosis: <u>Beginning stages of dementia, brought on by arteriosclerosis</u>

Main Symptoms: <u>Sentimentality, fussiness, weak judgment, and ineducable. Tendency toward drink. Argumentative, excitable.</u>

Bed-ridden yes/no <u>No</u> extremely restless <u>No</u> requires housing in secured bldg. <u>No</u>

Physically incurable illness yes/no <u>around 1917 hospitalized for optic nerve atrophy</u> war injuries yes/no <u>not detected at this time</u>

Schizophrenia: first case__condition__remitting well___

Feeblemindedness: moron__imbecile__idiot___

Epilepsy: psych. change__average frequency of seizures___

Senility: extreme confusion <u>No</u> poor personal hygiene <u>No</u>

Therapies (insulin, cardiazol, malaria, salvarsan, etc.) <u>n/a</u>
Long term success yes/no <u>n/a</u>

Admitted on the basis of §§51, 42b criminal code, etc:
<u>No</u> through ___

Punishable offenses: ___ Previous convictions: <u>Not known</u>

Type of occupation (Exact description of work and work abilities, i.e., farm work, can do little.—Metal worker, good skilled worker.—No vague descriptions, like housework, but rather clear examples: can clean rooms, etc. Also state whether patient can work continuously, often or only for shorter lengths of time.)
<u>Cannot work at all. Has very poor vision.</u>

Estimated future release: ___
Comments: <u>It is to be expected that his condition will worsen and that B—— will be even less able than in the past years to re-enter society. Will most likely never be able to be released.</u>

<u>Haina</u>, Town, Date <u>4 July 1941</u>

[initialed] <u>L</u>
[stamp]
Director and State Medical Adviser

[1]German or related blood (German blood), Jew, Jewish *Mischling*, I or II Degree, Negro (*Mischling*), Gypsy (*Mischling*) and so forth.

> — *Reproduced from* Verlegt nach Hadamar: Die Geschichte einer NS-"Euthanasie"-Anstalt *(Kassel, Germany, 1991), 73. Translation from the German by Neal Guthrie and Wendy Lower.*

"A DELIVERANCE"?

Once a patient had been designated for the "EUTHANASIA" program, the family was sent a letter notifying them of the patient's transfer to another medical care facility—in reality, a euthanasia facility. Once the patient had been killed, the family was notified with a standardized letter used by all euthanasia facilities. Relatives were falsely informed that the patient had died suddenly of an illness, and that the body had been cremated on the orders of the local police due to an epidemic at the facility, which consequently prevented visitations by relatives. The cremated remains and any personal effects were made available to the victim's family. The medical care facility from which the patient had been transferred for euthanasia was apprised of his or her real fate. An example of a fabricated notification of death is reproduced below.

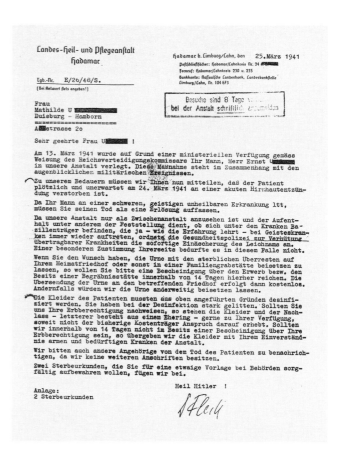

State Sanitarium and Care Facility
Hadamar
[. . .]

Hadamar by Limburg/Lahn, 25 March 1941
[. . .]

Mrs. Mathilde U——   Visits are to be announced in
Duisberg-Hamborn   writing 8 days in advance
A—— Street 20

Dear Mrs. U——

On 31 March 1941 your husband, Mr. Ernst U—— was transferred to our facility on the basis of the ministerial orders in accordance with the directives of the Commissar of Reich Defense. This measure is a result of the present military events.

It is with regret that we must inform you that the patient died suddenly and unexpectedly on 24 March 1941 as a result of acute meningitis.

Since your husband suffered from a severe incurable disease, you must view his death as a deliverance.

Since ours is only an interim facility, and residence here among other things depends on whether the patients are disease carriers (which, as experience has taught us, is often the case with the mentally ill), the Health Security Police has ordered the immediate cremation of all deceased for protection against communicable diseases. In this case special permission from you was not required.

If you wish to have the urn with the mortal remains interred in your local cemetery or in a family plot, please send notification within fourteen days that a plot has been acquired or is already in possession. The urn will be sent directly to the cemetery at no cost. If we do not hear from you, we will inter the urn elsewhere.

The patient's clothes have been disinfected for the reasons mentioned above. During disinfection, they were severely damaged. If you should prove to us your right of inheritance, the clothes and estate—this consists of a wedding ring—will gladly be put at your disposal, as long as no former creditors have any claim to them. Should we not be in possession of proof of your inheritance right within fourteen days, we will with your agreement deliver the clothes to the poor and needy patients of this institution.

We also ask you to inform other relatives of the death of the patient since we have no other addresses.

Please find enclosed two death certificates, which you should keep for possible presentation to the authorities.

Heil Hitler!
[signature] Dr. Fleck

Enclosures: 2 death certificates

— *Reproduced from* Verlegt nach Hadamar: Die Geschichte einer NS-"Euthanasie"-Anstalt *(Kassel, Germany, 1991), 108. Translated from the German by Neal Guthrie.*

A BISHOP SPEAKS OUT

By 1941, OPERATION T4 had become an open secret throughout Germany. Protestant and Roman Catholic clergy joined directors of various mental health facilities and other public figures to protest the program. The protest with the greatest public impact was a sermon given on August 3, 1941, by Clemens, Count von Galen, Roman Catholic bishop of Münster, excerpted in this selection. As a result of the sermon, which was immediately reproduced and distributed throughout Germany, many NAZI officials pressed for von Galen's arrest and imprisonment; Adolf HITLER demurred, however, fearing that the bishop could

A plume of smoke rises from the chimney of the crematorium at the HADAMAR State Psychiatric Hospital and Sanitorium in 1941. Hadamar was one of the busiest KILLING CENTERS of the infamous OPERATION T4 program; more than 15,000 mentally and physically disabled were slaughtered there. (Hessisches Hauptstaatsarchiv, Wiesbaden, Germany)

become an anti-Nazi martyr. Though the direct impact of von Galen's sermon is disputed, Hitler evidently bowed to public pressure and on August 24, 1941, ordered the program discontinued. Nevertheless, killing the mentally and physically handicapped continued on a more decentralized basis and in higher numbers until the very end of the war. The "EUTHANASIA" center at Kaufbeuren, however, continued in operation for several months after American forces occupied the town.

. . . As I am reliably informed, lists are being made up in the hospitals and nursing homes of Westphalia . . . of those patients who, as so-called unproductive citizens, are to be moved and soon thereafter killed. The first such transport left the institution of Marienthal near Münster this past week.

German men and women! Paragraph 211 of the German legal code still has the force of law. It states, "An individual who, acting with premeditation, kills another person shall . . . be punished by death for murder. . . ."

Here we are dealing with . . . our brothers and sisters —poor people, sick people—"unproductive people," if you will. But have they thereby forfeited the right to live? Have you, have I the right to live, only as long as we are productive, as long as we are recognized to be productive by others? . . . When it is once allowed that people have the right to kill unproductive persons and when it now falls first upon the . . . defenseless mentally ill, . . . the cripples incapable of work, the invalids of labor and war— then the murder of each of us when we are old and infirm, and thereby unproductive, is assured. . . .

— *Reprinted from Johann Neuhäusler,* Kreuz und Hankenkreuz: Der Widerstand gegen den Nationalsozialismus, *2 vols. (Munich, 1946), 2: 365–67. Translated from the German by Patricia Heberer.*

A 1945 photo of the Kaufbeuren Psychiatric Hospital, the "EUTHANASIA" facility in Bavaria where hundreds of people were killed in the euthanasia program from 1940 to 1945.
(Yivo Institute for Jewish Research, New York)

CHRISTMAS BONUS

The "Public Welfare Foundation for Institutional Care," whose letterhead appears on this correspondence, was in reality a camouflage organization for the administration of OPERATION T4. *Gottfried Scharz provided cremation services for the program; in this letter, he receives a bonus for his faithful work. The signature at the bottom of the letter, "Jennerwein," was the pseudonym of Viktor Brack. SS-Standartenführer (SS Colonel) Brack was a leading organizer of the "Operation T4" program and was redeployed by Heinrich* HIMMLER *in 1941 as a "gassing expert" in the construction of the* KILLING CENTERS *and* GAS CHAMBERS *in occupied Poland. Brack was sentenced to death on August 27, 1947, in the* <u>DOCTORS TRIAL</u>. *He was hanged in Landsberg prison on June 2, 1948.*

Public Welfare Foundation for Institutional Care

To: Mr. Gottfried **Schwarz**

<u>Bernberg</u>

On the occasion of the coming holiday season, I am pleased to inform you of the amount of your additional bonus that has been freely paid for by the Foundation during the course of the year. Your balance by the close of 1940 comes to

<u>440 Reichsmarks.</u>

I would like to take this opportunity to thank you for your faithful service, and hope that you will continue to make your full services available to the Foundation in the coming year. The amount of your balance should not be disclosed to your colleagues.

Berlin, 10 December 1940

[signature]
Jennerwein

— Reproduced from Ernst Klee, ed., Dokumente zur "Euthanasie," (Frankfurt am Main, 1985), 130. Translated from the German by Neal Guthrie.

Nurses of the HADAMAR Sanatorium, where thousands of people were killed during the "EUTHANASIA" Program from 1941 to 1945, pose in front of the building's gate. (NARA)

A NURSE'S STORY

Pauline Kneissler began working at the Grafeneck "EUTH-ANASIA" facility, one of the two earliest such facilities, soon after killings began there in early 1940. When the murder of the mentally and physically handicapped halted at Grafeneck in December of that year, she was transferred to HADAMAR and then finally to Kaufbeuren, a euthanasia facility in Bavaria. Kneissler continued to work at the facility after the war had ended. In July 1945, American military authorities discovered that killings at Kaufbeuren continued for at least a month after American forces occupied the area in late April 1945.

Sworn Statement

I, Pauline Kneissler, being duly sworn, depose and state:

1. I was born on 10 March 1900 at Kurdjomovka in southern Ukraine. In 1920 I became a German citizen. Between the ages of six and fifteen I had private instruction in my parents' house in Russia. In 1920 I moved to Duisburg on the Rhine, where I studied nursing. Until 1923 I trained for my job and on 4 January 1940 was placed in the Interior Ministry in Berlin. For fifteen years I was a municipal nurse with the magistrate of the city of Berlin. In April 1937, I joined the NSDAP. I was a member of the National Socialist Women's League, of the National Socialist Public Welfare Association, of the Reich Air Raid Protection League, and of the Reich Nurses' League.

2. Through my knowledge as a nurse and the fact that I had been working for many years in different German hospitals and nursing establishments in connection with the so-called euthanasia program, I am in a position to provide the following statement concerning this program.

3. In 1939 I was summoned by the police chief to report on 4 January 1940 to the Ministry of Interior, situated in the building of the Kolumbus-House. There a man named Blankenburg spoke to our group, which consisted of twenty-two or twenty-three people. He discussed the importance and secrecy of the euthanasia program and explained to us that the Führer developed a euthanasia law, which in consideration of the war was not to be published. It was abso-

lutely voluntary for those present to pledge their cooperation. None of those present had any objection to this program, and Blankenburg swore us in. We were sworn to secrecy and obedience, and Blankenburg called to our attention the fact that any violation of the oath would be punished by death. Dr. Bohne was present at this meeting.

4. After the conclusion of this meeting, we traveled by bus to Castle Grafeneck, where we were received by the director of this institution, Dr. Schumann. Our work at Grafeneck began in March 1940, but the male personnel had been working there before this.

5. It was one of my duties to travel with Mr. Schwenniger, who was also a member of the Charitable Foundation for Institutional Care, to the different institutions to pick up patients and bring them to Grafeneck. Mr. Schwenniger, who was in charge of our transports, had the lists of patients who were to be transferred. These lists had to correspond to the director's patients lists of the institutions from which the patients were to be transferred. The patients who were transferred by us were not all particularly serious cases. They were of course mentally ill, but very often in good physical condition. Each transport consisted of about seventy people, and we used to have such transports almost every day. My actual duty in connection with these transports was that of an accompanying nurse.

6. After the arrival of the patients at Grafeneck, they were housed in barracks, where Dr. Schumann and Dr. Baumhardt examined them superficially on the basis of a questionnaire. These two doctors gave the final word whether a patient should be gassed or not. In individual cases the patients were exempted from being gassed. In most cases the patients were killed within twenty-four hours of their arrival. I was at Grafeneck for nearly one year and know only of a few cases in which the patients were not gassed. In most cases the patients were given an injection of 2 cc of morphium scopolamine before the gassing. These injections were administered by the doctor. The gassing was car-ried out by specially selected men. Dr. Mennecke dis-ected some of the victims. Imbecile children between the

ages six and thirteen years were also included in this program. After the closing of Grafeneck I came to Hadamar and was there until 1943. In Hadamar the same work was continued, with the difference that gassing was stopped, and the patients were killed by vernal, Luminal, and morphium scopolamine. About seventy-five patients were killed per day. First Dr. Baumhardt and later Dr. Börneck was the director of Hadamar.

7. From Hadamar I was transferred to Irrsee near Kaufbeuren, where I continued my work. Dr. Valentin Falthauser was the director of this institution. There the patients were killed by injections as well as by tablets. This program continued until the collapse of Germany.

8. I know that, in the different institutions where I was, instructions were received from Mr. Blankenburg. During my job at Grafeneck, this institution was visited by Dr. Karl Brandt, Dr. Conti, Reich Leader Bouhler, and Mr. Brack. I know also that the Charitable Foundation for Institutional Care was also represented in certain institutions in Lublin.

I have read the above statement in the German language consisting of three (3) pages and declare that it is true and correct to the best of my knowledge and belief. I was given the opportunity to make changes and corrections in the above statement. This statement was given freely and voluntarily without any promise of reward, and I was subjected to no compulsion or duress of any kind.

[signature]
Pauline Kneissler

— *Reproduced from the National Archives and Records Administration, National Archives Collection of World War II War Crimes Records, Record Group 238, Office of the U.S. Chief of Counsel for War Crimes, Document NO-470. Translated from the German by Wendy Lower.*

THE AMERICAN HADAMAR TRIAL

The HADAMAR TRIAL (AMERICAN) was one of the first trials held in the American occupation zone of Germany after the end of the war. The seven defendants were tried for killing 476 ALLIED nationals diagnosed with tuberculosis and sent to HADAMAR for "EUTHANASIA." Although the prosecution team, headed by U.S. Army Colonel Leon JAWORSKI, had initially hoped to try the defendants for the murders of more than 15,000 Germans at the facility since it opened in December 1940, Allied military commissions discovered that, under international law, they were empowered to try only those cases in which the victims were Allied nationals. The Hadamar Trial received wide publicity both in Germany and abroad, as can be seen in this article from the New York Times.

— *Reproduced from* The New York Times, *October 9, 1945. Copyright © 1945 by the New York Times Company. Reprinted by permission.*

GERMANS DESCRIBE 400 SLAVES' DEATHS

2 Women in Reich Asylum Tell at Trial How Russians and Poles Were Poisoned

CASE SETS A PRECEDENT

Is First in U. S. Zone Dealing With Killing of Non-American Civilian Personnel

By DREW MIDDLETON
By Wireless to THE NEW YORK TIMES

WIESBADEN, Germany, Oct. 8 —Two German women calmly described today the businesslike manner in which 400 Polish and Russian slave laborers had been murdered by hypodermic needle and poison pills. They told their stories at the opening of the trial of seven Germans, one a woman, for mass murder at Landshaus.

The ugly picture of the doings in the three-story death house at Hadamar, where thousands of Germans also were exterminated, shared attention with the strong attack by United States officers conducting the defense against the legal basis for the trial. The attack, embodied in four motions, was denied by Col. John L. Dicks, head of the six-man military commission hearing the case.

Later Colonel Dicks prevented the defense from introducing testimony concerning the killing of Germans at Hadamar, a slaughter that Hans Guckert, once a patient at the mental institution, said had reached a total of 43,000 lives.

The 400 Russians and Poles murdered included women and some small children. Some, but not all, were suffering from tuberculosis or pneumonia as a result of long hours at hard labor, coupled with insufficient food. They were exterminated under the guise of receiving "medical treatment."

The Germans killed there generally, but not always, were suffering from mental illness.

2 Infants Among 16 Killed

"Only bodies came out," according to Nurse Nina Zachow, the first witness. She described how fourteen Polish and Russian women and two infants arrived at the institution, were undressed and put to bed and then treated with lethal injections by Henrich Rumoff, one of the defendants. "Nothing else happened. They were just picked up and carried out—they were dead," she said.

The court that has convened here has no precedent in the United States zone, for it is dealing with crimes committed against the nonmilitary personnel of another nation. The entire legal basis of the trial was sharply challenged by the defense's motions offered by Capt. Melvin R. Wintman of Chelsea, Mass. Captain Wintman, in his argument with Col. Leon Jaworski, the trial's judge advocate and head of the prosecution, read paragraphs from the "notes and comment" department of The New Yorker magazine of Sept. 15 in support of his contention that the alleged crimes were not covered by international law.

In asking for dismissal of all charges the defense claimed, first, that there was no rule of international law "for the purpose of trying persons for offenses committed prior to conquest." The second point was that the United States War Crimes Office was empowered to try only offenses committed against the United States, and therefore the United States had no right or authority in this case.

Prosecution Cites Eisenhower

Colonel Jaworski, who won convictions of six of the seven Germans tried at Darmstadt in July for the murder of six American airmen, declared in his reply that the unwritten international law and the Hague Convention of 1907 protected the citizens of occupied territory. The former Houston, Tex., corporation lawyer also cited a ruling by the United States Judge Advocate General that American jurisdiction is concurrent for offenses against United Nations citizens. He added that the case was being tried as a result of Gen. Dwight D. Eisenhower's directive, adding, "I don't think it is necessary to go much beyond that."

Captain Wintman then read from The New Yorker:

"We strongly suspect a long delay in the war trials, not so much because there is no solid floor under a certain court room as because there is no foundation under the new level of justice with which the victorious nations are now fumbling. * * * The chief thing to remember about international law is that it is not law and has never worked."

After a recess the commission denied each defense motion, but Captain Wintman said that he was willing to carry the case to the Board of Review, challenging American jurisdiction over such cases. He also believes that the defendants operated on orders from the German Government and believes that this is a case where the superior command is to blame rather than those who carried out its orders.

Trial Confined to Slaves

When, in questioning Nurse Zachow, Captain Wintman asked if she thought it wrong to kill German patients, Colonel Jaworsky objected, claiming that the defendants were not on trial for killing Germans, only slave workers.

Defense counsel replied that he planned to show that slave workers had received exactly the same treatment as Germans, but Colonel Dicks ordered him to confine his questioning to evidence dealing with the murder of Russians and Poles.

Captain Wintman said later that the defense's inability to have this testimony admitted would seriously curtail its efforts and give an incomplete picture of the case.

Lord Wright, chairman of the United Nations War Crimes Commission, was an interested spectator during the skirmishing between the prosecution and the defense.

Judith Thomas, a secretary in the mental institution, the second witness in the trial, told how death certificates had been filled out three or four weeks after the "patients" were received at the institution, and how the date and cause of death of Russian and Polish workers were always falsified.

"They died the day they were admitted," she said calmly. "Everybody knew that."

TRANSPORTS TO HADAMAR

Alfons Klein was the main defendant at the HADAMAR TRIAL (AMERICAN), *held in American-occupied Wiesbaden in October 1945. The thirty-five-year-old* NAZI *had been the chief administrator of the "*EUTHANASIA*" facility and in June 1944 had given orders to the Hadamar staff to murder the tubercular Soviet and Polish* FORCED LABORERS *transported to the institution. During the trial he testified about the murder of the* ALLIED *nationals, the basis for this prosecution. Alfons Klein was convicted and sentenced to death on October 15, 1945; on March 14, 1946, he was hanged for his crimes.*

ACCUSED KLEIN—During these proceedings several witnesses who did not belong to the Institution were asked whether they were very surprised or shocked to hear now that in the Landes-Heilanstalt [State Psychiatric Hospital and Sanitorium] at Hadamar over 470 Russians and Poles died by injections. This question was mostly answered in the affirmative. I want to talk about the motives underlying the cause of the law-makers to excuse them.

THE PRESIDENT—While this Commission is willing that you take all the time you need to make any statements, statements that are not pertinent to the issues . . . are not . . . relevant. . . . The laws of the German Reich are not a point at issue. Confine your statement to the points that I have just explained, namely, the killing of the Russians and Poles at Hadamar Institution between the dates of 1st July, 1944, and 1st April, 1945.

ACCUSED KLEIN—I want to talk about transports which were transferred to the Institution. I remember very well all details of the first big transport. As I stated before, this transport came from the labor camp in Hersfeld. I received all the transport lists and case histories from the leader of the transport in Limburg, and I looked through all medical papers specifically. It was to be seen from these medical papers without doubt that all sick people who arrived had been treated in hospitals for several months because of tuberculosis. Because they were not curable, they were released from these hospitals and brought back to the labor camps. After I had seen that from the papers, that evening I myself went up to the ward and I myself saw a great part of these sick people after they were undressed. All of the witnesses and also the accused must certify that, as far as the big transport is concerned especially, more than half of these diseased people had tuberculosis. In a large number of these diseased people, pus areas could be seen in the body the size of a hand. I remember a transport in which two children of the age of six arrived. This small transport arrived one afternoon and I saw it come towards the Institution. I looked at these small children who had pus extending on both arms. When the children came to this

A scene from the HADAMAR TRIAL (AMERICAN), where seven defendants were tried by a U.S. Military Commission headed by Colonel Leon Jaworski for the murder of 476 Russian and Polish forced laborers. On the right sits Alfons Klein, former superintendent at HADAMAR and chief defendant; next to him, Irmgard Huber, former chief nurse at Hadamar, confers with her attorney. (NARA)

Institution, they were crying already. I am of the sure conviction that if the gentlemen of the Commission had a chance to see such a transport it would not be difficult for them to judge whether the deeds which took place at Hadamar and whether this case can be looked upon as a violation of International Law. I myself believe it is cruel that such people who were incurable had to endure pain, if one would let them live longer, because this was a big danger to Eastern workers at that time. If these tubercular people remained in the camps, without doubt one would have to reckon that hundreds of thousands would be infected with tuberculosis. One had to consider that in part of these labor camps sanitary conditions are not of such a kind that such a disease can be treated.

BY THE PROSECUTION—There is nothing further that you wanted to say?

ACCUSED KLEIN—No.

— *Reprinted from United Nations War Crimes Commission,* The Hadamar Trial, *vol. 4 of* Law Reports of Trials of War Criminals, *Selected and Prepared by the United Nations War Crimes Commission (London, 1947–49), 198–200. Crown copyright. Reproduced with the permission of the Controller of Her Majesty's Stationery Office.*

DEATH BUS

The <u>Hadamar Trial (American)</u> convened by the Americans in October 1945, was the first opportunity for the German people to learn of the gruesome details of their former government's euthanasia *policy. The trial established the means by which the patients selected for euthanasia were transported from their place of confinement to the nearest euthanasia facility, in this case* Hadamar. *Buses used to transport all such patients belonged to a company deceptively named, the Non-Profit Patient Transport Corporation, denoted as "Hospital Transport AG" in this article from the* Frankfurter Rundschau *of November 13, 1945, after the defendants in the trial were convicted.*

The Death Buses of Hadamar
A report on Hitler's murder of Germans

A short while ago a court in Wiesbaden pressed charges against the care givers at the facility in Hadamar. They were found guilty of poisoning foreign workers. During the trial only a portion of the heinous crimes of these murderers came to light because Klein and his colleagues were tried only for the murder of citizens of Allied countries. The creatures, however, are responsible for an even greater number of murders of German citizens.

Those Germans, who according to Adolf Hitler were not considered worthy to live in the Nazi State, were murdered. At the beginning of the war the facility at Hadamar was vacated; it was to be used for "other purposes." It was soon evident what these purposes were: Hadamar was designated to be the death place for the sick and handicapped. A construction firm received the contract to deliver materials for the building of a crematorium, then they were forbidden to build it themselves; the hospital would take

A gray bus of the Public Patient Transport abbreviated in German as *Gekrat,* parked at the Eichberg state sanatorium, near Wiesbaden; summer 1941. These buses carried patients to the Hadamar "euthanasia" facility where they were gassed or poisoned.
(Hessisches Hauptstaatsarchiv, Wiesbaden, Germany)

Die Todesomnibusse von Hadamar
Ein Bericht über die Hitler-Morde an den Deutschen

Vor einiger Zeit trat ein Gericht in Wiesbaden gegen Pfleger der Anstalt von Hadamar zusammen, die für schuldig befunden wurden, Fremdarbeiter durch Gift getötet zu haben. In der Vernehmung wurde nur ein Teil der Schandtaten dieser Mörder aufgezeigt, denn Klein und Genossen wurden nur wegen Mordes an Staatsangehörigen alliierter Länder abgeurteilt. In noch viel größerem Ausmaße sind diese Kreaturen jedoch schuldig, deutsche Menschen gemordet zu haben.

el Ermordet wurden Deutsche, die, laut Adolf Hitler, nicht für würdig befunden wurden, im Nazi-Staat zu leben. Zu Beginn des Krieges wurde die Anstalt Hadamar geräumt; sie sollte „anderen Zwecken" zur Verfügung gestellt werden. Es zeigte sich bald, welchen Zwecken: Hadamar war ausersehen, die Todesstätte für Kranke und Sieche zu werden. Eine Baufirma bekam den Auftrag, Material zur Herstellung eines Verbrennungsofens zu liefern, dann wurde ihr untersagt, den Bau auszuführen; er wurde von der Anstalt selbst aufgebaut. Nach völliger Einrichtung der Anstalt begann der Antransport der Opfer. Fünf Omnibusse — sie liefen unter dem Decknamen „Krankentransport-AG" — waren unterwegs, und sie waren fleißig unterwegs.

Zuerst konnten diese Kranken noch aus den Fenstern der Omnibusse sehen, aber nach einiger Zeit wurden die Fenster verhängt, und später wurden die Sitze entfernt; die Menschen mußten sich auf den Boden legen. Man wollte damit ver- hindern, daß die Bevölkerung von Hadamar sich ein Bild von der Zahl der Kranken machen konnte. Denn ihr Schicksal war bald dem kleinsten Kind bekannt; die fünf Meter hohe Flamme, die aus dem Kamin des Ofens schlug, der dicke schwarze Rauch, der sich auf die Stadt niedersenkte, zeigten deutlich, was mit den Eingelieferten geschehen. Als im Jahre 1943 die Vergasung und Verbrennung der Bevölkerung bis zur Siedehitze gestiegen war, stellte die Anstalt die Vergasung und Verbrennung ein, man verwendete nun diesem Zeitpunkt an nur noch Spritzen, und verscharrte die Leichen.

Mit welchem Raffinement vorgegangen wurde, zeigt deutlich, daß nach kurzer Zeit die Anstalt ein eigenes Standesamt — was übrigens gesetzlich unzulässig ist — erhielt. Fünfzehn Angestellte hatten im Sekretariat zu tun, um die Totenscheine auszustellen. Als Ursache wurden immer dieselben Leiden angegeben: Lungenlähmung, Altersschwäche und Herzschlag. Die wahre Ursache war: diese Menschen waren krank; es wären Greise, Geisteskranke, Taubstumme, Blinde und Gelähmte. Sie waren nicht fähig, in einer Rüstungsfabrik zu arbeiten und durften, laut Beschluß Hitlers, nicht länger am Leben bleiben. Erschütternde Szenen spielten sich ab, wenn Angehörige eintrafen, um die Todgeweihten noch einmal zu sehen.

Für die Verkommenheit der Angestellten dieser Anstalt spricht, daß sie alte Menschen mit Fußtritten bedachten. Es war kein Wunder, daß diese Verbrecher immer rücksichtsloser und maßloser wurden. Sie standen unter dem Schutz des Staates, und keiner durfte es wagen, etwas gegen sie zu unternehmen. Sie wurden sehr gut bezahlt und warfen das Geld nur so zum Fenster hinaus. Zuerst besuchten sie nach Möglichkeit alle Lokale, aber bald fanden ihre Orgien nur noch beim Ortsgruppenleiter Gotthard statt. Es konnte doch möglich sein, daß sie im Rausch ausplauderten. Erschütternd ist es, wenn eine Schwester auf Vorhaltungen antwortet: „Ich handele doch nur auf Befehl, und ich stehe mich doch so besser." Kein Wunder, daß sie sich besser standen, man fand Ringe bei ihnen und ausgebrochene Goldzähne.

Die Alliierten haben Klein und Konsorten wegen Mordes an Staatsbürgern der Vereinten Nationen bestraft. Das Gericht hat es mit souveräner Geste abgelehnt, sich mit Verbrechen zu befassen, die an Deutschen begangen wurden. Das beweist nur, wie sehr wir selber uns erniedrigt haben. Wollen wir nicht jetzt, wo uns niemand daran hindert, zeigen, daß wir über ein Gewissen verfügen? Da gibt es immer noch Angestellte der Anstalt, die auf freiem Fuße sind, weil sie „nur" Deutsche ermordeten. Wann findet sich ein Staatsanwalt, der sie anklagt?

care of that on its own. After the institute was set up, the transport of victims began to arrive. Five buses, under the code name "Hospital Transport AG," were on the move—very diligently on the move.

At first the passengers could look through the windows of the buses, but soon they were covered up, and later the seats were removed; the passengers had to lie on the floor. One wanted to keep the number of passengers a secret from the citizens of Hadamar because even the youngest children knew the passengers' fate: the fifteen-foot-high flames rising out of the chimney of the ovens, the thick, black smoke that settled down onto the city, were clear indications of what was happening to the new arrivals. In 1942, when the mood of the population had reached the boiling point, the facility discontinued the gassings and burnings. They now started using injections and secretly burying the bodies.

With what cleverness this proceeded is clearly shown when, after a short time, the facility received its own registry office, which is not permissible by law. Fifteen people were employed to fill out the death certificates. The causes of death given were always the same: paralysis of the lungs, old age, and heart failure. The true cause was: these people were sick, they were elderly, mentally ill, deafmutes, blind, and handicapped. They were incapable of working in the armament factories and in accordance with Hitler's resolution; they were not allowed to remain alive. Deeply moving scenes were played out when relatives arrived to see the condemned one more time.

That they kicked old people speaks for the depravity of the staff of this facility. It was no wonder that these criminals became more and more ruthless and excessive. They stood under the protection of the state, and no one dared go against them. They were very well paid and spent money like water. At first they visited all the bars when possible, but soon their orgies took place only at District Group Leader Gotthard's home. It could very well be possible that they talked while drunk. It is shocking when a nurse, being reproached, answers, "I only follow orders, and I can live with myself more easily that way." No wonder they could live with themselves more easily; rings were found in their possession as well as broken off gold teeth.

The Allies punished Klein and his gang for the murder of citizens of the United Nations. With a superior gesture, the court declined to try crimes committed against German citizens. That only proves to what extent we alone have degraded ourselves. Do we not now want to show, now that no one prevents us, that we do have a conscience? There are still staff of the facility who are free to walk about because they killed "only" Germans. When will a prosecuting attorney turn up to accuse them?

> — *Reprinted from* Verlegt nach Hadamar. Die Geschichte einer NS-"Euthanasie"-Anstalt *(Kassel, Germany, 1991), 173. Translated from the German by Neal Guthrie.*

DEATH DOCTOR RELEASED

During the late 1950s and beyond, many West German courts reduced the sentences of convicted Nazi criminals. One of the more controversial commutations was that for Dr. Hans-Bodo Gorgass by Hessian President and Minister of Justice Zinn, who argued that Gorgass was "repentant" and "physically broken." In the HADAMAR TRIAL (GERMAN) in 1947, former SA member Gorgass had testified that mentally ill persons posed an emotional and financial burden on their relatives. Since the relatives were emotionally involved, the state should step in and relieve them of this burden by killing the mentally ill. After Gorgass was released from prison, he became an industrial pharmacist and continues to reside in Germany.

The Man Who Turned on the Gas Valve in Hadamar
Zinn Frees 1,000-fold Murderer
The Death Doctor Dr. Gorgass is Once Again among Us

The chief defendant of the Hadamar trial, Dr. Hans-Bodo Gorgass from Leipzig, who was sentenced to death in Frankfurt in 1947 for the murder of at least one thousand people and two years later had his sentenced reduced to life imprisonment, has now at the age of forty-seven been set free by the Hessian minister president and minister of justice. On 10 August 1956 Zinn had reduced the sentence of life imprisonment to fifteen years. Now Zinn, in response to Gorgass' wife's plea for mercy, has waived Gorgass' remaining sentence except for his loss of civil rights. After almost eleven years of imprisonment, Gorgass has been released from the Butzbach penitentiary.

Gorgass was the chief physician at the Hadamar Sanatorium near Limburg. Here some 10,000 people were gassed in the years between 1940 and 1941. When the mass murders became known, they were suspended due to the protest by the then bishop of Limburg, Antonius Hilfrich. The Fourth Great Criminal Court in session in 1947 under the chairmanship of Dr. Wirtzfeld, which was still allowed to sentence criminals to death in the first years after the war, clearly established after several days of evidence that not only the incurably ill but also healthy children from racially mixed marriages, psychopaths, concentration camp prisoners, asocials, and criminals were gassed in Hadamar.

Gorgass was the man who opened the gas bottle from outside and let the carbon monoxide gas stream into the "shower room" that held one hundred people. Then he cold-heartedly observed the agonizing death of his victims through a glass window.

Gorgass described himself to the court as a follower of euthanasia and cited in his defense an order received from Hitler. Dr. Wirtzfeld, in justifying the sentence, said the actual purpose of the organized mass murders was not the killing of the incurably ill but rather the removal of undesirable eaters and the clearing of the institution for other purposes. The murders committed in Hadamar are a disgrace that will be a burden on the German people for generations.

Even if the minister president has the right to grant clemency, we believe that the use of this right in the case of a thousand-fold murderer like Dr. Gorgass was inappropriate. It is inexplicable why Minister President Zinn, a representative of a democratic state and a democratic party, decided in favor of this act of clemency. This murderer, who has thousands of people on his conscience, deserves no mercy!

Limburger Neue Presse, 7 February 1958

> — *Reproduced from* Verlegt nach Hadamar: Die Geschichte einer NS-"Euthanasie"-Anstalt *(Kassel, Germany, 1991), 179. Translated from the German by Neal Guthrie.*

Jadwiga Dzido, a member of the Polish Resistance and former prisoner at the RAVENSBRÜCK concentration camp, displays wounds on her leg at the DOCTORS TRIAL; December 22, 1946. The injuries were caused by medical experiments conducted on her at that camp in November 1942. (NARA)

MEDICAL
EXPERIMENTS

Among the most notorious crimes committed by the NATIONAL SOCIALIST regime was the performance of medical experiments on human beings without their consent. Between September 1939 and April 1945, at least seventy medical research projects, involving several thousand prisoners, were conducted at various CONCENTRATION CAMPS and KILLING CENTERS throughout the REICH.

While medical experimentation utilizing human subjects is an acceptable and even necessary component of medical research, such experiments are traditionally subject to severe restrictions. According to these, humans may be used as test subjects only in those phases of an experiment for which they are deemed absolutely essential. Medical ethics prescribe that all human experimentation be conducted on a voluntary basis; subjects must be fully informed of all possible risks and must be free to halt the experiment at any time. While low-risk medications and treatment methods may be tried on healthy subjects, no person in good health should be deliberately infected with a dangerous disease to test a new medicine or effect a cure. In no case should the death or disfigurement of the test subject be a deliberate or essential element of the experiment.

In NAZI Germany, experimentation involving human subjects ignored these fundamental medical ethics. Concentration camp prisoners selected for medical research—among them Jews, GYPSIES, Poles, political prisoners, homosexuals, and Soviet prisoners of war—were forced to participate in dangerous and painful experiments. Many victims died as a direct result of the experimentation, while others were murdered immediately following the experimental phase so that scientists could determine all physiological effects of the experiment by postmortem examination.

In general, ethically questionable medical experiments carried out during the period of the THIRD REICH may be divided into three categories. The first category consists of experiments whose objectives aimed at facilitating the survival of AXIS military personnel under dangerous wartime conditions. At DACHAU concentration camp, Drs. Siegfried Ruff and Hans Romberg of the German Experimental Institute of Aviation, together with Dr. Sigmund RASCHER, a LUFTWAFFE and SS physician, conducted high-altitude experiments in order to determine the maximum altitude from which crews of damaged aircraft could parachute to safety. Some 70 to 80 prisoners perished from asphyxiation and internal injuries in low-pressure chambers designed to simulate the atmospheric conditions present at high altitudes. Parallel to these experiments were the so-called freezing experiments at Dachau that endeavored to establish the most effective treatment for victims of hypothermia, such as the German airman downed in icy waters or the infantryman exposed to frigid temperatures on the Russian front. In 1944, *Luftwaffe* researchers conducted a third battle-related experiment at Dachau involving tests of various methods to make seawater potable. By establishing a reliable process, the researchers hoped to improve survival rates of German

pilots and sailors stranded for many days at sea.

The second broad category of Nazi experimentation aimed at developing and testing pharmaceuticals, toxins, and treatment methods for injuries and illnesses that Axis soldiers encountered in the field. A large number of these experiments focused on the care of battle wounds and attendant infections. An effort to determine new therapies for severe bone fractures led to gruesome bone grafting experiments at the RAVENSBRÜCK concentration camp; here experiments under Dr. Karl Gebhardt involved breaking the leg bones of healthy Polish female prisoners and testing various treatments. Gebhardt, once president of the German Red Cross, also conducted fearsome experiments to test the efficacy of the antibacterial sulfanilamide against infection and putrefaction. Gebhardt had attended Reinhard HEYDRICH when the latter died of gangrene poisoning following an assassination attempt near Prague, and undertook the experiment after higher-ups hinted that Heydrich might have been saved had he been properly treated with sulfanilamide. Along the same lines, doctors at Dachau tested the effectiveness of a new coagulating agent on human subjects, while the AUSCHWITZ and BUCHENWALD concentration camps were sites of experimental treatment for second-degree, third-degree, and phosphorus burns.

Closely linked to research regarding treatment of battle wounds were experiments testing treatments for chemical warfare victims conducted under army auspices throughout the war years. In 1939, mustard gas experiments were carried out on prisoners of the SACHSENHAUSEN concentration camp, and in 1943–44, some fifty-two prisoners at Fort Ney near Strasbourg were exposed to phosgene gas, an insidious poison that causes suffocation and ultimately asphyxiation, in order to test a possible antidote, hexamythylene tetramine. Finally, the German concentration camps Sachsenhausen, Dachau, NATZWEILER, Buchenwald, and NEUENGAMME became sites of lethal experimentation involving immunization compounds and sera for the prevention and treatment of contagious diseases, including malaria, typhus, tuberculosis, yellow fever, and infectious hepatitis.

In the cases discussed above, Nazi doctors and scientists pursued research that—however vain—strove to save human lives. Their objectives thus complied with their professional obligations, yet the *methods* they employed breached all norms of medical ethics and violated the most accepted codes of professional conduct. In the final category of human experimentation, however, neither means nor ends were justified. This medical "research" sought specifically to underpin and advance the racial and ideological tenets of the Nazi worldview. The most infamous of these were the experiments by Dr. Josef MENGELE at Auschwitz. Mengele conducted a horrifying host of experiments involving twins, often killing them himself with chloroform injections following his experiments to examine their internal organs. Mengele hoped his "research" would establish the genetic cause for the birth of twins, which could thereby facilitate a eugenics program by which to double the Ger-

Dr. Klaus Karl Schilling, a physician at the DACHAU concentration camp, defends himself in the docket at the DACHAU TRIAL in December 1945. He was charged with infecting over one thousand prisoners with malaria in his experiments at the camp; hundreds died. Schilling admitted that his victims had not been volunteers, but finally maintained that his experiments had been for the good of mankind. The court sentenced him to death. (NARA)

man birthrate. Mengele also directed serological experiments on Gypsies at Auschwitz, as did Dr. Werner Fischer at Sachsenhausen, in order to determine how different "races" withstood various contagious diseases. The research of Dr. August Hirt at Strasbourg University had a similar purpose. Hirt accumulated a massive collection of Jewish skeletons; his victims, handpicked and gassed at nearby Natzweiler, were delivered to him, often still warm, so that Hirt could establish "Jewish racial inferiority" by means of anthropological study. Other heinous experiments meant to further Nazi racial goals were sterilization experiments, undertaken primarily at Auschwitz and Ravensbrück. There, scientists tested a number of methods in their effort to develop an efficient and inexpensive procedure for the mass sterilization of Jews, Gypsies, and other groups the Nazis determined racially or genetically undesirable.

The Nazi physicians and scientists who performed illegal medical experiments came from established institutions in the German medical profession. On October 25, 1946, twenty-three physicians and senior functionaries within the Nazi scientific community were tried by an American military tribunal at Nuremberg. In the first of these subse-

quent Nuremberg proceedings, the so-called DOCTORS TRIAL, the defendants stood accused of CRIMES AGAINST HUMANITY, WAR CRIMES, CONSPIRACY, and membership in CRIMINAL ORGANIZATIONS. Sixteen were found guilty, and seven, including chief defendant Dr. Karl BRANDT, were executed on June 2, 1948.

HYPOTHERMIA: PROGRESS REPORT

During the war, pilots forced down into the cold waters of the North and Baltic Seas and the Atlantic Ocean underscored the need to develop protective clothing and effective rewarming and resuscitation methods, for immersion in very cold water without protection causes shock and death. This problem led to the subsequent hypothermia and rewarming experiments conducted on DACHAU concentration camp prisoners by Dr. Sigmund RASCHER, a member of both the LUFTWAFFE and the SS. The goal of these experiments was to find the most successful means of reviving hypothermia victims. At the request of Heinrich HIMMLER, many of the earlier rewarming experiments conducted by Rascher utilized "animal" or body heat in order to rewarm severely chilled subjects. Throughout these experiments, Rascher sent regular reports to Himmler that described the progress of his research. The following is one such report, used by the prosecution at the DOCTORS TRIAL.

S. Rascher

Interim Report on Hypothermia Experiments in the
Dachau Concentration Camp
started on 15 August 1942

Experimental Procedure

The test subjects, dressed in complete flying uniform, winter or summer combination with an aviator's helmet, were placed in water. A life jacket of rubber or kapok was used to prevent submerging. The experiments were carried out with temperatures between 2.5° and 12°C [36° and 54°F]. In one of the experimental series the back of the head and neck were above water, while in another experimental series the neck (brain stem) and the back of the head were under water.

Electrical measurements gave hypothermia readings of 26.4°C [79.52°F] in the stomach and 26.5°C [79.7°F] in the rectum. Deaths occurred only when the brain stem and the back of the head were also chilled. Autopsies of such fatal cases always revealed substantial hemorrhaging, up to a half-liter, in the cranial cavity. The heart showed consistent extreme dilation of the right chamber. As soon as hypothermia reached 28°C [82.4°F] with these test subjects, they died without exception despite every effort at revival. The importance of heat-generating head and neck protection in the development of foam clothing was clearly proven by the described autopsy findings above.

Other important findings to be mentioned that were common in all experiments are: marked increase of the viscosity of the blood, marked increase of hemoglobin, an approximate fivefold increase of leukocytes, an invariable rise of blood sugar to twice its normal value. Auricular fibrillation appeared repeatedly at 30°C [86°F].

During attempts to save persons in the state of hypothermia, it was shown that rapid rewarming was in all cases preferable to slow rewarming because, after being removed from the cold water, the body temperature continued to drop rapidly. I think that for this reason we can dispense with the attempt to save hypothermic subjects by means of animal heat.

Gradual rewarming with animal or human bodies would be too slow. As measures to prevent hypothermia, only improvements in aviator clothing should be considered. First priority should be given to the German Textile Research Institute Mönchen-Gladbach, which produces foam suits with the appropriate neck protector. The experiments have shown that pharmaceutical measures are probably unnecessary if the flier is still alive at the time of rescue.

[signature] Dr. S. Rascher

Munich-Dachau, 10 September 1942

— *Reprinted from the National Archives and Records Administration, National Archives Collection of World War II War Crimes Records, Record Group 238, Office of the U.S. Chief of Counsel for War Crimes, Document 1618-PS. Translated from the German by Wendy Lower and Linda Bixby.*

HYPOTHERMIA: AN ASSISTANT TESTIFIES

Walter Neff was an Austrian political prisoner incarcerated at the DACHAU concentration camp. While there, he worked as an orderly in the infamous Experimental Block Number 5. In August 1942, he was assigned to assist in the hypothermia experiments conducted by Drs. Ernst Holzloehner and Ernst Finke, physiologists from the University of Kiel Medical School. Because he participated in these experiments, Neff was pardoned by Heinrich HIMMLER for his political crimes and employed as a medical assistant by the Office of the REICHSFÜHRER-SS Personal Staff (the bureau in charge of the Dachau medical experiments). Assigned to continue working in Dachau, Neff assisted Dr. Sigmund RASCHER, the physiologist in charge of hypothermia experiments at the camp after Holzloehner and Finke left in December 1942.

After the war, Neff was called to testify as a witness in the Nuremberg DOCTORS TRIAL. A portion of that testimony is reproduced below.

Q. Suppose you describe to the Tribunal exactly how these freezing experiments were carried out, that is what tests they made, how they measured the temperature and how the temperature of the water was lowered in the basin and so forth?

A. These basins were filled with water, and ice was added until the water measured 3°[C; 37.4°F], and the experimental subjects were either dressed in a flying suit or

SS-*Sturmbannführer* (SS Major) Dr. Sigmund RASCHER *(left)* and a LUFTWAFFE physician observe the reactions of a prisoner immersed for three hours in a tub of ice water, during experiments at the DACHAU concentration camp during 1942. REICHSFÜHRER-SS Heinrich HIMMLER authorized Dr. Rascher to conduct high-altitude and freezing experiments for the *Luftwaffe* on CONCENTRATION CAMP prisoners from 1941 to 1944.
(Süddeutscher Verlag Bilderdienst, Munich, Germany)

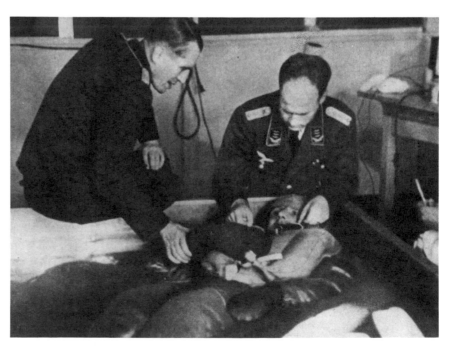

were placed into the ice water naked. During the period when Holzloehner and Finke were active, most experiments were conducted under narcotics because he maintained that you could not find the exact condition of the blood, and that you would exclude the will power of the experimental subject if he was under an anaesthetic. Now whenever the experimental subjects were conscious, it took some time until so-called freezing narcosis set in. The temperature was measured rectally and through the stomach through the Galvanometer apparatus. The lowering of the temperature to 32°[C; 89.6°F] was terrible for the experimental subject. At 32° the experimental subject lost consciousness. These persons were frozen down to 25°[C; 77°F] body temperature, and now in order to enable you to understand this problem, I should like to tell you something about the Holzloehner and Finke period. During the period when Holzloehner and Finke were active, no experimental subject was actually killed in the water. Deaths occurred all the more readily because during revival the temperature dropped even further and so heart failure resulted. This was also caused by wrongly applied therapy, so that in contrast to the low-pressure experiments, deaths were not deliberately caused. In the air-pressure chamber on the other hand, each death cannot be described as an accident, but as willful murder. However, it was different when Rascher personally took over these experiments. At that time a large number of the persons involved were kept in the water until they were dead.

— *Reprinted from "United States of America v. Karl Brandt, et al. (Case 1: 'Medical Case'),"* Trials of War Criminals Before the Nuernberg Military Tribunals Under Control Council Law No. 10, *15 vols. (Washington, D.C., [1949]), 1: 262–65.*

HYPOTHERMIA: ONLY TRAITORS OPPOSE EXPERIMENTS

The basis for using prisoners in lethal human experimentation was similar to the rationale for the "FINAL SOLUTION." The NAZI worldview dictated that the lives of Germans were infinitely more valuable than the lives of "the lower races." Therefore, Nazi physicians justified cruel human experimentation on CONCENTRATION CAMP *prisoners in the name of medical progress. In the following letter to Dr. Sigmund RASCHER, Heinrich HIMMLER, the* REICHSFÜHRER-SS, *discusses his opinion of human experimentation. It was introduced into evidence at the* DOCTORS TRIAL *in Nuremberg.*

Reichsführer-SS

Field Command Post, 24 October 1942

Dr. Sigmund **Rascher**
Munich
Träger Street 56

Dear **Rascher**!

Confidential Reich Affair
3 Copies
2nd Copy

I acknowledge the receipt of your letter of the 9th and 10th and both correspondences of 16 October 1942.

I have read with great interest your report about cooling experiments on humans. *SS-Sturmbannführer* [SS Major] **Sievers** should arrange the opportunity for an evaluation by institutes that are connected with us.

People who continue to disapprove of these human experiments would prefer to let brave German soldiers die of hypothermia; I regard them as guilty of high and capital treason, and I will not hesitate to report these men to the appropriate offices. I empower you to make my intentions known to the these offices.

I would like you to attend an oral lecture in November since unfortunately, in spite of my great interest, I will not get around to this sooner.

SS-Obergruppenführer [SS Lieutenant General] **Wolff** will be in contact with *General Feldmarschall* [General Field Marshal] **Milch**. The only non-physicians you are authorized to give reports to are *General Feldmarschall* Milch and, if he has time, of course to the Reich Marshal.

For warming those stranded at sea and picked up in boats or small vessels where there is no chance to place the hypothermic persons in a hot bath, I believe that blankets with heat packets or something similar sown into the lining are best. I assume that you are familiar with these heat packets, which we also have in the SS and which were used often by the Russians.

They are made of a material that develops a warmth of 70° to 80°C [158° to 176°F] after adding water and retains this temperature for hours.

I am very curious about the experiments with animal warmth. Personally I suppose that these experiments will perhaps bring the best and most lasting results. Of course, I could be mistaken.

Keep me informed about the ongoing research. We will see each other again in November.

Heil Hitler!
Yours,
signed **H. Himmler**

2.) *SS-Obergruppenführer Wolff*
Copy sent with request for acknowledgment.
I submit the report with the request for acknowledgment

and return, since the *Reichsführer-SS* in Munich wants the documents returned.

By order of
signed Brandt
SS-Sturmbannführer

— *Reproduced from the National Archives and Records Administration, National Archives Collection of World War II War Crimes Records, Record Group 238, Office of the U.S. Chief of Counsel for War Crimes, Document 1609-PS. Translated from the German by Wendy Lower and Linda Bixby.*

HIGH ALTITUDE: DR. RASCHER'S INTERIM REPORT

In spring 1942, Dr. Sigmund RASCHER began another area of research at the DACHAU concentration camp for the LUFTWAFFE: low-pressure or high-altitude experiments. In these tests, Rascher sought to simulate the atmospheric conditions that a pilot might encounter when falling from a plane without a parachute or oxygen mask. Using a specially designed low-pressure chamber provided by the German Air Force, Rascher locked victims inside the air-tight compartment and removed the oxygen source in order to observe the effects of sudden asphyxiation. Once the victims had either lost consciousness or died, their bodies were removed and held under water while autopsies were performed to determine the amounts of oxygen left in the brain and body cavities. On April 5, 1942, Dr. Rascher reported the earliest findings of these tests to Heinrich HIMMLER in the interim report reproduced below, used as evidence at the Nuremberg DOCTORS TRIAL. The cover letter is reproduced in facsimile.

Dr. Sigmund Rascher

Munich, 5 April 1942
Träger Street 56

[handwritten notation] 8 April

Highly esteemed *Reichsführer!*

Enclosed is the interim report on the low pressure experiments conducted so far in the Dachau concentration camp. May I respectfully ask you to treat the report as confidential.

A few days ago Reich Doctor-SS Professor Dr. Grawitz briefly viewed the experimental procedures. Since his time was very limited, no experiment could be demonstrated to him. *SS-Obersturmbannführer* [SS Lieutenant Colonel] Sievers took an entire day to watch some of the interesting standard experiments and may soon be reporting on this. I believe, highly esteemed Reichsführer, that you would be extraordinarily interested in these experiments. Is it not possible that on the occasion of a trip to southern Germany you would like to have some of the experiments demonstrated to you? If the obtained data continues to be confirmed, this would yield entirely new findings for science; likewise this would create a completely new perspective for aviation.

I hope that, thanks to the planned efforts of *SS-Obersturmbannführer* Sievers, the *Luftwaffe* will not pre-

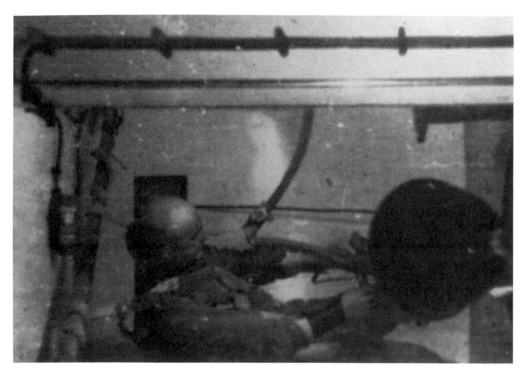

A DACHAU concentration camp prisoner hangs limply after a low-pressure experiment subjected him to air pressures equivalent to an altitude of 15,000 meters (ca. 49,000 feet). The purpose of these experiments, begun in 1942, was to determine the maximum altitude pilots could survive without oxygen.
(National Museum of Auschwitz-Birkenau, Oswiecim, Poland)

sent me with further difficulties. I am very much indebted to *SS-Obertsturmbannführer* Sievers, as he shows in every respect a very active interest in my work.

Respectfully, I thank you highly esteemed *Reichsführer,* for the generous fulfillment of my proposal to conduct such experiments of this kind in the concentration camp. With my best wishes for your personal well-being,

Heil Hitler!
Gratefully yours,
[signature] S. Rascher

First Interim Report on the Low Pressure Chamber Experiments in the Concentration Camp of Dachau

1. The question to be clarified is whether the theoretically established norms correspond with the results of practical experiments in regard to the duration of human life when breathing air with poor levels of oxygen and subjected to low pressure. It has been claimed that a parachutist who jumps from a height of 12 km [39,000 ft.] would suffer very severe injuries, probably even die, due to lack of oxygen. Practical experiments on this issue have always been discontinued after a maximum of 53 seconds, since very severe altitude sickness occurs or occurred.

2. Experiments testing the duration of life of a human above the normal breathing limits (4.5–6 km [15,000–20,000 ft.]) have not been employed at all since it has been an established conclusion that the human experimental subject would suffer death.

The experiments conducted by myself and Dr. Romberg indicated the following:

1. Experiments on parachute jumps proved that the lack of oxygen and the low atmospheric pressure neither at 12 nor 13 km [39,000 nor 43,000 ft.] altitude caused death. Altogether 15 extreme experiments of this type were carried out, in which none of the subjects died. Very severe altitude sickness with unconsciousness occurred, but completely normal functions of the senses returned when an altitude of 7 km [23,000 ft.] was reached on descent. Electrocardiograms taken during the experiments did show certain irregularities, but by the time the experiments were completed, the curves had returned to normal, and they did not indicate any abnormal changes during the subsequent days. The extent to which deterioration of the organism may occur due to continuously repeated experiments can only be established at the end of a series of experiments. The extreme, fatal experiments will be carried out on specially selected subjects; otherwise, it would not be possible to exercise the kind of control that is so extraordinarily important for practical purposes.

The subjects were brought under oxygen to an altitude of 8 km [26,000 ft.] and each had to do 5 knee bends with and without oxygen. After a certain interval of time, moderate to severe altitude sickness occurred, and the subjects became unconscious. However, after a certain period of accustoming themselves to an altitude of 8 km

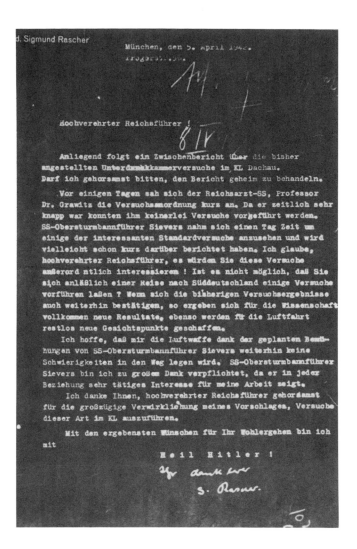

[26,000 ft.], all the subjects recuperated, regaining consciousness and the normal functions of their senses.

At first continuous experiments at altitudes higher than 10.5 km [34,000 ft.] resulted in death. These experiments showed that breathing stopped after about 30 minutes, while in 2 cases the electrocardiographically charted action of the heart continued for another 20 minutes after breathing had stopped.

The third experiment of this type took such an unusual course that I called an SS physician of the camp as witness, since I had worked on these experiments by myself. It was a continuous experiment without oxygen at an altitude of 12 km [39,000 ft], conducted on a 37-year-old Jew in good general condition. Breathing continued up to 30 minutes.

After 4 minutes the subject began to perspire and his head began to wobble; after 5 minutes there was cramping; between 6 and 10 minutes breathing increased and the subject became unconscious; from 11 to 30 minutes breathing slowed down to 3 breaths per minute, then finally stopping altogether. During this time severe cyanosis developed, along with foam appearing at the mouth.

EKGs were recorded in 3 variations at 5-minute intervals. After breathing had stopped, the recording of the

EKG continued until the heartbeat came to a complete stop. About ¹/₂ hour after breathing stopped, the autopsy began.

Autopsy Report:

When the chest cavity was opened, the pericardium was tightly filled (heart tamponade). Upon opening the pericardium, 80 cc of a clear, yellowish liquid streamed forth. The moment the tamponade stopped, the right auricle began to beat heavily, at first at the rate of 60 beats per minute, then progressively slower. Twenty minutes after the pericardium had been opened, the right auricle was opened by puncturing. For about 15 minutes a thin stream of blood spurted forth. Subsequently coagulation of the blood clogged the puncture wound in the auricle, and renewed acceleration of the right auricle's pulsing occurred.

One hour after breathing had stopped, the brain was removed with the spinal marrow being completely severed. As a result the movement of the auricle stopped for 40 seconds. It then renewed its movement, coming to a complete standstill 8 minutes later. A serious subarachnoid edema was found in the brain. A considerable quantity of air was discovered in the veins and arteries of the brain. In addition, the blood vessels in the heart and liver were enormously obstructed by embolisms.

The anatomical preparations will be preserved, so I will be able to evaluate them later.

The last-described case is to my knowledge the first one of this type ever observed on man. The above-described heart movements will gain particular scientific interest since the heart action was recorded with an EKG to the very end.

The experiments will be continued and further expanded. Another interim report will follow after new results have been obtained.

[signature] Dr. Rascher

— *Reproduced from the National Archives and Records Administration, National Archives Collection of World War II War Crimes Records, Record Group 238, Office of the U.S. Chief of Counsel for War Crimes, Document 1971a-PS. Translated from the German by Wendy Lower and Linda Bixby.*

SALT WATER: A GYPSY TEST SUBJECT TESTIFIES

Yet another type of medical experimentation inflicted upon CONCENTRATION CAMP *prisoners involved the forced ingestion of seawater. Commissioned by the* LUFTWAFFE *and the German navy, these tests sought to discover a way to make seawater potable for shipwrecked sailors and downed German fliers. Two separate water treatment processes were tested: the Konrad Schaefer method that purified salt water, and the Berka method that left the salt content of the water unchanged while masking the salt flavor. Because the Berka method was generally believed to be extremely toxic and most likely fatal, it was decided in May 1944 that this method would be tested on concentration camp inmates.*

Supervised by Dr. Wilhelm Beiglboeck, formerly the senior attending physician at the University Medical Clinic of Vienna, seawater experiments were conducted in Sigmund RASCHER'S *former laboratories at the* DACHAU *concentration camp during summer and fall 1944. Using a group of forty* GYPSIES *as human guinea pigs, Dr. Beiglboeck fed his*

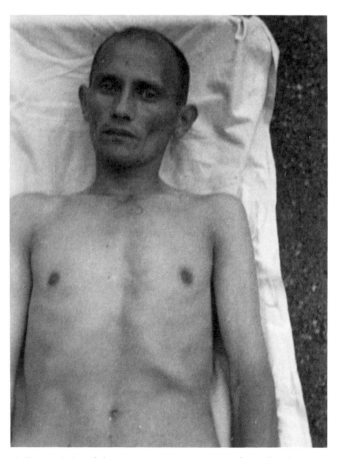

A GYPSY victim of the sea-water experiments performed at the DACHAU concentration camp from 1942 to 1944 in order to discover a method of making salt water potable. (NARA)

experimental subjects navy rations for two weeks and, during the next two weeks, fed them nothing save seawater treated by either the Schaefer or Berka methods. One of the test subjects, Karl Hoellenrainer, describes the experiment further in his testimony at the DOCTORS TRIAL.

Q. Now, will you, in detail, tell the Tribunal just what food the experimental subjects received prior to the experiments, during the course of the experiments, and after the experiments, and in doing so, Witness, kindly talk very slowly and distinctly so that the interpreters will be able to translate you more efficiently.

A. Yes. At first we got potatoes, milk, and then we got these cookies and dextrose and rusks. That lasted about 1 week. Then we got nothing at all. Then the doctor from the Luftwaffe said, "Now, you have to drink sea water on an empty stomach." That lasted about 1 or 2 weeks. This Rudi Taubmann [another prisoner], as I already said, got excited and didn't want to participate; and the doctor from the Luftwaffe said, "If you get excited and mutiny, I will shoot you," and then we were all quiet. Then we began to drink sea water. I drank the worst kind, that was yellowish. We drank two or three times a day, and then in the evening we drank the yellow kind. There were three kinds of water, white water, and [two kinds of] yellow water; and I drank the yellow kind. After a few days the people became raving mad; they foamed at the mouth. The doctor from the Luftwaffe came with a cynical laugh and said, "Now it is time to make the liver punctures." I remember one very well.

Q. Talk more slowly, Witness. Thank you.

A. Yes. The first row on the left when you came in, the second bed, that was the first one. He went crazy and barked like a dog. He foamed at the mouth. The doctor from the Luftwaffe took him down on a stretcher with a white sheet over him, and then he stuck a needle about this long (indicating) into his right side, and there was a hypodermic needle on it, and it bled, and it was very painful. We were all quiet and excited. When that was over, the other inmates took their turn. The people were crazy from thirst and hunger, we were so hungry—but the doctor had no pity on us. He was as cold as ice. He didn't take any interest in us. Then, one gypsy—I don't know his name any more—ate a little piece of bread once, or drank some water; I don't remember just what he did. The doctor from the Luftwaffe got very angry and mad. He took the gypsy and tied him to a bed post and sealed his mouth.

Q. Witness, do you mean that he put adhesive tape over this gypsy's mouth?

A. Yes.

Q. Go ahead, continue.

A. Then a gypsy, he was lying on the right, a big strong, husky fellow, he refused to drink the water. He asked the doctor from the Luftwaffe to let him go. He said he couldn't stand the water. He was sick. The doctor from the Luftwaffe had no pity, and he said, "No, you have to drink it." The doctor from the Luftwaffe told one of his assistants to

go and get a sun. Naturally, we didn't know what a sun was. Then one of his assistants came with a red tube about this long (indicating) and thrust this tube first into the gypsy's mouth and then into his stomach. . . . And then he pumped water down the tube. The gypsy kneeled in front of him and beseeched him for mercy but that doctor had none. . . .

Q. When you say "the doctor from the Luftwaffe" you mean the man you referred to as the "professor." The professor and the doctor from the Luftwaffe are the same or are they two different people?

A. Yes.

Q. I see. Thank you. Now, who performed the liver punctures?

A. The doctor from the Luftwaffe carried out the liver punctures himself. Some people were given liver punctures and at the same time a puncture in the spinal cord. The doctor from the Luftwaffe did that himself. It was very painful. Something ran out at the same time at the back. It was water or something—I don't know what it was.

Q. Well, did you receive a liver puncture?

A. Yes.

Q. Did the professor tell you for what reason he gave you that liver puncture?

A. The doctor from the Luftwaffe came to me and said, "Now, Hoellenrainer, it's your turn." I was lying on the bed. I was very weak from this water and from not having anything to eat. He said, "Now, lie on your left side and take the clothes off your right side." I held on to the bedstead on top of me and the doctor from the Luftwaffe sat down next to me and pushed a long needle into me. It was very painful. I said, "Doctor, what are you doing?" The doctor said, "I have to make a liver puncture so that the salt comes out of your liver."

Q. Now, Witness, can you tell us whether or not the subjects used in the experiments were gypsies of purely German nationality or were there some Polish gypsies, some Russian gypsies, Czechoslovak gypsies, and so forth?

A. Yes, there were about seven or eight Germans and the rest of them were all Poles and Czechs, Czech gypsies and Polish gypsies.

Q. Were any of the experimental subjects ever taken out of the station room to the yard outside the experimental barracks?

A. Yes, at the end when the experiments were all finished; and three people were carried out with white sheets over them on a stretcher. They were covered with sheets but I don't know whether they were dead or not. But we, my colleagues and I, talked about it. We never saw these three again, neither at work nor anywhere in the camp. We often talked about it and wondered where they were. We never saw them again. We thought that they were dead. . . .

— *Reprinted from "United States of America v. Karl Brandt, et al. (Case 1: 'Medical Case'),"* Trials of War Criminals Before the Nuernberg Military Tribunals Under Control Council Law No. 10, *15 vols. (Washington, D.C., [1949]), 1: 460–62.*

DRUG TESTS: "CURE-INDUCED" INFECTIONS

Wladyslawa Karolewska, a Warsaw elementary school teacher, became a member of the Polish RESISTANCE soon after World War II began. Captured and interrogated by the GESTAPO, she was sent, along with a transport of 700 Polish women, to the RAVENSBRÜCK concentration camp in fall 1941. There, beginning in August 1942, she and seventy-five other former resistance fighters became the test subjects for multiple operations and bacterial experiments designed to mimic battlefield wounds and treatments. Conducted at the suggestion of Dr. Karl Gebhardt, chief surgeon at the Hohenlychen Medical Institute, these experiments involved infecting healthy women with gangrene-causing bacteria and simulated shrapnel (glass and wood particles). The Ravensbrück physicians who performed these operations (Fischer, Oberhaeuser, Schiedlausky, and Rosenthal) then attempted to "cure" the resulting infection with the drug sulfanilamide. Between 1942 and 1944, Karolewska became permanently disabled as a result of six such procedures.

Herta Oberhauser, a physician at the RAVENSBRÜCK concentration camp and a defendant at the DOCTORS TRIAL, was convicted of involvement in sterilization and drug experiments on August 19, 1947. She was sentenced to 20 years in prison. (USHMM)

Reproduced below is a segment of Ms. Karolewska's testimony before the Nuremberg DOCTORS TRIAL, in which she describes the first two of these operations.

A. On 22 July 1942, 75 prisoners from our transport that came from Lublin were summoned to the chief of the camp. We stood outside the camp office, and present were Kogel, Mandel, and one person whom I later recognized as Dr. Fischer. We were afterwards sent back to the block and we were told to wait for further instructions. On the 25th of July, all the women from the transport of Lublin were summoned by Mandel, who told us that we were not allowed to work outside the camp. Also, five women from the transport that came from Warsaw were summoned with us at the same time. We were not allowed to work outside the camp. The next day 75 women were summoned again and we had to stand in front of the hospital in the camp. Present were Schiedlausky, Oberheuser, Rosenthal, Kogel, and the man whom I afterwards recognized as Dr. Fischer. . . . On the 14th of August, the same year [1942], I was called to the hospital and my name was written on a piece of paper. I did not know why. Besides me, eight other girls were called to the hospital. We were called at a time when executions usually took place and I thought I was going to be executed because some girls had been shot down before. In the hospital we were put to bed and the ward in which we stayed was locked. We were not told what we were to do in the hospital and when one of my comrades put the question she got no answer but an ironical smile. Then a German nurse arrived and gave me an injection in my leg. After this injection I vomited and I was weak. Then I was put on a hospital cot and they brought me to the operating room. There, Dr. Schiedlausky and Rosenthal gave me the second intravenous injection in my arm. A while before, I noticed Dr. Fischer, who left the operating theater and had operating gloves on. Then I lost consciousness and when I revived I noticed that I was in a proper hospital ward. I recovered consciousness for a while and I felt severe pain in my leg. Then I lost consciousness again. I regained consciousness in the morning, and then I noticed that my leg was in a cast from the ankle up to the knee and I felt very great pain in this leg and had a high temperature. I noticed also that my leg was swollen from the toes up to the groin. The pain was increasing and the temperature, too, and the next day I noticed that some liquid was flowing from my leg. The third day I was put on a hospital trolley and taken to the dressing room. Then I saw Dr. Fischer again. He had on an operating gown and rubber gloves on his hands. A blanket was put over my eyes and I did not know what was done with my leg but I felt great pain and I had the impression that something must have been cut out of my leg. Those present were Schiedlausky, Rosenthal, and Oberheuser. After the dressing was changed I was again put in the regular hospital ward. Three days later I was again taken to the dressing room, and the dressing was changed by Dr. Fischer with the assistance of the same doctors, and I was also blind-folded. I was then sent back to the regular hospital ward. The next dressings were made by the camp doctors. Two weeks later we were all taken to the operating theater again, and put on the operating tables. The bandage was removed, and that was the first time I saw my leg. The incision went so deep that I could see the bone. We were told then that there was a doctor from Hohenlychen, Dr. Gebhardt, who would come and examine us. We were waiting for his arrival for 3 hours, lying on our tables. When he came, a sheet was put over our eyes, but they removed the sheet and I saw him for a short moment. Then we were taken back to our regular wards. On 8 September I went back to the block. I couldn't walk. The pus was draining from my leg; the leg was swollen up and I could not walk. In the block, I stayed in bed for one week; then I was called to the hospital again. I could not walk and I was carried by my comrades. In the hospital I met some of my comrades who were there after the operation. This time I was sure I was going to be executed because I saw an ambulance standing outside the office, which was used by the Germans to transport people intended for execution. Then we were taken to the dressing room where Doctor Oberheuser and Doctor Schiedlausky examined our legs. We were put to bed again, and on the same day, in the afternoon, I was taken to the operating theater and the second operation was performed on my leg. I was put to sleep in the same way as before, having received an injection. This time I again saw Doctor Fischer. I woke up in the regular hospital ward, and I felt a much greater pain and had a higher temperature.

The symptoms were the same. The leg was swollen and the pus flowed from my leg. After this operation, the dressings were changed by Dr. Fischer every 3 days. More than 10 days afterwards, we were again taken to the operating theater and put on the table; and we were told that Dr. Gebhardt was going to come to examine our legs. We waited for a long time. Then he arrived and examined our legs while we were blindfolded. This time other people arrived with Dr. Gebhardt, but I don't know their names, and I don't remember their faces. Then we were carried on hospital cots back to our rooms. After this operation I felt still worse, and I could not move. While I was in the hospital, Dr. Oberheuser treated me cruelly.

— *Reprinted from "United States of America v. Karl Brandt, et al. (Case 1: 'Medical Case'),"* Trials of War Criminals Before the Nuernberg Military Tribunals Under Control Council Law No. 10, *15 vols. (Washington, D.C., [1949]), 1: 411–13.*

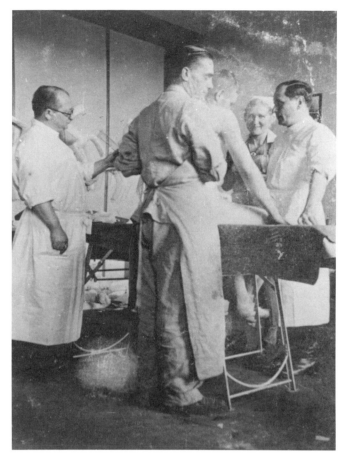

Dr. Carl Clauberg *(far left)* supervises the medical staff in the operating room of Block 10 at Auschwitz I concentration camp, where he experimented on Jewish female prisoners in order to discover an efficient and inexpensive method of mass sterilization; ca. 1944.
(Main Commission for Investigation of Nazi War Crimes, Warsaw, Poland)

STERILIZATION: HIMMLER'S ORDER

Nazi sterilization experiments generally fell into three categories: sterilization by medication, X rays, or injection. This last method, developed by Dr. Clauberg, the chief surgeon at the Ravensbrück concentration camp, was performed by injecting an irritating fluid, usually silver nitrate, directly into a woman's uterus. Injected without a woman's consent during a routine gynecological exam, the irritant caused severe pain and bleeding. Several thousand Jewish and Gypsy women were eventually sterilized in this manner.

In the following letter, Rudolf Brandt, Heinrich Himmler's personal assistant, writes to Dr. Clauberg initiating a new series of experiments testing the effectiveness of intrauterine injections. It was used as evidence at the Doctors Trial.

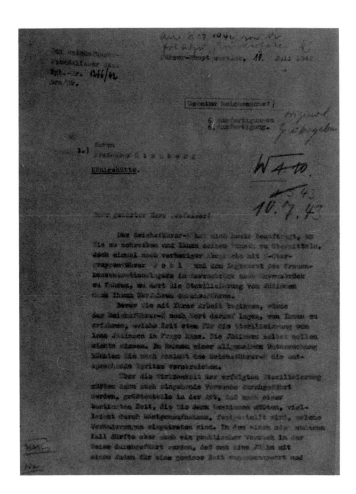

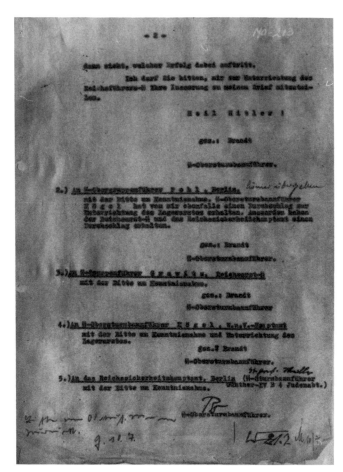

Reichsführer-SS   [handwritten remark]
Personal Staff   Returned
Journal Number 1266/42   31 October 1942
Bra/Dr.   by Pol. Administration K.

Führer's Headquarters, 10 July 1942

Confidential Reich Affair!

6 copies

6th copy

[handwritten remark]
Original handed to G.

1.) Professor **Glauberg**   [handwritten notations]
<u>Königshütte</u>   W 1.10
                               1.5.43
                             10.7.43

Dear Professor!

The *Reichsführer-SS* [Heinrich HIMMLER] authorized me today to write and transmit to you his wish that you proceed to Ravensbrück, after coordinating with *SS-Obergruppenführer* [SS Lieutenant General] **Pohl** and the camp physician of the women's concentration camp Ravensbrück, to perform there the sterilization of Jewesses using your method.

Before you begin your work, the *Reichsführer-SS* would be interested to learn from you how long it would take to sterilize a thousand Jewesses. The Jewesses them-

selves should not know about it. It is the understanding of the *Reichsführer-SS* that you could give the appropriate injection during a general examination.

The effectiveness of the sterilization will then have to undergo experiments, primarily of the type, perhaps through X rays, that would determine after a certain period of time what changes have taken place. In a few of these instances a practical experiment can be arranged by which a Jewess and a Jew can be locked up together

-2-

for a certain period of time; then it will be seen what results are achieved.

Please express to me your opinion about my letter for the information of the *Reichsführer-SS*.

Heil Hitler!
signed: Brandt
SS-Obersturmbannführer [SS Lieutenant Colonel]

2.) <u>To *SS-Obergruppenführer* [SS Lieutenant General] **Pohl**, Berlin</u>
for your information. *SS-Obersturmbannführer* **Kögel** also received a copy for the information of the camp physician. Likewise, the Reich Physician-SS and the Central Office for Reich Security received a copy.

signed: Brandt
SS-Obersturmbannführer

3.) To *SS-Gruppenführer* [SS Major General] **Grawitz,** <u>Reich Physician SS</u>

for your information.

> signed: Brandt
> *SS-Obersturmbannführer*

4.) To *SS-Obersturmbannführer* **Kögel,** <u>Central Office for Economy and Administration</u>

for your information and notification of the camp physician.

> signed: Brandt
> *SS-Obersturmbannführer*

5.) <u>To the Central Office for Reich Security, Berlin</u>
(*SS-Sturmbannführer* [SS Major] Günther—IVb4 Jewish Section)

for your information.

> [initialed] Br [Brandt]
> *SS-Obersturmbannführer*
> [handwritten, illegible]

— *Reproduced from the National Archives and Records Administration, National Archives Collection of World War II War Crimes Records, Record Group 238, Office of the U.S. Chief of Counsel for War Crimes, Document NO-213. Translated from the German by Gerald Schwab and Linda Bixby.*

STERILIZATION: A DOCTOR'S AFFIDAVIT

Although not a doctor, Rudolf Brandt was one of the main defendants in the Nuremberg <u>DOCTORS TRIAL</u>. *Formerly employed as the personal secretary to the* REICHSFÜHRER-SS, *Heinrich* HIMMLER, *Brandt headed Himmler's office at the Ministry of Interior. In the course of his duties, Brandt authorized the use of* CONCENTRATION CAMP *prisoners for medical experimentation conducted under Himmler's authority. The results of most experiments were reported directly to Brandt, who then passed this information on to Himmler. In the following affidavit, recorded by the United States Office of Chief of Counsel for War Crimes during its pretrial investigations for the Doctors Trial, Brandt sheds light on the many types of sterilization experiments that took place in concentration camps.*

SS-Gruppenführer (SS Major General) Karl BRANDT being sentenced to death on several counts, including participation in deadly medical experiments on thousands of concentration camp prisoners and official responsibility for the so-called EUTHANASIA program, at the <u>DOCTORS TRIAL</u>; **August 19, 1947.** (USHMM)

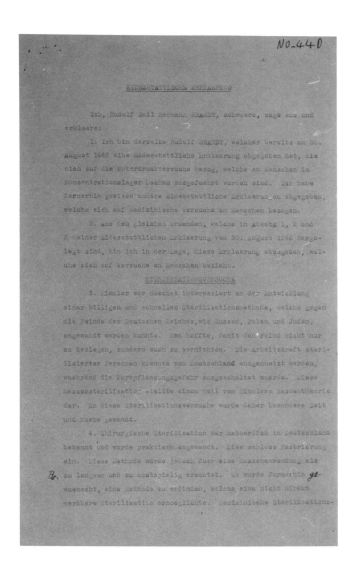

AFFIDAVIT

I, Rudolf Emil Herman BRANDT, duly sworn in, depose and state:

1. I am the same Rudolf BRANDT who already on 30 August 1946 furnished an affidavit concerning low pressure experiments that were conducted on persons at the Dachau concentration camp. I have furthermore furnished certain other affidavits concerning medical experiments on human beings.

2. For the same reasons set forth in paragraphs 1, 2, and 3 of my affidavit of 30 August 1946, I am in a position to make this declaration concerning experiments on human beings.

Sterilization Experiments

3. Himmler was extremely interested in the development of an inexpensive and rapid method of sterilization that could be used against the enemies of the German Reich, such as the Russians, Poles, and Jews. It was hoped thereby not only to defeat the enemy but also to annihilate him. The capacity for work of the sterilized persons could be exploited by Germany, while the danger of propagation would be eliminated. This mass sterilization represented part of Himmler's racial theory. As a result, considerable time and effort were devoted to these sterilization experiments.

4. Surgical sterilization was of course known in Germany and was applied. This included castration. This method was, however, considered too slow and too expensive for mass application. It was furthermore desired to create a procedure that would result in sterilization that was not immediately noticeable. Medical sterilization

begin page 2 of original

experiments were therefore conducted. Dr. Madaus had discovered that the drug "caladium seguinum," extracted from a North American plant *(Schweigrohr)*, caused sterilization when taken or injected. In late 1941, Dr. Adolf POKORNY drew Himmler's attention to this scientific research and suggested that it could be perfected and applied to Russian prisoners of war.

5. As a result of Pokorny's suggestion, experiments were conducted on concentration camp inmates in order to test the effect of the drug. Efforts were simultaneously made to cultivate the plant in large quantities. Oswald

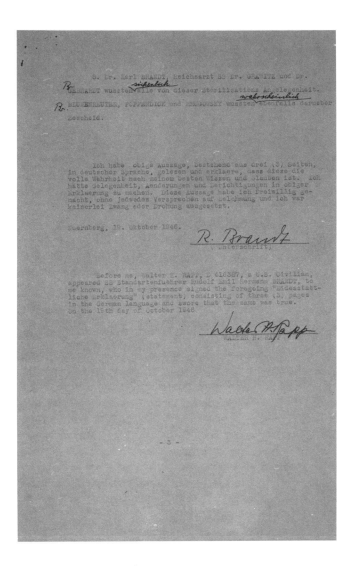

POHL, chief of the WVHA [SS CENTRAL OFFICE FOR ECONOMY AND ADMINISTRATION] took a personal interest in this matter. Greenhouses were used with a certain amount of success to cultivate this plant, and the experiments were continued. I do not believe, however, that it was possible to produce the drug in sufficiently large quantities to permit its large-scale application.

6. Dr. Glauberg also developed a method for the sterilization of women. This method was based on the injection of an irritating solution into the uterus. Glauberg conducted widespread experiments on Jewish women and Gypsies in the Auschwitz concentration camp. Several thousand women were sterilized by Glauberg in Auschwitz. Dr. Karl Gebhardt apparently conducted surgical sterilizations in the Ravensbrück camp.

7. Sterilization experiments were likewise conducted with X rays. Dr. SCHUMANN was working with this method in Auschwitz and sterilized a number of men.

begin page 3 of original

8. Dr. Karl BRANDT, Reich Physician-SS Dr. GRAWITZ, and Dr. GEBHARDT certainly knew about this sterilization matter. BLUMENREUTHER, POPPEN-

DICK, and MRUGOWSKY probably knew all about this as well.

I have read the above testimony containing three pages in the German language and state that, to the best of my knowledge and belief, this is the whole truth. I had the opportunity to make changes and corrections in the above affidavit. I made this statement voluntarily, without promise of reward, and I was subjected to no duress or threat of any kind.

Nuremberg, 19 October 1946

[signature] <u>R. BRANDT</u>
(Signature)

— Reproduced from the National Archives and Records Administration, National Archives Collection of World War II War Crimes Records, Record Group 238, Office of the U.S. Chief of Counsel for War Crimes, Document NO-440. Translated from the German by Gerald Schwab and Linda Bixby.

SKULLS AND SKELETONS: DEMAND

NAZI racial theory assumed a hierarchy of races in which the "superior ARYAN race" was involved in a struggle against the "inferior" Slavs, GYPSIES, Negroes, and Jews. This racist ideology eventually infected all academic disciplines within German society. Particularly corrupted by Nazi "racial science" were the medically related fields of anatomy, biology, and physiology. These sciences sought "scientific" methods to distinguish between the races.

One study, led by Dr. August Hirt, a professor of anatomy at the University of Strassburg, examined Jewish skulls for cranial differences between races. In search of subjects for his study, Hirt petitioned the AHNENERBE SOCIETY, an organization of the SS endowed to coordinate ethnological research in support of SS ideology. A research proposal written by Dr. Hirt and forwarded by Wolfram Sievers, the secretary general of the Ahnenerbe Society, to Rudolf Brandt, Heinrich HIMMLER's personal adjutant, on Dr. Hirt's behalf was introduced as evidence at the <u>DOCTORS TRIAL</u> held in Nuremberg. A page of the report is reproduced in facsimile.

Re: Securing Skulls from Jewish-Bolshevik Commissars for Scientific Research at the Reich University Strassburg.

There exists an extensive collection of skulls from nearly all races and peoples. Only from the Jews are there so few skulls available for scientific study that their evaluation does not allow reliable findings. The war in the East now presents us with the opportunity to remedy this shortage. By procuring the skulls of the Jewish Bolshevik commissars who personify a repulsive yet characteristic

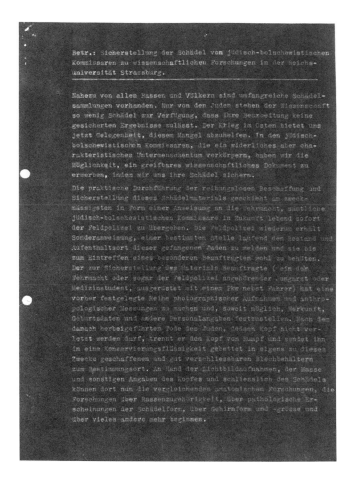

subhumanity, we have the opportunity to obtain tangible, scientific evidence.

The actual implementation of a smooth procurement and securing of these skulls could most practically be done through a directive to the *Wehrmacht*: that in the future all live Jewish Bolshevik commissars be turned over immediately to the field police. The field police in turn is to be issued special directives to continually inform a certain office of the number and place of detention of these captured Jews and to guard them well until the arrival of a special deputy. This special deputy (a junior physician belonging to the *Wehrmacht* or even the field military police, or a medical student equipped with car and driver), commissioned with the collection of the material, is to take a certain series of photographs and anthropological measurements and is to establish, as far as possible, the origin, date of birth, and other personal data of the prisoner. Following the subsequently induced death of the Jew, whose head must not be damaged, he will separate the head from the torso and will forward it to its destination point in a preservative fluid within a well-sealed tin container especially made for this purpose. Based on the photos, the measurements and other data on the head, and finally the skull itself, the comparative anatomical research, research on racial membership, the pathological features of the skull from the form and size of the brain, and many other things, can begin.

In accordance with its scope and tasks, the new Strassburg Reich University would be the most appropriate place for the collection and research on the skulls thus acquired.

— *Reproduced from the National Archives and Records Administration, National Archives Collection of World War II War Crimes Records, Record Group 238, Office of the U.S. Chief of Counsel for War Crimes, Document NO-085. Translated from the German by Wendy Lower and Linda Bixby.*

SKULLS AND SKELETONS: SUPPLY

The Anatomical Institute at the University of Strassburg, directed by Dr. August Hirt, collected and studied skeletons in a pseudoscientific attempt to identify physiological differences between the races. As Henri Henripierre, a laboratory assistant, describes below in his testimony at the Nuremberg DOCTORS TRIAL, *Dr. Hirt received bodies of carefully gassed "specimens" from the nearby* NATZWEILER *concentration camp. Upon arrival at the Institute, the bodies were specially preserved in vats of alcohol according to Hirt's instructions. Once preserved, Otto Bong, the Institute's autopsy technician, removed the flesh from some of the preserved bodies, and with the help of laboratory assistants Henripierre and Meier, cataloged the victims' skeletal measurements.*

Q. . . . Let's find out a little bit more about your job before then.

A. My employment was principally to preserve the corpses, to fetch these corpses at Mutzig, and also prepare for the lectures which were given to the students. . . .

In the month of July, 1943, Professor Hirt received a visit from the senior officer of the SS. I thought that he was a senior officer because he came in his own car, accompanied by his own driver. Now, to have a driver and a car, you would need to be a senior officer.

This officer came three times in the month of July. Professor Hirt took him and showed him the cellars of the laboratory. A few days later, Mr. Bong told me that he would have to prepare the tanks to receive a hundred and twenty corpses. We prepared the tanks. In these tanks there were synthetic spirits of 55 degrees.

The first convoy which we received was a convoy of thirty women. It was supposed to arrive at five o'clock in the morning, but it only arrived at seven. After having interrogated the driver about the delay, the driver gave answer, "They gave us a lot of trouble." These thirty corpses of women were unloaded by the driver and two assistants, also helped by Mr. Bong and myself.

The preservation of these corpses started straight away. The corpses arrived when they were still warm. The eyes were wide open and brilliant; they seemed congested and red, and they were popping out of the orbits. There were traces of blood at the nose and at the mouth, and there was evidence of fecal matter coming out. There was no rigor mortis apparent. At that moment I judged for myself that it was a case of victims who, in my opinion, had been poisoned or asphyxiated, because in the case of no victim of any previous preservation were there presented the symptoms and signs that these victims showed when they arrived. That is why I made a note of the serial numbers that the women had tattooed on their left forearm. I made a note of them on a piece of paper, and I kept them in secret in my house. The serial numbers consisted of five digits.

A few days later we received a second convoy of thirty men. These arrived exactly in the same state as the first, that is, still warm, with wide open eyes, congested, eyes brilliant, bleeding at the mouth and bleeding at the nose, and also losing their fecal matter.

The preservation of those thirty men was also proceeded with immediately, with one slight difference. The left testicle in each case was removed, which was sent to the Laboratory for Anatomy Number 2. That was a private laboratory run by Professor Hirt.

Some time later, thereupon, we received a third and last convoy, namely, of twenty-six men. They also arrived in the same state as the two previous cases.

I should like to make it clear once more—and I say this knowing it to be true—after the first convoy of women's bodies that we received, Professor Hirt, having met me at the door of an Anatomical Department, told me literally "Peter, if you don't hold your mouth, you won't get out of this." That is word for word what Professor Hirt told me.

Another peculiarity. Professor Hirt, some time before he received those bodies, said, in the basement of an Anatomical Department, talking to Mr. Bong, "They are going to drop like flies." All of this was a sign for me that it was literally a case of murder, I therefore was right in believing that those eighty-six victims which we had received had not died a natural death. . . .

Q. Do you know, witness, whether or not the people who were killed and delivered to you were Jews?

A. At the time that I saw these bodies I did not know whether they were Jews or not. I merely questioned Mr. Bong and I asked him what he thought those people were. It was Mr. Bong who said, "Das sind alles Juden," "They are all Jews."

Q. Now witness, will you tell the Tribunal just what happened to these bodies after they had been delivered to you and had been stored in the basement or in the cellar?

A. Once the bodies had been preserved, they were put into the tanks. They remained in the tanks for an entire year without anybody touching them. In the month of September, 1944, the Allies were advancing and therefore, at that time, Professor Hirt ordered Mr. Bong and Mr. Meier, the laboratory assistants, to cut up these eighty-six bodies and to have them cremated in the Strassbourg City Crematorium. The work having been accomplished by Mr. Bong and Mr. Meier in the actual room where these tanks were, I asked Mr. Bong the following morning if he had cut up all of the bodies. He replied, "We couldn't cut them all up, it was far too much work. We left some of the bodies at the bottom of the tanks." I then asked Bong, "Were all the corpses burned with their gold teeth?" At that moment Bong replied, "The gold teeth that were already found on the Jews were handed over to Professor Hirt by Mr. Meier."

The remaining corpses that were not put into coffins—because there weren't any coffins left—were tossed back into the tanks with the remainder of the others, so as to make people who would see them believe that they were the remains of anatomical defections.

— *Reprinted from National Archives and Records Administration, National Archives Collection of World War II War Crimes Records, Record Group 238, Nuernberg Trials Transcripts of the Proceedings, United States of America v. Karl Brandt, et al., 712–15.*

HOMOSEXUALS

Immediately after Adolf HITLER'S rise to power, homosexuals were persecuted by NAZI Germany. Viewed as sexual deviants and traitors to the THIRD REICH, homosexuals were arrested and jailed in prisons and CONCENTRATION CAMPS as early as 1933. By 1936, anti-homosexual legislation established the Reich Central Office for Combatting Homosexuality and Abortion. In conjunction with the police, this office organized the systematic registration and criminalization of all suspected homosexuals. Once incarcerated, homosexual prisoners were subjected to castration, medical experimentation, and murder.

The Danish endocrinologist Dr. Carl Vaernet, an alias for Dr. Carl Peter Jensen, performed some of the most brutal medical experiments on homosexuals jailed at the BUCHENWALD concentration camp. Vaernet believed that by first castrating his victims and then injecting them with massive doses of testosterone through a surgically implanted "male gland," he could medically change homosexuals into heterosexuals.

The letter reproduced below, and used as evidence at the Nuremberg DOCTORS TRIAL, was sent by Dr. Helmut Poppendick, chief surgeon in the SS CENTRAL OFFICE FOR RACE AND RESETTLEMENT and a defendant in the Doctors Trial, to Dr. Erwin Ding-Schuler, a Buchenwald concentration camp physician. Poppendick discusses Heinrich HIMMLER'S directives in preparation for Vaernet's hormone experiments.

[July 15, 1944]

By request of the Reichsfuehrer SS the Danish doctor SS Sturmbannfuehrer [SS Major] Dr. Vaernet has been given opportunity to continue his hormone research with

SS-*Standartenführer* (SS Colonel) Helmut Poppendick, the chief of personal staff of the Reich Physician SS and Police, was among twenty-three defendants at the DOCTORS TRIAL. Convicted of membership in a CRIMINAL ORGANIZATION, Poppendick was sentenced to ten years imprisonment; in 1951 his sentence was reduced to time served. (USHMM)

the SS, particularly the development of his artificial gland. The Reichsfuehrer SS anticipates certain results from the treatment of homosexuals with Vaernet's artificial gland. The technical preparations have come to such a point that experiments on human beings can be started within a reasonable space of time.

As SS Standartenfuehrer [SS Colonel] Dr. Lolling informed me, the concentration camp Weimar-Buchenwald has been directed to make available 5 prisoners for SS Sturmbannfuehrer Vaernet's experiments. These prisoners will be made available to SS Sturmbannfuehrer Vaernet by the camp physician at any time.

SS Sturmbannfuehrer Vaernet intends to go to Buchenwald shortly in order to make certain necessary preliminary tests on these prisoners. In case there will be special laboratory tests, you are requested to assist Vaernet within the scope of your possibilities.

Particulars on Vaernet's research were sent today to the camp physician of Weimar-Buchenwald for his information.

— *Reprinted from "United States of America v. Karl Brandt, et al. (Case 1: 'Medical Case'),"* Trials of War Criminals Before the Nuernberg Military Tribunals Under Control Council Law No. 10, *15 vols. (Washington, D.C., [1949]), 2: 251–52.*

A VERDICT

The Nuremberg DOCTORS TRIAL *was the first of twelve trials to be held before the* NUREMBERG MILITARY TRIBUNALS. *Lasting eleven months, this trial graphically recounted the horrific story of medical atrocities performed by physicians on unwilling victims, most of whom were concentration camp inmates. Exemplifying the process by which healers became murderers, the crimes of the nineteen medical defendants also created an international dilemma concerning medical ethics.*

The trial accused twenty-three defendants on four charges: CONSPIRACY, WAR CRIMES *in the form of medical experimentation on prisoners of war,* CRIMES AGAINST HUMANITY *through the murder or torture of thousands in the name of scientific research, and membership in* CRIMINAL ORGANIZATIONS *as defined by the* INTERNATIONAL MILITARY TRIBUNAL. *(The charge of conspiracy against all defendants was later dropped.)*

The following newspaper article recounts the results of the trial.

7 Nazi Doctors Get Death, 9 Jail Terms And 7 Are Acquitted

NUREMBERG, Aug. 20—The eight-month-old Nuremberg war crimes trial of 23 Nazi physicians and scientists ended here today with sentences of death by hanging for seven defendants, life imprisonment terms for five, four prison sentences ranging from 10 to 20 years and seven acquittals.

Defense counsels termed the trial extremely fair but said they will appeal for clemency to the United States Supreme Court.

Those sentenced to death were Karl Brandt, formerly Hitler's personal physician and a lieutenant general in the SS; Karl Gebhardt, personal physician to Himmler; Rudolf Brandt, former SS colonel; Joachim Mrugowsky, former chief hygiene officer in the SS; Wolfram Sievers, former head of the institute for military scientific research; Waldemar Hoven, former chief physician in the Buchenwald concentration camp, and Victor Brack, former SS general and official in Hitler's chancellery.

Guilty On Two Counts

All seven had been found guilty on counts 2 and 3 of the indictment, charging war crimes and crimes against humanity and all except Sievers guilty of membership in organizations declared criminal by the International Military Tribunal last fall, count 4.

Eight of the nine defendants sentenced to prison, including Herta Oberhauser, a woman doctor in the Ravensbrück concentration camp, were found guilty on counts 2 and 3. Helmut Poppendieck, former chief of staff of the SS medical office, drew 10 years for membership in a criminal organization.

Count 1 of the indictment charging conspiracy had been dropped.

— *Reproduced from* News of Germany, *August 21, 1947.*

A NEW MEDICAL OATH

The Nuremberg Doctors Trial not only forced the world to confront the atrocities committed by Nazi physicans but also created a crisis for medical ethics. Medical morality, traditionally articulated by the Hippocratic Oath, had clearly been corrupted or ignored by leading German physicians in the name of "research." As a result, at their 1948 Geneva meeting, the World Medical Association adopted a new version of the Hippocratic Oath that reemphasized a physician's primary responsibility: helping patients. This new Hippocratic Oath is now taken by all physicians on receipt of their diploma.

Now being admitted to the profession of medicine, I solemnly pledge to consecrate my life to the service of humanity. I will give respect and gratitude to my deserving teachers. I will practice medicine with conscience and dignity. The health and life of my patient will be my first consideration. I will hold in confidence all that my patient confides in me.

I will maintain the honor and the noble traditions of the medical profession. My colleagues will be as my brothers. *I will not permit consideration of race, religion, nationality, party politics or social standing to intervene between my duty and my patient. I will maintain the utmost respect for human life from the time of its conception. Even under threat I will not use my knowledge contrary to the laws of humanity.*

These promises I make freely and upon my honor.

— *Reprinted from Alexander Mitscherlich, M.D.,* Doctors of Infamy, *(New York, 1949), xxxviii–xxxix.*

Ilse Koch, wife of the former commandant of the BUCHENWALD concentration camp, *SS-Sturmbannführer* (SS Major) Karl Otto Koch, and known as "The Bitch of Buchenwald," points to a map of the camp during her testimony at the trial of former officials of the camp; April 1947. (NARA)

CONCENTRATION
CAMPS

In 1933, soon after the NAZIS began their rule, they established CONCENTRATION CAMPS at DACHAU and SACHSENHAUSEN. These were among the first of the most elaborate and criminal system of concentration camps and KILLING CENTER facilities in history. The main purpose of the camps was to confine and eventually exterminate "racial enemies" and political opponents of the REICH. By 1945, thousands of camps across German-occupied Europe were uncovered by the ALLIES, and the world came to know the real horror of Nazism and the "FINAL SOLUTION."

The history of the NATIONAL SOCIALIST camps began with the Nazi synchronization *(Gleichschaltung)* of German society in 1933. Communists, Jews, socialists, clergymen, pacifists, and others deemed a threat to German society were arbitrarily arrested and interned in newly established concentration camps such as Dachau, Oranienburg, and Lichtenburg (a women's camp). Nazi officials claimed that these individuals were being taken into "protective custody" or were being held for "reeducational" purposes. In July 1933, six months after Adolf HITLER gained power, about 27,000 persons were held in these "detention centers," which came under the command of Heinrich HIMMLER's SS in 1934.

From 1939 on, the Germans expanded the concentration camp system. They needed to "accommodate" the growing

Spanish Republican prisoners used as draft animals at the MAUT-HAUSEN concentration camp in 1942. Many Spanish Republican refugees fled Spain after the Fascist victory in that country's civil war in 1939. Most were arrested by the Germans following their internment in France and then transferred to CONCENTRATION CAMPS. (NARA [Francisco Boix])

The infamous quarry at the MAUTHAUSEN concentration camp as it appeared in 1942 in a photo taken by a German official of the camp. Thousands of prisoners died in the quarry. (NARA [Francisco Boix])

number of "enemies" within both the THIRD REICH and those territories coming under German control. They also wished to exploit prisoner labor for the expanding war effort. In German-occupied Poland, killing centers were established as the final destination for Jews, GYPSIES, and Soviet prisoners of war. In the Third Reich, a growing number of prisoners from categories including political opponents, homosexuals, and "ASOCIALS" were incarcerated, tortured, starved, and worked to death in notorious Nazi camps like Dachau, RAVENSBRÜCK, MAUTHAUSEN, GROSS-ROSEN, FLOSSENBÜRG, and BUCHENWALD. During the course of the Third Reich, about 1.6 million persons were interned in concentration camps; this figure does not include those who perished in the killing centers.

Concentration camps were often centers for various SS enterprises that used SLAVE LABOR. Many camps were built near quarries, brickyards, or armament factories to facilitate production. Later, during 1943–44, the German Ministry of Armaments, the SS, and German industry collaborated to bring the armaments works near or into the camps. At Mauthausen, a camp which Reinhard HEYDRICH classified in the harshest category, about 1,500 to 3,500 political opponents of the Third Reich worked in a 300-foot-deep quarry pit, hauling 60- to 130 -pound stones on their backs up 186 stone steps while punishments squads *(SS-Straf-kommandos)* brutalized them. More than 119,000 prisoners died at Mauthausen between 1939 and 1945.

Though living conditions varied from camp to camp, a common regime was strictly observed. Such conditions were defined by Dachau commandant Theodor Eicke, who was named inspector of concentration camps in 1934. Eicke commanded the dreaded SS Death's Head Units, which guarded the concentration camps. When prisoners entered Dachau, they lost all legal status, were stripped of all possessions, and underwent degrading examinations to assign their racial and political category. Their heads were shorn, and they were usually given striped fatigues bearing

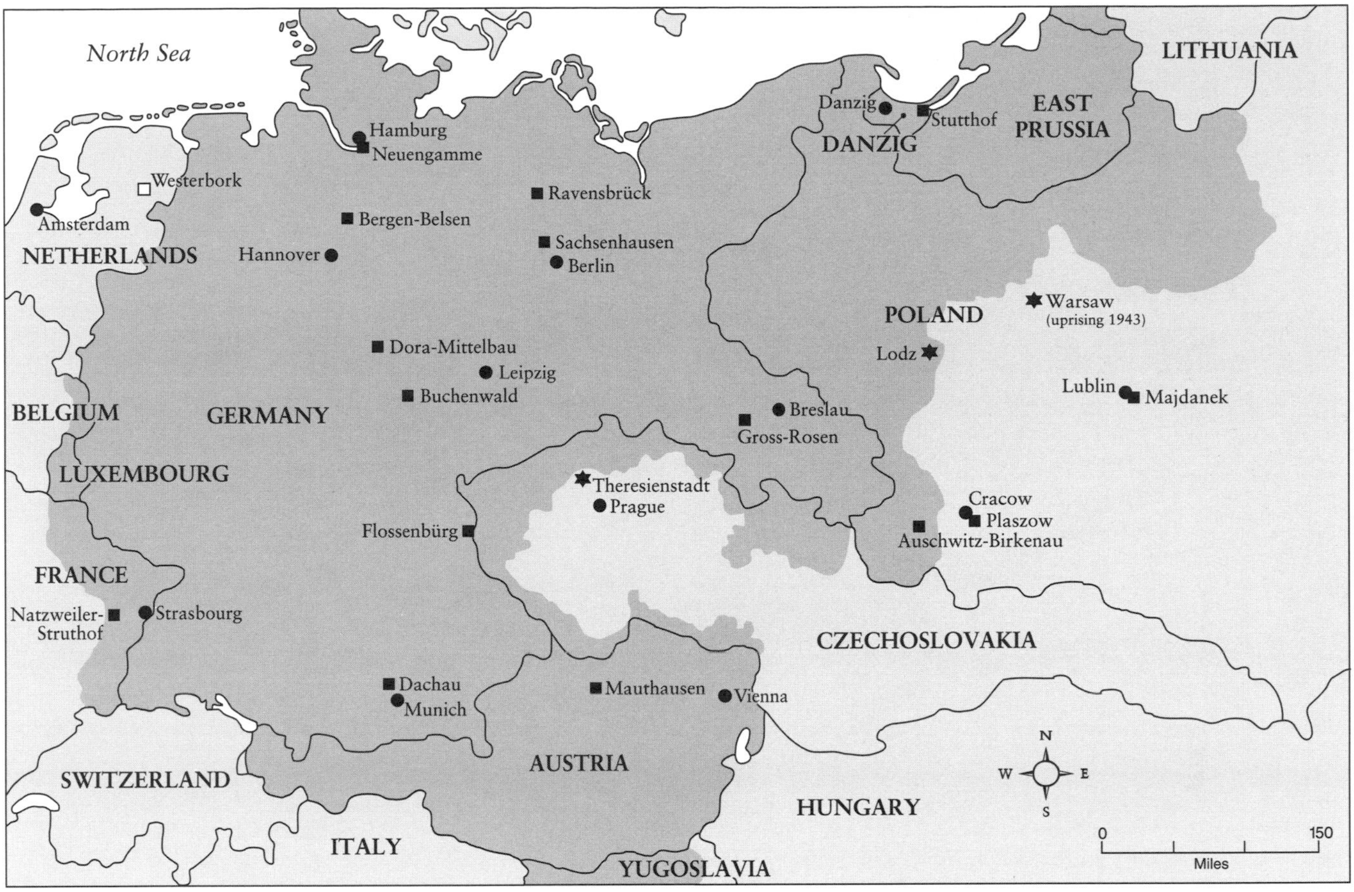

Major Concentration Camps, Transit Camps and Ghettos, 1944

■ Concentration Camps
□ Transit Camp
✱ Ghetto
● Cities
German Reich early 1944
Europe 1937 Boundaries

their new identity: a serial number and a colored triangle designating their "criminal" category and nationality.

A typical day in a concentration camp commenced with early morning roll call; prisoners stood outside, sometimes for hours, in all types of weather while guards counted and recounted the prisoners. Often guards arbitrarily singled out individual prisoners to harass and torture. Prisoners labored up to eleven hours per day building roads or working in gravel pits, workshops, or armaments factories. Daily food rations of watery turnip soup and "sawdust" bread were just enough to sustain life, but not enough to satisfy prisoners' hunger or to fortify them against the harsh conditions and recurrent epidemics. Prisoners fell under the constant scrutiny of SS guards or fellow inmates assigned as block leaders *(BLOCKÄLTESTE)* and *KAPOS*, who often treated them brutally. After evening roll call, prisoners were sent to overcrowded barracks that were often filthy and unheated.

The mortality rate in the camps was extremely high. In 1942, more than 57,000 or sixty percent of an average camp population of 95,000 persons, perished during a six month period. Survival depended on factors such as the prisoner's political or racial category, the whim of camp administrators, and favorable labor assignments. Such assignments—those requiring less demanding physical labor, or assignment to a kitchen or agricultural work party where additional food might be obtained—were essential for survival.

From fall 1944 to spring 1945, conditions in concentration camps deteriorated swiftly. Camps in the path of the advancing ALLIES were quickly evacuated, and the prisoners were forced to march to camps in Germany's interior. Those who survived these marches were forced into camps such as Ravensbrück and Bergen-Belsen, where food and medical supplies were scarce, disease rampant, and conditions overcrowded. Of the 700,000 persons in concentration camps in January 1945, from 250,000 to 300,000 people perished during spring 1945.

Among the first WAR CRIMES trials held in Allied-occupied Germany were the BERGEN-BELSEN TRIAL at Lüneberg in the British zone, and the DACHAU TRIAL at Dachau in the American zone, convened in late 1945. Both set the precedent for subsequent war crimes trials that prosecutions of war criminals in the early postwar period would deal primarily with the activities of perpetrators in the Nazi camps. Only more recently has attention turned to the killings outside the camps.

Two Dutch prisoners lie dead after being shot near the fence in the MAUTHAUSEN concentration camp in 1942. A "death zone" was proclaimed near the fences enclosing all CONCENTRATION CAMPS; any prisoner found inside the area was shot. Prisoners were often forced into the zone by guards and "shot while trying to escape."
(NARA [Francisco Boix])

PUNISHMENT REGULATIONS

CONCENTRATION CAMP *life was brutal. Punishments for prisoners were prescribed for even the most minor infractions, real or imagined. Guards often indulged their sadistic inclinations, injuring and even killing prisoners. The regulations for the treatment of prisoners reproduced here are the official guidelines that were issued over the signature of Heinrich* HIMMLER, *head of the* SS, *which controlled and administered the concentration camps. In reality, any and all means of punishment, even death, were used. These guidelines were used as evidence by the prosecution at the* INTERNATIONAL MILITARY TRIBUNAL. *The cover and last page are reproduced in facsimile.*

Dv.:LO.KL.
Secret   No. 005

Service Directive
for
Concentration Camps
(Camp Regulations)

Berlin 1941

Printed by the Central Office for Reich Security

[. . .]

The following punishments shall be administered:

1. Disciplinary Punishments

(a) Warning with threat of punishment,

(b) Extra work during free time under supervision of an *SS-Unterführer* [SS noncommissioned officer],

(c) Prohibition to write or receive private letters,

(d) Deprivation of midday meal while remaining fully employed,

(e) Assignment to a punishment company,

(f) Hard bed in a cell after a day of work.

2. Detention Punishments

(a) Confinement, medium, Level I, up to 3 days. Implementation of punishment: wooden plank bed, lighted cell
Food: water and bread

(b) Confinement, intensive, Level II, up to 42 days. Implementation of punishment: wooden plank bed, darkened cell
Food: water and bread, full rations every 4th day

(c) Confinement, severe, Level III, up to 3 days. Implementation of punishment: No opportunity to sit or lie down, darkened cell
Food: water and bread

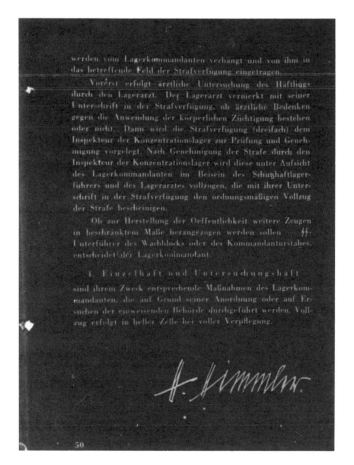

Level III can be applied as individual punishment or can be used on a day-by-day basis as a further intensification of Level II.

3. Corporal Punishments:

Five to 25 blows can be administered, namely on the rump or the thigh. The number of blows is to be determined by the camp commander and recorded by him in the appropriate space on the sentencing decree.

First the prisoner is given a medical examination by the camp physician. The camp physician records with his signature on the sentencing document whether medical considerations exist against the application of corporal punishment. The sentencing document is then submitted (in triplicate) to the inspector of the concentration camp for review and approval. After approval of the sentence by the inspector of concentration camp, the sentence is carried out under the supervision of the concentration camp commander in the presence of the leader of the protective custody section and the camp physician, who verify the orderly execution of the sentence by their signatures in the sentencing document. Whether, for the sake of being more public, a limited number of further witnesses should be added—the *SS-Unterführer* of the camp block or of the commander's office staff—will be determined by the camp commander.

4. Solitary Confinement and Detention (pending trial) are appropriate measures under the control of the camp commander depending on his orders or the wishes of the committing authority. They are to be carried out in a bright cell with full rations.

[signature] H. Himmler

— *Reproduced from the National Archives and Records Administration, National Archives Collection of World War II War Crimes Records, Record Group 238, Office of the U.S. Chief of Counsel for War Crimes, Document USSR-011. Translated from the German by Gerald Schwab.*

A JEWISH PRISONER'S STATEMENT

Those Jews deemed capable of work by the Germans were not immediately dispatched to the GAS CHAMBERS of the KILLING CENTERS of OPERATION REINHARD or AUSCHWITZ-BIRKENAU. Instead they were initially sent to either one of the major CONCENTRATION CAMPS or one of the latter's numerous sub-camps which proliferated throughout the REICH. Blizyn, mentioned in this selection, was a LABOR CAMP located in Radom, Poland. MAJDANEK was a labor camp as well as a concentration camp and killing center. When Majdanek was about to be liberated by the Soviet Army in July

1944, many prisoners were forcibly marched or transported to other concentration camps within the Reich. Thousands of prisoners died during these FORCED EVACUATIONS, *as stated in this affidavit by David Wajnapel, a Polish Jew, used at the* INTERNATIONAL MILITARY TRIBUNAL.

A few weeks after the entry of the German troops into Radom, Police and SS arrived. At the very moment of their arrival, the conditions became immediately worse. The house in the Heromskist, where their headquarters were, became a menace to the entire population. People who were passing this street were dragged into the gateway and ill-treated by merciless beatings and by the staging of sadistic games. All members of the SS, officers as well as other ranks [enlisted men], took part in this. Being a physician, I often had the opportunity to give medical help to seriously injured victims of the SS.

After a short time the SS uniform became a menace to the population. I myself was beaten up until I bled by four SS men in the street in spite of my doctor's armlet. Later on two ghettos were established in Radom. In August, 1942 the so-called "deportation" took place. The ghettos were surrounded by many SS units who occupied all the street exits. People were driven out to the streets, and those who ran away were fired at. Sick people at home or in hospitals were shot on the spot, among others also the inmates of the hospital where I was working as a doctor. The total number of people killed amounted to about 4,000. About 3,000 people were spared and the rest—about 20,000 people—were sent to Treblinka. The whole action was directed and executed by the SS. I myself saw that the SS staff were on the spot forming groups and issuing orders. In the streets and in the houses SS men ill-treated and killed people without waiting for orders. After the "deportation" the remaining people were massed in a few narrow lanes and we came under the exclusive rule of the SS and became the private property of the SS who used to hire us out for payment to various firms. I know that these payments were credited to a special SS account at the Radom Bank Emisyjny. We were visited by SS men only. Executions carried out by the SS in the ghetto itself were a frequent occurrence. On 14 January 1943 another deportation to Treblinka took place. On 21 March 1943 in the whole district there took place the so-called action against the intelligentsia, which action, as far as I know, was decided upon at an SS and Police Fuehrers' [leaders'] meeting in Radom. In Radom alone about 200 people were shot at that time; among others, my parents, my brother and his 9 month old child met their deaths. On 9 November of the same year all Jewish children up to 12 years of age as well as the old and sick were gathered from Radom and from camps situated near Radom and shot in the Biala Street in Radom. Both SS officers and other ranks participated in this. From March 1943 on I stayed 18 months in Blizyn Camp. The camp was entirely under the SS and the Radom Police Chief's control. Its commander was Unterstuerm-fuehrer [SS 2d Lieutenant] Paul Nell, the guards were composed of SS privates and NCOs [noncommissioned officers]. The foremen were Waffen-SS men who had been wounded at the front. Both behaved in an inhuman manner by beating and ill-treating us. Shootings of people were frequent occurrences. Originally, sentences were passed by the SS and Police Fuehrer, later on by the camp commander. The SS other ranks knew very well about the bloody deeds which were committed by the SS in Poland, in particular they told me personally about mass murders of Jews in Maidanek [CONCENTRATION CAMP] (in Nov. 1943). This fact was no secret; it was common knowledge among the civil population as well as among the lowest-ranking SS men. When the camp was taken over by the Maidanek Concentration Camp, new guards were sent to our camp, but there was no difference between them and the previous ones. In July 1944 the whole camp including myself was sent to the Auschwitz [concentration] camp, which could be entered only by SS men. The conditions of this camp are well known. I escaped during the evacuation of this camp into Germany. On the way the SS escort machine-gunned exhausted prisoners and later on the rest of the marching column (near Rybnik [Poland]). Several hundred people were killed at that time. When I saw that the situation was hopeless, I fled under fire into a wood, where shortly I was liberated by the Soviet Army.

— *Reprinted from* Trial of the Major War Criminals Before the International Military Tribunal. *42 vols. (Nuremberg, 1947), 20: 382–86.*

MURDER OF SOVIET PRISONERS

More than three million Soviet prisoners of war died as prisoners of the Germans during World War II through execution, starvation, exposure, and mistreatment. Some Soviet prisoners were sent to the MAUTHAUSEN *concentration camp, one the worst camps in the* CONCENTRATION CAMP *system. Their plight was witnessed by Francisco Boix, also a prisoner at Mauthausen, who described their fate at the* INTERNATIONAL MILITARY TRIBUNAL *in the testimony reproduced here.*

Francisco Boix was a Spanish Republican who had fled to France in 1939 after the Fascist victory in the Spanish Civil War. He fought as a volunteer with the French Army in 1940. Captured by the Germans, he became a prisoner of war. Transferred to the Mauthausen concentration camp, he worked in the camp photographic section developing photographs taken by SS *men. He and several other prisoners managed to save many of these photos; some, used as evidence at the International Military Tribunal and later at the* MAUTHAUSEN TRIAL, *are reproduced in this chapter.*

Thirty emaciated Soviet officer prisoners of war stand for roll call in the MAUTHAUSEN concentration camp; 1942. A special barrack was reserved for Soviet prisoners of war imprisoned in Mauthausen. (NARA [Francisco Boix])

BOIX: . . . I would like to note that there were cases when Soviet officers were massacred. It is worth noting because it concerns prisoners of war. I would like the Tribunal to listen to me carefully.

THE PRESIDENT: What is it you wish to say about the massacre of the Soviet prisoners of war?

BOIX: In 1943 there was a transport of officers. On the very day of their arrival in the camp they began to be massacred by every means. But it seems that from the higher quarters orders had come concerning these officers saying that something extraordinary had to be done. So they put them in the best block in the camp. They gave them new prisoner's clothing. They gave them even cigarettes; they gave them beds with sheets; they were given everything they wanted to eat. A medical officer, Sturmbannfuehrer [SS Major] Bresbach, examined them with a stethoscope.

They went down into the quarry, but they carried only small stones, and in fours. At that time Oberscharfuehrer [SS Sergeant] Paul Ricken, chief of the service, was there with his Leica taking pictures without stopping. He took about 48 pictures. These I developed and five copies of each, 13 by 18 [cm., 5 in. by 6.5 in.], with the negatives, were sent to Berlin. It is too bad I did not steal the negatives, as I did the others.

When that was done, the Russians were made to give up their clothing and everything else and were sent to the gas chamber. The comedy was ended. Everybody could see on the pictures that the Russian prisoners of war, the officers, and especially the political commissars, were treated well, worked hardly at all, and were in good condition. That is one thing that should be noted because I think it is necessary.

And another thing, there was a barrack called Barrack Number 20. That barrack was inside the camp; and in spite of the electrified barbed wire around the camp, there was an additional wall with electrified barbed wire around it. In that barrack there were prisoners of war, Russian officers and commissars, some Slavs, a few Frenchmen, and, they said, even a few Englishmen. No one could enter that barrack except the two Fuehrer who were in the camp prison, the commanding officers of the inner and outer camps. These internees were dressed just as we were, like convicts, but without number or identification of their nationality. One could not tell their nationality. . . .

THE PRESIDENT: Very well. Is there any other particular incident you want to refer to?

BOIX: Yes, about Block 20. Thanks to my knowledge of photography I was able to see it; I had to be there to handle the lights while my chief took photographs. In this way I could follow, detail by detail, everything that took place in this barrack. It was an inner camp. This barrack, like all the others, was 7 meters wide [23 ft.] and 50 meters long [164 ft.]. There were 1,800 internees there, with a food ration less than one-quarter of what we would get for food. They had neither spoons nor plates. Large kettles of spoiled food were emptied on the snow and left there until it began to freeze; then the Russians were ordered to get at it. The Russians were so hungry, they would fight for this food. The SS used these fights as a pretext to beat some of them with bludgeons.

— *Reprinted from* Trial of the Major War Criminals Before the International Military Tribunal, 42 vols. *(Nuremberg, 1947),* 6: 275–77.

Prisoners, most Yugoslavian PARTISANS, as they appeared after their interrogation in the political section of the MAUTHAUSEN concentration camp; 1943. (NARA [Francisco Boix])

EXECUTION OF AMERICAN PRISONERS OF WAR

American prisoners of war were also held in CONCENTRA-TION CAMPS. In fall 1944, twelve American servicemen of the OFFICE OF STRATEGIC SERVICES fought with Slovakian insurgents who had risen against the Germans in August in support the Soviet Army's advance into the area. They were captured that December after the Germans crushed the revolt and sent to the MAUTHAUSEN concentration camp, where they were brutally interrogated by the camp staff and later executed on the orders of Ernst KALTENBRUNNER on January 24, 1945. At the <u>MAUTHAUSEN TRIAL</u>, Wilhelm Ornstein, a Pole imprisoned in Mauthausen who worked in the camp CREMATORIA, testified about these executions. The SS men mentioned in his testimony—ZIEREIS, Altfuldisch, Niedermayer, Proksch, Trum, and Stretwiesser —were members of the camp senior staff; all except Ziereis, who was killed at war's end, were defendants at the Mauthausen Trial.

Q. Will you describe to the Court, please, the method whereby these neck shots were carried out, Mr. Ornstein?

PROSECUTION: Excuse me, may he sit down?

PRESIDENT: Yes. (Whereupon the witness resumed the stand.)

QUESTIONS BY PROSECUTION (Continued):

Q. All right, sir, will you describe that procedure to the Court, Mr. Ornstein?

A. The neck shots were carried out in different ways. They were performed differently against Americans in high offices and women, and it was performed differently

towards prisoners. In the case of American officers and women there was always a screen which was put up there and was supposed to show a camera. Furthermore, after every neck shot the SS men would get rid of the blood so that the next one coming in there would not see the blood. That is in comparison with the execution of prisoners, where from eight to ten (8 to 10) prisoners were executed in succession, and only after that all the blood was removed. Those SS people who took part in the executions had their various functions. One [SS man] was in the clothing room and sent the people, the others were in the hallways from the clothing room to the execution room; one was at the door and always called out "next one"; one was at the camera and called out "photograph"; one of them always prepared the ammunition and loaded the weapon; the others held the innocent victims by the hand if they struggled and didn't want to turn around. The hangings were done differently.

Q. Will you describe, please, the method and procedure that was followed in the hanging of prisoners while you were there in Mauthausen, in that room?

A. Yes. That was in an iron traverse, on an iron rod. There was a rope wrapped around, and three people at a time were hanged. Under the rod there was a chair set up with springs in it. Those that were sentenced had to stand up on the chair, had to put the rope around their own necks, one SS man secured the rope on one side, pressed the spring, the chair fell down and those sentenced remained hanging in the air. They hanged about ten minutes on the rope, and afterwards they had to be taken into the cooling room.

Q. The Americans that you testified to who were executed, did they know they were going to be executed?

A. No. There were signs saying to the bath on the doors which they entered.

Q. I thought you testified that they were placed before a camera.

A. The first room they entered was labeled "bath." Then later when they were already undressed and had to enter the next room, somebody, Ziereis was always yelling "photograph, photograph."

Q. Do you know whether or not these Americans were tried by court martial?

A. No, I don't know.

Q. Did you ever see Trum shoot anybody at an execution?

A. No.

Q. Was Ziereis present at all executions?

A. Yes. The performance of the execution was done only by officers. Only in the last few days [before the camp was liberated in May 1945] the executions or rather the gassings were performed under the direction of Altfuldisch, Niedermayer, Proksch, Streitwieser.

— *Reprinted from National Archives and Records Administration, Overseas Commands, Record Group 338, Records of USAREUR, War Crimes Branch, War Crimes Case Files 1945–49, Cases Tried, Case 000-50-5, Box 342.*

A MURDERER'S DEATHBED CONFESSION

Franz ZIEREIS was the commandant of the MAUTHAUSEN concentration camp for most of the war. He was shot and wounded by American troops while trying to escape arrest in May 1945 and made several confessions of his crimes to ALLIED intelligence officers while confined to a hospital bed before his death on May 24, 1945. The confession reproduced below was transcribed by a Polish doctor and passed through several hands before it arrived at the British prosecution staff during the INTERNATIONAL MILITARY TRIBUNAL. It was later used as evidence at the MAUTHAUSEN TRIAL. "Action K" used in this document refers to "Aktion Kugel" (Operation Bullet), a secret order of March 1944 that decreed that all prisoners of war incapable of labor, except for American and British prisoners, were to be shot while "attempting to escape."

United Nations War Crimes Commission
(Research Office) . . .
February, 1946.

Note: The following translation of Ziereis' confession has been amended in places, as regards the wording of English, for greater clarity; otherwise, the text is reproduced as it was received. It is not always clear whether certain statements are made by Ziereis himself or by the secretaries or other deponents. . . . Chief Research Officer. . . .

Record of statements taken from SS-Standartenführer [SS Colonel] Franz Ziereis, former commandant of the Concentration Camp Mauthausen-Gusen-Linz etc.

I, Franz Ziereis, was born 13.7.1905 [July 13, 1905] in Munich. My father was killed in the first world war; my mother is living in Munich.

I have one brother Rudolf who is 38 years old, a steam engine machinist, and two sisters Margarete 47 years old and Wilhelmine 32 years old. I am a merchant by profession. During my long unemployment I worked as a carpenter.

I performed my military service from 1.4.24 to 30.9.36 [April 1, 1924 to September 30, 1936] in a Bavarian Regiment, in which I held the rank of Sergeant. I left the Army with the rank of Lieutenant, and I came to the SS on August 30th 1936 with the rank of Obersturmführer [SS First Lieutenant] and I was assigned to the 4th Standarts SS in Oranienburg, as a teacher, for schooling the men.

I was sent to Mauthausen on 17.11.39 [November 17, 1939] in succession to the previous camp commandant, Sauer. I owe my rapid rise to the fact that I often volunteered for front line service; but my commanding officer, under the SS Reichsführer Himmler, compelled me to remain as a camp commandant at Mauthausen. The proportion of SS troops to the number of prisoners was 1 to 10.

The greatest number of prisoners in the camp at Mauthausen was 17,000 over and above other camps [presumably "the other camps" of the Mauthausen group]. The greatest number of prisoners in the other camps, excluding Mauthausen, was 76,000 prisoners, and the total came to 95,000. The number of deaths was over 65,000. The number of SS troops was about 5,000; they were called "Totenkopfverbande" (Deaths-Head-Units). They were divided into sections of guards and command-staff. The rest of the SS (over 6,000 men) came from the Air Force (Luftwaffe); they were dressed in SS uniforms, and many of them were so called "Volksdeutsche."

Prisoners of German nationality—in all about 450 men—were also assigned to the SS troops under orders given by Himmler. These prisoners might be required to fight against the enemy, especially against the Russians. They were mostly volunteers; the rest were conscripted by the commanders without my knowledge.

Orders to burn all the prisoners' documents were given in the last days of April (1945) and in the first days of May; the order was issued by the Office D in Berlin by Groupleader SS Gluecks. [*Office D* (SS CENTRAL OFFICE FOR ECONOMY AND ADMINISTRATION) controlled the camps.] The order to kill the prisoners was given by SS Reichsführer Himmler. During his visit to Mauthausen, Himmler himself gave orders that the prisoners were to be made to carry big stones 45-50 kg. each, as an example of how they might be liquidated.

Personally I have murdered many hundreds of prisoners, perhaps about 400 by consigning them to the penal

SS-Standartenführer (SS Colonel) Franz ZIEREIS, commandant of the MAUTHAUSEN concentration camp in Austria from 1939 to the camp's liberation in May 1945. (NARA)

company (Strafkompanie), where many were tortured and killed every night, according to orders from Berlin. I have personally participated in the executions.

In 1940, 320 Poles from Warsaw were massacred by orders received from Gruppenführer [Major General] Mayerich. On several occasions I had to shoot at prisoners because the new SS troops (Volksdeutsche) shot so badly with small arms. The order that they were to be shot with small arms came from Gruppenführer Gluecks. A shooting-stand was installed in the camp at Sachsenhausen, by his orders, where the prisoners were shot without warning from behind (Genickschuss), while a radio loud-speaker blared out.

According to orders issued by Hauptsturmführer [SS Captain] Lonauer and Dr. Renault, "incorrigible criminals of profession" were certified "insane" and sent to Hartheim [a euthanasia facility] near Linz [Austria], where they were annihilated by a special process of Dr. Krebsbach's.

The majority of the first few thousand prisoners to be murdered, were killed by SS-Hauptsturmführer Bachmayer in the Camp at Mauthausen. Many others were killed by camp leader Seidler at Gusen. Seidler and Chmielewski had the skins (from murdered bodies) prepared and made into satchels, lampcovers, bookcovers, etc. I did not have any skins prepared for myself because it was forbidden by Berlin.

The "action K" consisted of prisoners, who were not allowed to have contact with anybody, and were liquidated by Himmler's orders. Chmielewski, the first Camp Gusen commandant, had murdered several thousand prisoners. I am not responsible for this, because the orders were given by Berlin. . . . Furthermore, I received orders to kill all the prisoners at Gusen I and II by blowing up the vaults (Kellerbau) at a time when the prisoners would be in them, in case the Russian Army should advance into the neighbourhood. If the USA Army were to come first the prisoners were to be set free. In February 1945 SS-Gruppenführer Pohl had given instructions that the prisoners were to be led into the woods where they were to be murdered in different ways, by certain means; this was also to be done if the war was lost. My wife was shocked, and exerted her influence on me so that I began to ignore Berlin. I had recognized that the orders from Berlin were senseless, but it made me nervous. Mauthausen-Gusen were the last camps to which the camps at Buchenwald, Dachau, Auschwitz etc. were finally evacuated. Thousands of prisoners were sent to us unexpectedly, men, women and children—and there was no food for them. I asked Berlin to stop this cruelty and they, my superiors, criticized me. In every convoy there were 600–800 dead prisoners. Shortly before the end of the war they sent us a convoy of 4,800 prisoners from Dachau, and only 180 of them arrived, the others had died from starvation on the way, because they had been given no food. In the last days, just before the end of the war, the crematorium crews at Mauthausen and Gusen were murdered by SS-Hauptsturmführer Bachmeyer because they knew too much. Continuing his statements Ziereis mentioned many names of high SS officials, among them Eigruber, the Gauleiter of

A view of Gusen CONCENTRATION CAMP, one of more than fifty subcamps of the MAUTHAUSEN concentration camp, taken by a German photographer in 1942. (NARA [Francisco Boix])

Upper Austria [apparently an interrogator's comment]. When I met Himmler for the last time, he said, it was in Vienna, 7–8 weeks ago. I believe that he is hiding somewhere in Czechoslovakia. In reply to my question as to whether he realized that the war was lost for Germany, he said "Yes." Now I realize what a disaster has been brought on 80 million Germans by one stupid man, Hitler, and the results.

At this point the interrogation came to an end because of Ziereis' weakness and his difficulty in speaking. Franz Ziereis made the above statements as he lay in bed, having been seriously wounded by two shots, one in the stomach and one in the left shoulder.

All the questions asked him in German by two Intelligence agents he answered consciously and without any compulsion.

— *Reprinted from National Archives and Records Administration, Overseas Commands, Record Group 338, USAREUR, War Crimes Branch 1945–49, Case Files-Cases Tried, Record Group 338, Case 000-50-5, Box 337.*

THERESIENSTADT

As the "FINAL SOLUTION" became a reality, the Germans found it necessary to camouflage the ultimate purpose of the DEPORTATION of Jews to the East: death by mass execution or gassing in KILLING CENTERS. Such a plan would have been met with hostility by the citizens of western Europe. The deception chosen to obscure the killing was to describe the deportations as "EVACUATIONS" for labor in eastern Europe. However, even dedicated NAZIS could hardly believe that older Jews and disabled war veterans could perform heavy labor. A TRANSIT CAMP to hold these Jews, and those with important connections, was established in fall 1941: the THERESIENSTADT ghetto. They were soon joined by Jews from the PROTECTORATE OF BOHEMIA AND MORAVIA. Eventually some 140,000 Jews from central and western Europe, including the Danish Jews in 1943 mentioned in this selection, were deported from their homelands to this GHETTO during the war. Most were later transported to AUSCHWITZ-BIRKENAU, where they perished in the camp's GAS CHAMBERS.

Mordechai Ansbacher was a teenaged German Jew when he was sent to live with relatives in Belgium in 1939. After the Germans conquered that country in 1940, he returned to Germany, where he was assigned to perform FORCED LABOR for several months before he was deported to Theresienstadt with his mother in September 1942. At the EICHMANN TRIAL, he testified about his experiences in this ghetto.

Q. Please describe to the Court your daily life in Theresienstadt.

A. Originally I lived together with my mother in house No. L206. The Theresienstadt Ghetto was divided into large buildings, barracks and blocks of houses. Each block of houses had its own specific number. There was an office called *"Evidenz"* (Registration). There we were given a slip of paper after we arrived with the transport from Würzburg, on the way from Silesia. This was the place where they took away from everyone those things that were considered forbidden, such as thermos flasks, beverages, cigarettes and toilet paper.

After we had waited a long time in the blazing sun, they transferred us on foot to house L206. We were allocated the attics, for all the rooms were already full, and they said: This is where you will sleep, this is your place.

Q. Was this beneath the roof?

A. Beneath the roof.

Q. How many of you were there altogether?

A. I remember in our building there were people from Würzburg in the early days, for a week later half the people died right away—amongst those who died was Director Mandelbaum. . . .

Presiding Judge Please do not diverge from the question.

Witness Ansbacher Then there were about 100–200 of us.

State Attorney Bar-Or Why do you say that a large number of them died right away?

Witness Ansbacher There was terrible hunger, and the hygienic conditions were most awful.

Q. Did they attend to the people?

A. Not at all. People were unable to wash themselves—there was no water. With difficulty a little water was brought from another building, and that was supposed to suffice both for drinking and for washing.

Q. How long did you remain there in the attic?

A. I remained in the attic for about four weeks. Afterwards I received a place on the floor in the room below, also together with aged and sick people—no one knew who was lying next to him.

Presiding Judge Was this regarded as being an improvement?

Witness Ansbacher Not necessarily, but upstairs it was so full and additional transports had arrived, and they compressed more people inside. In the attics there was neither air nor light. Later on, they set aside special places for the sick. In every building there was one special room for the sick. Whoever went into the room for the sick—it was called *"Krankenstube"* at first, and afterwards *"Revier"*—in most cases never came out again alive. Everyone had to work in the ghetto. And, in fact, from this, from having been inactive and then having to work, from this people died. For in addition to the hunger, they were not able to stand it. There were various kinds of work. For example, my mother was living with me. She was registered as a nurse, but there she was given the job of looking after the toilet. It was called *"Klowache."* It was considered to be very respectable work, for then one received extra food, and this was something very important.

State Attorney Bar-Or I want you to describe to the Court what happened to you. How old were you when you reached Theresienstadt?

Witness Ansbacher Fifteen years old.

Q. Please describe your life in Theresienstadt.

A. For some time I stayed in the same building, in L206. Afterwards an order came stating that the children were to be concentrated in youth hostels. I was moved with my possessions to a youth hostel in Lange Strasse—it was L414. There were several youth hostels: One mainly for children from Czechoslovakia, one for the children of people from Germany and Czechoslovakia, and one for girls only. In the youth hostels the situation was much better. We received food which was totally different, there were sanitary facilities, and we were forced to wash. Every morning there was a roll-call where the children were counted, given instructions, and the work divided amongst them. Once I worked in agriculture, another time in building. They sent us out to all kinds of work. The best thing was when they sent us to bring food, for then we were able to *"schleusen."* That was the expression for purloining. . . .

Q. What was *"schleusen"*?

A. This was the most common word in Theresienstadt.

Q. For what?

A. If anyone was able to purloin food, then he was master of the situation. It was called *schleusen.* One did *schleusen* with wood, for there were no chairs; one did *schleusen* with water, *schleusen* with potatoes—everything needed *schleusen.* . . .

State Attorney Bar-Or What work were you engaged in during the period you were in Theresienstadt?

Witness Ansbacher There were many kinds of work. First of all, a boy who had not yet reached the age of sixteen could study. Although it was absolutely forbidden by the German authorities, there were schools in all the youth hostels nonetheless.

Q. Was this forbidden in Theresienstadt?

A. It was forbidden to set up a school, but we organized lessons. There were excellent teachers, and they devoted some of their time after work or during work, they obtained special authority from Edelstein, who viewed this favourably and supported the idea of maintaining lessons. . . .

Q. Do you remember the time when Jews from Denmark came to Theresienstadt?

A. Yes.

Q. Please tell the Court about it.

A. I do not remember the exact date.

Q. I did not ask you for the date.

A. I remember well that we were terribly shocked, we actually cried when we saw these people arriving.

Q. Why?

A. Every day we saw the transports which arrived. These were always people who came with their rucksacks, with bags, with strong clothing. For there were special instructions on behalf of the Reich Association of Jews about what was needed in the camps, what was worthwhile taking and what was worthwhile leaving behind, although these instructions were usually not observed. Everyone had more or less what was required in the camp—there were stout shoes and so on. Suddenly there appeared a group of people with top hats, frock coats, with patent leather shoes, with walking sticks, as if they were strolling on some promenade abroad. We could not bear to see this, we cried. We said: "How can it happen that these people are being brought here unaided, without anything?" They had no idea at all what was happening to them. Later on they told us that they were literally dragged from the streets, that the Danish people helped them and objected to their being taken. Thus it happened that, while people were attending to their affairs, going to court or some other place, they were actually kidnapped in the street and put into trucks, and they were no longer seen by their friends. Among them were two companions by the name of Rubin, who were together with me until they were moved to the building for prominent people. This was something special where only privileged people lived. Generally, the *Dienststelle* [administrative office] in Berlin gave orders that these people had to be kept separately.

Q. When did you hear for the first time that you would have to leave Theresienstadt?

A. I heard all the time that I would have to leave Theresienstadt. Everyone who was in Theresienstadt was included in the transports. One always found some reason to be released. We passed through a terrible experience at night—they were nights of fear. Here was a transport, they were preparing the coupons [deportation orders for AUSCHWITZ]: "Have you received yours?" "No." "Did you receive one?" "No." "You have not received one? I have already received an order to report." They were thin coupons, those fateful vouchers. The number of the transport was written there, and the personal number.

Q. Who issued these vouchers?

A. They were sent by the *Evidenz-Abteilung*, a registration office, the department responsible to the SS for the condition of the Jews.

Q. When did you get such a coupon?

A. I received such a coupon, as I have mentioned, several times, but I was always released. I received my fateful coupon during the High Holidays in the year 1944.

— *Reprinted from Ministry of Justice, State of Israel,* The Trial of Adolf Eichmann, *5 vols. (Jerusalem, 1992), 2: 680–83.*

A PRISONER'S CAMP ODYSSEY

Dr. Ludwig Soswinski was a leading member of the Austrian Communist Party before the war. Arrested immediately after the German annexation of Austria in 1938, he spent the next seven years in CONCENTRATION CAMPS. *At war's end he made the following report for the American* OFFICE OF STRATEGIC SERVICES *describing this experience. His description of his years of incarceration begins with the* DACHAU *concentration camp, where he was sent in 1938. He was later transferred to concentration camps at* FLOSSENBÜRG, AUSCHWITZ-BIRKENAU, *and* MAJDANEK *(designated here as Lublin), ending the war in* MAUTHAUSEN. *Such transfers of prisoners between camps were not unusual if a prisoner survived long enough; there were thousands of concentration camps and sub-camps in the German camp system.*

In the camp itself [Dachau] the forced labor was frightful and many preferred to go over the guarded fence (Fostenkette), that is, to certain death. Many were brought beyond the guarded limits technically when one [a guard] indicated a work place to them, afterward guarded limits would be reduced so that the work place remained out of the guarded limits whereupon the convict would be shot. Cause of death: shot during flight! The barracks in which we lived were meticulously clean but thereby also a source of the most frightful camp punishments. For example, one day the "Schutzhaft" [protective custody] camp leader SS-Hauptsturmfuhrer [SS Captain] Kegel, later camp commandant of the women's concentration camp Ravensbruck and of concentration camp Flossenburg, came to block 5 in black SS gala uniform. The order was that the floor must be washed clean, polished and completely free of dust. He entered the barracks, lay down on the floor of the dwelling room and must have found upon getting up a few dust particles upon his uniform. Punishment: the whole block personnel (5 men) one hour of "Baum" [hanging prisoners by their arms]. Since I myself have twice had the opportunity to hang for an hour I can describe this torture exactly. The wrists are held fast together with a chain. The other end of the chain is hooked onto a hook located 1.90 m [6 ft. 3 in.] above the ground and thereupon the step upon which one formerly stood is removed. Thereupon one hangs with hands chained backwards, wrists approximately at the height of a man's head with the toes 10 to 15 cm [4–6 in.] above the ground. One hour—60 minutes—

Dr. Eugen Kogon, a former Austrian prisoner at the BUCHENWALD concentration camp, testifies for the prosecution at the WAR CRIMES trial of former camp officials held at DACHAU in April 1947. Dachau had become a site for American war crimes trials. Dr. Kogon wrote *The Theory and Practice of Hell*, one of the earliest books to examine the German CONCENTRATION CAMP system. (NARA)

3600 seconds. This procedure takes place in the open air and so I hung for the second time on 5 March 1940 at 15 degrees centigrade [59°F]. If, for example, the later camp commandant SS-Hauptsturmfuhrer Zillschlecht was so disposed, then he came himself to the court yard (arresthof) and set the people up to swing: if he was angry then he loosed a savage dog upon those hanging in arrest which then snapped after their feet and sexual parts. All these miseries had to be endured weeks long, many months long, with complete lack of feeling in the arms from the shoulders to the ends of the fingers.

On 25 January 1939 a convict escaped. Penalty for the whole camp: After returning from work at six o'clock in the evening the whole camp must go to the roll call ground without eating. And there we stood at attention without caps, without gloves which each had to put down on the ground, for 36 hours without interruption. For hours long we had to hold the hands stretched out in front. At the roll call place there were immediately dead: 25. I don't know how many died in the hospital as a consequence. I pass over here the special treatment of the Jews because they paled as contrasted to those which I later experienced in concentration camp Auschwitz.

In the winter 1939–40 I was in the concentration camp Flossenburg. In coarse (Zwilch) clothing with a coat out of paper material I stood high up in the quarry eight hours daily without pause at 30° centigrade [*sic*] [86°F]. I had to dig away and shovel down snow, ice, and earth. The food: 250 grams [about 9 ounces] of bread per day, one liter of beet water (Rubenwasser) with five small potatoes and 100 grams [3 ounces] of vegetable sausage, that it to say, without meat. The punishment for knocking the hands in stone breaking was: treadmill! On a slope with 45° inclination upon the whole width of which the water from the latrine flowed down there was a circular "way," that is, between blocks of stone and puddles of urine. Then one received a 15–20 kg. [33–44 lb.] stone on the shoulder and then it went as follows. Double time, march, march, lie down! Up, march, march, lie down! Eight hours daily. For some days long, for some months long. . . .

We returned to Dachau. Here we received bread and money from the outside with the help of an SS man, Engle Murach. Another SS man came afterwards and the consequence was that I and 16 comrades and the SS man were arrested. We each received an hour "Baum," 25 lashes (stockhiebe)—(beating on the seat, kidney blows)—that is, fifty because two SS men struck simultaneously—(blows were with an ox tail wrapped with wire)—45 days arrest—(food every third day, the other days 200 grams [7 ounces] bread and water) made more severe by a hard bed, dark cell without a window, one year penal company. The SS man was on account of clemency punished with arrest. . . .

In January 1944 I came to the concentration camp Lublin in the slave business German Armament Works, one of the enterprises of the possession of the SS. This Lublin business, there was such a business in each concentration camp, was discontinued in November, 1943. Why? Because on the morning of 3 November 1943 the District of Lublin was made free of Jews. On this day was collectively shot the somehow [*sic*] confined Jews. 25,000 men, women, and children. I have received many reports of eye and ear witnesses of convicts and civilians: they marched naked early in the morning into the so-called "Splinter graves" which had been erected in the previous weeks. The first row must lie down on the ground in the graves and was dispatched by shots, thereupon the next row had to lie down on the dead and half dead and was likewise dispatched by shooting, until the grave was full and then to the next grave.

Lublin-Majdanek. The world must know these names. The total number of dead in this camp amounts on an estimate to 700,000 numbered and unnumbered convicts.

At the evacuation of this camp in July 1944 all footsick and weak who could not go further were of course shot on the march. I request if perhaps one already doubts my mental ability to calculate, not to read the following numbers any more. I wish I were an insane person who thought out the following, poor lunatic who made up such a story as this. And the world would be spared this. . . .

[*Soswinski was evacuated to the Auschwitz-Birkenau concentration camp complex, where he remained until the evacuation of that camp in January 1945.*]

We were evacuated out of Auschwitz; march out, the usual picture; footsore and weak were dispatched. After a train trip with up to 100 men at 15° centigrade [59°F] in an open coal car, we came on 25 January 1945 to the concentration camp Mauthausen.

Comparisons never agree, but if I must compare Auschwitz with Mauthausen then the difference is approximately that between a big business and a cunningly established little business. The total death number of the whole auxiliary camp: 80,000. A bit of gas, a bit of "squirts," that is to say poison injections, stone breaking with jumping down sixty meters [197 ft.], a bit of beating to death, a bit of shooting, a bit of starving. Yes, Herr SS-Standartenfuhrer [SS Colonel] Ziereis, Herr Obersturmfuhrer [SS 1st Lieutenant] Trum, Herr Obersturmfuhrer Rachmayer: you yet have a specialty: on 16 February 1945 you have at -10° centigrade [14°F] 200 convicts let stand and freeze naked from noon until evening in the cold. In the evening they were bathed warm again and put out again naked. Then they were with the help of a hose sprayed with cold water. On the morning of 17 February 1945 they were dead.

In the hospital camp are located seven barracks for sick persons. These barracks were designed for stables because they have only four windows and a skylight which, however, cannot be opened. These barracks are 8 meters wide [26 ft.] and 25 meters long [82 ft.]. Three beds one above the other: 800 to 1000 men to a barracks, 5 convicts in one bed. Washing none. A Phlegmone corpse lies upon a corpse with odaman [*sic*] and so forth. Dozens of men go through the barracks at night because they cannot lie down. Two out of one bed go casually to the WC [toilet] which is not in the same barracks covered in the best cases by one blanket: then they certainly find on their return that their bed is occupied for some have observed the opportunity and laid themselves down. Then there is noise and now the others wander. It also happens that the stronger, a man 1.70 m. [6 ft.] tall and weighing 48 kg. [106 lb.] simply throws out of bed another equally tall but with only 44 kg. [97 lb.]

Nourishment: 80 gr. [3 ounces] bread, a half liter of water with some dried vegetables.

Now what comes no man will believe.

One morning bodies were found eaten by their own bedmates. . . .

It is a part cut out of my personal life and experiences in 7 years detention and five concentration camps. Thereupon I draw for myself the following conclusion:

If I find my relatives still living, I do not know. I do not know whether I still have a family. But I know for certain that I will go for a period of my life without respect to my personal fate, at home and everywhere where with my whole strength I can help fight and rout out fascist rule!

Fascism means: Murder, barbarism, sadism, hunger, war!

— *Reprinted from National Archives and Records Administration, Overseas Commands, Record Group 338, Records of USAREUR, War Crimes Branch, War Crimes Case Files, Cases Tried 1945–49, Case 000-50-5, Box 337.*

A PERPETRATOR FROM DACHAU

The DACHAU *concentration camp was the oldest* CONCENTRATION CAMP *in Germany; it was constructed in 1933. During its twelve-year existence it was known as a "political" camp, since most prisoners were political prisoners. They helped to make Dachau as brutal as any other concentration camp in Germany.*

Sebastion Schmid was an SS *man at Dachau serving as a driver in the camp from mid-1938 to 1941. He was tried by a U.S. General Military Government Court at Dachau during 1947 in the* SCHMID TRIAL. *Convicted and initially sentenced to life imprisonment, the sentence was eventually reduced to time served in 1951; however, Schmid was not released until 1953.*

Reductions of sentences of convicted war criminals were a policy of the American occupation government in Germany as the Cold War escalated at the time of the Korean War. Schmid's arrest card with his "mug shot" and the review of his sentence conducted by the court of the American military government that reviewed his case are reproduced here.

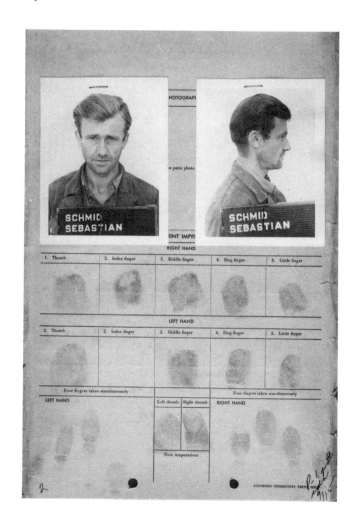

— Reproduced from the National Archives and Records
Administration, Overseas Commands, Record Group 338,
USAREUR, War Crimes Branch, War Crimes Case Files,
Cases Tried 1945–1949, Case number 000-Dachau-2,
Box 271.

THE DORA-MITTELBAU TRIAL

The DORA-MITTELBAU concentration camp, referred to in
this selection as Nordhausen, was originally a sub-camp
of the BUCHENWALD concentration camp until it became
an independent camp in November 1944. The infamous
V-2 guided missile was assembled in plants within the
Dora-Mittelbau camp complex. From 1945 to 1948 the
United States military conducted almost 500 war crimes
trials at the site of the former DACHAU concentration
camp. Among them was the DORA-MITTELBAU TRIAL
described in this article from News of Germany, the major
American newspaper printed in the American Zone of
occupation in Germany.

A prosecution witness testifies at the DORA-MITTELBAU TRIAL on
September 25, 1947. He is pointing to a defendant, a camp doctor
who denied medical care to prisoners. (NARA)

15 Are Found Guilty Of Camp Atrocities In Last Dachau Trial

DACHAU, Dec. 31 — The U. S. War
Crimes Commission here, rounding out two
years of work yesterday, pronounced sentences in the last of its trials, that of 15 former officials and guards of the Nordhausen
concentration camp.

All the defendants were found guilty of
committing atrocities. Hans Möser, former
SS 1st lieutenant, was sentenced to death by
hanging, seven others received life imprisonment and the remainder prison sentences
ranging from five to 25 years. Heinz Dettmer,
another 1st lieutenant, who previously had
been sentenced to 15 years in prison for
crimes committed at Dachau, received an additional seven years.

In the two years of its activities, the Dachau
war crimes commission found guilty 1,414 of
the 1,664 persons indicated for war crimes.
Of these, 425 were sentenced to death, 199
to life imprisonment and 790 received prison
sentences. There were 486 trials.

Sentences are being served in the Landsberg war crimes prison.

— Reprinted from News of Germany, January 1, 1948.

THE HELL OF BERGEN-BELSEN

The BERGEN-BELSEN concentration camp was first established in spring 1943 on the site of a former prisoner-of-war camp. Originally constructed as an internment camp to hold candidates for prisoner exchanges, by mid-1944 prisoners from other CONCENTRATION CAMPS began to be transferred to Bergen-Belsen; the camp eventually became a full-fledged concentration camp by the end of the year. In early 1945, thousands of prisoners had arrived from other camps; conditions deteriorated quickly and life became a living hell for the prisoners.

Dora Sazfran, a Polish Jew arrested in May 1943, was first imprisoned in the MAJDANEK and later in the AUSCHWITZ concentration camps. During the evacuation of Auschwitz in January 1945, she was part of a FORCED EVACUATION on which hundreds died. She arrived at Bergen-Belsen later in the month, where she remained until its liberation by British troops in April 1945. She gave the following testimony about conditions in the camp just before its liberation at the BELSEN TRIAL in 1945.

Subsequently did you go to Belsen?—On 18th January I arrived at Belsen and was put into Block 28 [a barrack]. The conditions were so bad that it is impossible to find words in this world. In half a barracks there were 600 to 700 people. We were lying on the floor covered with lice and every other kind of vermin one could imagine. Our food depended very largely on the efforts of the senior of the block. If she was energetic we might get a quarter basin of soup at mid-day, if not, we might get it at three o'clock. There was no bread for four weeks before the arrival of the British troops. During the whole time I was at Belsen, people were not taken for baths nor were their clothes changed. Towards morning there were several hundred corpses in the blocks and around the blocks. When the Lager Kommandant or [defendant Irma] Grese came along to inspect people, the corpses were cleared away from the front of the blocks, but inside they were full of corpses.

What employment had you in Belsen?—I worked in the kitchen from three o'clock in the morning till nine o'clock at night in order to have a bed and a little more soup.

You have already pointed out No. 16 (Karl Francioh) [another defendant] as the man in charge of your particular kitchen. Do you remember what happened the day before the British arrived?—When the S.S. ran away on that day and when they returned, the man I pointed out [Francioh] fired from the kitchen, through the window, killing several women.

Was he the only person firing?—From the other half of the kitchen there was another cook firing. About 50 people were killed altogether. . . .

When did you go to Belsen?—At the beginning of January we were evacuated from Auschwitz to Belsen and quite a lot of people met their death on the way, for anybody who could not keep up was shot. We marched on foot day and night without receiving food and we were beaten at every step by the S.S. After eight days we were loaded on to open trucks, and, as the weather was cold and frosty, a large number of women died. At Belsen we were chased into the frost with just a nightdress on and had to parade for the shower-baths. We stood about outside lightly dressed for a very long time before we received any soup, and then we were sent to an empty hut. We should have received three-quarters of a litre of soup each day, but actually we only got half a litre, which was normally issued towards evening, and a crumb of bread. At the beginning we got this bread daily, but later on not at all.

Did you see any persons beaten at Belsen?—One evening I saw how a young woman was being beaten, Kramer, Volkenrath and another female being present. She was kicked and beaten with a wooden stick. In the bath-house I remember how a woman officer beat the naked bodies of the women there with a rubber truncheon. I also saw Volkenrath and two others—one of whom I recognize as No. 8 (Herta Ehlert) [a defendant]—undress and severely beat a girl in a small hut where two Blockführerinnen [women barracks leaders] slept. . . .

When you were at Belsen did the conditions in the camp with regard to food and accommodation get worse gradually or suddenly?—They deteriorated gradually. By the beginning of March things had got into a very critical state.

Is it true that many of the people were very ill, and that many arrived dead with the transports?—No, when they arrived at Belsen they were alive, but after a short time many of them died.

— *Reprinted from Raymond Phillips,* Trial of Josef Kramer and Forty-four Others (The Belsen Trial) *(London, 1949), 85, 91–93.*

SIMON WIESTENTHAL OFFERS HIS SERVICES

The ALLIED governments were not the only ones concerned with apprehending war criminals. Survivors, such as Simon Wiesenthal, the famed "NAZI hunter," also took part in the search. In the decades since the war, Wiesenthal has helped to locate a number of war criminals, including Franz Stangl, former commandant of SOBIBOR and TREBLINKA killing centers. A Jewish architect from Poland, Wiesenthal had lost his entire family during the Holocaust. Soon after his liberation from the MAUTHAUSEN concentration camp in May 1945 he offered his services to the American Military Government officials.

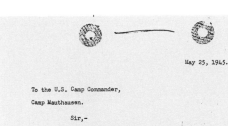

May 25, 1945.

To the U.S. Camp Commander,

Camp Mauthausen.

Sir,-

Having spent a number of years in thirteen Nazi concentration camps, including Mauthausen from which I was liberated by the American forces on May 5th and where I still am staying at the present, and desirous to be of help to the U.S. authorities in their effort to bring the Nazi criminals to account, I take the liberty of submitting the following:

1. As all of the camps where I was confined are located in the zones taken by the Soviet armies, it is my conviction that those responsible for the atrocities committed therein by the SS men are not to be found in the eastern parts of Europe but should be sought either in Southern or Western Germany.

2. I am enclosing a brief list of those whom I have seen in these various camps and whom I can recognize on sight. Many of these have caused incalculable sufferings to myself as well as to my fellow inmates. Many of these I have personally seen commit murder phantastic both in number and method. As shown, some of them had either their homes or relatives living in localities now under Allied occupation.

3. With all of the members of my family and of my nearest relatives killed by the Nazis, I am asking of your kindness to place me at the disposal of the U.S. authorities investigating war crimes. Although I am a Polish citizen and would like to return to my homestead, I feel that the crimes of these men are of such magnitude, that no effort can be spared to apprehend them. I also feel that it is my duty to offer my services either for the purpose of furnishing the description of their misdeeds or as an eyewitness in case identification is needed.

4. To furnish you with the personal data regarding my person, a brief curriculum vitae is attached.

Respectfully,

/s/ Ing. Wiesenthal Szymon
Szymon Wiesenthal
(Camp Mauthausen, 127371).

Curriculum Vitae
of
Ing. WIESENTHAL, Szymon   CLASSIFICATION CANCELLED
by authority of U.S.F.E.T.

Born on December 31, 1908, in Buczacz, Poland. My education comprises public and high schools in that city, Institute of Technology in Prague where I received the degree of Engineer in Architecture (1932), State diploma in Architectural Engineering in Poland (1939) with simultaneous degree of Free Artist from the Polish Academy of Art in Lemberg (1937).

After the outbreak of the war I stayed in Lemberg and after the entry of the Red Army continued my work as a construction engineer and a designer of refrigerating plants and other various constructions as well as private dwellings. During this period I invented an artificial insulation material for which the Soviet Government awarded me a premium of 25,000 rubles.

When after the outbreak of the German-Soviet war that city was taken by the German troops, I was immediately arrested on July 13, 1941, as one of the Jewish intelligentsia. Of independent means, through a bribery I succeeded in getting out of the prison. Because of the anti-Jewish restrictions I could not continue my profession of an architect, and worked for a while as a painter in the railroad shops in Lemberg. On October 20, 1941 I was again arrested for the reason of not having declared my engineering degree which I in fact did not wish to disclose, not willing to work for the Germans. After four weeks I was sent back to work at the same railroad shop as a draftsman where I was kept for almost two years among other 1500 Jews compelled to labor like myself. It was during this time that my life was several times placed in extreme danger, and that I lost both of my parents who were killed by the Nazis. It was also during this time that I saw mass destruction of Jews in that city, although my own wife managed to escape to Warzsaw. Of her I have not heard since and may only assume that she perished in that city during the uprising in August, 1944, when 200,000 Jews lost their lives there. It was only through working in the railroad shop that I managed to survive in the end.

When it became clear to me that Nazis have launched their policy of the wholesale anihilation of Jews, I escaped on October 18, 1943, from the Lemberg hard labor camp where I was kept as a prisoner during my two years of labor at the railroad works (as a prisoner I was sent to the shop daily under guard with the others) and went into hiding until joining Jewish partisans on November 21, 1943, who operated there. It was while fighting in the partisan ranks against the Nazis that we managed to collect and bury for safekeeping considerable amount of evidence and other materials proving the crimes committed by Nazis. When the partisans were dispersed by the Germans I fled to Lemberg on February 10, 1944, and again went into hiding. On June 13, 1944, I was found during a house to house search and was immediately sent to the famous Lacki camp, near that city. Since there was no escape for the partisans who were caught, I attempted suicide by cutting the veins on my arms but was saved.

With the beginning of the Russian offensive, I was sent from one concentration camp to another as the result of constant German retreat. These camps include Przemysl, Dobromil, Chyrow, Sanok, Dukla, Grybow, Neu-Sandes, Krakow-Plashow, Grossrosen, and Buchenwald. To Mauthausen I came on February 15, 1945.

/s/ Ing. Wiesenthal Szymon
Ing. Szymon WIESENTHAL

— Reproduced from Archives, Research Institute, United States Holocaust Memorial Museum, RG 06.005.05, War Crimes Investigation and Prosecution, U.S. Case Files, Concentration Camp Cases Not Tried, Reel 6.

Defendants on trial for barbarities committed at the BUCHENWALD concentration camp are assembled by American military police before entering the courtroom; April 16, 1947. (NARA)

At PLASZOW concentration camp in Poland, women prisoners pull railcars loaded with stones from the quarry up a steep incline, the so-called Industry Street; 1944. (USHMM)

SLAVE LABOR

The German SLAVE LABOR program, initiated in 1937 in all CONCENTRATION CAMPS, was essentially an emergency solution to an acute shortage of manpower. By 1939, labor shortages had become especially severe. Rearmament and mobilization within Germany prior to the outbreak of war had shifted many agricultural laborers into essential war industries and now threatened to jeopardize the NAZI'S public popularity because of imminent shortages of consumer goods. The situation was exacerbated by the WEHRMACHT draft for the invasion of Poland in September that occurred at the high point of the harvest. In response, Nazi policy makers, loath to fill the vacated positions with unemployed women, opened labor offices in several Polish towns three days after German troops marched into Poland and called for volunteer eastern workers. By October 1939, almost 110,000 Polish civilian workers were employed in German fields and factories. Polish soldiers, captured as prisoners of war, were forced into agricultural service.

Buoyed by the huge success of the volunteer Polish labor mobilization and by the swift defeat of the Polish army, German social engineers seized the opportunity to extract more workers from the Polish population. Laws were promulgated that dictated working conditions and forced all Polish men between 14 and 60 into compulsory service. New laws made it legal for Nazi recruiters to seize potential workers off the street and ship them to Germany in work gangs. By May 1940, all Polish prisoners of war were demobilized and ordered to report for work.

Although most Poles were initially used in Germany for agricultural labor, they also worked in other sectors of the economy. Women and young girls were compelled to work as nannies and domestic servants in German households. Chain gangs rebuilt roads, bridges, and buildings in need of repair or damaged by the war. Mining and other occupations involving backbreaking physical labor employed Polish prisoners of war. Eventually, as the German army subdued and controlled ever larger areas of western and eastern Europe, and as the *Wehrmacht's* supply needs increased, the methods for recruiting FORCED LABOR used in Poland were implemented in all other occupied territories.

Generally, the THIRD REICH forced laborers fell into three categories: "voluntary" foreign workers, prisoners of war, and concentration camp prisoners. Representing every European nationality, foreign workers, sometimes euphemistically called "guest workers," were effectively owned by the German government and leased to private industry or agriculture. Firms facing labor shortages approached the SS and, using a combination of money, connections, and influence, competed for the privilege of employing forced labor.

German Labor Minister Fritz SAUCKEL ordered that "all [foreign workers] must be fed, sheltered, and treated in such a way that they produce to the highest possible extent at the lowest conceivable degree of expenditure." Using this guideline, firms provided their foreign laborers only the barest minimums in food, clothing, and shelter, leaving workers defenseless to the ravages of disease, malnutrition, and exposure. Nonetheless, some minimal effort was made by both the Nazi state and German industries to keep these workers alive. This same standard did not apply to the treatment of concentration camp workers, especially Jews, GYPSIES, and Soviet prisoners of war.

The first corporation to fully integrate concentration camp labor into modern industrial production was the chemical conglomerate I.G. FARBEN. Known in German corporate circles as a model enterprise, I.G. Farben built

REICHSFÜHRER-SS Heinrich HIMMLER and entourage during an inspection tour of the construction of the I.G. FARBEN works at AUSCHWITZ III, July 17–18, 1942. Left to right are *SS-Obergruppenführer* (SS General) Rudolf Brandt, Himmler's personal adjutant; *Bauleiter* (Construction superintendent) Max Faust, I.G. Farben's chief engineer; and *SS-Obersturmbannführer* (SS Lieutenant-Colonel) Rudolf HÖSS, commandant of the Auschwitz concentration camp. (Main Commission for the Investigation of Nazi War Crimes, Warsaw, Poland)

and ran sections of the AUSCHWITZ concentration camp (Auschwitz III) devoted to the production of fuel and synthetic rubber. Eventually employing 30,000 workers before the end of the war, Farben's treatment of its SLAVE LABORERS was brutal but not atypical of German firms utilizing such labor.

I.G. Farben corporate officers estimated that the average new Farben "employee"—a prisoner selected for slave labor from the Auschwitz concentration camp complex—lost between nine and twelve pounds a week eating the meager rations provided for workers. At that rate, most workers forced to do exhaustive labor and endure concentration camp conditions died of malnutrition, starvation, or exhaustion within three to six months of initial "employment." These figures can be applied to most concentration camp and prisoner-of-war slave labor. Borrowing a phrase from Benjamin Ferencz, author of this volume's introductory essay, these forced laborers were "less than slaves." Sent to work only in order to extract labor from victims before they died, the workers were not viewed as productive property but were seen as disposable commodities. Selection for labor instead of the gas chambers only postponed the inevitable: death.

Only four major cases against slave labor profiteers ever came to trial after the war. Of these, three trials indicted industrialists and corporate officers (the FARBEN TRIAL, KRUPP TRIAL, and FLICK TRIAL); and the fourth, known as the POHL TRIAL, charged members of SS organizations that allocated slave labor. In most cases, defense attorneys did not attempt to deny the facts indicting their clients. Instead, they argued that the use of slave labor within a war economy was not unlawful. This defense claimed that modern, "total war" legitimized the use of forced labor as a military or economic necessity. During the war against the Soviet Union, the defense argued, the capitalistic use of slave labor in war production defended the economic and ideological integrity of the West against the spread of Communism.

Although the "legitimate" use of slave labor was rejected by the Nuremberg courts, it is unlikely that the defense counsels expected this argument to work. Instead, they sought to convince the courts of their clients' innocence. Not only did the suited and somber defendants fail to fit the public perception of mass murderers and slavers, but in the Cold War atmosphere of the postwar period, Communists often seemed far more dangerous than Nazis. By claiming that the wholesale participation of German industry in forced labor programs was not criminal, the defense tried to preempt later prosecutions of hundreds of as-yet uncharged German businesses. This defense, which only partially succeeded inside the courtroom, was enthusiastically embraced by both the German and American publics. By 1951, all industrialists convicted of slave labor charges by Nuremberg courts were pardoned and released.

SS-Hauptsturmführer (SS Captain) Amon Goeth, commandant of PLASZOW concentration camp from February 1943 to September 1944, stands on the balcony of his camp villa, holding a rifle he used to shoot prisoners. (USHMM)

AMON GOETH: SCHINDLER'S NEMESIS

Amon Goeth, the commandant of the PLASZOW concentration and LABOR CAMP from early 1943 to fall 1944, was tried by the Supreme National Tribunal of Poland soon after the end of World War II for crimes committed in the areas of Cracow, Tarnow, Szebnie, and Plaszow. This trial sought to broaden the legal definition of GENOCIDE, first established by the INTERNATIONAL MILITARY TRIBUNAL. By introducing evidence detailing the NAZI mechanism for the systematic destruction of European Jews, Polish prosecutors were able to further develop the economic, social, and cultural implications of genocide that had only been superficially addressed by the court at Nuremberg.

The following selection contains portions of the indictment, trial, and judgment from the GOETH TRIAL. He was found guilty of all charges and sentenced to death by hanging on September 5, 1946.

[*From the indictment:*]
(1) The accused as commandant of the forced labour camp at Plaszow (Cracow) from 11th February, 1943, till 13th September, 1944, caused the death of about 8,000 inmates by ordering a large number of them to be exterminated.
(2) As a SS-[Haupt]Sturmführer [SS Captain] the accused carried out on behalf of SS-Sturmbannführer [SS Major] Willi Haase the final closing down of the Cracow ghetto. This liquidation action which began on 13th March, 1943, deprived of freedom about 10,000 people who had been interned in the camp of Plaszow, and caused the death of about 2,000.
(3) As a SS-Hauptsturmführer [SS Captain] the accused

carried out on 3rd September, 1943, the closing down of the Tarnow ghetto. As a result of this action an unknown number of people perished, having been killed on the spot in Tarnow; others died through asphyxiation during transport by rail or were exterminated in other camps, in particular at Auschwitz.

(4) Between September, 1943, and 3rd February, 1944, the accused closed down the forced labour camp at Szebnie near Jaslo by ordering the inmates to be murdered on the spot or deported to other camps, thus causing the death of several thousand persons.

(5) Simultaneously with the activities described under (1) to (4) the accused deprived the inmates of valuables, gold and money deposited by them, and appropriated those things. He also stole clothing, furniture and other movable property belonging to displaced or interned people, and sent them to Germany. The value of stolen goods and in particular of valuables reached many million *zlotis* at the rate of exchange in force at the time. For those acts the accused was arrested by the German authorities on 13th September, 1944, but he was not brought before any German court. He was later extradited to Poland by the Allied authorities in Germany. . . .

[*From a summary of the case:*]
The criminal activities of the accused Amon Goeth in the Cracow district were but a fragment of a wide action which aimed at the extermination of the Jewish population in Europe. This action was to be carried out by stages. In the first stage the personal and economic freedom of the Jews was only partly restricted; then they were completely deprived of personal freedom and confined in so-called ghettoes. From there they were gradually transferred to concentration camps and eventually murdered in a wholesale manner by shooting and in gas-chambers. Large numbers of Jews perished in each stage of this action also through inhuman treatment and torture or were individually murdered by German and Ukrainian henchmen. . . .

[*From the judgment:*]
His criminal activities originated from general directives that guided the criminal Fascist-Hitlerite organization, which under the leadership of Adolf Hitler aimed at the conquest of the world and at the extermination of those nations, which stood in the way of the consolidation of its power.

The policy of extermination was in the first place directed against the Jewish and Polish nations.

This criminal organization did not reject any means of furthering their aim at destroying the Jewish nation. The wholesale extermination of Jews and also of Poles had all the characteristics of genocide in the biological meaning of this term, and embraced in addition the destruction of the cultural life of these nations. . . .

— *Reprinted from United Nations War Crimes Commission,*
   Law Reports of Trials of War Criminals *(New York, 1992),*
   118–19, 126.

Women inmates march inside the PLASZOW concentration camp in Poland; ca. 1943–44. (USHMM)

PLASZOW SLAVE LABOR CAMP

In June 1942, construction began on the PLASZOW concentration and labor camp in the suburbs of Cracow, the capital of the GENERAL GOVERNMENT. Designed to be a collection point for all Jews remaining in the General Government, Plaszow prisoners served as FORCED LABORERS until their deportation to KILLING CENTERS or CONCENTRATION CAMPS. The first Plaszow workers constructed the camp itself by laboriously removing the headstones from the Jewish cemetery on which the camp was built. As the camp population increased, however, prisoners were employed in the production of glass, metal, clothing, brushes, and other goods in industries around the city of Cracow. It was this camp and its commandant, Amon Goeth, who were portrayed in the 1993 film Schindler's List.

The following testimony by Dr. Moshe Beisky, describing life in the Plaszow camp, was given during the EICHMANN TRIAL *in Jerusalem in 1961.*

Q. How many people were there in the camp?

A. At the beginning of January there were two thousand. Those who went outside the camp went under armed guard. During the first period, the guard was not so heavy, but there was no great fear that people would escape, for a simple reason, namely that where in a particular group that went outside the camp someone escaped, the penalty was the killing of some or most of the group, I shall quote some such cases.

Presiding Judge How many people were there in the group?

Witness Beisky In the group to which I belonged it varied. There were days when we went out in a group of 70–90. It depended on the work. That same firm, Strauch, had 700–800 men whom it was entitled to divide up amongst the places of work which it managed in Cracow. The work was from the early hours and it consisted of loading coal.

Attorney General What do you mean by "early hours"?

Witness Beisky Rising time was 4:30 in the morning. Before we left for work there was a morning roll-call. All the occupants of the hut were lined up on the camp ground, until the person in charge of the camp, the commander, appeared, and was given a report on the number of people alive, and the number who had died—if there were deaths —how many were killed, what was the state of the sick and the state of the healthy.

Q. Where did they die and where were they killed?

A. In the course of these events, it is difficult for me— and I am also thinking of the others who were in the same camp—to remember the days on which people did not die or were not killed. I now pass to our lot, that is to say the lot of those who went outside to work. It might be thought to have been easier, for at least from the moment that we left the precincts of the camp until the moment when we returned to it, we were involved in work. Although the work was hard, it was work. But at the same time the people of the camp who remained inside were subjected to things which I later on experienced personally—for I myself had to endure them.

They had to set up a camp. Only afterwards did we know the reason for this. The work went on from the early hours of the morning until the late hours of the evening, always under supervision, and of course very hard labour. When it was necessary to lift heavy stones from the tombs, they were not given more people for it than the number who could carry this out only with supreme efforts. And if something was not done properly by such groups, then individuals and also complete groups of 30 to 40 people were executed in various ways.

I said earlier: "It might be thought that our lot was good." The food in the camp was bad and scarce, and therefore the people who went outside could not resist the temptation to obtain some food from outside for themselves and the members of their family. And since for a considerable part of the people this was close to Cracow where they had friends, they used to buy things. The danger arose daily when they came back, for on their return they were searched at the gate. If food was found, it ended —in the best of circumstances—with whippings, between 25 and 100 lashes on the naked body. . . .

A group that appeared with food in its possession— and I shall quote a concrete instance—that was a particular group of the *Abladekommando*, a unit that was in charge of the offloading of goods from the railway station —when this group returned and food was found in its possession, the camp commander came up (at that time it was Untersturmführer [SS 2d Lieutenant] Amon Goeth) and asked whose food it was. When no one answered, he took a gun from a guardsmen standing next to him and shot a young man whose name was Nachmansohn—his brother lives in Tel Aviv—he shot him. On the same occasion he shot another man, Disler. And then someone had a bril-

liant idea and said that he had brought the food. Then everyone in the group received 100 lashes. It was a group of 20 men or more. One of the men is living today in Tel Aviv—his name is Mandel, who was wounded in the course of the shooting and remained lying there until the group was taken to the parade ground, and there everyone received his "desserts." He himself had to count the blows and if he made an error in the counting, he had to go back to the beginning and start all over again. There was an instance with that group where one of the older men was beaten and cried out a great deal, and after that had to go to the camp commandant and to inform him that he had received his punishment and he thanked him for it. When he turned around, he shot him and he, too, was killed. . . .

Attorney General . . . Perhaps you would describe the living conditions in Plaszow?

Witness Beisky There were various periods. In the first period there was a little more space. We lived in huts. There were bunks on three levels. In a regular hut there were, generally speaking, between 200 and 250 persons, according to the size of the hut. There was no mattress. But it is true that each one took with him some kind of blanket and that was spread out on the bunk. For those who went outside there was always the danger of being killed on their return, for someone would always smuggle in something on reaching the camp. Those who were inside were in a situation of working always on the run.

Q. What do you mean by "on the run"?

A. The "*Vorarbeiter*" (workers in charge) and SS men stood there and kept you running: "Run, do it on the double, hurry." And I will give you the example of the two engineers who, owing to the fact that a hut was not erected quickly enough—it was the late Mrs. Reiter, an engineer from Cracow, and the engineer Ingber—were shot dead, and killed because of that fact. . . .

— *Reprinted from State of Israel, Ministry of Justice, The Trial of Adolf Eichmann, 5 vols. (Jerusalem, 1992), 1: 346–48.*

DESTRUCTION OF THE POLES

Whether recruited voluntarily, conscripted as FORCED LABOR, *or deported to* CONCENTRATION CAMPS, *Poles made up a large percentage of the German foreign work force. Considered racially inferior by* NAZI *ideology, these slave laborers were subjected to brutal treatment and exploitation by the German war industry. Workers who did not immediately comply with orders or who seemed reluctant to work were considered to be saboteurs, and thus deserving of harsh punishment and death.*

In his speech to concentration camp commandants on March 15, 1940, Heinrich HIMMLER *outlined the role of the Polish forced laborer employed by Germany industry. Portions from that speech were then reproduced and circulated as Nazi propaganda. The following excerpts were later introduced as evidence at the* INTERNATIONAL MILITARY TRIBUNAL.

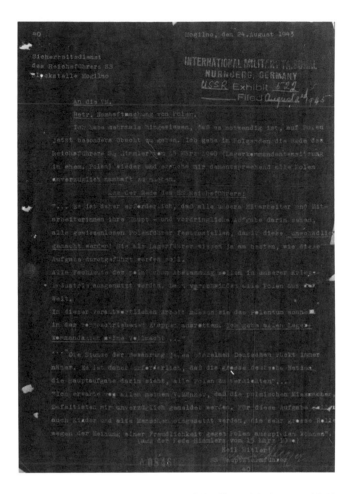

Mogilno, 24 August 1943

Security Service
of the Reichsführer SS
Mogilno

    To the Secret Agents
    Subject: Arrest of Poles
    I have repeatedly pointed out that it is necessary now to be especially careful of Poles. I am enclosing the speech of the Reichsführer SS Himmler of 15 March 1940 (meeting of camp commandants in former Poland) and accordingly request that I be provided immediately with the names of all Poles.

        From the speech of the SS Reichsführer
    ". . . It is therefore necessary that all our male and female colleagues recognize that their primary and immediate task is to apprehend all unscrupulous Polish leaders so that they can be rendered harmless! You as camp commandants know best how this task should be carried out.

"All skilled workers of Polish descent are to be exploited in our war industry. Then all Poles will disappear from the world.

"In this responsible task you must quickly eradicate Polish consciousness in the prescribed stages. I give all camp commandants my authorization . . ."

". . . The hour of trial is near at hand for every German. It is therefore necessary that the great German nation sees its main task to annihilate all Poles . . ."

"I expect from all my agents that the Polish dissidents and defeatists are reported to me without delay. For these tasks children and the elderly can be put to use; they can play a large role because of their impression of friendliness towards the Poles."

Heil Hitler
[signature illegible]
SS-Hauptsturmführer [SS Captain]

    — *Reproduced from the National Archives and Records Administration, National Archives Collection of World War II War Crimes Records, Record Group 238, Office of the U.S. Chief of Counsel for War Crimes, Document USSR-522. Translated from the German by Gerald Schwab and Linda Bixby.*

Young Polish men and women forced to build an autobahn in Germany as Germans supervise them; 1941.
(Bildarchiv Preussischer Kulturbesitz, Berlin, Germany)

THE MISTREATMENT OF RUSSIAN POWs

One of the many groups of people forced to work in German industry as SLAVE LABOR *were Soviet prisoners of war. In stark contrast to the* GENEVA CONVENTION *international agreement on the treatment of captured enemy soldiers, German policies deliberately sought to kill prisoners of war through work and starvation. In accordance with this strategy, Krupp, an armaments firm, employed several thousand Soviet prisoners of war in its steel works near the German city of Essen. Noted for its particularly harsh treatment of Russian slave laborers, the Krupp concern maintained hundreds of labor camps similar to Raumastrasse* LABOR CAMP, *described in the affidavit below.*

Apolinary Gotowicki, a Polish prisoner of war and physician, made the following statement about his observations in several Krupp factories. It was used by the prosecution at the INTERNATIONAL MILITARY TRIBUNAL.

13 October 1945

Sworn Statement

I, the undersigned Dr. Apolinary Gotowicki, physician in the Polish Army, on 3 January 1941 came into German captivity and remained so until the entry of the Americans. I gave medical help to the Polish, Russian, and French prisoners of war who were forced to work in different parts of the Krupp factories. I personally visited the Russian prisoner of war camp on Rauma Street in Essen, which had a capacity of about 1800 men. In this camp there was a great hall that normally could accommodate 200 men; about 300–400 men were thrown together and housed here in such a catastrophic manner that no sanitary conditions were possible. The floor was made of concrete, and the straw sacks that served as beds were filled with bugs and lice. On cold days the rooms were never heated, and it appeared to me, a physician, to be unworthy for humans, that people were in such a condition. It was also impossible to keep the places clean; because of the overcrowding the men found hardly any room to move. Every day up to 10 men were brought to me whose bodies were covered with bruises because of continual beatings with rubber hoses, steel rods, or sticks. The men were often writhing in such agony that it was impossible for me to give them even a little medical aid. In spite of the fact that I protested, made complaints, and often intervened, it was impossible for me to protect the people or to see that they got a day off from work. It was difficult for me to see how such suffering men were forced to do heavy work. Under personal danger, I visited gentlemen of the Krupp administration as well as gentlemen from the Krupp Directorate to get help. It was strictly forbidden because the camp was directed by the SS and Gestapo, and according to well-known instruction, I had to keep silent, otherwise I myself could have been

Prisoners filling carts at the MAJDANEK **concentration camp; ca. 1942–44.**
(Main Commission for the Investigation of Nazi War Crimes, Warsaw, Poland)

brought to a concentration camp. On innumerable occasions I brought my own bread ration, which was even meager for me, and tried to give it to the prisoners if possible. From the beginning, in the year 1941, the conditions did not improve, but rather they became worse. The diet consisted of a watery soup that was dirty and sandy, and often the prisoners of war had to eat cabbage that was rotten and stank. Everyday I noticed people who were dying like animals of hunger or mistreatment. Often the dead lay for two or three days on their straw sacks, until their bodies stank so badly that fellow prisoners took them outside and buried them somewhere. The bowls from which they ate, they also used as toilets because they were too tired or too weak from hunger to be able to stand up from their plank beds and go outside. At 3 o'clock in the morning they were wakened. The same bowl was used for washing and later again for eating. This system was common knowledge. Anyway it was impossible for me to get even elementary help or relief to get rid of epidemics, illnesses, or cases of starvation. There was no medical aid for the prisoners to speak of; I never received any medical supplies. I alone cared for the people medically in 1941, and of course as the only help, it was impossible for me to care for so many people, and added to that, I had hardly any medical resources. Of the 1800 persons who daily came to me crying and complaining, I did not know what to do. I myself often collapsed each day, and in spite of this I had to take everything on my shoulders and watch how the people perished and died. A report was never done about how and why the prisoners of war died. With my own eyes I saw how the Russian prisoners of war returned from their work at Krupp and how they collapsed during the march home and how a number of them had to be wheeled back on carts or carried by their comrades. It was in this manner that the men came back to their camp. The work they had to do was very difficult and dangerous, and the men frequently had cuts on their fingers, hands, or legs. The accidents were very serious, and the men came to me and asked for medical

Inmates of the MAJ-DANEK concentration camp working as SLAVE LABORERS. (Main Commission for the Investigation of Nazi War Crimes, Warsaw, Poland)

help. But it was not possible for me to keep them from work for even one or two days, though I often went to the Krupp Directorate and requested permission for this. By the end of 1941, two men died daily; in 1942 the death rate increased to three to four men daily. I was placed under Dr. May and after strong complaints often succeeded in getting him to come to the camp to see the terrible conditions, but even for him it was impossible to get medical help from the Medical Department of the German Army or from Krupp, nor could he improve conditions, treatment, or food.

I also witnessed a conversation with Russian women who explained to me personally that they worked in the Krupp factories and that they were beaten daily in a barbaric manner. The food there also consisted of a watery soup that was dirty and not fit to eat and whose terrible smell one could notice from far away. Their clothing was ragged and torn; on their feet they wore rags and wooden shoes. Their treatment was, as far as I could tell, the same as that given the Russian prisoners of war. Beating was a daily occurrence. The conditions lasted for years, from the beginning until the arrival of the American troops. The people constantly lived in horrible fear, and it was a great danger for them to describe to anyone anywhere the conditions that prevailed in their camp. The directives they received were such that they immediately could have been killed if any of the guards, the SS, or Gestapo became aware that this occurred. It was for me, as a physician, possible to speak with the people more closely; they had

trust in me and knew that as a Pole I would never betray them to anyone.

[signature] Dr. Apolinary Gotowicki
residing Essen-Steele, Bochumer St. 55

[signature] Albert D. Friar, Capt.
Court President

[stamp]
Military Government
Summary Court Essen
130 Det.

— *Reproduced from the National Archives and Records Administration, National Archives Collection of World War II War Crimes Records, Record Group 238, Office of the U.S. Chief of Counsel for War Crimes, Document D-313. Translated from the German by Wendy Lower and Linda Bixby.*

A DOCTOR'S REPORT

Although entitled to state health care according to German social insurance laws, foreign workers were frequently unable to obtain medical help because of discriminatory practices and medical supply shortages. In order to keep foreign laborers at work, companies employed physicians to care for FORCED LABORERS and to oversee health conditions in LABOR CAMPS. Nevertheless, negligence, insufficient food, long hours, harsh treatment, and poor conditions exposed foreign workers to life threatening illnesses and death without hope for medical comfort.

In the following affidavit, introduced as evidence at the INTERNATIONAL MILITARY TRIBUNAL, *Dr. Wilhelm Jaeger describes the conditions in a few of the labor camps run by the Krupp steelworks, a division of that major German munitions manufacturer. Krupp controlled fifty-five such camps in the area around the German city of Essen alone.*

Posen, 15 October 1945

I, Dr. Wilhelm Jäger, am a general practitioner in Essen, Germany, and its surrounding communities. I was born in Germany on 2 December 1888 and now live at Sengenholz 6, Kettwig, Germany.

I make the following statement of my own free will and without force. I was not promised reward of any kind.

On 1 October 1942, I became senior camp doctor in the Krupp workers' camps for foreigners and had the responsibility for the medical supervision of all of Krupp's workers' camps in Essen. One of my duties was to report on the sanitary and health conditions of the workers' camps to my superiors at the Krupp works.

In fulfilling my responsibilities I visited all of the Krupp camps that housed foreign civilian workers, and I am therefore able to make this statement on the basis of personal knowledge.

My first official responsibility was to make a thorough inspection of the various camps. At that time, in October 1942, I discovered the following conditions: The eastern workers and Poles—from this point on I will use the term "eastern workers" for both eastern workers and Poles—who labored in the Krupp works at Essen were kept in camps at Seumann Street, Spenle Street, Grieper Street, Heer Street, Germania Street, Kapitän-Lehmann Street, Dechen School, and Krämer Square.

All of these camps were surrounded by barbed wire and were closely guarded.

Conditions in all of these camps were extremely bad. The camps were overcrowded. In some camps there were twice as many people in a barrack as health conditions allowed.

At the camp at **Krämer Square**, the inhabitants slept in triple-tiered bunks, and in other camps they slept in double-tiered bunks. The health authorities require a minimum distance of 50 cm [19 inches] between beds. In these camps the distance between beds was 20–30 cm [8–12 inches] at the most.

Food for the eastern workers was altogether insufficient. The eastern workers received 1,000 calories a day, which was less than the minimum for any German. When German workers engaged in strenuous work, they received 5,000 calories a day; the eastern workers, who did the same type of work, received only 2,000 calories a day. The eastern workers were given only 2 meals a day plus their bread ration. One of these two meals consisted only of a thin, watery soup. I was not sure that the eastern workers

in fact received the required minimum. Later, in 1943, while I was checking the food prepared by the kitchens, I discovered a number of instances where food was withheld from the eastern workers.

The diet was composed of a small portion of meat per week. Only inferior meats, such as horse meat or tuberculin-infested meat, was allowed. This meat was usually cooked into a soup.

The clothing of the eastern workers likewise was inadequate. They worked and slept in the same clothing in which they had arrived from the East. Almost none of them had coats and were forced, therefore, to use their blankets as coats in cold and rainy weather.

The shortage of shoes forced many workers to go to work in their bare feet, even in winter. A number of wooden shoes were provided, but their quality was such that they hurt the workers' feet. Many workers preferred to go to work in their bare feet rather than endure the suffering caused by the wooden shoes. Apart from the wooden shoes, no clothing of any kind was issued to the workers until the latter part of 1943, when a blue suit was issued to some of them. To my knowledge, this was the only issuance of clothing to the workers from the time of their arrival until the American forces entered Essen.

The sanitary conditions were especially bad. At Krämer Square, where approximately 1,200 eastern workers were crowded into the rooms of an old school, the sanitary conditions were atrocious. Only 10 children's toilets were available for the 1,200 inhabitants. At the Dechen School, 15 children's toilets were available for the 400–500 eastern workers. Excrement contaminated the floors of these lavatories. There were also limited facilities for washing.

The supply of medical instruments, bandages, medicine, and other medical supplies at these camps likewise was completely insufficient. Therefore, only the very worst cases were treated. The number of eastern workers who were ill doubled that of the German workers. Tuberculosis was especially widespread. The percentage of tuberculosis among the eastern workers was 4 times the rate of the Germans (Germans at 0.5%, eastern workers at 2%).

At the Dechen School approximately 2.5% of the eastern workers suffered from active tuberculosis. The Tatars and Kirghiz suffered the most due to this illness. As soon as they were affected, they dropped like flies. The reason was due to bad living conditions, poor quantities of food, overwork, and insufficient rest.

The workers were likewise afflicted with spotted typhoid. Lice, the carrier of this disease, together with countless fleas, bugs, and other vermin, tormented the inhabitants of these camps. As a result of the filthy conditions of these camps, nearly all eastern workers were afflicted with skin diseases. The shortage of food also caused many cases of starvation edema, nephritis, and shighakruse [dysentary].

When sick, the workers had to continue to go to work unless a camp doctor wrote that they were unfit for work. At Seumann Street, Grieper Street, Germania Street,

Kapitän-Lehmann Street, and Dechen School, there were no daily office hours. At these camps, the doctors would only be there every second or third day. As a result, workers were forced to go to work, despite being ill, until they were able to see the doctor. I did my best to improve conditions as much as possible. I insisted on the building of new barracks in order to relieve the overcrowded conditions of the camps. Despite this, the camps were still overcrowded, but not as much as before. I tried to remedy the poor sanitary conditions at the Krämer Square and at the Dechen School by bringing about the installation of some emergency toilets. But the number was not enough to make a difference in the terrible conditions. I ordered more sanitary equipment.

When the heavy air raids began in March 1943, conditions in the camps deteriorated even more. The problem of housing, food, and medical attention became more acute than ever. The workers lived in the ruins of their former barracks. Medicine and bandages were used up, lost, or destroyed, and were difficult to replace. At time, the water supply at the camps was completely shut off for periods of 8–14 days. We installed a few emergency toilets in the camps, but there were not enough of them to remedy the situation.

After the air raids in March 1943, many eastern workers were housed at the Krupp factories. Boards separated a corner of the building in which they worked. The day shift slept there during the night and the night shift during the day in spite of the loud, constant noise in the factory. I believe that these conditions continued until the American troops entered Essen.

As the air raids increased in Essen, conditions became worse. On 28 July 1944, I reported to my superiors that:

"The district barrack in Rabenhorst is in such bad condition that it cannot even be considered a district barrack. The rain leaks through every corner and side. Housing of the sick there is therefore impossible. The necessary labor for production is in danger because the sick are not able to recuperate. . . ."

— *Reproduced from the National Archives and Records Administration, National Archives Collection of World War II War Crimes Records, Record Group 238, Office of the U.S. Chief of Counsel for War Crimes, Document D-288. Translated from the German by Linda Bixby.*

Prisoners of the MAJDANEK concentration camp working as SLAVE LABORERS. The *Ost* emblem identified east European workers.
(Main Commission for the Investigation of Nazi War Crimes, Warsaw, Poland)

A KRUPP WORKER'S OBSERVATIONS

In early summer 1944, Krupp representatives selected 520 female Jewish prisoners from the Gelsenkirchen CONCENTRATION CAMP, a sub-camp of the BUCHENWALD concentration camp, to work in the main Krupp steel mill near Essen, Germany. The selected prisoners, between fourteen and twenty-five years of age, had been deported from Hungary, Romania, and Czechoslovakia. Originally sent to the AUSCHWITZ camp complex, the girls had already survived several SELECTIONS which had doomed their fellow deportees to death in the GAS CHAMBERS. Once in Essen, the girls were housed in barracks on Humboldtstrasse, 4 1/2 miles from the steel mill. Forced to walk to the Krupp factory in all types of weather, they were beaten with dog whips during the march to and from work. Fearing the arrival of the ALLIES in spring 1945, the Krupp management evacuated the SLAVE LABORERS on a ten-mile forced march to Bochum, a nearby town. From there the women were deported back to Buchenwald on March 17. Eventu-

ally liberated from BERGEN-BELSEN *concentration camp by the British army, only a handful of these women survived the war.*

A Krupp machinist describes these women in the following affidavit used as evidence in the KRUPP TRIAL.

Affidavit

I, Peter Gutersohn, residing at Essen-West, Bockmuhlen-weg 2, after having been warned that I shall be liable to punishment for making false statements, herewith declare the following under oath of my own free will and without coercion:

I have been with Krupp [the largest German arms manufacturer] since 1912. I worked in Machine Construction 9, a plant which built tank and gun turrets. Plant leader Wunsch of Machine Construction 9, resident in Sythen near Haltern, Stockweise [in Germany], treated the foreigners, prisoners of war, or civilians working there in a very brutal manner.

I have personally experienced how Wunsch in Machine Construction 9 beat and kicked the buttocks of Russian prisoners of war and eastern workers in order to drive the people to work. These people who were very weak anyway often fell to the ground under the weight of these blows and bled at the nose. The food of the Russians consisted of practically nothing but watery soup.

Although the French civilians working in Machine Construction 9 were treated somewhat better than the eastern workers, they were handled rather severely. Wunsch also refused the French civilians their accumulated leave on numerous occasions, on the grounds that some of them did not return from their leave.

Wunsch once caught eastern workers engaging in personal jobs, that is, they were making rings and the like out of waste metal. Thereupon he summoned all the eastern workers in the plant (there must have been 150 of them at the time); he searched them and beat them. He related this to us himself in an air raid shelter during an air raid. Following the middle of October 1944 we also received an allocation of concentration camp women, Hungarian Jewesses. These women were in very reduced circumstances. They had to load rubbish and cart it away on wheelbarrows and carry iron girders; they were also employed on other cleaning-up activities. These Jewesses had neither work clothes nor protective gloves for these jobs. Their entire clothing consisted of one ragged dress made of burlap. They wore wooden slippers on their naked feet. The huts in which these Jewesses lived were severely damaged during an air attack, so that the huts were no longer waterproof. Thus in winter the Jewesses had to come to work in the worst weather, dressed in their wet rags, with simply their thoroughly soaked blankets on their shoulders. I have witnessed this myself on many occasions. If, in these conditions, the women wanted to dry themselves out a little at a coal fire, or if they tried to wash some of their rags, they were immediately driven away by Wunsch.

The Jewish concentration camp women were accompanied to their work by two SS-women, and at their work

Prisoners building the Krupp works at the AUSCHWITZ **camp complex; 1942.**
(Main Commission for the Investigation of Nazi War Crimes, Warsaw, Poland)

they were guarded by an armed member of the Wehrmacht. At the various jobs themselves they were supervised by the competent members of the staff.

One day at the beginning of March, 1945, these Jewish concentration camp women did not come to work, and since that time I have heard nothing more of them. . . .

— Reprinted from National Archives and Records Administration, National Archives Collection of World War II War Crimes Records, Record Group 238, Office of the U.S. Chief of Counsel for War Crimes, Document NI(K)-8766.

INFANTS OF SLAVE LABOR

In January 1943, Hans Kupke, the supervisor for all Krupp LABOR CAMPS *and later a defendant in the* KRUPP TRIAL, *established a new camp near the German town of Voerde. The camp, also known as Buschmannshof, occupied barracks which Krupp Industries had taken over from* ORGANIZATION TODT, *the construction corps for the German army. Designed to house the children of eastern workers, Buschmannshof was later expanded to house pregnant women immediately before and after giving birth. As soon as they were able, new mothers were forced to go back to work, leaving their infants behind. Neglected, malnourished, and abused, very few of these children lived past the age of two. Although reports vary, statistics provided during the Krupp Trial revealed that many of Buschmannshof's infant population died before the camp was evacuated to the East in February 1945.*

The testimony of Ernst Wirtz, a Krupp employee and former supervisor of foreign workers, describes conditions at Buschmannshof during the Krupp Trial.

Q. Where were you in January 1945?

A. In January 1945, I was in Kulmbach in Oberranken [Germany].

Q. What was the order that Director Hupe [another Krupp employee] gave you in Kulmbach regarding the transport of eastern workers from Voerde?

A. In January 1945, I had to go to Essen—the beginning of January—and I had to pick up a consignment of eastern workers. In Essen I was told by Mr. Dollwein that I had to go to Voerde in order to set up the transport of eastern workers.

Q. What was in Voerde?

A. In Voerde we had a former camp of the Organization Todt. . . .

Q. How many people were in this camp?

A. I assume about 4,000.

Q. Were these men and women?

A. Mixed—men, women, and children.

Q. From among these women and children did you pick the people for Kulmbach?

A. Yes.

Q. What did you see in the barracks in which the children lived?

A. The children were undernourished. There was no child at all whose arms or hands were thicker than my thumb.

Q. How old were those children?

A. From babies up to the age of 2 years.

Q. Were these the children of eastern workers?

A. Yes, they had been born in the camp.

Q. How were these babies housed in the Voerde camp when you saw them?

A. In sort of prison bunks. They had paillasses [straw mattresses] with rubber sheets, and the children were there quite naked.

Q. Could you see definite signs of undernourishment in these children?

A. Yes; many of them had swollen heads. . . .

Q. Mr. Witness, were you surprised about this pitiable state of the children?

A. Yes.

Q. What did you tell the camp leader?

A. I told the girls in charge of the children—I asked them how it came about that these children were so undernourished, and I was told that these children had very little to eat.

Q. Were these female eastern workers?

A. Yes.

Q. And they told you that these children didn't get enough food?

A. Yes.

Q. Did these female eastern workers also tell you how many children died every day?

A. Yes. Fifty or sixty children died every day, and as many were born every day, because there was a constant influx of eastern female workers with children.

Q. You said 50 to 60 children died every day?

A. Yes.

Q. And there was a steady influx of new ones?

A. Yes.

Q. Were these eastern female workers who had children married for the greater part?

A. Yes.

Q. What happened to the children of the female eastern workers—did they tell you what happened with the children who died?

A. I asked the interpreter to ask them how it came about that so many children died, and if the children were buried; and the interpreter told me the children were cremated inside the camp. . . .

Q. Do you know how long—do you know during which time, how long a time it was during which Krupp administered the camp at Voerde?

A. I can't tell you in detail, but I assume since 1943.

Q. Since 1943?

Women slave laborers digging gravel at the AUSCHWITZ **camp complex; 1943.**
(National Museum of Auschwitz-Birkenau, Auschwitz, Poland)

A. Yes.

Q. But if you say that the female workers told you 50 or 60 children died every day, you didn't mean that this number of children died over the whole period?

A. No.

Q. This only referred to a short period?

A. Yes.

Q. Could you give us an estimate concerning which period approximately?

A. There was January 1945—it may have been for 1 year.

Q. At the most for 1 year?

A. Yes. . . .

Q. . . . Witness, do you know what happened to the children of a female worker who worked for Krupp?

A. As soon as the eastern worker had given birth to the child, she was allowed 6 weeks; and after these 6 weeks, she went back to work; and the child was kept in the camp so that the female worker could go to work again. She saw that child only after work.

Q. Was this child separated from the mother?

A. Yes.

— *Reprinted from "United States of America v. Alfred Krupp, et al." (Case 10: 'Krupp Case'), Trials of War Criminals Before the Nuernberg Military Tribunals Under the Control Council Law No. 10, 15 vols. (Washington, D.C., 1950), 19: 1112–17.*

VIENNA "WELCOMES" HUNGARIAN JEWS

After the assassination of Reinhard HEYDRICH in 1942, Ernst KALTENBRUNNER was promoted to replace Heydrich as the head of the CENTRAL OFFICE FOR REICH SECURITY, or RSHA. A large umbrella organization, the RSHA was heavily involved in overseeing the evacuation of Jews and other "negative elements" from eastern territories slated for GERMANIZATION. Once expelled, these deportees were used as SLAVE LABORERS throughout German-occupied territory or sent directly to CONCENTRATION CAMPS and KILLINGS CENTERS. Ultimately, those laborers who did not die from overwork or ill treatment were victims of "SPECIAL TREATMENT," the NAZI euphemism for murder.

In the following letter written to the Nazi mayor of Vienna, Kaltenbrunner discusses a transport of Jewish workers possibly sent to Vienna to repair air raid damage. This letter was used by prosecutors at the INTERNATIONAL MILITARY TRIBUNAL.

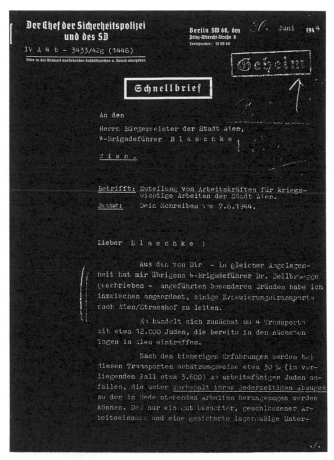

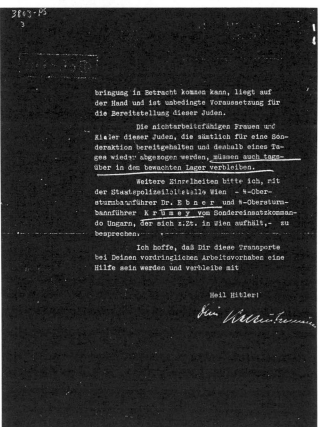

Berlin SW 68, 30 June 1944
Prinz-Albrecht Street 8
Telephone: 12 00 40

The Chief of the Security Police
and the Security Service
IV A 4 b - 3433/42g (1446)

In reply please refer to above office
stamp and date

[stamp] Secret

Express Letter

To the
Mayor of the City of Vienna
SS-Brigadeführer [SS Brigadier General] **Blaschke**

<u>Vienna</u>

<u>Re:</u> The Assignment of Labor Forces for Militarily
Important Work in the City of Vienna.

<u>Ref.:</u> Your letter of 7 June 1944

Dear **Blaschke**!

Because of your stated specific reason—by the way,
SS-Brigadeführer Dr. Dellbuegge wrote me regarding the
same issue—I have ordered an evacuation transport to go
to Vienna/Strasshof.

It consists first of four transports with 12,000 Jews
who are prepared to arrive in Vienna in the next few days.

According to recent experience roughly 30 percent of
these transports will make available (in this case about
3,600) able-bodied Jews for work who are to be <u>kept ready
for their departure at any time</u> and are to be employed in
the work we discussed. That only a well-guarded, closed-
labor assignment and a secure, camp-like quarters can be
considered is obvious and is an absolute requirement for
providing these Jews.

The Jewish women and children who are not able to
work will be kept ready together for a "Sonderaktion"
[special operation] and therefore one day will be relocated
again; they must also remain in the guarded camp.

For further details I request that you confer with *SS-
Obersturmbannführer* [SS Lieutenant Colonel] Dr. **Ebner**
at the State Police Office in Vienna and *SS-Obersturmbannführer* **Krumey** of the Special Operation Detachment
Hungary, who is at this time in Vienna.

I hope that these transports will be of help to your
urgent labor plans, and I remain

Heil Hitler!
[signature]
your Kaltenbrunner

— *Reproduced from the National Archives and Records
Administration, National Archives Collection of World War
II War Crimes Records, Record Group 238, Office of the U.S.
Chief of Counsel for War Crimes, Document 3803-PS. Trans-
lated from the German by Wendy Lower and Linda Bixby.*

OSWALD POHL'S TRIAL BEGINS

Oswald POHL was the administrative head of the SS CENTRAL OFFICE FOR ECONOMY AND ADMINISTRATION, or WVHA. This office sought financial independence for the SS from the NAZI PARTY and the state by making SS programs profitable. To this end, Pohl arranged to "lease" CONCENTRATION CAMP prisoners as SLAVE LABOR to German industry in exchange for fees. Desperately short of workers, corporations coveted these forced laborers as a means of achieving higher productivity. This program was so successful that the WVHA was unable to provide enough cheap labor to meet industry demands. Supplies of slave workers were therefore often "auctioned" to companies willing to pay the highest fees or those with the best SS connections.

After the war, Oswald Pohl and other WVHA employees were tried for these and other CRIMES AGAINST HUMANITY connected with the slave labor program. Pohl was found guilty by a NUREMBERG MILITARY TRIBUNAL during the POHL TRIAL and sentenced to death by hanging.

Slave Labor Killing Of PWs Is Revealed As Pohl Trial Opens

NUREMBERG, April 9 — A Nazi plan to kill prisoners of war by literally working them to death was disclosed here at the trial of SS Gen. Oswald Pohl and 17 of his major aides in the SS central economics and administration office. As chief of that office, Pohl had been the head of the entire Nazi concentration camp system.

At the opening of the trial yesterday before U. S. Military Tribunal No. 2, presided over by Justice Robert M. Toms, Prosecutor McHaney declared the group of 18 defendants had been responsible not only for the operation of the concentration camps from 1942 on, but also for the killing of military prisoners through slave labor.

Documents showed that under an agreement between Himmler and the justic ministry, McHaney said, certain categories of prisoners were to be turned over to the SS which was to force them to work until they died of exhaustion.

The prosecutor pointed out this was the first trial of leaders of a Nazi organization termed criminal by the International Military Tribunal.

— *Reproduced from* News of Germany, *April 10, 1947.*

Jewish SLAVE LABORERS who built an autobahn in Geppensdorf, Germany; November 1940. The photo's donor, Abram Stone, is fourth from left. (USHMM)

In Kraigonev, U.S.S.R., a German firing squad discharges a volley into Russians kneeling at the edge of a ditch already littered with corpses; ca. 1941–43. (NARA)

MASS EXECUTIONS
AND REPRISALS

The murder of civilians in wartime has been endemic to man's conflicts for centuries; the twentieth century has witnessed the worst atrocities to date. During the Second World War, Germany's occupation brought terror and death to the nations it conquered, beginning with the conquest of Poland in September 1939. The SS began mass executions in an attempt to eliminate the Polish classes it perceived as the immediate enemies; thousands were shot in the first few years of the occupation. But such brutal acts were only the precursor to crimes of unimagined magnitude committed a short time later.

With the German invasion of the Soviet Union in June 1941, killing operations motivated by NAZI racial ideology began on a massive scale; the extermination of the Jews of that nation was a step toward the "FINAL SOLUTION." These mass executions were committed chiefly by SS units called EINSATZGRUPPEN that followed the German Army's advance. Their aim was to exterminate all Jews, GYPSIES, Communist functionaries, and the institutionalized mentally and physically handicapped individuals. To facilitate this murderous end, a formal agreement was reached before the invasion between the WEHRMACHT and the CENTRAL OFFICE FOR REICH SECURITY (RSHA) that defined exactly how the SS would carry out the killings with the German army's cooperation. In forward areas recently conquered by the Wehrmacht, the Einsatzgruppen operated with the army's acquiescence and sometimes its active participation. Proximity to the victims was a necessity if the Einsatzgruppen were to catch and kill as many as possible.

Four Einsatzgruppen were formed, designated with the letters A to D, to exterminate the Jews and Gypsies of the Soviet Union and the Baltic republics (Latvia, Lithuania, and Estonia). Each Einsatzgruppe was composed of members of the SECURITY POLICE and the SD and used subordinate units called EINSATZKOMMANDOS to carry out much of the killing. The latter included members of the German police, WAFFEN-SS and numerous auxiliary police units recruited by the Germans from the local populations of Ukraine, Belorussia, and the Baltic republics. The executions followed a general pattern. Shootings took place outside a town or city alongside ditches or mass graves, where the victims were immediately buried. Jews were rounded up by a variety of ploys usually connected with a requirement for them to "register for resettlement." Once gathered, they would be led in groups to the execution site, stripped of their valuables, and shot. Although secrecy was desired, it was not unusual for German and local bystanders to observe the executions, sometimes actually taking part themselves or photographing the proceedings. Such witnesses fed rumors of the massacres that shortly began to circulate throughout the East.

There were thousands of such mass executions in the East, varying in size from several victims to thousands; their magnitude is staggering. In late September 1941, more than 33,000 Jews were killed at Babi Yar, near the Ukrainian city of Kiev, by SS men of Einsatzgruppe C with the active assistance of members of the Ukrainian auxiliary police recently formed for "security" duties. Some 75,000 Jews were killed in Odessa in October 1941, when SS men of Einsatzgruppe D assisted their Rumanian allies in a massive POGROM that swept that city. Since many of the Soviet Union's Jews were concentrated in the western part of the country, the number of victims killed after the invasion began in June reached more than 100,000 a month by December 1941. The victims were not just Soviet citizens; by late 1941 Jews who had been deported from western Europe to the East swelled the numbers killed in these bloody massacres.

After killing hundreds of thousands of people, the Germans concluded that mass shootings were "inefficient," both because of the effort involved and the serious psychological effect the cold-blooded murders at close range often had on the perpetrators. In early 1942, GAS VANS were introduced as a "less disturbing" means of dispatching the victims. Asphyxiating the victims with the vehicle's exhaust spared the "sensibilities" of the executioners. The gas vans, which saw service with the Einsatzgruppen in Russia, never completely supplanted shooting as the basic form of execution, which continued to the war's end in all areas the Germans occupied. Not all such shootings were carried out by the SS; the Wehrmacht could and did occasionally participate in executions organized by the Einsatzgruppen.

After the initial wave of killings during 1941, the SS still had to deal with the thousands of Jews who had been missed in the first murderous onslaught. Some were herded into GHETTOS in the occupied portions of the Soviet Union, most of which were eventually liquidated and their residents killed or deported. Some ghettos became a source of FORCED LABOR for the German war effort. The economic contribution that skilled Jewish labor could make became more important as the war in the East dragged on; the murder of hundreds of thousands of these laborers adversely affected Germany's ability to wage war against the Soviet Union. By the time the Soviet Army liberated their country in 1944, more than a million skilled workers and other civilians had been killed in mass executions by the Einsatzgruppen and their accomplices.

Mass shootings were not restricted to the East; they occurred all over Europe. Massacres were perpetrated throughout the war under the guise of "security" operations as the Waffen-SS and German army attempted to ferret out resistance fighters, or PARTISANS, who operated behind German lines in the Soviet Union, the Balkans, Italy, and France. The innocent civilians killed in these actions helped to swell the official count of "partisans" killed. In Yugoslavia there were massacres of civilians throughout the period of German occupation, including those committed during the massive roundups of Jews in that country in 1942. In retaliation for the May 1942 assassination of Reinhard HEYDRICH, the town of LIDICE, Czechoslovakia, was razed in June and its male inhabitants killed. All its women were

Three generations of Jewish females, including a nine-year-old girl, stand in front of clothing taken from some of the 2,800 Jews slaughtered at the fishing village of Skeden, near Liepaja, Latvia, between December 15 and 17, 1941. The Jews were forced to undress at a temperature of 23° F and were then shot in groups of ten by Germans and Latvians. Women were compelled to clasp their babies to make them better targets. Pits had been dug to hold the corpses. This photo was found in the GESTAPO files in Liepaja.
(Yad Vashem, Jerusalem, Israel)

deported to the RAVENSBRÜCK concentration camp and its children to the WARTHEGAU, where eight were selected for GERMANIZATION and adopted by SS families. Two years later, in June 1944, approximately 700 people were massacred by a *Waffen-SS* unit in Oradour-sur-Glane in southern France in retribution for the disappearance of an SS officer. The wholesale shooting of innocent civilians as reprisal became a trademark of German occupation during World War II.

Comparatively few of the perpetrators of these crimes have been brought to justice. The KRASNODAR TRIAL saw several members of *Einsatzgruppen D* tried in absentia for their crimes in the Soviet Union. The EINSATZGRUPPEN TRIAL of 1947–48 brought many of the top officials of the *Einsatzgruppen* to justice. But not until the late 1950s were some of the many lower ranking Germans directly involved in such mass executions brought to trial in German courts. The Soviets tried several cases of a similar nature during the 1950s and 1960s; the MERE TRIAL of 1961 is an example. Unfortunately, such trials have accounted for only a fraction of the WAR CRIMINALS who killed millions throughout German-occupied Europe.

DEATH NEAR RIGA

During the opening phases of the German invasion into the Soviet Union in June 1941, Jews, GYPSIES, and Communists were massacred from Estonia on the Baltic Sea to Odessa on the Black Sea. Outside Riga, Latvia, shootings of Jews occurred in the Rumbuli Forest during late November and early December 1941, when some 25,000 Jews were shot in pits by the SS. On November 30, as described below, more than 10,000 Jews were killed. Most were from the Riga GHETTO; one thousand of these victims were from a transport of German Jews recently deported from the REICH.

A portion of the judgment from the TUCHEL TRIAL, in which several of the massacre's perpetrators were tried and convicted, is reproduced below.

The actual site of execution lay about five miles outside Riga in the direction of Dünaburg [Daugavpils], between the highway and the railroad, both of which connect Riga and Dünaburg. The railroad tracks and the road there run a near-parallel course, with the railroad tracks running to the north of the road. The site lies in the vicinity of the railroad station at Rumbuli; its terrain is sandy and slightly hilly, sparsely wooded, and forms part of the Rumbuli Forest. In the center of this site was a densely forested area; this was the location of the actual execution site, with prepared pits designed to accommodate about thirty thousand bodies. The approaching columns of Jews coming from Riga along the highway between Riga and Dünaburg had to turn left from the highway onto a dirt track which led up to the small patch of woods. In the process they were funneled into a narrow cordon, which was formed by SS units, a contingent of the Special Task Unit Riga, and Latvian units.

The columns of Jews advancing from Riga, comprising about one thousand persons each, were herded into the cordon, which was formed in such a way that it narrowed greatly as it continued into the woods, where the pits lay. The Jews first of all had to deposit their luggage before they entered the copse; permission to carry these articles had only been granted to give the Jews the impression that they were taking part in a resettlement. As they progressed, they had to deposit their valuables in wooden boxes, and, little by little, their clothing—first overcoats, then suits, dresses, and shoes, down to their underclothes, all placed in distinct piles according to the type of clothing.

On this particular day (30 November 1941), the air temperature in Riga measured at two meters [6.5 ft.] above ground, was -7.5°C [18.5°F] at 7:00 A.M., -1.1°C [30°F] at 1:00 P.M., and 1.9°C [35.4°F] at 9:00 P.M. On the previous evening, 29 November 1941, there had been an average snowfall of seven centimeters [2.7 in.]. On 30 November between 7:00 A.M. and 9:00 P.M. it did not snow.

Stripped down to their underclothes, the Jews had to move forward along the narrow path in a steady flow toward the pits, which they entered by a ramp, in single file and in groups of ten. Occasionally the flow would come to a standstill when someone tarried at one of the undressing points; or else, if the undressing went faster than expected, or if the columns advanced too quickly from the city, too many Jews would arrive at the pits at once. In such cases, the supervisors stepped in to ensure a steady and moderate flow, since it was feared that the Jews would grow edgy if they had to linger in the immediate vicinity of the pits. . . .

In the pits the Jews had to lie flat, side by side, face down. They were killed with a single bullet in the neck, the marksmen standing at close range—at the smaller pits, on the perimeter; at the large pit, inside the pit itself—their semi-automatic pistols set for single fire. To make the best of available space, and particularly of the gaps between bodies, the victims next in line had to lie down on top of those who had been shot immediately before them. The handicapped, the aged, and the young were helped into the pits by the sturdier Jews, laid by them on top of the bodies, and then shot by marksmen who in the large pit actually stood on the dead. In this way the pits gradually filled.

— *Reprinted from Gerald Fleming,* Hitler and the Final Solution *(Berkeley, 1982), 78–79. Courtesy University of California Press.*

WITNESS' STATEMENT

As they invaded the Soviet Union, the Germans sought Jews, GYPSIES, *and political officers, called commissars, among the Soviet prisoners of war as well as in the civil population. The* WAFFEN-SS, *mentioned in this statement by a Polish Jew drafted into the Soviet Army, was the military branch of the* SS *that fought alongside the German army and participated in massacres of both prisoners of war and civilians.*

After the initial wave of killings by the EINSATZGRUPPEN *during 1941 and early 1942, these units settled down in specific areas throughout the occupied Soviet Union and*

A German shoots a Polish prisoner in Radogoszcz, Poland; 1942.
(Main Commission for the Investigation of Nazi War Crimes, Warsaw, Poland)

continued their work. Jews who had been overlooked in the first wave of killings were caught and killed, as were those who had been concentrated in GHETTOS *in numerous towns in the Baltic republics, eastern Poland,* BELORUSSIA, *and Ukraine.*

The statement reproduced below was introduced as evidence at the INTERNATIONAL MILITARY TRIBUNAL.

Report
of Witness Examination

carried out by the public prosecutor and member of the Central Committee for Investigating German Crimes in Poland, Dr. Stanislaw Piotrowski, in Nuremberg on the 29 July 1946.

On the basis of the regulations of Polish law, the witness was informed of the responsibility for false testimony and took the oath.

Name:	Goldberg, Mojzesz
Age:	36 years
Birthplace:	Radom
Occupation:	Merchant
Religion:	Jewish
Address:	Stuttgart, Bismarck Street 138
Relationship to the Parties:	——

The Witness states the following:

1) On 23 June 1941, I was drafted in Lemberg [L'viv] into the Soviet Army. In mid-July I was taken prisoner by the Germans. In a village five kilometers [three miles] from Podwoloczysk, the SS companies sought out the Jews from the entire mass of prisoners and shot them on the spot. I remained alive since they did not recognize me as a Jew. I stress that this was done by the *Waffen-SS*.

2) After I was released from prison; I lived in Radom and worked in the period from June 1942 until July 1944 for the *Waffen-SS* in three positions: SS Veterinarian Reinforcement Department, Kosciuszki Street; the Garrison Administration of the Waffen-SS, Planty 11; and the Building Department of the Waffen-SS, Slovakia Street 27. Since I worked so long for the SS, I know very well the names and faces of all the officers and non-commissioned officers of the above mentioned departments of the *Waffen-SS*. The head of the SS Veterinary Reinforcement Department was *SS-Sturmbannführer* [SS Major] Dr. Held and *SS-Hauptsturmführer* [SS Captain] Schreiner; the head of the Garrison Administration was SS-*Obersturmführer* [SS 1st Lieutenant Colonel] Grabau (presently at the Dachau concentration camp); and the head of the Building Department was *SS-Oberscharführer* [SS Staff Sergeant] Seiler. All the persons mentioned, together with their companies, took a direct part in the implementation of the evacuations in Radom on 5, 16, and 17 August 1942, during which several thousand persons were shot on the spot. I know that SS Veterinarian Reinforcement companies themselves went

into the provincial cities with the purpose of carrying out the "evacuations" of Jews. I heard how individual soldiers boasted about the number of Jews they had killed. I know from their own stories that these same companies participated in the operations against Polish partisans, as well as the setting on fire of surrounding Polish villages.

[signature] Goldberg
[signature] Piotrowski

The report was read aloud to me.

— *Reproduced from the National Archives and Records Administration, National Archives Collection of World War II War Crimes Records, Record Group 238, Office of the U.S. Chief of Counsel for War Crimes, Document GB-565. Translated from the German by Wendy Lower and Linda Bixby.*

A GERMAN EYEWITNESS

Not all Germans supported the murderous activities of the EINSATZGRUPPEN. *The spectacle of such executions did offend the basic decency of some Germans, as shown in the official report written by a German army officer who witnessed a massacre near Zhytomyr in Ukraine, in July 1941. Such sentiments, however, were rarely expressed. The cover letter to the report is reproduced in facsimile.*

[stamp]
Secret!

[stationery]
The Deputy Commanding General
of the 9th Army Corps
and
the Commander in Military District IX

Kassel, 17 January 1942

Nr. 370/42 secret

[stamp]
21 January 1942
Nr. 402/42 secret-1

[stamp]
High Command of the Army
20 January 1942

To the
Chief of Army Armaments - Commander of the
Reserve Army -
Berlin

Re: Atrocities toward the civilian population in the East.
/1 Enclosure

Because of rumors circulating about mass executions in Russia, I investigated their origins because I thought them extremely exaggerated.

Enclosed is a report by Major **Roesler** that fully confirms the rumors. When such actions take place in such openness, it will be unavoidable that they will become known and criticized in the homeland.

[signature, illegible]

Copy

Roesler, Major   at present Kassel, 3 January 1942

Report

The following "Behavior toward the Civilian Population in the East" by the Replacement Infantry Regiment 52 gives me cause to report the following:

At the end of July 1941, the infantry regiment 528 led by me was on the way from the West to Zhytomyr, where we were supposed to move into rest quarters. When I and my staff had occupied my staff quarters on the afternoon of our arrival, we heard gunfire at regular intervals from a short distance that, after a short time, were followed by pistol shots. I decided to investigate, and together with my adjutant and orderly (*Oberleutnant* [1st Lieutenant] von Bassewitz and *Leutnant* [2nd Lieutenant] Müller-Brodmann) set out on a search in the direction of the gunfire. We soon had the impression that a terrible scene must have taken place here because after a while we saw numerous soldiers and civilians streaming towards a railway embankment ahead of us, behind which, we were

told, continual shooting took place. During this entire time, we were unable to see over the embankment. After a certain amount of time, however, we could hear the sound of a trilling whistle and then a 10-unit gun salvo that was later followed by pistol fire. When we had finally climbed the railway embankment, we saw on the other side a picture whose inhuman atrocity had a shocking effect on the unprepared interloper. A 7–8-meter long [23–26 feet] and maybe 4-meter wide [13 feet] trench had been dug into the ground. The removed earth was piled to one side. This pile and the trench walls beneath it were completely sullied with streams of blood. The pit itself was filled with an inestimable number of human bodies of all kinds and of both sexes so that the depth of the pit remained uncertain. Behind the heaped pile of earth was a police commando led by a police officer. There was blood on their uniforms. Within a broad vicinity, numerous soldiers were standing around, some units already resting, some in bathing suits as spectators, as well as numerous civilians with their wives and children. Only by forcing my way through the crowd was I able to get a look at the pit, an image I am still unable to forget even today. Among others an old man with a white beard was lying in the trench. He still had a small walking stick hanging over his left arm. Since this man continued to pant and puff, I tried to get a policeman to put an end to his life; he said to me with a laughing expression, "I've already given it to him seven times in the belly; he'll croak on his own." The shot bodies in the trench were not laid out in order but rather laid where they had fallen from the trench wall after being shot. All of these people had been shot in the nape of the neck and finished off with pistols. Because of my participation in the First World War as well as in the French and Russian offensives of this war, I have by no means become soft. Also during my activities with the Free Corps in 1919 I lived through more than mere unpleasantness; still, I cannot remember having witnessed a scene like the one I just described. It is for me irrelevant that court decisions ordered these executions. I consider it to be incompatible with our previous understanding of discipline and culture that here in complete openness, like on an open-air stage, mass slaughtering of people took place. I would also like to mention that, according to statements from soldiers who frequently witnessed these executions, several hundred people were shot daily.

Proofread true copy
[signature, illegible]
Major

signed **Roesler**

— *Reproduced from the Archives, Research Institute, United States Holocaust Memorial Museum, Records Relating to the Soviet Union under Nazi Occupation, Record Group 22.001*01. Translated from the German by Neal Guthrie.*

Soviet citizens, possibly Ukrainians, are herded into a ravine in Sdolbunov, U.S.S.R., before they are to be shot en masse by Germans; October 14, 1942.
(Main Commission for the Investigation of Nazi War Crimes, Warsaw, Poland)

REPORT ON A MASSACRE

Among the most compelling of the millions of documents left by the Germans were the Operational Situation Reports of the EINSATZGRUPPEN. *A total of 195 such reports were written between June 1941 and June 1942. They describe in gruesome detail the murderous activities of the* Einsatzgruppen *throughout the occupied areas of the Soviet Union.* Sonderkommando 4a, *a unit from* Einsatzgruppen C *active in northern Ukraine, perpetrated one of the most notorious massacres near the city of Kiev in late September 1941. The explosion of a number of delayed-action mines left throughout the city after the Soviet Army's retreat was used as a pretext for the murder of 33,000 Jews in a series of ravines at Babi Yar. German policemen serving in a police regiment used to secure rear areas also participated, as did Ukrainian auxiliary police; the latter were formed by the* SS *to provide security behind the frontline.*

A complete set of Einsatzgruppen *Operational Situation Reports was found by the* ALLIES *at the end of the war. Several were introduced as evidence at the* INTERNATIONAL MILITARY TRIBUNAL *and later at the* EINSATZGRUPPEN TRIAL, *where this document was used in evidence by the prosecution.*

NO - 3140

- 15 -

ordentlich gross. Hinzu kommt, dass Juden sich nachweislich an der Brandlegung beteiligt hatten. Die Bevölkerung erwartete deshalb von den deutschen Behörden entsprechende Vergeltungsmassnahmen. Aus diesem Grunde wurden in Vereinbarung mit dem Stadtkommandanten sämtliche Juden Kiews aufgefordert, sich am Montag, den 29.9. bis 8.00 Uhr an einem bestimmten Platz einzufinden. Diese Aufrufe wurden durch die Angehörigen der aufgestellten ukrainischen Miliz in der ganzen Stadt angeschlagen. Gleichzeitig wurde mündlich bekanntgegeben, dass sämtliche Juden Kiews umgesiedelt würden. In Zusammenarbeit mit dem Gruppenstabe und 2 Kommandos des Polizei-Regiments Süd hat das Sonderkommando 4a am 29. und 30.9. 33 771 Juden exekutiert. Geld, Wertsachen, Wäsche und Kleidungsstücke wurden sichergestellt und zum Teil der NSV zur Ausstattung der Volksdeutschen, zum Teil der kommissarischen Stadtverwaltung zur Überlassung an bedürftige Bevölkerung übergeben. Die Aktion selbst ist reibungslos verlaufen. Irgendwelche Zwischenfälle haben sich nicht ergeben. Die gegen die Juden durchgeführte "Umsiedlungsmaßnahme" hat durchaus die Zustimmung der Bevölkerung gefunden. Dass die Juden tatsächlich liquidiert werden, ist bisher kaum bekanntgeworden, würde auch nach den bisherigen Erfahrungen kaum auf Ablehnung stossen. Von der Wehrmacht wurden die durchgeführten Massnahmen ebenfalls gutgeheissen. Die noch nicht erfassten, bzw. nach und nach in die Stadt zurückkehrenden geflüchteten Juden werden von Fall zu Fall entsprechend behandelt.

Gleichzeitig konnten eine Reihe NKWD-Beamter, politischer Kommissare und Partisanenführer erfasst

II.

Executions and Other Measures

Partly because of the better economic situation of the Jews under the Bolshevik regime and their activities as informers and agents of the NKVD [People's Commissariat of Internal Affairs], and partly because of the explosions and resulting fires, the public feeling against the Jews was especially strong.

begin page 15 of original

Added to that, it was proved that Jews had participated in the arson. The people therefore expected from the German authorities adequate retaliatory measures. For this reason, all Jews in Kiev were requested, in agreement with the city commander, to appear Monday, 29 September, by 8 A.M., at a designated place. These summonses were posted across the entire city by members of the assembled Ukrainian militia. It was simultaneously announced verbally that all Jews in Kiev were to be resettled. In collaboration with the group staffs and two commandos of the Police Regiment South, Special Detachment 4a executed 33,771 Jews on 29 and 30 September. Money, valuables, underwear, and clothing were secured and in part placed at the disposal of the NSV [NATIONAL SOCIALIST PEOPLES' WELFARE SOCIETY] to be used by ethnic Germans, and in part given to the city administration authorities for the needy population. The operation went smoothly. No type of unforeseen incidents occurred. The "Resettlement Measure" against the Jews was approved throughout by the population. The fact that in reality the Jews were liquidated was hardly known until now and would also, according to current experiences, hardly have been objected to. The measures carried out were also approved by the *Wehrmacht*. The Jews who had not yet been apprehended as well as those who gradually returned to the city from their flight were in each case treated accordingly.

At the same time, a number of NKVD officials, political commissars, and partisan leaders were seized and liquidated.

— *Reproduced from the National Archives and Records Administration, National Archives Collection of World War II War Crimes Records, Record Group 238, Office of the U.S. Chief of Counsel for War Crimes, Document NO-3140. Translated from the German by Wendy Lower.*

AN *EINSATZGRUPPE'S* "BALTIC ROUNDUP"

Einsatzgruppe A, *one of the four* EINSATZGRUPPEN *used in the Soviet Union for mobile killing operations, murdered Jews,* GYPSIES, *Communists, and other civilians as they marauded throughout the Baltic republics that the Soviets had illegally occupied and annexed in 1940. A top secret draft memorandum to the* CENTRAL OFFICE FOR REICH SECURITY *in Berlin, with an accompanying map, describes the results of their killing operations in late 1941. This document was introduced in evidence during the* INTERNATIONAL MILITARY TRIBUNAL.

This map entitled "Jewish Executions Carried Out by Einsatzgruppe A" and stamped "Secret Reich Matter" shows the number of Jews executed in the Baltic states and Belorussia by late 1941. The legend near the bottom states that "the estimated number of Jews still on hand [was] 128,000." The coffin is a symbol for the number of dead Jews in each designated area.

— *Reprinted from National Archives and Records Administration, National Archives Collection of World War II War Crimes Records, Record Group 238, Office of the U.S. Chief of Counsel for War Crimes, Document 2273-PS.*

Jews

The systematic mopping up of the Eastern Territories embraced, in accordance with the basic orders, the complete removal, if possible, of Jewry. This goal has been substantially attained—with the exception of White Russia—as a result of the execution up to the present time of 229,052 Jews. . . . The remainder still left in the Baltic Provinces is urgently required as labour and housed in ghettos.

To attain this object various kinds of measures were necessary in the different areas of the Eastern Territories (Ostland).

In the three Baltic States of Estonia, Latvia, and Lithuania, Jewry did not make itself decisively felt until Bolsheviks had come into power there. But even before that the Jewish influence on the one hand and the anti-Jewish feeling of the population on the other hand, were very strong.

In the following the various areas of the Eastern Territories will be dealt with separately:

1) Estonia

. . . At the beginning of 1940 there were living in Estonia about 4,500 Jews out of a total population of 1.2 million. Their influence on the economic life of the country was considerably stronger than the proportion of Jews to the whole population. . . .

With the advance of German troops the majority of the Jews, together with the Soviet-Russian authorities, left the country. Approximately 2,000 Jews remained behind in the country. Out of these almost 1,000 lived in Reval alone.

The Estonian Self Protection Movement (Selbstschutz) [units of armed local citizens soon controlled by the Germans], formed as the Germans advanced, did begin to arrest Jews, but there were no spontaneous pogroms. Only

by the Security Police and the SD were the Jews gradually executed as they became no longer required for work.

Today there are no longer any Jews in Estonia.

2) Latvia

. . . The total number of Jews in Latvia amounted in June 1935 to 93,479 or 4.79% of the total population. . . .

When the German troops marched in there were still 70,000 Jews in Latvia. The remainder fled with the Bolsheviks. The Jews left behind were actively engaged in sabotage and setting fire to places. In Dünaburg [Daugaupils] so many fires of this kind were started by the Jews that a large part of the Town was destroyed.

After the terror of the Jewish-Bolshevik rule—altogether 33,038 Letts [Latvians] were transported, imprisoned or murdered—an extensive pogrom carried out by the population might have been expected. In fact, however, only a few thousand Jews were eliminated by local forces on their own initiative. In Latvia it was necessary to carry out extensive mopping-up operations by means of the Sonderkommandos with the help of forces picked from the Latvian Auxiliary Police (mostly relations of the Letts who had been carried off or murdered).

Up to October 1941 approximately 30,000 Jews had been executed by these Sonderkommandos. The remaining Jews who were still indispensable from the economic point of view were collected in ghettos, which were established in Riga, Dünaburg and Libau.

As a result of punishments instituted for not wearing the Jewish star, black market, thieving, fraud, but also to prevent the danger of epidemics in the ghettos, further executions were subsequently carried out. In this way 11,034 Jews were executed in Dünaburg on 9.11.41 [9 November 1941], and, as the result of an action ordered and carried

A German Army firing squad shoots six PARTISANS in the Soviet Union; summer 1942. Such executions were commonplace throughout German-occupied Europe during Workd War II.

(Bundesarchiv Koblenz, Germany)

out by high authorities and Police chiefs, 27,800 were executed in Riga at the beginning of December 1941, and, in the middle of December 1941, 2,350 were executed in Libau. At the moment there are in the ghettos (other than Jews from the Reich) Latvian Jews in

Riga approximately 2,500
Dünaburg approximately 950
Libau approximately 300.

These are indispensable at the moment as they are specialized workers necessary for maintaining the country's economy.

3). Lithuania

. . . When German troops marched in the Lithuanians expressed their hatred of the Jews in active pogroms, at the same time Jewish communist youths set fire to many towns, through which the German armoured units had passed leaving them little damaged, by means of tins of petrol [gasoline] which they had previously put ready.

As a result of the pogroms carried out by the Lithuanians, who were nevertheless substantially assisted by Sipo [SECURITY POLICE] and SD, 3,800 Jews in Kauen [Kovno] and 1,200 in the smaller towns were eliminated.

Where Jews were able to escape, they were not infrequently handed over to the authorities by the farmers.

These spontaneous mopping-up actions were, however, insufficient to stabilize this rear section of the Front, and at the same time the enthusiasm of the local inhabitants waned.

Therefore by means of selected units—mostly in the proportion of 1:8—first of all the prisons, and then systematically district by district the Lithuanian sector was cleansed of Jews of both sexes. Altogether 136,421 people were liquidated in a great number of single actions. It is worthy of note that many of the Jews used force against the officials and Lithuanian auxiliaries who were carrying this out, and before their execution still expressed their Bolshevik convictions by cheering Stalin and abusing Germany.

As the complete liquidation of the Jews was not feasible as they were needed for labour, ghettos were formed which at the moment are occupied as follows:

Kauen approximately 15,000 Jews,
Wilna [Vilnius] approximately 15,000 Jews,
Schaulen [Siauliai] approximately 4,500 Jews.

These Jews are used primarily for work of military importance. For example up to 5,000 Jews are employed in three shifts on the aerodrome near Kauen on earthworks and work of that sort.

— *Reprinted from National Archives and Records Administration. National Archives Collection of World War II War Crimes Records, Record Group 238, Office of the U.S. Chief of Counsel for War Crimes, Document 2273-PS, pp. 2–5.*

A unit of *EINSATZGRUPPE A* prepares to shoot Lithuanian Jews near Kovno, Lithuania; late 1941 or early 1942.
(Jewish State Museum of Lithuania, Vilnius, Lithuania)

CALCULATING THE KILLING

Regular administrative reports were one of the features of EINSATZGRUPPEN *operations and a vital means of documenting the Holocaust. This message to Einsatzgruppe A, operating in the Baltic republics and the northern Soviet Union, lists the murders committed in Lithuania by* Einsatzkommando 3, *one of its subordinate units.*

Commanding Officer of the Security Police and the Security Service
Kauen [Kovno] [handwritten] 107.12

Received				Place for Incoming Stamp	Forwarded			
Time	Date	Month	Year		Time	Date	Month	Year
					9 February 1942 [handwritten] 128			
to			through		to			through
					[handwritten, illegible]			
				Telegram— Radio Message— Teletype Telephone Message	Notice of Delay [handwritten, illegible]			
Message No. 412								

To Group A <u>in Riga</u>

<u>Re:</u> Executions up to 1 February 1942 by the Einsatzkommando 3

<u>Ref.:</u> Your message: No. 1331 of 6 February 1942

A: Jews 136,421

B: Communists 1,064 (among them 1 commissar, 16 [illegible], 5 [illegible]

C: Partisans 56

D: Mentally ill 653

E: Poles 44; Russian prisoners of war 28; Gypsies 5;
    Armenians 1.

Total: <u>138,272</u>, among them 55,556 women, 34,464
children.

[signature] [Karl] Jäger
SS-[title, illegible]

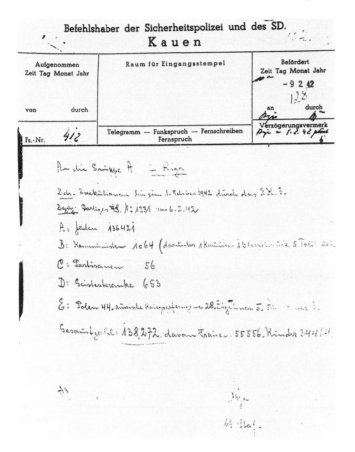

— *Reproduced from the Archives, Research Institute, United
States Holocaust Memorial Museum, Record Group 11.001,
Selected records of the "Osoby" Archive in Moscow, Reel
183, file 500-1-25, 128. Translated from the German by
Gerald Schwab.*

DEFINING
JURISDICTIONS

*Massacres of Jews in the East often became public specta-
cles in which bystanders were either voyeurs or active participants. Besides the* SS, *German police, local auxiliaries,
and* WEHRMACHT *soldiers, members of the many German
governmental organizations active in the East could and did
take part in the killings. The document reproduced below
relays an order on this subject from Alfred* ROSENBERG,
*Reich commissar for the Occupied East, to the headquar-
ters of the* CENTRAL OFFICE FOR REICH SECURITY. *The*

*"eastern officials" mentioned in the text are staff members
of Rosenberg's ministry.*

    *This document was introduced as evidence by the pros-
ecution at the* <u>EINSATZGRUPPEN TRIAL</u>.

2 P 739/42g   Kovno, 11 November 1942

To
Main Office I
Main Office II
Main Office III
Main Office Technical   [stamp] SECRET

<u>Settlement Staff Kovno</u>

<u>Re:</u> Participation of Officials in Executions

I request that the following decree of the Reich
Commissar for the Occupied East be brought to the
attention of the staff in the appropriate manner:
    "In view of a particular case, I hereby prohibit the
    active participation of officials of the eastern adminis-
    tration in executions of any kind. The carrying out
    of executions, especially in the liquidation of Jews, is
    the task of the Security Police and the SD."

[signature illegible]

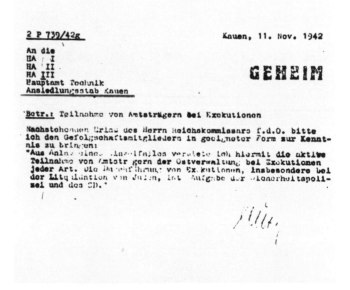

— *Reproduced from the National Archives and Records
Administration, National Archives Collection of World War II
War Crimes Records, Record Group 238, Office of the U.S.
Chief of Counsel for War Crimes, Document NO-2673.
Translated from the German by Wendy Lower.*

Execution of residents of Bochnia, Poland, in Uzbornia Grove near the town; December 18, 1939. A German firing squad shot fifty-one inhabitants of the area after members of a resistance group *Orzel Bialy* (White Eagle) attacked a German police station two days earlier.
(Main Commission for the Investigation of Nazi War Crimes, Warsaw, Poland

The prisoners are marched to the execution site.

German police line up the victims.

The execution.

A MASSACRE OF POLES

The conquest of Poland in September 1939 saw the "pacification" of the entire country by the German army, the EINSATZGRUPPEN *of the* SS, *and* ETHNIC GERMAN *paramilitary groups. The SS were particularly brutal as they hunted Polish and Jewish elites, ostensibly to quell resistance to the German conquerors but in reality to eliminate so-called enemies of the* REICH. *In so doing, they often interfered with the occupation policy of the German military and civil administration in Poland, including* WARTHEGAU, *an area of Poland incorporated into the Reich in October 1939. Portions of a report by a German army general to the German Army High Command about such operations were introduced as evidence at the* INTERNATIONAL MILITARY TRIBUNAL *and are reprinted here in translation.*

Copy of Copy
Military District Command XXI

Posen, 23.11.1939

I c 86/39 Secret
SECRET!
To

Commander of the Command

The Warthegau is to be regarded as pacified. Repeated rumors of resistance have not been confirmed. The reason for this is not a change in the mood of the Polish population but the recognition of the hopelessness of a revolt. The dangers inherent from the large number of released prisoners and other returning Polish soldiers is not to be underestimated and needs constant observation, especially since many officers have not yet been apprehended. The control of this danger is only possible through the military occupation of the country in its present form; the civil authorities are totally unable to do so with the currently available police units.

The extensive reconstruction in all areas is not helped by the intervention of SS formations that are given "national political special assignments" and are not under the jurisdiction of the Reich representatives in the states. As a result, there is a tendency [for the SS] to interfere over and above these assignments in all parts of the administration and to form a "state within a state." This factor is not without repercussions on the troops, who are outraged by the way the assignments are carried out and, as a result, find themselves in conflict with the [civil] administration and the party. I will prevent the danger of serious conflicts through strict orders. It must be recognized that this will make serious demands on the discipline of the troops.

In nearly all the larger villages, shootings have occurred in the open by the mentioned organizations. Selection for these shootings varied significantly and was often incomprehensible; the discharge was in many cases unjustified.

In many districts, all Polish estate owners have been arrested and interned with their families. Arrests were almost always accompanied by plundering.

Evacuations were carried out in the cities, with entire blocks of houses indiscriminately evacuated, and the occupants loaded on trucks and brought to concentration camps during the night. Here, too, plundering was a constant accompaniment. The accommodations and food in the camps were such that the troop's medical officer feared the outbreak of epidemics that would present a danger to the troops. As a result of my intervention, remedial action will be taken.

In several cities, operations were carried out against Jews that resulted in extreme excesses. On 30 October 1939, under the command of a higher SS leader, 3 SS trucks drove through Turok from which people on the street were indiscriminately hit over the head with cowhide and long whips. Ethnic Germans were among the victims. Finally a group of Jews were herded into the synagogue and were forced to sing and crawl through the benches, all the while being constantly hit by SS men with whips. They were then forced to drop their pants and were hit on the naked buttocks. One Jew, who out of fear had defecated in his pants, was forced to smear the excrement into the face of other Jews.

In Lodz it was confidentially reported that the *SS-Oberführer* [SS Colonel] Mehlhorn had given the following orders:

1.) Effective 9 November, Poles and Jews will no longer be paid unemployment compensation; only forced labor will be recompensed. (This measure has already been confirmed.)
2.) Jews and Poles will as of 9 November be excluded from the allocation of food and coal rations.
3.) Unrest and incidents should be provoked to make implementation of the national political policy easier.
4.) The fire brigade is to be reinforced at once so that, in the event of accidental fires in Jewish or Polish residential quarters and factories, an undesirable spreading to other properties can be prevented. . . .

signed **Petzel**
General of Artillery

for the certification of the copy
[signature, illegible]

Oberstleutnant [Lieutenant Colonel]

— Reproduced from the National Archives Record Administration, National Archives Collection of World War II War Crimes, Record Group 238, Office of the U.S. Chief of Counsel for War Crimes, Document D-419. Translated from the German by Gerald Schwab and Linda Bixby.

THE ECONOMIC CONSEQUENCES OF THE KILLING

Many of the Jews killed in the massacres were workers whose skills had been of increasing importance to the Germans as the war continued. Logistical support for the German armies in the Soviet Union was provided by many small industries and factories in the conquered territories, including the armaments industry. The killing of skilled workers adversely affected the output of these small plants and exacerbated tensions among the numerous German administrative units attempting to exploit the newly conquered East. In this document, the German army's armament inspector in Ukraine describes such circumstances to the chief of the Economic Armaments Office at the WEHRMACHT *High Command.*

This document, whose second page is reproduced in facsimile, was introduced as evidence at the INTERNATIONAL MILITARY TRIBUNAL.

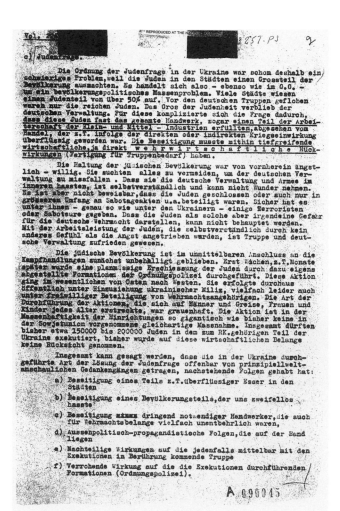

c) Jewish Question.

The regulation of the Jewish question in Ukraine was already a difficult problem because the Jews in the cities constituted a large portion of the population. This means that, as in the General Government [occupied Poland], we are dealing with a great problem of population politics. Many cities had a Jewish population of over 50%. Only the rich Jews had fled from the German troops. The bulk of Jewry remained under German administration. The latter became complicated by the problem <u>that these Jews represent nearly all trade</u> and even <u>a section of manpower that fills small and middle industries</u>, not including the trade that at this time had become superfluous as a direct or indirect result of the war. <u>The liquidation, therefore, had far reaching economic and even direct consequences for the **armaments industry**</u> (production for supplying the troops).

The attitude of the Jewish population from the start was anxious—willing. They tried to avoid everything that might displease the German administration. That they inwardly hated the German administration and army is understandable and cannot be surprising. However, it is not evident that the Jews as a whole or even in large part had participated in sabotage or other similar acts. Certainly there were some terrorists or saboteurs among them—just as among the Ukrainians. But it cannot be said that the Jews as such represented a danger to the German armed forces. The output produced by Jews, who, of course, were prompted by nothing but the feeling of fear, was satisfactory to the troops and the German administration.

At first the Jewish population remained unmolested during the immediate military operation of annexation. Just weeks or in some cases months later, a planned shooting of Jews was carried out by assigned formations of the Order Police. This operation went essentially from the east to the west. It occurred completely in the open with the use of Ukrainian militia, and often unfortunately also with the voluntary participation of members of the armed forces. The manner of implementing these operations, which included men, the elderly, women, and children of all ages, was horrible. The great numbers executed make these operations more gigantic than any other operation undertaken thus far in the Soviet Union. Altogether about 150,000 to 200,000 Jews may have been executed in the part of Ukraine belonging to the Reich Commissariat Ukraine. No consideration was given to economic interests.

Altogether it can be said that the type of solution to the Jewish question applied in Ukraine, openly and principally based on ideological theories, has had the following effect:

    a) Liquidation of a section of the partly superfluous eaters in the cities.

    b) Liquidation of a portion of the population that undoubtedly hates us.

    c) Liquidation of badly needed tradesmen, who were

A Polish priest, Father Piotr Sosnowski from the village of Tuchola, stands before a firing squad in the notorious forest near Piasnica Wielka, Poland; late 1939. More than 12,000 people were shot here between November 1939 and April 1944; those who survived the shooting were beaten to death with rifle butts. (Main Commission for the Investigation of Nazi War Crimes, Warsaw, Poland)

also often indispensable for the armed forces.

d) Foreign political-propaganda consequences, which are obvious.

e) Adverse effects on the troops that come in contact with the executions.

f) Brutalizing effect on the formations (Order Police) that carry out the executions.

A skimming off of the agricultural surplus from Ukraine for the purpose of feeding the Reich is, therefore, only conceivable if the Ukrainian domestic trade is suppressed to a minimum. The attempt will be made to achieve this:

1. by eliminating the superfluous eaters (Jews, the population of Ukraine's major cities that, like Kiev, overall obtain no food rations);

2. by an extreme reduction of the rations allocated to the Ukrainians in the remaining cities;

3. by reducing the consumption by the farming population.

One must be clear that in Ukraine, only the Ukrainians can produce economic values by labor. If we shoot the Jews, let the prisoners of war perish, condemn the urban population in large part to death by starvation, and also lose a part of the farming population in the coming year through starvation, the question remains unanswered: **Who then is supposed to produce economic values here?** In view of the manpower shortage in the German Reich, there is no doubt that the necessary number of **Germans** will not be available either now or in the near future. If the Ukrainian is supposed to work, then he must be kept in physical condition, not because of sentiment but instead because of very unemotional economic considerations. An essential part of this is the creation of an orderly relationship between money, price of goods, and wages.

(Summary)

Population

The attitude of the Ukrainian population is still obliging in spite of the deterioration of its economic situation over the last months.

The ethnic Germans in Ukraine do not constitute an element on which the administration and the economy of the country can lean.

A considerable proportion of the Jews, who represented more than half of the population in the cities of the Reich Commissariat Ukraine, has been executed. Therefore, the majority of tradesmen has been eliminated; this also hurts the interests of the armed forces (supplies for troops, lodging).

Lodging, food, clothing, and health of the prisoners of war is bad; mortality is very high. The loss of tens of thousands, even hundreds of thousands, during this winter is to be expected. Among them is manpower that could have been utilized successfully for the Ukrainian economy, also skilled specialists and tradesmen.

— *Reproduced from the National Archives and Records Administration, National Archives Collection of World War II War Crimes Records, Record Group 238, Office of the U.S. Chief of Counsel for War Crimes, Document 3257-PS, pp. 2–3. Translated from the German by Wendy Lower.*

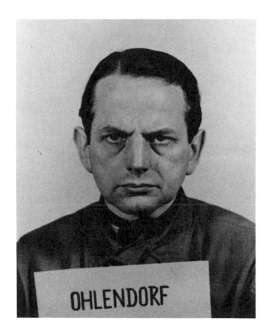

A "mug shot" of Otto Ohlendorf, commander of
EINSATZGRUPPE D and one of the defendants at the
EINSATZGRUPPEN TRIAL. (NARA)

A PERPETRATOR'S TESTIMONY

One of the commanders of the four EINSATZGRUPPEN *active in the Soviet Union was Otto Ohlendorf, a lawyer who had joined the* NAZI PARTY *and* SS *in the mid-1920s. Joining the* SD *in 1936, he was on the staff of the* CENTRAL OFFICE FOR REICH SECURITY *by 1939, and became the commander of* Einsatzgruppen D *in June 1941. His* Einsatzgruppe *swept through the southern Ukraine to the Crimea and the northern Caucasus, killing Jews,* GYPSIES, *and Communist functionaries. The largest single massacre of Jews took place in his operational area, in Odessa (Ukraine), during October 1941, when up to 75,000 Jews and Communists were killed by troops of Germany's ally, Romania, with the help of SS troops under Ohlendorf's command.*

After the war, Ohlendorf testified quite freely to the murders committed by his Einsatzgruppe *at the* INTERNATIONAL MILITARY TRIBUNAL, *as is shown by his testimony below. A year later he was one of the defendants at the* EINSATZGRUPPEN TRIAL, *where he was convicted and sentenced to death. Ohlendorf was hanged for his crimes in 1951.*

COL. AMEN: Do you know how many persons were liquidated by Einsatz Group [*sic*] D under your direction?

OHLENDORF: In the year between June 1941 to June 1942 the Einsatzkommandos reported 90,000 people liquidated.

COL. AMEN: Did that include men, women, and children?

OHLENDORF: Yes.

COL. AMEN: On what do you base those figures?

OHLENDORF: On reports sent by the Einsatzkommandos to the Einsatzgruppen.

COL. AMEN: Were those reports submitted to you?

OHLENDORF: Yes.

COL. AMEN: And you saw them and read them?

OHLENDORF: I beg your pardon?

COL. AMEN: And you saw and read those reports, personally?

OHLENDORF: Yes.

COL. AMEN: And it is on those reports that you base the figures you have given the Tribunal?

OHLENDORF: Yes.

COL. AMEN: Do you know how those figures compare with the number of persons liquidated by other Einsatz groups?

OHLENDORF: The figures which I saw of other Einsatzgruppen are considerably larger.

COL. AMEN: That was due to what factor?

OHLENDORF: I believe that to a large extent the figures submitted by the other Einsatzgruppen were exaggerated.

COL. AMEN: Did you see reports of liquidations from the other Einsatz groups from time to time?

OHLENDORF: Yes.

COL. AMEN: And those reports showed liquidations exceeding those of Group D; is that correct?

OHLENDORF: Yes.

COL. AMEN: Did you personally supervise mass executions of these individuals?

OHLENDORF: I was present a two mass executions for purposes of inspection.

COL. AMEN: Will you explain to the Tribunal in detail how an individual mass execution was carried out?

OHLENDORF: A local Einsatzkommando attempted to collect all the Jews in its area by registering them. This registration was performed by the Jews themselves.

COL. AMEN: On what pretext, if any, were they rounded up?

OHLENDORF: On the pretext that they were to be resettled.

COL. AMEN: Will you continue?

OHLENDORF: After the registration the Jews were collected at one place; and from there they were later transported to the place of execution, which was, as a rule, an antitank ditch or a natural excavation. The executions were carried out in a military manner, by firing squads under command.

COL. AMEN: In what way were they transported to the place of execution?

OHLENDORF: They were transported to the place of execution in trucks, always only as many as could be executed immediately. In this way it was attempted to keep the span of time from the moment in which the victims knew what was about to happen to them until the time of their actual execution as short as possible.

COL. AMEN: Was that your idea?

OHLENDORF: Yes.

COL. AMEN: And after they were shot what was done with the bodies?

OHLENDORF: The bodies were buried in the antitank ditch or excavation.

COL. AMEN: What determination, if any, was made as to whether the persons were actually dead?

OHLENDORF: The unit leaders or the firing-squad commanders had orders to see to this and, if need be, finish them off themselves.

COL. AMEN: And who would do that?

OHLENDORF: Either the unit leader himself or somebody designated by him.

COL. AMEN: In what positions were the victims shot?

OHLENDORF: Standing or kneeling.

COL. AMEN: What was done with the personal property and clothing of the persons executed?

OHLENDORF: All valuables were confiscated at the time of the registration or the rounding up and handed over to the Finance Ministry, either through the RSHA [CENTRAL OFFICE FOR REICH SECURITY] or directly. At first the clothing was given to the population, but in the winter of 1941–1942 it was collected and disposed of by the NSV [NATIONAL SOCIALIST PEOPLE'S WELFARE SOCIETY].

COL. AMEN: All their personal property was registered at the time?

OHLENDORF: No, not all of it, only valuables were registered.

COL. AMEN: What happened to the garments which the victims were wearing when they went to the place of execution?

OHLENDORF: They were obliged to take off their outer garments immediately before the execution.

COL. AMEN: All of them?

OHLENDORF: The outer garments, yes.

COL. AMEN: How about the rest of the garments they were wearing?

OHLENDORF: The other garments remained on the bodies.

COL. AMEN: Was that true of not only your group but of the other Einsatz groups?

OHLENDORF: That was the order in my Einsatzgruppe. I don't know how it was done in other Einsatzgruppen.

COL. AMEN: In what way did they handle it?

OHLENDORF: Some of the unit leaders did not carry out the liquidation in the military manner, but killed the victims singly by shooting them in the back of the neck.

COL. AMEN: And you objected to that procedure?

OHLENDORF: I was against that procedure, yes.

COL. AMEN: For what reason?

OHLENDORF: Because both for the victims and for those who carried out the executions, it was, psychologically, an immense burden to bear.

COL. AMEN: Now, what was done with the property collected by the Einsatzkommandos from these victims?

OHLENDORF: All valuables were sent to Berlin, to the RSHA or to the Reich Ministry of Finance. The articles which could be used in the operational area, were disposed of there.

COL. AMEN: For example, what happened to gold and silver taken from the victims?

OHLENDORF: That was, as I have just said, turned over to Berlin, to the Reich Ministry of Finance.

During a roundup in Poland, German police guard prisoners who are forced to kneel against a wall; 1941. (USHMM)

COL. AMEN: How do you know that?

OHLENDORF: I can remember that it was actually handled in that way from Simferopol.

COL. AMEN: How about watches, for example, taken from the victims?

OHLENDORF: At the request of the Army, watches were made available to the forces at the front.

COL. AMEN: Were all victims, including the men, women, and children, executed in the same manner?

OHLENDORF: Until the spring of 1942, yes. Then an order came from Himmler that in the future women and children were to be killed only in gas vans.

COL. AMEN: How had the women and children been killed previously?

OHLENDORF: In the same way as the men—by shooting.

COL. AMEN: What, if anything, was done about burying the victims after they had been executed?

OHLENDORF: The Kommandos filled the graves to efface the signs of the execution, and then labor units of the population leveled them.

COL. AMEN: Referring to the gas vans which you said you received in the spring of 1942, what order did you receive with respect to the use of these vans?

OHLENDORF: These gas vans were in future to be used for the killing of women and children.

COL. AMEN: Will you explain to the Tribunal the construction of these vans and their appearance?

OHLENDORF: The actual purpose of these vans could not be seen from the outside. They looked like closed

trucks, and were so constructed that at the start of the motor, gas was conducted into the van causing death in 10 to 15 minutes.

COL. AMEN: Explain in detail just how one of these vans was used for an execution.

OHLENDORF: The vans were loaded with the victims and driven to the place of burial, which was usually the same as that used for the mass executions. The time needed for transportation was sufficient to insure the death of the victims.

COL. AMEN: How were the victims induced to enter the vans?

OHLENDORF: They were told that they were to be transported to another locality.

COL. AMEN: How was the gas turned on?

OHLENDORF: I am not familiar with the technical details.

COL. AMEN: How long did it take to kill the victims ordinarily?

OHLENDORF: About 10 to 15 minutes; the victims were not conscious of what was happening to them.

COL. AMEN: How many persons could be killed simultaneously in one such van?

OHLENDORF: About 15 to 25 persons. The vans varied in size. . . .

COL. AMEN: Did you receive reports from those who were working on the vans?

OHLENDORF: I received the report that the Einsatzkommandos did not willingly use the vans.

COL. AMEN: Why not?

OHLENDORF: Because the burial of the victims was a great ordeal for the members of the Einsatzkommandos.

— *Reprinted from* Trial of the Major War Criminals before the International Military Tribunal, *42 vols. (Nuremberg, 1947),* *4: 319–23.*

German soldiers in the act of killing a prisoner in the Soviet Union. (NARA)

AN "ANTI-PARTISAN" OPERATION

Massacres of innocent civilians and prisoners of war occurred throughout the territory controlled by the Germans. Often in the guise of "anti-PARTISAN" operations ostensibly intended to destroy the resistance or partisans, German army and SS units would round up and kill Jews, GYPSIES, and civilians found in areas where the RESISTANCE was active. Yugoslavia was the scene of many brutal massacres by the Germans and their allies, the Croatian USTACHI. The level of resistance there was so high that the country was considered a war zone by the German military. The Prince Eugen Division mentioned below was a WAFFEN-SS unit trained for combat but more than willing to partake in the slaughter of innocent civilians.

A young Soviet PARTISAN is hanged with two other Belorussian resistance fighters in Minsk as a German officer tightens a noose around the neck of one of victims; October 26, 1941.
(Central State Archives for Film and Photography, Minsk, Belarus)

The statement reprinted below is the testimony of Leander Holzter, an ETHNIC GERMAN and former SS member, taken October 27, 1945, by a Yugoslav war crimes commission and introduced as evidence during the INTERNATIONAL MILITARY TRIBUNAL.

In August 1943, by the order of battalion leader *SS-Obersturmbannführer* [SS Lieutenant Colonel] Wagner, the 23d Company under the command of company leader *SS-Untersturmführer* [SS 2nd Lieutenant] Schuh set fire to a village on the Jablanica—Prozor railway line, during which the inhabitants of the village were shot. In August 1943, on the orders of the same person, the 23d Company set fire to a village on the Niksic—Avtovac railway line, and the inhabitants of the village were shot. The order for the shootings came from Jablanica, and the villages were already burned to the ground by morning. The shootings in Pancevo were carried out by the police agent Gross, a former master dyer, and Brunn, a former master miller from the SS Division Prinz Eugen, from Pancevo. The latter received a reward of 20,000 dinars for the hangings at the cemetery. . . .

— *Reproduced from the National Archives Records Administration, National Archives Collection of World War II War Crimes, Record Group 238, Office of the U.S. Chief of Counsel for War Crimes, Document GB-566. Translated from the German by Wendy Lower.*

A PRECEDENT

Not all shootings and massacres took place in eastern Europe. In March 1944, fifteen American soldiers, captured in northern Italy while on a sabotage mission for the OFFICE OF STRATEGIC SERVICES, were executed by the German army. The DOESTLER TRIAL was convened to try Anton Doestler, the German army general who had ordered the killings. Doestler maintained that he had only followed his superior's orders (Adolf HITLER'S) in carrying out the infamous "Commando Order," which allowed for the execution of any ALLIED soldiers captured on intelligence or sabotage missions in German-occupied territory. Clearly in violation of the HAGUE CONVENTION, which forbade the execution of soldiers captured in uniform, Doestler's defense was rejected. This precedent was used only one month later when a similar defense arose at the INTERNATIONAL MILITARY TRIBUNAL.

NEW YORK: SATURDAY, OCTOBER 13, 1945.

Dostler Sentenced to Die For Shooting of OSS Men

German General's Counsel Plans Appeal— Observers See Precedent Ruling Out Plea Based on Obedience to Superiors

By VIRGINIA LEE WARREN
By Wireless to THE NEW YORK TIMES.

ROME, Oct. 12 — Gen. Anton Dostler, the first officer of the German General Staff to be tried before an American military commission on a wartime charge, was today sentenced to death by a firing squad.

Dostler, who has been in the German Army since he was 18 years old, stood stiffly in the scarlet-trimmed uniform of a full general of the Wehrmacht, his hands lightly clenched, as Maj. Gen. Lawrence C. Jaynes announced the verdict.

[General Jaynes told the defendant that at least three-fifths of the court had concurred in his guilt and voted the death sentence by secret ballot, The Associated Press said.]

The full report of the presiding officer's pronouncement reached the condemned man with agonizing slowness since, after every few words, a GI interpreter standing beside him had to translate each phrase into German.

Dostler, who was convicted of ordering the shooting of fifteen American soldiers without trial when they were captured while on a mission for the Office of Strategic Services in March, 1944, betrayed no emotion when General Jaynes' inflection dropped as he came to the end and the interpreter, himself an OSS man, translated what most of the spectators had already heard—"to be shot to death by musketry."

The court room, in the great dank Palace of Justice, was gaudily illuminated by photographers' spotlights and packed with several hundred Italian as well as Allied soldiers and military observers, Red Cross workers and a number of American civilians attached to various agencies here.

But there was no demonstration of any kind. The one person who seemed perhaps most affected was the interpreter, Corp. Albert

Continued on Page 6, Column 2

DEATH IS VERDICT IN DOSTLER TRIAL

Continued From Page 1

Hirschman of Berkeley, Calif., who turned pale as he had to utter the death sentence and left the scene afterward without a word.

Trial Sets Precedent

The record of the four-day trial in which Dostler attempted to prove that he ordered the summary shooting of the Americans because he was at the mercy of his superiors, including Adolf Hitler, will be turned over to Gen. Joseph T. McNarney on appeal of his defense counsel. His review is expected to take at least two weeks, which means that the execution is not likely to take place for nearly a month.

The case is considered important largely because the verdict, no matter which way it went, was bound to set some sort of precedent for the subsequent mass of war crime trials.

Most observers felt that if Dostler were sent before a firing squad it would mean that pressure from Hitler would not be acceptable in future courts as an excuse for flouting the international laws of warfare and that to attribute one's acts to one's superiors would not absolve the actual perpetrator of responsibility for such acts.

To put it simply, if every German now held by the Allies could get off easy by blaming Hitler there would be no point in having war crime trials.

On the other hand, some observers point out that Dostler's conviction sets a precedent whereby such persons, as the chiefs of execution squads, and anyone else who had anything to do with carrying out an order handed down by Hitler or other high officers, are involved and should be treated accordingly.

Defense Handicapped

In the trial, which ended with the pronouncement of the death sentence at 9 o'clock this morning, the defense was admittedly hampered by the failure of the American military authorities to find Dostler's chief of staff, the commanding officer of the Fortress Brigade which was entrusted with the actual execution of the Americans, and several other high ranking members of the Wehrmacht. These had been sought at Dostler's express request.

As the trial progressed it soon became apparent that junior German officers were not loath to testify against their former superiors.

Immediately after sentence was pronounced Dostler, with his counsel, Col. Claudius O. Wolfe of San Antonio, Tex., and Maj. Cecil K. Emery of Des Moines, Iowa, left the court room by a small side door through which the prisoner had always entered.

After twenty minutes' consultation Dostler, wearing a long gray coat, reappeared and as he was being escorted toward the exit he noticed in the almost empty court room Lieut. Wiliam T. Andress Jr. of Dallas, Tex., who helped prosecute the case, Dostler asked permission to speak to him. He wanted to know whether between now and the time of his execution he would continue to be considered a prisoner of war or be treated as a "criminal."

The answer was that upon his return to the detention camp at Aversa his status would technically change but that his surroundings would remain the same.

— *Reproduced from* The New York Times, *October 13, 1945.*
Copyright © 1945 by the New York Times Company.
Reprinted by permission.

German General Anton Doestler, just before he was executed; December 1, 1945. He was sentenced to death for ordering the execution of fifteen American soldiers. (NARA)

A SOVIET TRIAL

Many executions of Jews and Gypsies *took place in the Soviet Union. The Soviets tried the perpetrators both during the war (in proceedings such as the* Krasnodar Trial*) and after. The postwar trials involved Soviet citizens who had actively participated in such atrocities. The* Mere Trial*, described here, was one such trial, noteworthy because one of the defendants, Ain-Ervin Mere, then living in Great Britain, was not extradited by the British government. As this article about the trial from* The New York Times *reports, the wave of extermination that swept the former Soviet Union from 1941 to 1944 could not have been carried out without the willing participation of local accomplices.*

ESTONIAN ADMITS DEATH CAMP ROLE

Tells Soviet Court He Shot 'Once' During Murder of 125,000 by Nazis

TALLINN, U.S.S.R., March 6 (AP)—A Soviet court put on trial today three Estonians accused in the murder of 125,000 East Europeans, most of them Jews, in Nazi death camps during World War II. One of the defendants calmly related to the court how the extermination had been carried out by shooting.

Ralf Gerrets and Jan Vijk pleaded guilty at the start of the trial. A third man, Ain Erwin Mere, escaped to Britain after the war and the British have refused to grant a Soviet extradition request. He is being tried in absentia.

The Soviet Government, which has controlled Estonia since World War II, invited foreign correspondents from Moscow to attend the trial in this capital of the Estonian Republic.

Gerrets, standing ramrod straight in a gray suit and blue shirt, testified that he was a prison employe under the Germans after they conquered Estonia in 1941.

He worked at the Jagala camp near here. He said trains arrived there regularly from Czechoslovakia with prisoners. At a typical execution, he testified, a busload of forty prisoners would be driven from the camp to a ten-foot trench dug near by and a guard would order them to undress.

Gerrets said groups of six to ten would be marched into the trench, ordered to lie down side by side and then shot to death. The victims who followed, he said, would be ordered to lie down on the bodies of the dead to be shot in turn.

He had the job of taking their valuables, watches and jewelry, all to be turned over to a benefit fund of the security police.

Admits Shooting Once

The court repeatedly sought to connect Gerrets with the actual shootings, but he said that only once did he fire his pistol at men and women in a pit.

He said he was standing near the pit watching a shooting when he heard a woman's voice coming from deep down among the pile of bodies.

"I thought how horrible it would be down there among all that blood, so I drew my pistol and fired it in the direction of the voice coming up through the pile of bodies," he said. "I had such a small pistol that I believe it did not reach her. She went right on talking."

The trial is expected to continue until the end of the week.

— *Reprinted from* The New York Times, *March 7, 1961.*
Courtesy Associated Press.

GYPSY EXECUTIONS IN ESTONIA

At the MERE TRIAL, defendant Ralf Gerrets testified about the killing of a group of GYPSIES near Tallin, Estonia, in March 1943. They were bused from Jägala CONCENTRATION CAMP near Tallinn to the execution site of Kalevi-Liiva, where hundreds of prisoners from the camp had already been killed. Gerrets was a member of the Estonian Security Police, who worked in concert with the German SS, as did Jaan Viik, another defendant; Lieutenant Laak was the commandant of Jägala.

Prosecutor: By whom were they shot?

Gerrets: By Lieutenant Laak.

Prosecutor: All alone?

Gerrets: Yes, all alone.

The last to be slain was an invalid, an old woman who had no legs. The warders were drunk; they seized her and dragged her, like a sack, along the ground. It was only when she gave them her gold ring and some money that they lifted her up and threw her "gently" into the pit . . . . When Gerrets opened the door of the second car, it turned out that there were small children there.

Prosecutor: How old were they?

Gerrets: Something between three and five, not more. They were crying.

Prosecutor: What was done with them?

Gerrets: The warders came and took them away.

Prosecutor: Where?

Gerrets: To the pit. There were seven men, each of them carrying two children. Two children were left in the bus. I took them. I was about five or six metres [ca. 16–19 ft.] from the pit when the warder Purka ran to meet me and took the children from me. I myself did not get quite near to the pit.

Prosecutor: But you took the children out of the car?

Gerrets: Yes. A warder wanted to help me, but I said it was not necessary, I'd manage by myself.

Prosecutor: Who shot the children?

Gerrets: When I took a glance at the pit, I saw that Laak was standing on the right, Viik on the left, both with automatic guns in their hands.

When we had got back to the camp, we sat down to dinner and the commandant brought a bottle of vodka. Viik, too, came there, having already emptied his bottle. Laak praised him: "You were a brave man, Viik, to be the first to shoot!"

— *Reprinted from Raul Kruus,* People, Be Watchful, *(Tallinn, 1962), 35.*

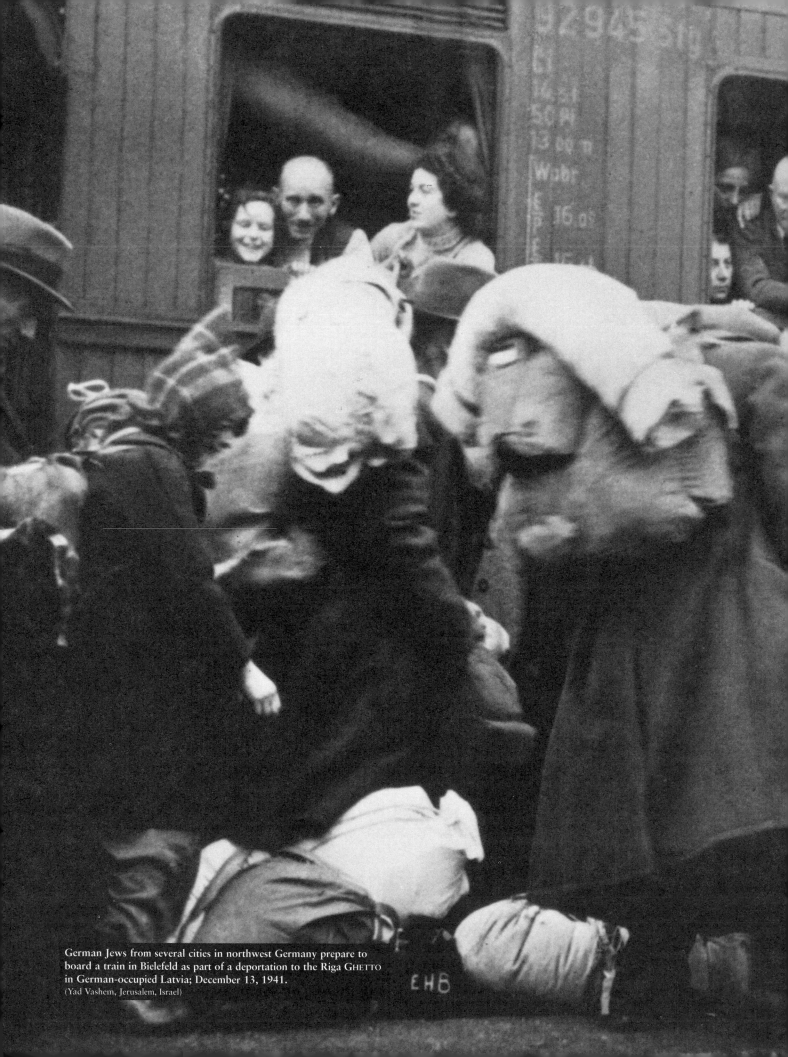

German Jews from several cities in northwest Germany prepare to
board a train in Bielefeld as part of a deportation to the Riga GHETTO
in German-occupied Latvia; December 13, 1941.
(Yad Vashem, Jerusalem, Israel)

DEPORTATIONS

The dislocation of much of Europe's population reached major proportions during World War II. This tragedy had its beginning with Adolf HITLER'S belief that the German nation could never regain the power or prestige lost after World War I without first becoming *judenrein,* or cleansed of Jews. Soon after their seizure of power in 1933, Hitler and the NAZI regime began measures to implement this concept. By the mid-1930s, Nazi organizations compelled German Jews to emigrate by terror, legislation, and discrimination. This policy was later changed to include forced DEPORTATIONS and extermination.

The first attempted plan for the systematic removal of Jews from Germany was geographically based. The conquest of Poland in 1939 provided the possibility of using former Polish territory as a dumping ground. The Germans designated the area around Lublin in eastern Poland as the site for a Jewish "reservation." The resulting Lublin Plan represented only a small part of the vaster scheme to restructure Europe along racial lines. Concurrent with the actions in Lublin, the Nazis also implemented similar plans for the deportation of thousands of Poles and GYPSIES.

The man responsible for the first deportations to the Lublin reservation was Adolf EICHMANN. As the head of the Jewish division of the CENTRAL OFFICE FOR REICH SECURITY, Eichmann directed deportations of several thousand Jews and Gypsies from Vienna and other German-controlled cities to Nisko, a town south of Lublin. Despite Eichmann's hopes for the Lublin Plan and Nisko settlement, deportations were abruptly halted soon after they had begun. The area was not suited to receive thousands of deportees. Neither facilities nor housing were readily available. Elsewhere, the Germans were having difficulty expelling Poles in order to provide housing for arriving ETHNIC GERMAN re-settlers. Consequently, Poles were also being deported into the Lublin area. The resulting confusion forced the premature end to Eichmann's operation and forced the Nazis to seek alternative methods of "cleansing" Germany of "undesirables."

Meanwhile, deportations were occurring throughout the THIRD REICH. More than 70,000 French residents of Alsace-Lorraine, including French Jews, Gypsies, the handicapped, and Blacks, were transported to VICHY-controlled France. More than 380,000 Poles were forced to evacuate their homes throughout Poland and deported into the GENERAL GOVERNMENT. Gypsies were regularly rounded up and herded into guarded camps. In September 1941, Hitler ordered the removal of all remaining Jews from Germany, thus achieving his ideal *judenrein* nation. Although deportations of German Jews began in November 1941, it was not until the following summer, when the newly constructed KILLING CENTERS started operations, that large-scale deportations began in earnest throughout Europe.

As massive transfers of people became common, the administrative divisions within the Central Office for Reich Security became more specialized. During this period, Eichmann was reassigned to head DEPARTMENT IVb4 which combined two areas of responsibility: evacuations and Jews. In October 1941, Eichmann ordered the transportation of 50,000 German Jews to various eastern GHETTOS. Many were sent to occupied areas of the Soviet Union and were shot immediately upon arrival; others were deported to ghettos in Poland to replace former inhabitants who had been deported to the first killing center at CHELMNO.

Once the major killing centers had opened in late spring 1942, deportations increased in volume and frequency. Coordinated by Eichmann's office, transports to the killing centers required complicated negotiations with the railroads, the SS, the German military, foreign governments, and camp administrators. Many individuals throughout German-controlled territory—military personnel, public servants, and civilians—were involved with these plans. By working with Department IVb4 branch offices in occupied countries,

Clothing and other possessions litter the area behind Jewish women and a child who await deportation from the Soviet Union; 1942.
(Hessisches Staatsarchiv Darmstadt, Germany)

Eichmann ensured that roundups proceeded smoothly and transport trains departed on time. In this manner, Eichmann also coordinated the arrival of trains at the killing centers.

Although German and some western European Jews were deported in third-class passenger coaches during 1941 and 1942, the deportees were usually transported as cargo in freight cars. As many as 80 to 100 people were locked into each unheated boxcar. This meant that a typical transport train carried between 2,000 and 5,000 people. The space aboard the trains became so cramped that many victims suffocated or were trampled to death long before their arrival at the killing centers. Deportees were not provided with food, water, or sanitation facilities during the entire length of their two- to seven-day journey. Because of this, starvation and dehydration also claimed countless lives. As a result, the SS expected as many as one-quarter to one-third of the passengers on each train to die during the journey before arrival.

As the war drew to a close the killing centers ceased operations, and both CONCENTRATION CAMPS and killing centers began to be liberated by the advancing ALLIES. The Germans attempted to move prisoners to Germany using FORCED EVACUATIONS by train and on foot. During such forced marches, many prisoners too weak to maintain the pace were shot and killed. Others died of illness, exposure, and exhaustion as they walked many miles each day for several weeks. Without food or shelter, these victims were simply left along the roads. While precise figures are unknown, historians estimate that up to 250,000 victims died in these DEATH MARCHES during the last year of the war alone.

After the war, the deportation of unwilling people was classified both as a WAR CRIME and a CRIME AGAINST HUMANITY in the INTERNATIONAL MILITARY TRIBUNAL. In later trials, such as in the RuSHA TRIAL, deportations were listed solely as crimes against humanity. These crimes, however, paled in comparison to the planned murder of millions, of which the deportations were often a component. Courts rarely charged those responsible only for the deportations. This changed after the EICHMANN TRIAL in 1961, in which Adolf EICHMANN was tried by an Israeli court for the deportation of Jews, Poles, and Gypsies, found guilty, and later hanged. Eichmann's well-publicized trial initiated the investigation of others who had participated in deportations. As a result, both Wilhelm Harster, Eichmann's representative in the Netherlands, and Kurt Asche, a Department IVb4 employee in Belgium, were tried for their roles in deportation actions in the HARSTER TRIAL of 1967 and the ASCHE TRIAL in 1980.

A series of photographs found in the offices of the Gestapo in Würzburg after the conquest of Germany in 1945. The captions read *(this page)* "... our people had to work hard once again during the loading of their baggage! ... If I must, if I must, leave this little town. ..." (lyrics of a traditional, German folk song used to satirize the victims) and *(opposite page)* "... Exodus of the Children of Israel from beautiful Würzburg!" (NARA)

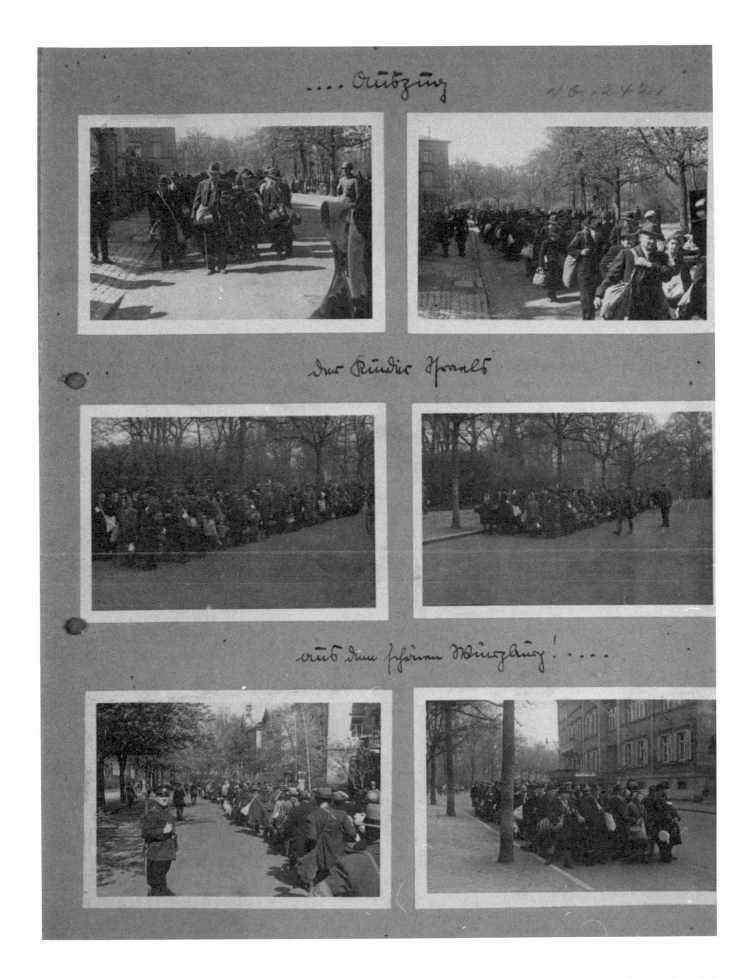

LETHAL TIMETABLES

Although most victims of the "FINAL SOLUTION" were destined to perish in the GAS CHAMBERS, the murders often began on their journey to the KILLING CENTERS. Jews and other Nazi victims were transported to Nazi death camps in so-called Sonderzüge or special transport trains. While German Jews as a rule arrived at Auschwitz and other killing centers in normal third-class passenger wagons, most non-German Jews were not as fortunate. Most passengers of the transport trains were crowded into freight cars, often one hundred to a car. In summer, the cars were intolerably hot; in winter, unbearably cold. Many deportees, especially the elderly, the young, the ill, and the infirm perished en route before the trains reached their final destinations.

The train schedules reproduced below list the departure and arrival times for special transport trains destined for the TREBLINKA killing center, where more than 5,000 victims arrived daily. These timetables were found after the war and were used by the Polish Main Commission for the Investigation of Nazi Crimes as evidence in several WAR CRIMES trials. The schedule for August 25, 1942, is reproduced in facsimile.

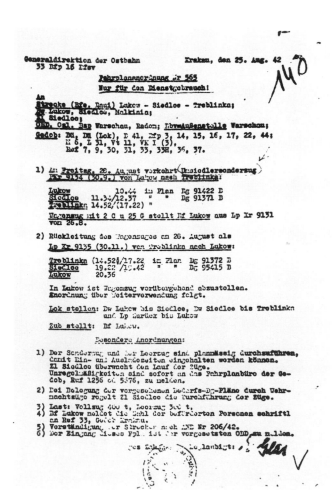

General Headquarters   Cracow, 25 August '42
Eastern Railway

33 Bfp 16 Bfsv

Instructions for Timetable No.565
For official use only! . . .

1) On <u>Friday, 28 August</u> Resettlement Special Train <u>PKr 9134 (30.9.)</u> runs from Lukow to Treblinka:

Lukow	10.44	according to timetable	Dg91422 D
Siedlce	11.34/12.37	" "	Dg91371 D
Treblinka	14.52/(17.22)	" "	

[. . .]

2) Return of the freight train on August 28 as <u>Lp Kr 9135 (30.11) from Treblinka to Lukow</u>:

Treblinka	14.52/17.22	according to timetable	Dg91372 B
Siedlce	19.22/19.42	" "	Dg 95415 B
Lukow	20.36		

[. . .]

In Lukow the freight train is to be shunted temporarily. Instructions about further use are to follow.

Special Instructions:

1) The special train and the empty train are to be run through according to schedule so that loading and unloading times can be observed. Zl Siedlce supervises the running of the trains. Irregularities are to be immediately reported to the scheduling office of the General Headquarters, Eastern Railway, tel. 1756 or 5676.

2) In case the designated times are required by army trains, Zl Siedlce coordinates the running of the trains.

3) Cargo: full train 400 tons, empty train 300 tons.

4) Train station Lukow reports in writing the number of transported persons to dept. 33, General Headquarters, Eastern Railway, Cracow.

5) Notification about lines according to ANB No. 206/42.

6) The receipt of this timetable is to be reported to the Eastern Railway Headquarters.

    signed Zahl [illegible]   certified [signature] Glas

      [stamp]
General Director of the Eastern Railway

General Headquarters Eastern Railway
Cracow, 3 August 1942
33 Bfp 15 Bfsv

Instructions for Timetable No. 548

After 6 August 1942, until further notice, another special train with resettlers from Warsaw Danz station to Treblinka and the return of the empty train will run as follows: . . .

Warsaw Danz station—Malkinia—Treblinka

Warsaw Danz station		dep. 12:25	by timetable Dg 913—
Warsaw Marki	arr. 12:42	12:59	" "
Tluszcz		14:00	12:27	" "
Malkinia		15:54	16:13	by timetable Dg91368
Treblinka	arr. 16:20		

[. . .]

Treblinka—Malkinia—Warsaw Danz station

Treblinka		dep. 19:00	by special timetable
Malkinia	arr. 19:07	19:32	by timetable Dg91342
Tluscz		20:55	21:38	" "
Warsaw Marki		22:35	23:02	" "
Warsaw Danz station arr. 23:19			

[. . .]

— Reprinted from the Archives, Research Institute, United States Holocaust Memorial Museum, Records Relating to Nazi Genocide in Poland from the Main Commission for the Investigation of Crimes against the Polish Nation—Institute of National Memory, Record Group 15.006.01. Doc. 17. Translated from the German by Wendy Lower.

GYPSIES

Soon after Germany conquered Poland in September 1939, Adolf EICHMANN, the SS officer in charge of Jewish affairs for the SD, began implementing plans for the creation of a Jewish reservation. Located near the Polish town of Nisko, a large swampy region in the Lublin district was selected to become the center of a new camp or GHETTO containing "racially undesirable" elements. Hoping eventually to expel all Jews, GYPSIES, and Slavs from the THIRD REICH into this territory between the German and Russian borders, Eichmann wanted the initial DEPORTATION to Nisko to serve as a model for all future deportations. In the end the Nisko plan was aborted, in part because insufficient preparations had been made to settle arriving Jewish deportees.

The first transport to Nisko included trains from three separate German-controlled areas: Vienna, Austria; the towns of Kattowice in annexed Poland; and Mährisch Ostrau (Ostrava, Czech Republic). Because the deportations came from several areas, complex negotiations took place between Hans Günther (an SS captain in charge of the CENTRAL OFFICE FOR REICH SECURITY, [RSHA], office for Jewish Affairs in Prague), Rolf Günther (Eichmann's deputy), Arthur Nebe (chief of the criminal police in the RSHA and the transport organizer in Vienna), and Josef Wagner (the GAULEITER of Silesia). Wagner, an ardent Roman Catholic and also Gauleiter of Westphalia, was relieved of his posts in 1941 and expelled from the NAZI PARTY in 1942. Arrested following the attempt on Adolf HITLER'S life in July 1944, he was later executed.

The following two cables, the second reproduced in facsimile, detail the logistical arrangements for the first Nisko transport.

Secret State Police [Gestapo]—State Police Agency, Berlin Reports Transmission

Received	Place for Incoming Stamp	Forwarded
Day Month Year Time 16 October 1939 8:10 P.M. to through [handwritten, illegible]		Day Month Year Time to through
Message Nr/ [handwritten] 7180	VERY URGENT TO BE DELIVERED EVEN AT NIGHT	
	Telegram-Radio Message-Teletype Telephone Message	

GYPSY women tend their children at an assembly point following their expulsion from Germany's western border; ca. August 1938.
(Bundesarchiv Koblenz, Germany)

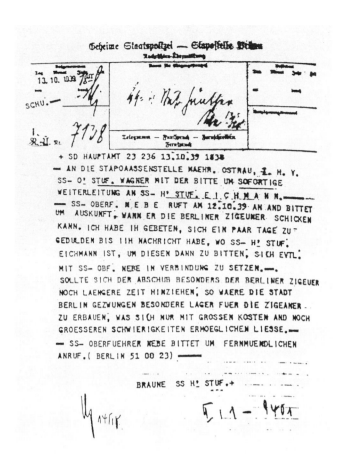

GUENTER, VIENNA 4, PRINZ-EUGEN STREET 22, AND FOR THE AREAS OF MÄHRISCH OSTRAU AND KATTOWICE WITH *SS-H[auptsturmführer]* GUENTER IN THE SERVICE BUILDING OF THE STATE POLICE BRANCH OFFICE, SO THAT THOSE INDIVIDUALS DIRECTLY COMMISSIONED BY ME MAY HANDLE THE DETAILS FOR IMPLEMENTING THESE MEASURES.

Secret State Police [Gestapo]—State Police Agency, Berlin
Reports Transmission

Received				Place for Incoming Stamp	Forwarded			
Day	Month	Year	Time		Day	Month	Year	Time
13	October	1939	6:55 P.M.					
to SCHU.		through [hand-written, illegible]			to		through	
Message Nr/ [handwritten] 7138				[handwritten, illegible]				
				Telegram-Radio Message-Teletype Telephone Message				

TO THE STATE POLICE BRANCH OFFICE MÄHRISCH OSTRAU [Ostrava], ATTENTION *SS-O[bersturmführer* (1st Lieutenant)] WAGNER, WITH THE REQUEST THAT HE IMMEDIATELY TRANSMIT TO *SS-H[auptsturmführer]* EICHMANN.

SS-OBERFÜHRER [SS Colonel] NEBE TELEPHONED ON 12 OCTOBER 1939 AND ASKED FOR INFORMATION ABOUT WHEN HE CAN SEND THE BERLIN GYPSIES. I HAVE ASKED HIM TO HAVE PATIENCE FOR A FEW DAYS, UNTIL I HAVE NEWS CONCERNING WHERE *SS-H[auptsturmführer]* EICHMANN IS, IN ORDER TO ASK THE LATTER AT THAT TIME IF HE MAY PERHAPS PUT HIMSELF IN COMMUNICATION WITH *SS-O[berführer]* NEBE. IF THE DELAY CONCERNING THE BERLIN GYPSIES WILL BE DRAWN OUT FOR A LONGER PERIOD, THEN THE CITY OF BERLIN WOULD BE FORCED TO ERECT SPECIAL CAMPS FOR THE GYPSIES, WHICH WILL ONLY BE REALIZED WITH GREAT COST AND STILL GREATER COMPLICATIONS.

SS-OBERFÜHRER NEBE REQUESTS AN ANSWER BY TELEPHONE (BERLIN 51 00 23).

BRAUNE, *SS-H[auptsturmführer]*
[signature, illegible]

> — *Reprinted from Romani Rose, ed.,* Der nationalsozialistische Völkermord an den Sinti und Roma *(Heidelberg, 1995), 89–90. Recently published in English as* The Nazi Genocide of the Sinti and Roma. *Translated from the German by Patricia Heberer.*

FROM SECURITY OFFICE DANUBE REGION NO. 7743

TO THE STATE POLICE BRANCH OFFICE, MÄHRISCH OSTRAU [Ostrava] ATTENTION *SS-H[auptsturmführer* (SS Captain)] GUENTER, MÄHRISCH OSTRAU

IN REFERENCE TO THE EARLIER CABLE FROM CHIEF OF THE SECURITY POLICE, *SS-OBERFÜHRER* [SS Colonel] NEBE, IT IS REQUESTED TO TELEGRAPH TO *SS-OBERFÜHRER* NEBE AN ANSWER TO THE FOLLOWING TEXT:

CONCERNING THE DEPORTATION OF GYPSIES, IT IS REPORTED THAT ON FRIDAY, 20 OCTOBER 1939, THE FIRST TRANSPORT OF JEWS FROM VIENNA DEPARTS. THREE TO FOUR RAILWAY CARS FILLED WITH GYPSIES COULD BE ATTACHED TO THIS TRANSPORT.

CONTINUOUS TRANSPORTS NOW DEPART REGULARLY FOR THE TIME BEING FROM VIENNA FOR THE AREAS OF AUSTRIA, FROM MÄHRISCH OSTRAU FOR THE PROTECTORATE [formerly part of Czechoslovakia], AND KATTOWICE FOR THE FORMER POLISH TERRITORIES.

REGARDING FURTHER TRANSPORTS OF GYPSIES, I SUGGEST ON HIS END THAT THE TOP OFFICIAL OF THE CRIMINAL POLICE OFFICE VIENNA PUT HIMSELF IN CONTACT WITH *SS-H[auptsturmführer]*

German police guard a column of Jews during a deportation in Amsterdam; February 22, 1941. Approximately 400 Jews between the ages of 25 and 35 were rounded up during the operation. (Rijksinstituut voor Oorlogsdocumentatie, Amsterdam, Netherlands)

The Dutch Jewish deportees are crammed into waiting trucks by the German police for deportation to the MAUTHAUSEN concentration camp. None returned at war's end. (Rijksinstituut voor Oorlogsdocumentatie, Amsterdam, Netherlands)

ANNE FRANK

During the German occupation of the Netherlands, Dr. Wilhelm Harster headed the SECURITY SERVICE (SD) in that country, working closely with the Dutch branch office of the CENTRAL OFFICE FOR REICH SECURITY, DEPARTMENT IVB4. Although Harster did not personally participate in the deportations, his office expelled victims from their homes throughout the Netherlands and sent them to the TRANSIT CAMP of WESTERBORK, near the German border. From there, trains full of prisoners bound for German KILLING CENTERS departed weekly. On September 3, 1944, the last train to leave Westerbork for AUSCHWITZ concentration camp carried Anne Frank, a teenage Jewish girl who had lived in hiding with her family for more than two years.

After the war, Harster was charged and convicted for his role in the deportation of more than 102,000 Dutch Jews in what became known as the HARSTER TRIAL. The following article discusses that trial and the difficulty prosecuting similar NAZI desk murderers.

— *Reprinted from* Newsweek, *January 30, 1967. © 1967, Newsweek Inc. All rights reserved. Reproduced by permission.*

REGULATIONS

The CENTRAL OFFICE FOR REICH SECURITY (RSHA) was the main organization through which the Germans coordinated the police and government bureaucracy against "enemies of the state." One division of the RSHA, DEPARTMENT IVB4, headed by Adolf EICHMANN, combined two areas of responsibility: DEPORTATIONS and Jewish Affairs. While working in Department IVb4, Eichmann, along with SS and police leaders, developed and managed the methods, regulations, travel schedules, and finances involved with virtually every deportation transporting Jewish victims from across Europe to German CONCENTRATION CAMPS and KILLING CENTERS.

The following selection, originally prepared by Eichmann's office, contains the top secret instructions for SS and SD personnel involved with the deportation of Jews to the AUSCHWITZ concentration camp. It was used as evidence at the VENTER TRIAL.

V. Reception

The Commander of the Security Police and of the Security Service in Cracow is responsible for receiving the evacuated persons in the General Government. To complete the receiving process he will make use of the headquarters of the Higher SS and Police Leader in the district of Lublin.

VI. System of Registration

The travel times (departure times) determined by the Reich Rail are binding and can no longer be changed; therefore, they are to be followed exactly by the dispatch headquarters. Also the unscheduled special trains are to be used fully.

The departure of every transport train is to be announced immediately by urgent teleprint or telegram according to the given example (Enclosure 1)

a/ to the Central Office for Reich Security, Reference IVb4,
b/ to the Commander of the Security Police and the Security Service, *SS-Oberführer* [SS Colonel] Dr. **Schöngarth**, Cracow,
c/ to the Higher SS and Police Leader in the Lublin District, *SS-Brigadeführer* [SS Brigadier General] **Globocnik**, Lublin

The arrival of the transports and the orderly overtaking at the final destination will be reported by the receiving headquarters (SS and Police Leader in the Lublin District) by teleprint or telegram according to the given example (Enclosure 2) and given to the Central Office for Reich Security. Reference IVb4.

Upon completion of the entire action, a total report containing numerical documentation (classification into sex, age, and occupation groups) is to be presented to the Central Office for Reich Security by the dispatching headquarters as well as from the receiving headquarters.

Jews being deported from the German town of Mainfranken sometime between 1941 and 1943. This photo was found in the offices of the GESTAPO in Würzburg by the ALLIES in 1945 as they swept into Germany. It was used as evidence at the INTERNATIONAL MILITARY TRIBUNAL. (NARA)

VII. Evacuation Costs

The calculation of evacuation costs is regulated by Ordinance II C 1/2—No. 650/41—238–10 from 10 January 1942.

VIII. Treatment of property of the evacuated

Guidelines for treatment of the property of the evacuated will be sent at the appropriate time.

Guidelines classified "secret" also sent to the State Police and State Police Central Office in the Reich on 20 February 1943 are as follows:

Guidelines
for the technical accomplishment
of the evacuation of Jews to the East
(Concentration Camp Auschwitz)

For the evacuation of Jews from the territory of the Reich and Bohemia and Moravia to the East, the guidelines under the nullification of the previous ordinance have been established which are to be followed exactly:

I. Responsible Offices

The execution falls on the State Police (Central) Office (in Vienna as before the Central Settlement Office for Jewish Emigration, Vienna, in collaboration with the State Police Office, Vienna. In the Protectorate it falls on the Commander of the Security Police and the Security Service, Central Office for the Regulation of the Jewish Question in Bohemia, Moravia, Prague).

The responsibility of these offices, in addition to the gathering and personal registration of the groups of persons to be evacuated, is the transport of Jews in special German Reich Railway trains in accordance with the Central Office for Reich Security, and in agreement with the schedule arranged by the Reich Transportation Ministry, and the regulation of property rights matters.

II. Determining the groups of persons to be evacuated

To be included in these evacuations are all Jews (§5 of the First Decree to the Reich Citizenship Law of 14 November 1935 Reich Law Gazette I, p. 1333), save for the time being the following exceptions:

1./ Jews living in German-Jewish mixed marriages as well as

a/ Jewish spouses of terminated German-Jewish mixed marriages, in accordance to §5 para. (a) of the Police Decree on the marking of Jews dated 1 September 1941 (Reich Law Gazette I, p. 547), who are freed from wearing the obligatory marking.

b/ Jewish *Mischlinge* [mixed-breeds] who, according to §5 (2) of the First Decree to the Reich Citizenship Law of 14 November 1935 (Reich Law Gazette I, p. 1333), count as Jews as long as they are not married to a Jew.

2./ Jews, who on the basis of special ordinances of the Central Office for Reich Security, IVb4, are to be exempted for now from evacuation.

3./ Jews older than 65 years of age. In a Jewish marriage in which one spouse is under the age of 65 and the other over the age of 65, both can be evacuated.

4./ Recipients of the Wound Badge and medals awarded for bravery (Iron Cross I, Gold Medal for Valor, etc.).

5./ For Jews and racial Jews to whom the following so-called hardship cases apply, in accordance with the proposal of the Reich Minister of the Interior enclosed here, further treatment, i.e., examination, is to be planned at the appropriate time:

a/ Leaving the Jewish faith is allowed only after the deadline date (15 September 1935) but before the reunification of Austria with the German Reich. (Applies only to former Austrian citizens.)

b/ It is plausible that the half-Jew could have left the Jewish faith in time, i.e., at the latest before the unification of Austria with the German Reich, if the Austrian Law of 25 May 1868 on the interconfessional conditions of citizens (Code of Civil Law for Austria 1868, p. 99) had not hindered him from doing so since this law forbade a change of religious confessions for individuals between 8 and 14 years of age. (Applies only to former Austrian citizens.)

c/ The desire *truly to leave* the Jewish faith before the deadline date (15 September 1935) is *proven*, however the formal departure from the Jewish faith in accordance with the set state laws was not or was incorrectly completed for <u>justifiable</u> reasons.

7./ [sic] A separation of spouses as well as children under 14 years of age from their parents is to be avoided wherever possible.

With regard to the treatment of <u>Jews with foreign citizenship</u>, special directives will be enacted.

<u>III. Transport</u>

It is recommended to confine the Jews to be transported. Each transport will consist of at least 1,000 Jews each in agreement with the schedule established by the Reich Transportation Ministry, which is being forwarded to the participating offices.

<u>Each person must take along:</u>

Marching rations for ca. 5 days,
1 suitcase or backpack with the following equipment:
1 pair of sturdy work boots,
2 pairs of socks,
2 shirts,
2 pairs of underwear,
1 set of work clothes,
2 wool blankets,
2 sets of bed clothes (covers with sheets),
1 food bowl,
1 drinking cup,
1 spoon, and
1 sweater.

<u>The following may not be taken along:</u>

Stocks and bonds, foreign currency, savings books, etc., valuables of any kind (gold, silver, platinum—with the exception of wedding rings), living animals, food ration cards (to be taken and given over to the regional Economic Offices).

Before departure, deportees are to be searched for weapons, ammunition, explosives, poison, foreign currency, jewelry, etc.

In order to maintain peace and order during the trip and for cleaning the cars after exiting the train, Jewish supervisors are to be assigned.

When reporting the Jews' change of address, do not enter the destination in the registration books at the registration offices but rather "moved to an unknown address."

<u>IV. Transport Escorts</u>

For the security of the transports every transport train is to be assigned a suitably equipped escort party (ordinarily Order Police in numbers of 1 leader and 15 men) who with reference to the continuous escape attempts, are to be instructed in detail about their assignments and necessary measures in dealing with escape attempts.

> — *Reproduced from the Archives, Research Institute, United States Holocaust Memorial Museum, War Crimes Cases from the Archives of the Staatsanwaltschaft Berlin, Record Group 06.009.04 A03, pp.55–60. Translated from the German by Neal Guthrie.*

A FUNCTIONARY IS CONVICTED

Kurt Asche, a low level NAZI *bureaucrat serving in Brussels, Belgium, worked for the* CENTRAL OFFICE FOR REICH SECURITY *(RSHA). The head of a small branch office of RSHA,* DEPARTMENT IVB4, *Asche was the local contact for the Department's central office headed by Adolf* EICHMANN *in Berlin. In charge of imposing all German anti-Jewish measures on the Belgian population, Asche organized the* ARYANIZATION *of Jewish business, the confiscation of Jewish property, and the collection of Jews for* SLAVE LABOR. *Beginning on August 4, 1942, Asche also supervised the* DEPORTATION *of 34,000 Belgian Jews to* AUSCHWITZ *and other* KILLING CENTERS *and* CONCENTRATION CAMPS.

In November 1980, thirty-five years after the war, Asche was tried for his role in the deportation of Belgian Jews. The following newspaper article by Patricia Clough reports on the results of the ASCHE TRIAL.

'Desk murderer' walks free from Nazi trial

From Patricia Clough, Kiel, July 8

Kurt Asche walked out of court a free man yesterday after being sentenced to seven years imprisonment for his part in the murder of the 26,000 Belgian Jews deported to Auschwitz during the German occupation.

The man described during his trial as Belgium's Eichmann is aged 72, and was freed pending confirmation of the sentence because there seemed little chance of his evading justice.

The public prosecutor, lawyers for 49 co-plaintiffs and the defence all said they would apply to the High Court for a review of the verdict. It therefore appears unlikely that Asche will enter jail before the end of this year, at the earliest.

Dr Rudolf Dann, the presiding judge, said no sentence could match. Asche's crimes or atone for what he had done. If it were possible for Germans to make up for the Nazi past, the courts were not the place to do it.

The sentence was merely symbolic, the expression of the court's clear disapproval of what the accused had done, he said.

Seated below a dusty plaster relief of the goddess Justitia, with the scales of justice in one hand and a sword in the other, Dr Dann was evidently painfully aware of the importance of West German justice before the crimes of the holocaust.

As Dr Dann had evidently foreseen there were vehement protests at the sentence. As soon as the judge's comments were over a babble of voices rose in the foyer as former Auschwitz inmates and co-plaintiffs whose parents and relatives had died in the gas chambers, expressed their disgust.

" A great *Schweinerei* ", commented Mme Miriam Wald, a former Auschwitz captive with her camp number tattooed on her forearm.

" It is scandalous ", protested Mme Sophie Rechtman, whose mother, grandmother and other relatives died at Auschwitz. " It is a scandal for the dead, for the Jews and for the German people. It is not possible that he should be allowed to leave the court a free man ", she said.

Maitre Serge Klarsfeld, a lawyer for the co-plaintiffs who, with his wife, Beate, had played an important part in getting this and similar cases before the courts, said he was satisfied and that the sentence was fair. " It was a fair trial ", he said.

Asche's greyish face with its sharp features, remained expressionless during the verdict as it had done throughout the trial. As in other Nazi crime trials, onlookers had difficulty in associating this unobtrusive-

looking pensioner in his neat, grey suit with the horrors recounted by witnesses.

The trial is the last of several of the " desk murderers ", the SS officials who, with a stroke of their pens, sent thousands of Jews to their deaths without laying their hands on a single one.

Asche was the head of the Jewish office of the German security police in Brussels and was responsible for the registering, rounding-up and deporting of Jews in cattle trucks to the death camps.

Originally there had been two other defendants, Ernst Boje Ehlers and Dr Konstantin Canaris, nephew of the wartime Admiral. Both of these former SS colonels had been the heads of security police at different times in Brussels and were Asche's immediate superiors. Ehlers committed suicide the month before the trial opened and Dr Canaris, aged 74, has been certified too sick to stand trial.

It is now 18 years since proceedings opened. The investigations started late, were pursued slowly and much time was lost in appeals when an earlier court refused to send Asche for trial on the grounds that the evidence was not strong enough.

Maitre Klarsfeld and his wife had expedited the proceedings by producing documents and by protests, including the ransacking of Ehlers's home, to draw the public's attention to the delays.

Throughout the trial, Asche insisted that he had played an insignificant role, that his work consisted mainly of going over old documents and that, above all, he had no idea that the Jews were being sent to their deaths. He said he thought they were simply being sent to work camps.

The court found that he supervized everything to do with the rounding-up and deporting of the Jews and that he must have known where they were going.

Jewish and German witnesses who had been in Brussels at the time, testified that they either knew or suspected the real purpose of the deportation. If the little people knew, the court could not imagine that the head of the Jewish office, who had discussed the deportations with the main Jew hunter Adolf Eichmann, could not have known.

The court's view of Asche amounted to a thumbnail sketch of so many middle-sized cogs in the holocaust machine. Unemployed, he had joined the Nazi Party not out of conviction but in the hope that he would thus find work.

— Reprinted from The Times *(London), July 9, 1981.*
© *Times Newspapers Limited, London, 1981.*

A CONSULATE DOES NOT OBJECT

Adolf EICHMANN, *head of* DEPARTMENT IVb4 *of the* CENTRAL OFFICE FOR REICH SECURITY (RSHA), *was given responsibility for overseeing the* DEPORTATION *of Jews from all countries occupied by the* THIRD REICH. *In this capacity, Eichmann worked closely with the German Foreign Ministry in order to coordinate the deportations across national borders. Franz Rademacher, the deputy minister of the* Abteilung Deutschland *(German Department), became Eichmann's counterpart in the Foreign Ministry in order to facilitate the transport of Jews to the* KILLING CENTERS *in the East.*

In the following letter, addressed to Eichmann's department, Rademacher responds to the request by RSHA Department IVb4 to begin deportations of French Jews.

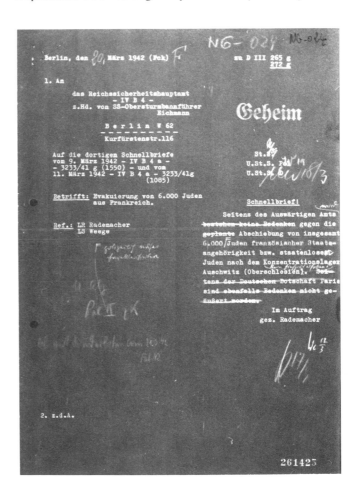

Berlin, 20 March 1942 (Fck)   to be filed under 265 secret
272 secret

1. To
    The Reich Security Main Office
        - IVb4 -
      attention: *SS-Obersturmbannführer*   [stamp]
      [SS Lieutenant Colonel] Eichmann   SECRET

As a film is about to be shown as evidence at the EICHMANN TRIAL in Jerusalem, Adolf EICHMANN sits in the glass booth designed for his protection during the trial; June 8, 1961. Eichmann was the mastermind of the SS DEPORTATION plans for countries from central and western Europe.
(Government Press Office, Jerusalem, Israel)

Berlin W 62

- - - - - - - - - - - - - -

Kurfürsten Street 116

Regarding the express letter
from 9 March 1942 - IVb4 a -
- 3233/41 g (1550) and from
11 March 1942 - IVb4 a - 3233/41g
(1085)

St.S [State Secretary]
U.St.S. Pol [Under State Secretary Political Division]
U.St.S. D [Under State Secretary Germany Division]

Re: Evacuation of 6000 Jews from France.

Ref.: LR [Legation Councillor] Rademacher
LS [Legation Secretary] Weege
[handwritten, illegible]

> Express Letter!
> The Foreign Office has no objections regarding the planned deportation of a total of 6,000 Jews of French citizenship and stateless Jews to the Auschwitz Concentration Camp (Upper Silesia). The German Embassy in Paris has not expressed objections either.
>
> By order
> signed Rademacher
> [handwritten, illegible]

2. For the Files

> — Reproduced from the National Archives and Records Administration, National Archives Collection of World War II War Crimes Records, Record Group 238, Office of the U.S. Chief of Counsel for War Crimes, Document NG-024. Translated from the German by Wendy Lower.

WESTERN DEPORTATIONS

On June 11, 1942, Adolf EICHMANN called an important meeting in Berlin for DEPARTMENT IVb4 of the CENTRAL OFFICE FOR REICH SECURITY (RSHA). Eichmann's deputies from IVb4 divisions in three German-occupied countries were also present at this meeting. They were Kurt Asche from Brussels, Belgium; Wilhelm Zoepf from The Hague, Netherlands; and Theodor Dannecker from Paris, France. Each of these men served as liaison officers with Eichmann's main headquarters in Berlin by heading SS and SD forces with whom they coordinated the round up and registration of local Jewish populations. Eichmann's June 11 meeting set the starting date for combined mass DEPORTATIONS of Jews from all three occupied nations to AUSCHWITZ-BIRKENAU.

Reproduced below is a copy of Dannecker's notes from this historic Berlin meeting. Introduced by the prosecution during the ASCHE TRIAL, the document also provided incriminating evidence during the HARSTER TRIAL.

IV J-SA 24
Dan./Ge.
Paris, 15 June 1942
Ref: Additional Jewish transports from France

1. Note: Par. Hagen

On 11 June 42 a meeting took place in the RSHA-IVb4 at which besides the undersigned (*SS-Hauptsturmführer* [SS Captain] Dannecker) also the officials of Jewish affairs from Brussels and the Hague participated.

a) <u>Topic</u>

For military reasons, during the summer a deportation of Jews from Germany to the eastern deportation territory cannot take place.

RFSS [Himmler] therefore ordered that a large number of Jews from either the southeast (Rumania) or from the occupied western territories will be transferred to the concentration camp Auschwitz for the purpose of labor.

A basic condition is that the Jews are (of either sex) between 16 and 40 years old. Ten percent of Jews incapable of work can be shipped with them.

b) <u>Arrangement</u>

It was agreed that 15,000 from the Netherlands, 10,000 from Belgium and from France, including of the unoccupied territory, a total of 100,000 Jews will be deported.

As suggested by the undersigned [Dannecker], besides the age limit it was determined that the group of those to be deported will only encompass those Jews who are required to wear the Jewish star, as long as they do not live in mixed marriages.

c) <u>Technical Implementation</u>

I. In regards to the furnishing of transport materials, contact is to be established on the order of the RSHA through the undersigned with ETRA, Paris (*Generalleutnant* [Major General] Kohl). At the same time the question of the required ten transport trains for Belgium should be answered. After 13 July 1942, the transports—approximately three per week—should roll. . . .

Section IVb4 of the RSHA—*SS-Obersturmbannführer* [SS Lieutenant Colonel] Eichmann—has ordered that the participating officials have to report again in Berlin for a final meeting on 2 July 1942. . . .

signed Dannecker
SS-Hauptsturmführer [SS Captain]

— *Reprinted from Eckhard Colmorgen, Maren Wulf, and the Working Group for the Asche Trial, Dokumente der Asche-Prozess (Kiel, 1985), 70. Translated from the German by Wendy Lower.*

THE PRICE OF DEPORTING JEWS

The Independent State of CROATIA was established in 1941 by Germany and Italy during the dismemberment of Yugoslavia. Soon after its creation, Germany exerted pressure on the new government to deport all Croatian Jews to CONCENTRATION CAMPS and KILLING CENTERS. As an economic incentive for such DEPORTATIONS, Siegfried Kasche, the German ambassador, negotiated an agreement with the Croatian Minister of Finance, Vladimir Kosak, that allowed the Croatian government to keep all revenues derived from the sale of confiscated Jewish property. In exchange, Croatia agreed to pay Germany a fee for the transportation cost of each deportee.

Only in the Italian occupation zone of Croatia were Jews spared this fate. In these areas along the Dalmatian coast, the Italian government protected approximately 5,000 people by continually delaying negotiations and deportations.

The following telegram details the Kasche-Kosak financial agreement on the deportation of Croatian Jews.

[stamp]
Foreign Office
Germany Section III 892 g [secret]
rec'd. 15 Oct 1942
encl. 2 carbon copies

<u>Telegram</u>
(not coded)

Agram, 14 October 1942
Arrived: 14 October 1942   7:25 P.M.

<u>No. 2955 of 14 October 42</u>

On 9 October 1942, Finance Minister Kosak agreed to make thirty Reichsmarks available for every evacuated Jew. Written confirmation as well as payment will be arranged by Foreign Minister Lorkovic. Preparatory measures for the Evacuation of Jews from the Italian occupied zones and for the

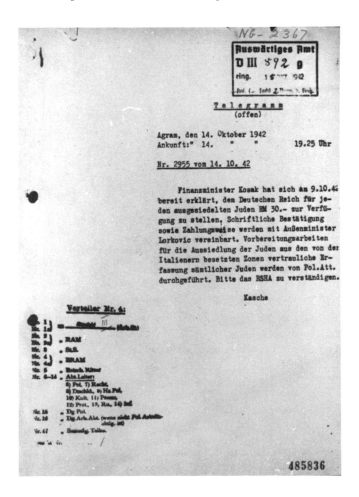

Jews being marched out of Krakow during a DEPORTATION in March 1943. Round ups of Jews took place in towns, villages, and GHETTOS throughout occupied Poland as part of OPERATION REINHARD. It is unlikely that many of the people in this photograph survived the war.
(Main Commission for the Investigation of Nazi War Crimes, Warsaw, Poland)

confidential registration of all Jews is being carried out by the political attachés. Please inform the Central Office for Reich Security.

Kasche

[stamp]
Distribution list No.4
No. 1 Germany III (work sheet)
No. 1a
No. 2 Reich Foreign Minister
No. 2a
No. 3 State Secretary
No. 4. Office of the Foreign Minister
No. 4a
No. 5. Ambassador Ritter
No. 6-14 Department Chiefs:
6) Political, 7) Justice,
8) Germany, 9) Trade Policy,
10) Culture, 11) Press,
12) Protocol, 13) Broadcasting, 14) Information,
No. 15 Deputy Chief Political Division
No. 16 Deputy Chief Operational Division (if not the Political Division)
No. 17 Files of Telegram Correspondence

— *Reproduced from the National Archives and Records Administration, National Archives Collection of World War II War Crimes Records, Record Group 238, Office of the U.S. Chief of Counsel for War Crimes, Document NG-2367. Translated from the German by Wendy Lower.*

THE DISAPPEARANCE OF POLISH FARMERS

The TREBLINKA killing center was originally constructed as a penal colony northeast of Warsaw in the Sokolow sub-district of the GENERAL GOVERNMENT. Established in the summer of 1941, the prison camp held between 1,000 and 1,200 Polish and Jewish inmates who were used as FORCED LABOR in a nearby quarry. It was these same laborers who, in spring 1942, built the GAS CHAMBERS and CREMATORIA for Treblinka.

As the following announcement indicates, the fear of deportation to Treblinka and other LABOR CAMPS was regularly used by German officials to terrorize and threaten the local Polish population into submission.

Notice No. 150

NOTICE

Farmers, my patience is over. For the past few weeks I have repeatedly urged you to follow my orders.

Despite this, a certain number of you still believe you did not need to follow these orders. For this I am giving you the following penalty to be carried out on Friday 10 October 1941.

<u>Thirty-six farmers and the Soltys [village administrator] from the village of Stoczek, thirty-seven farmers from the village of Brzozka, municipality of Stoczek, and thirteen other Soltyse and villagers in positions of trust are to be deported to the labor camp at Treblinka.</u>

In the next few days the same fate will befall those who continue to sabotage my orders.

Sokolow, 13 October 1941

The District Leader in Sokolow
GRAMSS

— Reprinted from Czeslaw Pilichowski, No Time Limit for These Crimes! *(Warsaw, 1980), n.p. Courtesy Wydawnictwo Interpress, Warsaw. Translated from the German by Neal Guthrie.*

THE WARSAW GHETTO UPRISING

On April 19, 1943, the first day of the Passover holiday, armed German troops entered the WARSAW GHETTO *with the intention of deporting all remaining Jews to* KILLING CENTERS. *Instead of becoming the relatively simple task anticipated by the Germans, this operation sparked the most famous act of armed Jewish resistance during the war. Fighting with makeshift weapons from hidden underground bunkers, resistance fighters eluded capture and death for several weeks. Eventually, more than 2,000* SS *soldiers and police units using anti-aircraft guns and armored vehicles under the command of SS-Obersturmbannführer (SS Lieutenant Colonel) Jürgen* STROOP *were required to pacify and destroy the ghetto.*

After the war, Stroop was jailed in Poland along with Gustav Schielke, a low level NAZI, *and Kazimierz Moczarski, a former leader in the Polish resistance. While Stroop was awaiting the* STROOP TRIAL (POLISH), *these three men discussed their roles during the war. In the following conversation, later published by Moczarski, Stroop describes the Warsaw Ghetto uprising.*

"At seven A.M. [on the second day of the deportation operation] the first assault units reentered the Ghetto. I'd broken them into groups of thirty-six men, each with its own officer. Police Major Sternhagel knew his orders: carefully reoccupy the area taken the day before, clean up the *Restghetto*, then comb the entire walled area. I thought we could complete the bulk of our job that Tuesday, and use the third and following days for mopping up. As things turned out, I was wrong."

Schielke cut in. "What do you mean *Restghetto*?"

"The portion of Warsaw's Jewish quarter which was voluntarily vacated by its inhabitants in July 1942," Stroop replied mechanically [the *Restghetto* was the last remnant of the Warsaw Ghetto].

I couldn't believe my ears. "What do you take us for, *Herr General*," I shouted. "Exactly where did those departing Jews go? And *voluntarily* at that. On July twenty-second, 1942, your people began the deportation of Warsaw's Jews to extermination camps. Some three hundred and twenty thousand people were sent to Treblinka's gas chambers. Not to mention those who were murdered back in the Ghetto. How can you dare—" . . .

"We weren't able to clean out the *Restghetto* that day," Stroop continued. "We encountered pockets of resistance every inch of the way, including hideaways concealed within living quarters. I ordered up two assault units. The tank sent along to protect them drew heavy fire, and one of its treads was damaged. The fighting dragged on. We managed to capture several strongholds but in the process suffered two wounded, both of them *Panzer Grenadiers* from the *Waffen-SS*.

"Our SS men had their hands full knocking out enemy defense positions, but it was the *Wehrmacht* engineers and flamethrowing crews who bore the brunt of the job. We were obliged to blow up the bunkers to force those Jewish fighters out. One of the principal defense centers at that point in the fighting was a block of buildings that housed the Army Quartermaster's factories and workshops. Can you believe that those buildings, controlled by General Schindler's *Wehrmacht* men, were riddled with Jewish bastions, both above and below ground? My Chief of Staff, *SS-Sturmbannführer* [SS Major] Max Jesuiter, ordered the German administrator to evacuate all Jews from the houses and workshops immediately. Reputedly there were some four thousand or so of the scum hidden there, but only twenty-eight showed their noses. The rest lay low, fled through those rat holes of theirs, or offered armed resistance. I must admit they fought well and hard, keeping us at a distance and inflicting losses. That's what forced me to bring in the engineers and the antiaircraft guns."

"What caliber were the guns?" Schielke inquired.

"Light. Twenty millimeter. Fast firing. But you can imagine, gentlemen, the potency of guns like that shooting straight ahead at targets no more than two hundred or three hundred meters away. The Jews responded with grenades and automatic fire aimed at our gun crews. The snipers must have been low on ammunition because they made each shot count. . . .

"The next day, the Wednesday before Easter, we attacked the block again, making several assaults. With the help of the engineers and heavy armor, we succeeded in cleaning up part of the area, uncovering close to *seventy* bunkers in the process. During the fierce fighting, the enemy hammered us with grenades, mines, Molotov cocktails, and pistol fire. You should have seen those Jews dashing from one hiding place to the next, agile as wildcats, through those narrow tunnels of theirs. I must admit, their communications setup was admirable. Our engineers were finally forced to blow up all the enemy strongholds and passages they could find. They then set the whole block on fire. We literally smoked those Jews out. Surrender was better than frying. I'll never forget how they shrieked. Some committed suicide, but we deported the rest to Treblinka by rail on the spot.

"We captured five thousand Jews in the Quartermaster's Fort that day. Unfortunately an equal number escaped. We knew there were still Jews and bunkers deep underground, but we didn't know how to reach them. Every time we swept the area, we found more strongholds and hiding places to be stormed.

"The dust, stench, and smoke turned the entire block into a living hell. It was hard to believe that in Lazienki Park near my residence strollers were enjoying a warm spring day and the first flowers."

— *Reprinted from Kazimierz Moczarski,* Conversations with an Executioner, *ed. Mariana Fitzpatrick (Englewood Cliffs, N.J., 1981), 126–28, 130–31.*

HUNGARIAN DEPORTATIONS

German troops occupied Hungary on March 19, 1944. Soon thereafter plans were drawn up for the systematic plunder of Jewish property, the concentration of Jews in hastily constructed GHETTOS, *and, finally, the* DEPORTATION *of all Hungarian Jews. The first area of the country in which German anti-Jewish measures were initiated was the Transcarpathian Ukraine. By April, seventeen ghettos imprisoning 144,000 people had been set up in this area of the Carpathian Mountains. In accordance with plans implemented by Edmund Veesenmayer, the German diplomatic envoy working with Adolf* EICHMANN'S *division of the* CENTRAL OFFICE FOR REICH SECURITY (RSHA), *deportations of Carpathian Jews began on May 15. By June 7, 1944, all Carpathian Jews had been sent to the* AUSCHWITZ-BIRKENAU *camp complex.*

The telegram below, sent by Veesenmayer, describes the deportation plans for Hungary. After the war, this document was used as evidence against Veesenmayer and others by the prosecution during the MINISTRIES TRIAL.

[stamp]
Foreign Office
INL II 764 secret
rec'd. 24 April 1944
encl. (copies) carbon copies.

Telegram
(Secret-Teletype)

Budapest, 23 April 1944 1:30 A.M.
Received: 23 April 1944 8:00 P.M.

Nr. 1022 from 23 April Secret!

Also for Ambassador Ritter.

In connection with telegraphic report No. 117 from 19 April.

In connection with telegraphic report No. 117 after speaking with the appropriate officials, I inform you of the following:

On 16 April ghettoization began in the Carpathian region. 150,000 Jews already registered. The operation will probably be completed by the end of next week. Approximately 300,000 Jews. Following that, similar work is planned and already in preparation for Siebenbürgen [Transylvania] and other communities bordering Rumania. An additional 250,000–300,000 Jews are to be registered. After this the adjacent communities in Serbia and Croatia will be registered, and finally, ghettoization of the interior, concluding with Budapest.

Negotiations for transport have begun and provide for daily shipments of 3,000 Jews mainly from the Carpthian area beginning 15 May. Later, if transportation facilities permit, there will be simultaneous transports from other ghettos. Receiving station Auschwitz. Provisions have been made so that far-reaching consideration will be taken in the implementation of this operation. In order not to jeopardize the implementation of this operation, it appears advisable to postpone the transport of the 50,000 Jewish workers from the Budapest area, whose shipment has been demanded by me and has been agreed on by the government; in view of the existing transportation difficulties this will be necessary anyway. Transport by foot is not practical, since it entails great difficulties for supplying food, shoes, and guards. Since the Jewish operation is a complete whole, I consider the above-sketched plan as correct, and I request wired orders if you have any doubts or special requests.

Veesenmayer

[distribution stamp]
State Secretary Keppler
Under State Secretary Political Division
Ambassador Ritter.
"   Gaus
Chief   Personnel
"   Trade Political Division
"   Legal Division
"   Cultural Political Division
"   Press Division
"   Radio   "
"   Protocol
"   Deputy Chief Political Division
Group Chief Inland I
"   II
Minister Schnurre
"   Benzler
"   Frohwein
"   v. Grundherr
Senior Legation Councillor Melcher
Dr. Megerle
Work Copy! File with Inland II
S. Hungary

— *Reproduced from the National Archives and Records Administration, National Archives Collection of World War II War Crimes Records, Record Group 238, Office of the U.S. Chief of Counsel for War Crimes, Document NG-2233. Translated from the German by Wendy Lower.*

A DEPORTATION train is checked by men from the Hungarian Gendarmerie before departing from Koszeg, Hungary; June 1944.
(Yad Vashem, Jerusalem, Israel)

DEPORTATION DEATH MARCH

The Jews of Budapest, Hungary's capital, were not deported until fall 1944, after a right-wing government was installed following a German-engineered coup that October. The last series of DEPORTATIONS from Budapest, began on November 8, 1944. Because gassing operations at AUSCHWITZ-BIRKENAU and other KILLING CENTERS were being phased out as the Soviet army rapidly approached, these Jews were sent west into Austria on foot. Brutally forced to walk more than 125 miles to the Hungarian border station at Hegyeshalom, those too physically exhausted to march were shot or left to die along the roadside. On November 10, Aviva Fleischmann, a Hungarian Jew, was forced from her home with her family and taken to a brick factory in Budapest, a collection point for the deportation of Budapest's Jews. After several days she became part of a forced march toward the German REICH, which she described in her testimony at the EICHMANN TRIAL reproduced here. Jews who survived the DEATH MARCH were sent to LABOR CAMPS throughout Germany.

A. Early the next morning, we had to line up in rows, and we walked past a committee which included several SS officers and several men in civilian clothes.

Q. Were they German SS?

A. Yes. They lined us up in rows, and we began walking.

Q. Did you know where you were bound for?

A. No. They said we were going to work. We walked from early in the morning until the dark of night. There were many people who already on the first day fell by the wayside—they were unable to walk.

Q. What happened to them?

A. They remained on the road; either they shot them, or they beat them until they died, or they simply left them dying until they were finished.

Q. Did you yourself see such cases?

A. I saw more than one case.

Q. For how many hours did you walk each day?

A. I don't know. My watch was taken from me. But we walked from the earliest light until darkness fell.

Q. Were you given food?

A. In the evening, we were given some dirty water. They said it was soup.

Q. Where did you sleep?

A. Wherever darkness overtook us. Once it was a stable into which we were crowded. There was no possibility of lying down, we merely sat down, huddled together. Once, it was in the open, when we did not reach any place where there was a farm, or a village or something. On one occasion they put us into a cargo lighter.

Q. How many people were there in this group in which you were walking?

A. About 1,500–2,000 people. We walked in fours.

Q. How many days were you on the road?

A. The march lasted about eight days, excluding the fifth day, when we came to a camping place, as it were. It was a large farmstead for raising pigs, and there they cleared one pigsty for us.

Q. Where was this—do you remember the name of the place?

A. It was near Györ. There they put us into these stalls which were designed for pigs. We were herded together

Raoul Wallenberg *(right, hands clasped behind his back)* standing among a crowd of Jews awaiting DEPORTATION at Budapest's Josef Varos station; November 1944. He is flanked by an officer of the Hungarian Gendarmerie *(on his left)*, the Hungarian police organization that actively aided the Germans in rounding up and deporting Hungarian Jews. A Jew holding a Swedish *Schutzpass* (safe-conduct pass) stands at right. (Thomas Veres)

Exhausted Hungarian Jews pause somewhere in Austria on their DEATH MARCH from Budapest to SLAVE LABOR and CONCENTRATION CAMPS in the German REICH; November 1944.
(Yad Vashem, Jerusalem, Israel)

there all night; by then large numbers of people had already contracted dysentery, and their feet were injured. Then the gendarmerie which had accompanied us that day—for they changed them every day—selected a group. There were about twenty of us who still managed somehow to remain on our feet, and we had to remain there every morning to clean up after the sick and bury the dead.

Presiding Judge Were there men and women in this group?

Witness Fleischmann Both men and women; however, there were only a few men, since the men had already been taken by then for forced labour. There were only those whom they caught on the way or who managed to escape, who thought they had managed to escape, or those who were on leave and were taken.

State Attorney Bach Was there a doctor at this place, in Györ, in this pigsty?

Witness Fleischmann There was no doctor. We had a professor in our group.

Q. A professor of what?

A. He was the chief doctor in a hospital for lung patients. He was already an elderly man; he fell sick with dysentery and could not walk. He remained there, on the spot.

Q. Who attended to him?

A. We did. What attention did he get? We were able to give him water. Two days later, he came across his daughter there. She arrived with a fresh transport that night.

Q. How old was this girl?

A. She was a girl of fifteen. It was a tragic encounter. Two days later, the father died.

Q. Was the daughter with him during these two days?

A. Yes, she remained with us. Amongst the men, there were lawyers and engineers.

Q. How long were you there?

A. We were there from 15 November until 3 December.

Q. Did you have medicines?

A. No. We also did not receive food. We stood there and watched while they gave the gendarmerie their food.

Presiding Judge What did you eat?

Witness Fleischmann Occasionally, one of them had pity on us and threw us a bit of bread.

State Attorney Bach Was this place a kind of way station?

Witness Fleischmann Yes, it was an overnight stop. Every evening new transports arrived there, and in the morning they continued on their way.

Q. They continued in the morning, and only you people remained because you had to clean up?

A. Yes. To clean the place, since most of them suffered from dysentery.

Q. What treatment could you give these patients, if any?

A. None. We had to rake together sand and the straw from inside, together with the filth, and burn it.

Q. How many people died there during the time you were there?

A. Hundreds.

— *Reprinted from Ministry of Justice, State of Israel*, The Trial of Adolf Eichmann, *9 vols. (Jerusalem, 1992), 3: 1108–09.*

After disembarking at the BIRKENAU killing center, Hungarian Jews await the confiscation of their last few possessions by the "Canada" commando, the teams of prisoners who sorted clothing and possessions; May 1944. (Yad Vashem, Jerusalem, Israel)

KILLING CENTERS

The culmination of NATIONAL SOCIALIST anti-Jewish policy was the "FINAL SOLUTION," the effort to exterminate Europeans Jews on a comprehensive and universal scale. The systematic mass murder of Jews began with the German invasion of the Soviet Union in June 1941. Operating behind the German army as it advanced into Soviet territory were SS *EINSATZGRUPPEN* units whose men shot hundreds of thousands of Jews in their initial phase of operation. This method of killing ultimately proved slow and inefficient; the protracted shootings of unarmed victims, many of whom were women and children, exacted a heavy psychological toll on the perpetrators, and it was virtually impossible to keep the process a secret. Thus, senior SS administrators sought to devise another, more efficient means of killing. In the end they turned to gassing, a technique with which NAZI officials had already had considerable experience, as lethal gassing had been extensively employed in the mass murder of the mentally and physically handicapped in the first phase of the "EUTHANASIA" program. It was, in part, the success of several gassing experiments that led SS authorities in charge of the "Final Solution" to construct six KILLING CENTERS, all located in German-occupied Poland. These camps differed radically from the CONCENTRATION CAMPS that had proliferated throughout the German REICH and in German-occupied territories. The sole purpose of such killing centers was the rapid and efficient murder of Jews, irrespective of age, sex, or capacity for work.

CHELMNO (or Kulmhof), forty-seven miles west of Lodz, was the first killing center. It was destined to serve as the chief extermination site for the Jews of the Lodz Ghetto and for the entire WARTHEGAU region of Poland, which had been annexed by the Reich. In November 1941, one or more GAS VANS that had been used by *Einsatzgruppen* units operating in Ukraine arrived in Chelmno; on December 8, 1941, mass gassings of Jews in the vans began. More than 320,000 Jews from Poland, the German Reich, the PROTECTORATE OF BOHEMIA AND MORAVIA, and Luxembourg perished at Chelmno, as did 5,000 Austrian GYPSIES.

There were no barracks to accommodate the large number of Jews brought by the transports to Chelmno; the camp was not a source of FORCED LABOR for the German war effort. Only small crews of Jewish laborers were selected at intervals to empty and clean the gas vans after each gassing and to bury the victims in mass graves in nearby forest clearings. This prototype, refined and improved in the succeeding months, was to serve as the model for the killing centers of OPERATION REINHARD, the systematic extermination of Jews in the GENERAL GOVERNMENT of occupied Poland.

To support such a massive killing operation, three Operation Reinhard extermination camps—BELZEC, SOBIBOR, and TREBLINKA—were established in 1942. The first, Belzec, was opened on March 17, 1942, on the site of a former LABOR CAMP about 100 miles southeast of Warsaw on the Lvov-Lublin railway line. Belzec was the first killing center to employ fixed and permanent GAS CHAMBERS. Like Chelmno, nearly all of its victims were Jews; approximately 600,000 were gassed with carbon monoxide exhaust during its one-and-a-half-year period of operation. Only a handful of people is known to have survived.

The second Reinhard camp, Sobibor, began to receive its first trainloads of deportees in May 1942. Here, as elsewhere, railroads transported most victims to the extermination site. Like Belzec, it was strategically placed along a main railroad line in a small village near Lublin in the General Government of occupied Poland. At least 250,000 Jews died at Sobibor. Daily transports brought about 1,500 to 2,000 Jews, many of them children, to be immediately gassed in the five carbon monoxide gas chambers located at the camp. Heinrich HIMMLER ordered the closing of the camp on July 5, 1943, as most of the Jews in the General Government had already been killed; a prisoner revolt in October of that year hastened its closing. Some 50 Jews who had escaped during the Sobibor uprising survived the war and were able to relate the horrors they experienced there.

Treblinka was perhaps the most efficient of the Operation Reinhard killing centers. At least 800,000 persons perished in the camp's thirteen gas chambers in a little more than a year's time. Construction of the camp began in May 1942, and by July the first transports of Jews arrived at the killing center. Himmler himself chose the Treblinka site as the final destination for the Jews of the WARSAW GHETTO, just fifty miles away. In the camp's first three months of operation, more than a quarter-million Jews from the Ghetto perished there. Jews also arrived from other parts of Europe, including Germany, Austria, Czechoslovakia, Holland, Belgium, and Greece. At Treblinka, camp officials employed the lessons they had learned at the other Reinhard camps. Deception, they had discovered, was an important tool. Treblinka's gas chambers were situated

Photographs belonging to Jews deported from Western Europe to the MAJDANEK concentration camp were among the personal possessions discovered in the camp after its liberation in July 1944.
(Central State Archives of Film, Photo, and Phonographic Documents, Krasnogorsk, Russia)

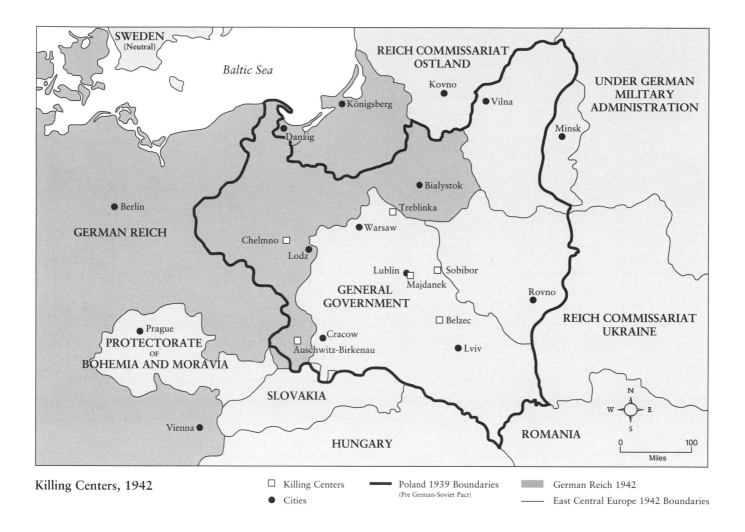

Killing Centers, 1942

□ Killing Centers
● Cities

━━━ Poland 1939 Boundaries
(Pre German-Soviet Pact)

▨ German Reich 1942

─── East Central Europe 1942 Boundaries

beyond the flower-adorned facade of a railroad station. On the roof of one gas chamber the Nazis placed a large Star of David. The chambers themselves were equipped with pipes and phony shower nozzles to give the impression that they were really bathhouses. The processing of each transport was executed with the maximum efficiency: it took only 45 minutes to lead the victims from the boxcars to the gas chambers, which could hold the entire human cargo of 20 freight cars at one time. After a prisoner revolt in August 1943, the number of transports declined considerably; as with Sobibor, the uprising speeded the final liquidation of the camp. Following its closure in November 1943, the Germans made a substantial effort to camouflage the site. The mass graves were opened and the corpses of Treblinka's victims burned; the buildings were leveled, and trees were planted on the site. Finally, the area was turned into a farm, and a Ukrainian peasant family was settled there.

In the Nazi camp system, one may distinguish MAJDANEK and AUSCHWITZ from the killing centers of Operation Reinhard because the former two camps combined elements of the traditional concentration camp—an installation for SLAVE LABOR—with the machinery of the "Final Solution." For prisoners capable of heavy or skilled labor,

the killing process was simply extended; countless numbers of prisoners were worked to death instead of being immediately gassed. At Majdanek, originally a labor camp with a projected prisoner population of about 250,000, gassings began in fall 1942; together with shootings, drownings, and hangings, approximately 360,000 Jews, Gypsies, Poles, and Soviet prisoners of war were killed there. Very few prisoners survived Majdanek; indeed one's possibility for survival was greater at Auschwitz.

The Auschwitz concentration camp complex was the largest Nazi extermination facility. This enormous killing enterprise claimed the lives of an estimated 1.1 million Jews, and some 116,000 non-Jewish prisoners, including 75,000 Christian Poles, 21,000 Gypsies, and 15,000 Soviet prisoners of war. Established by an order from Himmler in April 1940, Auschwitz, like Majdanek, served as a concentration camp until September 3, 1941, when the prussic acid mixture ZYKLON B was tested on six hundred Soviet prisoners of war. The efficiency with which Zyklon B killed its victims prompted Nazi leaders to expand Auschwitz into a vast complex that included the killing center at Birkenau (Auschwitz II) and the labor camp at Monowitz (Auschwitz III). Birkenau became the central extermination site with four CREMATORIA equipped with gas chambers that could hold 2,000 persons at one time. A smaller crematorium gassing facility at Auschwitz I did not continue to operate for long once Birkenau's gas chambers were in operation.

The main goals at the Auschwitz complex were the exploitation of labor and the extermination of Jews. Unlike the killing centers of Operation Reinhard, camp officials at Auschwitz employed the infamous "SELECTION" process, whereby arriving Jewish deportees were divided into two groups: those destined for immediate gassing and those who might survive for a short time as slave laborers. Selections occurred on the ramp where the transport trains were unloaded; small children, the elderly and infirm, and many women were routinely sent immediately to the gas chambers. When the Soviets liberated Auschwitz on January 27, 1945, they found only 5,000 prisoners in the camp; the other prisoners had been forcibly evacuated to concentration camps within the shrinking borders of the Reich.

In part because the Soviet Army had liberated or uncovered all the Nazi killing centers, early trial proceedings for the crimes committed in the six killing centers took place in the East. From 1946 to 1948, a court in Lublin, Poland, tried 95 SS men who had participated in crimes at the Majdanek killing center. In 1947, a Polish court in Warsaw likewise tried and convicted Rudolf HÖSS, the former commandant of Auschwitz; he was hanged before the commandant's villa at Auschwitz that same year. Most killing center trials, however, were conducted in the 1960s and 1970s before West German courts. Franz Stangl, former commandant of Sobibor and Treblinka, was identified in Brazil in 1967 and extradited to West Germany; tried in Düsseldorf for crimes committed at Treblinka, he was sentenced to life imprisonment in 1970. Various camp personnel were tried at the TREBLINKA, SOBIBOR, and MAJDANEK TRIALS and in three separate AUSCHWITZ TRIAL proceedings. Nevertheless, hundreds of guards, SS camp officials, technicians, and planners responsible for these factories of death have escaped trial and punishment.

THE FIRST TRIAL

The first major war crimes trial of the Second World War was conducted in the Soviet Caucasus city of Krasnodar in July 1943. Twenty-four members of EINSATZGRUPPE D *were tried for the murder of 7,000 people during the 1942 German advance. The Germans were tried in absentia since they were not in Soviet custody during the trial. Soviet accomplices were tried on a charge of treason for their collaboration with the Germans in the murders of Jews,* GYPSIES, *Soviet commissars, and patients institutionalized in three hospitals in the Krasnodar region.*

The following New York Times *article reporting the* KRASNODAR TRIAL *proceedings was one of the earliest reports about atrocities committed by the* Einsatzgruppen *to reach the American public.*

11 RUSSIANS ON TRIAL AS ATROCITY AIDES

Moscow Says Nazis Used Motor-Cars for Mass Suffocations

MOSCOW, July 15 (Æ)—Tass, official Soviet news agency, said today that hearings have started in the military trial of eleven persons charged with high treason for complicity in alleged atrocities committed during the German occupation of Krasnodar in the Caucasus.

The news agency declared that investigations had established that Russian prisoners had been burned alive, hospital patients massacred and "many thousands" of citizens suffocated with carbon monoxide "in specially equipped motor-cars" in Krasnodar and the adjacent territory.

Tass said the alleged atrocities were committed by units of the Seventeenth German Army under command of Col. Gen. Richard Ruof, the Gestapo "and their accomplices" late in 1942, before the territory was retaken by the Russians.

The hospital massacres were said to have taken place at the Krasnodar Municipal Hospital, the Berezan Hospital Colony and a territorial children's hospital in the Labinsnaya district.

Tass reported the motor-cars used in the suffocations, which it said the population nicknamed "murderesses," were closed five and seven ton trucks equipped with grates in the floors connected with the exhaust pipes. Sixty to eighty victims, Tass said, were herded into the trucks at a time, the doors closed and the motors turned on for a few minutes.

Then the trucks were driven to anti-tank ditches, where the bodies were dumped, Tass said the investigation revealed.

— From The New York Times, *July 16, 1943. Reprinted with the permission of Associated Press.*

Jews awaiting death in a GAS VAN at the CHELMNO killing center; early 1942. (Main Commission for the Investigation of Nazi War Crimes, Warsaw, Poland)

GAS VANS: MOBILE ASPHYXIATION

In the early stages of the German war with the Soviet Union, the EINSATZGRUPPEN killed thousands of civilians by shooting. Realizing that such efforts expended much needed war materiel and exposed the executioners to intense "mental anguish," their superiors at the CENTRAL OFFICE FOR REICH SECURITY began to search for more efficient methods of mass murder. The first to find such a method was Arthur Nebe, commander of Einsatzgruppe B. Nebe, discovering that one could kill groups of individuals quickly by channeling exhaust gas from a truck into a sealed chamber, reported his success to Berlin. In response, the Technical Department of the Central Office for Reich Security, headed by Walter Rauff, developed the GAS VAN; by piping carbon monoxide exhaust from the truck's engine into the large sealed rear cabin, Rauff had created a mobile gas chamber with an innocuous exterior. Capable of killing up to 60 persons at one time, at least 30 gas vans were employed in the occupied East by mid-1942. Prone to numerous malfunctions, as described in the report and cable reproduced below, the problematic nature of the gas vans encouraged German technicians to develop perma-

nent gassing facilities. The cable is reproduced in facsimile; both documents were introduced as evidence at the INTER-NATIONAL MILITARY TRIBUNAL.

Field Post number 32 704   Kiev, 16 May 1942
[handwritten] B Nr 40/42

                   [stamp] Secret Reich Matter!
To
SS-Obersturmbannführer [SS Lieutenant Colonel] **Rauff** in **Berlin**
Prinz Albrecht Street 8

[handwritten] R 29/5 pers. evl Pradel n.R. b/R
[handwriting left margin illegible]

The overhauling of vans by Groups D and C is completed. While the vans of the first series can also be used when the weather is not so bad, the vans of the second series (Saurer) break down completely in rainy weather. If it has rained for instance for only one-half hour, the van cannot be used because it simply skids. It is only usable in completely dry weather. The question is whether the van can only be used while standing at the place of execution. First the van has to be brought to this place, which is possible only in good weather conditions. The place of execution is usually 10–15 km [6–9 miles] away from the roads and is difficult to access because of its location; in damp or wet weather it is not accessible at all. If the persons to be executed are driven or led to this place, they realize immediately what is going on and get restless, which is to be avoided as much as possible. There is only one way remaining; to load them at the collecting point and to drive them to the spot.

I had the vans of Group D camouflaged as house trailers by putting one set of window shutters on each side of the small van and two on each side of the larger vans, such as one often sees on farm houses in the country. The vans became so well known that not only the authorities but also the civilian population called them the "death van" as soon as one of those vehicles appeared. It is my opinion that the van cannot be kept secret for any length of time, even camouflaged.

The Saurer van I transported from Simferopol to Taganrog suffered damage to the brakes on the way. The Security Command in Mariupol found the cuff of the combined oil-air brake broken at several points. By persuading and bribing H.K.P. [army vehicle park] we managed to have a form machine made, on which two cuffs were cast.

When I reached Stalino and Gorlowka a few days later, the drivers of the vans complained about the same defects. After having talked to the commandants of these commands, I went again to Mariupol to have more cuffs also made for these vans. As agreed, two cuffs will be made for each van: six cuffs will stay in Mariupol as replacements for Group D, and six cuffs will be sent to *SS-Untersturmführer* [SS 2d Lieutenant] ERNST in Kiev for the vans of Group C. The cuffs for Groups B and A could be acquired from Berlin because transport from Mariupol to the north would be too complicated and would take too long. Lesser damage to the vans will be repaired by experts from the commandos, that is by the groups in their own repair shops.

Because of the rough terrain and the indescribable road and street conditions, the caulkings and rivets loosen in the course of time. I was asked if in such cases the vans should be brought to Berlin for repair. The transport to Berlin would be much too expensive and would demand too much fuel. In order to save these expenses I ordered smaller leaks soldered, and if that should no longer be possible, to notify Berlin immediately by radio that van police no. —— is broken down. Besides that I ordered that during the gassings all men are to be kept as far away from the vans as possible so they should not suffer ill effects from the gas that could possibly escape. I would like to take this opportunity to bring the following to your attention: several commands have had their own men do the unloading after the gassing. I brought this to the attention of the commanders of those *Sonderkommandos* that due to this work, these men can suffer enormous emotional and physical harm, if not immediately then possibly at a later date. The men have complained to me about headaches that occurred after each unloading. In spite of this they do not want to change the procedure because they fear that prisoners doing this could use this as an opportunity to flee. I request orders be issued to protect the men from harm.

The gassing is usually not carried out correctly. In order to conclude this issue as quickly as possible, the driver should press the accelerator to the fullest extent. By doing this, the persons to be executed suffer death from suffocation and not death after unconsciousness as planned. My instructions now have proved that by correctly adjusting the lever, death comes faster, and the prisoners are put to sleep peacefully. Distorted faces and excretions, such as could be seen before, are no longer noticed.

Today I shall continue my journey to Group B, where I can be reached with further news.

[signature] Dr. Becker
SS-Untersturmführer

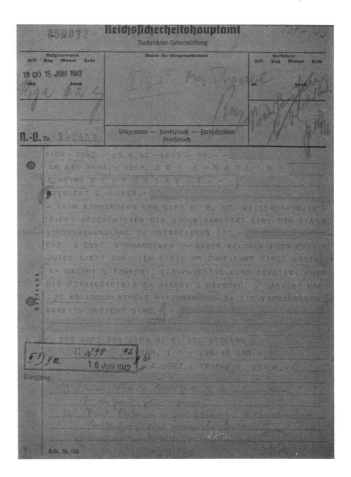

CENTRAL OFFICE FOR REICH SECURITY [handwritten] 501-JS
Reports Transmission

Received	Place for Incoming Stamp	Forwarded
Time Day Month Year 7:00 P.M. 15 June 1947 [handwritten] IID 3a Maj Pradel		Time Day Month Year
to through Riga E 2		from through
[handwritten, illegible]		
Message Nr. 152452	Telegram— Radio Message— Teletype Telephone Message	

RIGA 7082 - 15 JUNE 1942 - 6:55 P.M.- BE. - -
TO THE CENTRAL OFFICE FOR REICH SECURITY -
ROOM. 2 D 3 A - BERLIN
TOP SECRET REICH
SUBJECT: S. VANS—

A TRANSPORT OF JEWS WHICH IS TO UNDERGO
SPECIAL TREATMENT ARRIVES WEEKLY AT THE
OFFICE OF THE COMMANDER OF THE SECURITY
POLICE AND SECURITY SERVICE IN WHITE
RUTHENIA.

THE 3 S-VANS ON HAND ARE NOT ADEQUATE
FOR THIS TASK. I REQUEST ASSIGNMENT OF
ANOTHER S-VAN (5 TONS). AT THE SAME TIME IT
IS REQUESTED TO SEND 20 GAS HOSES FOR THE
3 S-VANS ON HAND (2 DAIMOND, 1 SAURER),
SINCE THE ONES ON HAND ARE LEAKING.

THE COMMANDER OF THE SECURITY POLICE AND
THE SECURITY SERVICE
OSTLAND
ROEM. 1 T - 126/42 GRS.
A. SIGNED TREUHE *SS-HAUPTSTURMFÜHRER* [SS
Captain]

[stamp]
[handwritten]
No. 240/42
II D 3a 16 June 1942

Procedure:
[handwritten]
1) When can we count on having another S-van ready?
2) Are gas hoses on hand, ordered, or when to be delivered?
3) Request answer.

[handwritten] 501-ps
R 16/6

— *Reproduced from the National Archives and Records
Administration, National Archives Collection of World War II
War Crimes Records, Record Group 238, Office of the U.S.
Chief of Counsel for War Crimes, Document 501-PS. Trans-
lated from the German by Wendy Lower and Linda Bixby.*

GENOCIDE

*The atrocities committed by the Germans in attempting to
exterminate the Jews of Europe led to the development of
a new vocabulary to describe the horrors they perpetrated.
One of the most important such words, "genocide," was
coined by Professor Raphael Lemkin in his book* Axis Rule
in Occupied Europe, *published in 1944. Lemkin examined
German occupation policies in relation to existing international law and explored possible means of adjudicating the
crimes associated with those policies, particularly the*

*attempt to exterminate Europe's Jews in the "FINAL SOLU-
TION." The term quickly gained wide usage in the English
language.*

*Raphael Lemkin was a prominent Polish Jewish lawyer
who supported international penalties for crimes of genocide. He escaped from Poland in 1941, where most of his
family had been killed, after serving with the Polish RESIS-
TANCE, and eventually reached the United States where he
taught at Duke and Yale Universities. After the war he was
instrumental in the passage of a United Nations resolution
on the prevention and punishment of genocide.*

New Word 'Genocide' Used In War Crime Indictment

By The Associated Press.

LONDON, Oct. 21—An arti-
cle in The Sunday Times said
today that last week's United
Nations indictment against German war criminals had brought
a new word into the English
language—genocide—and that
it has been coined by a Duke
University professor.

The word occurs in count 3 in
which it is stated that all twenty-four defendants "conducted
deliberate and systematic genocide, viz., the extermination of
racial and national groups,
against the civilian populations
of certain occupied territories."

The article said that it had
been coined by Prof. Raphael
Lemkin of Duke, who is now in
London, from the ancient Greek
word "genos," meaning race or
tribe, and the Latin "cidere,"
meaning to kill.

— *Reproduced from* The New York Times, *October 22, 1945.
Copyright © 1945 by the New York Times Company.
Reprinted by permission.*

IT TOOK FIFTEEN MINUTES

At the TREBLINKA killing center, as at other OPERATION REINHARD killing centers, victims were selected for the GAS CHAMBERS immediately upon arrival at the camp's train station. Those who were too weak to be crowded into the gas chambers were separated from the arriving deportees and then taken to the so-called infirmary (the "Lazarett"), a shed concealing a trench in which the ill or enfeebled prisoners were shot and their bodies burned. The rest of the arrivals were told that they had come to a TRANSIT CAMP and would undergo a disinfection before continuing on their journey to work sites. Instructed to undress and leave their valuables, the victims were then led to the gas chambers, which had been disguised as showers. Once there, the door of the chamber was sealed and the victims were asphyxiated with carbon monoxide gas.

In the following testimony from the INTERNATIONAL MILITARY TRIBUNAL, Shmuel Rajzman, a Polish Jew deported to Treblinka from the WARSAW GHETTO in August 1942, describes the arrival procedure.

MR. COUNSELLOR SMIRNOV: I beg you to describe this camp to the Tribunal.

RAJZMAN: Transports arrived there every day; their number depended on the number of trains arriving; sometimes three, four, or five trains filled exclusively with Jews from Czechoslovakia, Germany, Greece, and Poland. Immediately after their arrival, the people had to leave the trains in 5 minutes and line up on the platform. All those who were driven from the cars were divided into groups—men, children, and women, all separate. They were all

forced to strip immediately, and this procedure continued under the lashes of the German guards' whips. Workers who were employed in this operation immediately picked up all the clothes and carried them away to barracks. Then the people were obliged to walk naked through the street to the gas chambers.

MR. COUNSELLOR SMIRNOV: I would like you to tell the Tribunal what the Germans called the street to the gas chambers.

RAJZMAN: It was named Himmelfahrt [Ascension] Street. . . .

MR. COUNSELLOR SMIRNOV: Please tell us, how long did a person live after he had arrived in the Treblinka Camp?

RAJZMAN: The whole process of undressing and the walk down to the gas chambers lasted, for the men 8 or 10 minutes, and for the women some 15 minutes. The women took 15 minutes because they had to have their hair shaved off before they went to the gas chambers.

MR. COUNSELLOR SMIRNOV: Why was their hair cut off?

RAJZMAN: According to the ideas of the masters, this hair was to be used in the manufacture of mattresses for German women.

THE PRESIDENT: Do you mean that there was only 10 minutes between the time when they were taken out of the trucks and the time when they were put into the gas chambers?

RAJZMAN: As far as men were concerned, I am sure it did not last longer than 10 minutes.

MR. COUNSELLOR SMIRNOV: Including the undressing?

RAJZMAN: Yes, including the undressing.

MR. COUNSELLOR SMIRNOV: Please tell us, Witness, were the people brought to Treblinka in trucks or in trains?

RAJZMAN: They were brought nearly always in trains, and only the Jews from neighboring villages and hamlets were brought in trucks. The trucks bore inscriptions, "Expedition Speer," and came from Vinegrova Sokolova and other places.

MR. COUNSELLOR SMIRNOV: Please tell us, what was the subsequent aspect of the station at Treblinka?

RAJZMAN: At first there where no signboards whatsoever at the station, but a few months later the commander of the camp, one Kurt Franz, built a first-class railroad station with signboards. The barracks where the clothing was stored had signs reading "restaurant," "ticket office," "telegraph," "telephone," and so forth. There were even train schedules for the departure and the arrival of trains to and from Grodno, Suwalki, Vienna, and Berlin.

MR. COUNSELLOR SMIRNOV: Did I rightly understand you, Witness, that a kind of make-believe station was built with signboards and train schedules, with indications of platforms for train departures to Suwalki, and so forth?

RAJZMAN: When the persons descended from the trains, they really had the impression that they were at a very good station from where they could go to Suwalki, Vienna, Grodno, or other cities.

MR. COUNSELLOR SMIRNOV: And what happened later on to these people?

RAJZMAN: These people were taken directly along the Himmelfahrtstrasse to the gas chambers.

MR. COUNSELLOR SMIRNOV: And tell us, please, how did the Germans behave while killing their victims in Treblinka?

RAJZMAN: If you mean the actual executions, every German guard had his special job. I shall cite only one example. We had a Scharführer [SS Sergeant] Menz, whose special job was to guard the so-called "Lazarett" [infir-mary]. In this "Lazarett" all weak women and little children were exterminated who had not the strength to go themselves to the gas chambers.

MR. COUNSELLOR SMIRNOV: Perhaps, Witness, you can describe this "Lazarett" to the Tribunal?

RAJZMAN: This was part of a square which was closed in with a wooden fence. All women, aged persons, and sick children were driven there. At the gates of this "Lazarett," there was a large Red Cross flag. Menz, who specialized in the murder of all persons brought to this "Lazarett," would not let anybody else do this job. There might have been hundreds of persons who wanted to see and know what was in store for them, but he insisted on carrying out this work by himself.

Here is just one example of what was the fate of the children there. A 10-year-old girl was brought to this building from the train with her 2-year-old sister. When the elder girl saw that Menz had taken out a revolver to shoot her 2-year-old sister, she threw herself upon him, crying out, and asking why he wanted to kill her. He did not kill the little sister; he threw her alive into the oven and then killed the elder sister.

Another example: They brought an aged woman with her daughter to this building. The latter was in the last stage of pregnancy. She was brought to the "Lazarett," was put on a grass plot, and several Germans came to watch the delivery. This spectacle lasted 2 hours. When the child was born, Menz asked the grandmother—that is the mother of this woman—whom she preferred to see killed first. The grandmother begged to be killed. But, of course, they did the opposite; the newborn baby was killed first, then the child's mother, and finally the grandmother.

— *Reprinted from* Trial of the Major War Criminals before the International Military Tribunal, 42 vols. *(Nuremberg, 1947),* 8: 325–27.

Hungarian Jews selected for gassing—women, children, the old, and infirm—await their end in a grove near one of the four CREMATORIA at the BIRKENAU killing center.
(Yad Vashem, Jerusalem, Israel)

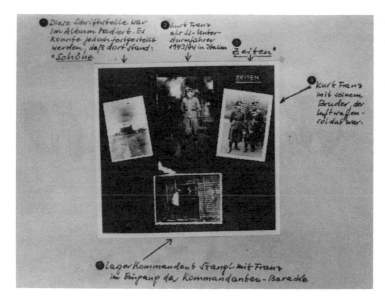

A page from the photo album of Kurt Franz, the last commandant of the TREBLINKA killing center. The railroad station at Treblinka is shown at upper left, Franz himself top center, Franz and his brother at right, and Kurt Franz with Franz Stangl at the bottom. Stangl was a former commandant of Treblinka; he was convicted in the STANGL TRIAL. Franz labeled this photo montage "Schöne Zeiten" (Wonderful Times).
(Bildarchiv Preussicher Kulturbesitz, Berlin, Germany)

INTERVIEW WITH A MURDERER

Franz Stangl was the commandant of the TREBLINKA killing center during most of its operation. A police inspector before the ANSCHLUSS, Stangl became police superintendent of Hartheim, a "EUTHANASIA" facility in Austria, in 1940. In spring 1942, Odilo GLOBOCNIK, head of OPERATION REINHARD, assigned Stangl to the SOBIBOR killing center. During his short tenure as commandant, construction of the camp was completed. Soon thereafter, Stangl was transferred to Treblinka, where he served as commandant until the KILLING CENTER was closed in August 1943.

At the end of World War II, Stangl escaped American internment and, with a RED CROSS passport, reached Syria. In 1951, he settled in Brazil, registering under his own name at the Austrian consulate. Tracked down in 1967, Stangl was extradited that year and tried before a German court in 1970 for mass murder at Treblinka. Sentenced to life imprisonment at the conclusion of the STANGL TRIAL, he consented to an extended interview with journalist Gitta Sereny, excerpted below, in which he discussed his role as the commandant of both Sobibor and Treblinka. Hermann Michel, mentioned in the text, formerly served as an orderly at Hartheim and later worked with Stangl at Sobibor.

After an eight months' trial, considered by the Germans the most important Nazi-crime (NS) trial to be held in Germany since Nuremberg, Franz Stangl, "Kommandant" of the extermination camp Treblinka in Poland from August, 1942, to August, 1943, (and Sobibor for the preceding four months), was sentenced on December 22, 1970, to life imprisonment for co-responsibility for the murder of 400,000 men, women and children in Treblinka during the year of his command. While the evidence presented in the course of the trial did not prove Stangl himself to have committed specific acts of murder, it did prove to the satisfaction of the Judges that by virtue of his attitude and the orders he gave, enforced and/or approved in his role of camp commander, he was an active participant in the murder of the prisoners.

It was quite clear to me that the whole story of his beginnings in Poland (and some of the Euthanasia phase) was in part fabrication, rationalization and partly an evasion: but having pressed him on it repeatedly, on several occasions, I hoped that if I didn't press him on it any further at this point, he would find it possible a little later along in his story, to revert to telling me the truth about the rest of it, however difficult. As it turned out I was right.

He next told me about the Polish workers and that he found them to be "a lackadaisical lot." Within two or three days he obtained a Jewish "Work commando" of 25 men, and some Ukrainian guards from a nearby training camp.

"There really was nothing there, no amenities for anybody. Those first weeks we all bunked in together."

"What do you mean 'all together'? The German staff, the Ukrainian guards and the Jews?"

"At first we just used one hut, while we were working on the others: we slept on the floor in the kitchen, and the others in the loft."

"When did you first find out what the camp was really for?"

"Two things happened: when I'd been there about three days I think, Michel came running one day and said he'd found a funny building back in the woods. 'I think there is something fishy going on here,' he said. 'Come and see what it reminds you of.'"

"What did he mean 'in the woods'?"

"It was about ten—even 15 minutes—walk away from the railway station where we were building the main camp. It was a new brick building with three rooms of three by four metres. The moment I saw it I knew what Michel meant: it looked exactly like the gas chamber at Schloss Hartheim."

"*But, who had built this? How could you possibly not have noticed it before? Or seen it on the plans?*"

"The Poles had built it—they didn't know what it was. Neither Michel nor I had had any time yet to go for walks in the woods. We were very busy. Yes, it was on the plans, but so were lots of other buildings . . ." The sentence trailed off.

"*All right, you hadn't known: but now you knew. What did you do?*"

His face had gone red. I didn't know whether because he had been caught out in a lie, or because of what he was about to say next: it was much more usual for him to blush in advance than in retrospect.

"The second thing I mentioned happened almost simultaneously. A transport officer—a sergeant—arrived from Lublin and said, to me, (he sounded angry even now) that Globocnik was dissatisfied with the progress of the camp and had said to tell me that 'if these Jews don't work properly, just kill them off and we'll get others.'"

"*What did that indicate to you?*"

"I went the very next day to Lublin to see Globocnik. He received me at once. I said to him, 'How can this sergeant be permitted to give *me* such a message? And anyway I am a police officer. How can I be expected to do anything like that?' Globocnik was very friendly. He said I had misunderstood; I was just overwrought. 'We'd better get you some leave,' he said. 'You just go back for the moment and get on with the building. You are doing fine.' And then he said 'Perhaps we can arrange to have your family come out for a bit.' So I went back. What else could I do?"

"*Did you ask Globocnik about the gas chamber?*"

"There was no opportunity," he said firmly. "I went back to Sobibor and talked it over with Michel. We decided that somehow we had to get out. But the very next day Wirth came. He told me to assemble the (German) personnel and he made a speech—just as awful, just as vulgar as his speech had been at Hartheim. He said that any Jews who didn't work properly here would be 'eliminated.' 'If any of you don't like that,' he said to us, you can leave. But under the earth,' he added in his heavy wit, 'not over it.' And then he left. I went back to Lublin the next morning. *Sturmbann-fuehrer* (Major) Hoefle, Globocnik's aide, kept me waiting in the office all day, and again the next morning. Then he finally told me that the General would not be available for me. [Hans Hoefle, Deputy Director of the *Einsatz Reinhard* (Operation Reinhard), hanged himself while awaiting trial in the Vienna Remand prison in August, 1962.] I went back to Sobibor. Four days later a courier came from Lublin with a formal letter from Globocnik informing me that Wirth had been appointed Inspector of Camps and that I was to report to him at Belsec [Belzec] forthwith."

Wirth had by then commanded both Chelmno, where the old-fashioned method of gas vans was found to be impractical for the huge task at hand, and Belsec where the first large-scale gas exterminations in gas chambers were begun as early as October [*sic*], 1941.

"I can't tell you what it was like," Stangl said: he spoke slowly now, in his more formal German, his face strained and grim. He passed his hand over his eyes and rubbed his forehead. "I went there by car. As one arrived one first reached Belsec railway station, on the left side of the road. The camp was on the same side but up a hill. The *Kommandantur* was 200 metres [656 ft.] away, on the other side of the road. It was a one-storey building. The smell . . ." he said, "Oh God, the smell. It was everywhere. Wirth wasn't in his office, they said he was up in the camp. I asked whether I should go up there, and they said 'I wouldn't if I were you—he's mad with fury, it isn't healthy to go near him.' I asked what was the matter. The man I was talking to said that one of the pits had overflowed. They had put too many corpses in it, and putrefaction had progressed so fast that the liquid underneath had pushed the bodies on top up and over, and the corpses had rolled down the hill. I saw some of them—oh God, it was awful. A bit later Wirth came down. And that's when he told me. He said that was what Sobibor was for. And that he was putting me officially in charge. I said I couldn't do it. I simply wasn't up to it. There wasn't any argument, or discussion. He just said my reply would be reported to HQ and for me to go back to Sobibor. In fact I went to Lublin, tried again to see Globocnik, again without success: he wouldn't see me. When I got back to Sobibor, Michel and I talked and talked about it. We agreed that what they were doing was a crime. We considered deserting—we discussed it for a long time. But how? Where could we go? What about our families?"

He stopped. He stopped now, just as he and Michel must have stopped talking about it then, because as long as there was nothing they could or dared to do, there was nothing else to say.

"*But you knew that day that what was being done was wrong?*"

"Yes, I knew, Michel knew. But we also knew what had happened in the past to other people who had said no. The only way out we could see was to keep trying in various and devious ways to get a transfer. The direct way was impossible. As Wirth had said, that led 'under the earth.' Wirth came back the next day. He ignored me; he stayed several days and organized everything. Half the workers were detailed to finish the gas chambers."

It appears that Wirth tested their potential efficiency by, as Stangl said, "pushing our 25 worker Jews in one afternoon and gassing them."

"*What were you doing?*"

"I continued the construction of the camp. Michel had been put in charge of carrying out the gassings."

"*So now the exterminations had really started: it was happening right in front of you. How did you feel?*"

"At Sobibor one could avoid seeing almost any of it—it all happened so far away from the camp buildings. All I could think of was that I wanted out. I planned and planned. I heard there was a new police unit at Mogilev. I went back to Lublin and filled out an application blank for transfer. I asked Hoefle to help me get Globocnik's signature. He said he would do what he could, but I never heard of it again. Two months later—in June—my wife wrote that she had been requested to supply details about the children's ages: they were going to be granted a visit to Poland."

"Did you want them to come there?"

"I wanted to see them, of course. But don't you see what this signified? Globocnik had said to me, months before, that I needed 'leave.' But they weren't going to let me go home, like other people. I was in danger, it was quite obvious. And they were making damn sure I knew about it.". . .

"I got up at dawn," he began. "The men used to be livid because I made my first round at five a.m. It kept them on their toes. I first checked the guards—the British were supposed to have dropped parachutists in the region and I had had to secure the camp against the outside. We had put up a second fence of steel anti-tank obstacles. And then I went up to the *Totenlager* [death camp]."

"What were you doing at the Totenlager *at five a.m.?"*

"It was a *round*: I went everywhere. At seven I went into breakfast. After a while I had them build our own bakery. One of the worker-Jews was a wonderful Viennese baker. He made delicious cakes, very good bread. After that we gave our army issue bread to the *Arbeitsjuden* [worker-Jews] of course."

"Of course? Did everybody?"

"I don't know. I did. Why not—they could use it. I tried other ways to get them food too: you know the Poles had ration books which allowed them an egg a week, so much fat, so much meat. Well, it occurred to me that if everybody in Poland had the right to ration tickets—if that was the law—then our *Arbeitsjuden* were in Poland too and also had the right to ration tickets. So I told Maetzig, my bookkeeper, to go to the town council and request 1,000 ration books for our thousand worker-Jews."

"What happened?"

He laughed. "Well, in the surprise of the moment they gave him 1,000 rations for that week. But afterwards the Poles—the town council—complained to somebody at HQ and I was hauled over the coals for it. Still, it was a good try and we did get something out of it: they had 1,000 eggs that week."

"Getting back to your daily routine, what did you do after breakfast?"

"At about eight I'd go to my office."

"What time did the transports arrive?"

"Usually about that time."

"Didn't you attend their arrival?"

"Not necessarily. Sometimes I went."

"How many people would arrive on a transport?"

"Usually about 5,000. Sometimes more."

"Did you ever talk to any of the people who arrived?"

"Talk? No. But I remember one occasion—they were standing there just after they'd arrived, and one Jew came up to me and said he wanted to make a complaint. So I said yes, certainly, what was it. He said that one of the Lithuanian guards (who were only used for transport duties) had promised to give him water if he gave him his watch. But he had taken the watch and not given him any water. Well, that wasn't right, was it? Anyway, I didn't permit pilfering. I asked the Lithuanians then and there who it was who had taken the watch, but nobody came forward. Franz—you know, Kurt Franz—whispered to me that the man involved could be one of the Lithuanian officers—they had so-called officers—and that I couldn't embarrass an officer in front of his men. 'Well,' I said. 'I am not interested what sort of uniform a man wears. I am only interested in what is inside a man.' Don't think *that* didn't get to Warsaw in a hurry. But, what's right is right, isn't it? I made them all line up and turn out their pockets."

"In front of the prisoners?"

"Yes, what else? Once a complaint is made it has to be investigated. Of course, we didn't find the watch—whoever it was had got rid of it."

"What happened to the complainant?"

"Who?"

"The man who had lodged the complaint about the watch?"

"I don't know," he said vaguely. "Of course, as I said, usually I'd be working in my office: there was a great deal of paperwork—till about 11. Then I made my next round, starting on top at the *Totenlager*. By that time they were well ahead with the work up there." ['*Da hat der Betrieb schon gelaufen.*']

What he meant was that by this time the 5,000 people who had arrived that morning were dead: the "work" he referred to was the disposal of the bodies which took most of the rest of the day. I knew this but I wanted to get him to speak more directly about the *people* and asked where the people were who had come on the transport. But his answer was still evasive: he still avoided referring to them as "people."

"Oh, by that time of the morning everything was pretty much finished in the lower camp. A transport was normally dealt with in two or three hours. At 12 I had lunch and after that about half an hour's rest. Then another round and more work in the office."

"What did you do in the evenings?"

"After supper people sat around and talked. When I first came they used to drink for hours in the mess. But I put a stop to that. Afterwards they drank in their rooms."

"What did you do? Did you have any friends there, anyone you felt you had something in common with?"

"Nobody. Nobody with whom I could really talk. I knew none of them."

"Even after a while? A month?"

He shrugged his shoulders. "What's a month? I never found anybody there—like Michel—with whom I felt I could speak freely of what I felt about this *Schweineri* [big mess]. I usually went to my room and went to bed."

"Did you read?"

"Oh no. I couldn't read there. It was too unquiet . . . The electricity went off at ten—after that everything was quiet. Except of course when the transports were so big that the work had to continue in the night."

"Well now, this was your routine. But how did you feel? Was there anything you enjoyed—you felt 'good' about?"

"It was interesting to me to find out who was cheating. As I told you, I didn't care who it was: my professional ethos was that if something wrong was going on, it had to be found out. That was my profession: I enjoyed it. It fulfilled me. And yes, I was ambitious about that: I won't deny that."

"Would it be true to say that you got used to the liquidations?"

He thought for a moment. "To tell the truth," he then said slowly and thoughtfully, "one did become used to it."

"In days? Weeks? Months?"

"Months. It was months before I could look one of them in the eye. I repressed it all by trying to create a special place: gardens, new barracks, new kitchens, new everthing—barbers, tailors, shoemakers, carpenters. There were hundreds of ways to take one's mind off it: I used them all."

"Even so, if you felt that strongly, there had to be times, perhaps at night in the dark, when you couldn't avoid thinking about it?"

"In the end the only way to deal with it was to drink. I took a large glass of brandy to bed with me each night and I drank."

"I think you are evading my question."

"No, I don't mean to: of course thoughts came. But I forced them away. I made myself concentrate on work, work and again work."

"Would it be true to say that you finally felt they weren't really human beings?"

"When I was on a trip once, years later in Brazil," he said, his face deeply concentrated, and obviously reliving this experience, "my train stopped next to a slaughterhouse. The cattle in the pens, hearing the noise of the train, trotted up to the fence and stared at the train. They were very close to my window, one crowding the other, looking at me through that fence. I thought then 'look at this; this reminds me of Poland'; that's just how the people looked, trustingly, just before they went into the tins . . ."

"You said 'tins,'" I interrupted. "What do you mean?" But he went on without hearing or answering me.

". . . I couldn't eat tinned meat after that. Those big eyes . . . which looked at me . . . not knowing that in no time at all they'd be dead." He paused. His face was drawn. At this moment he looked old and worn and real—it was his moment of truth.

"So you didn't feel they were human beings?"

"Chattels," he said tonelessly, "they were chattels." He raised and dropped a hand in a gesture of despair. Both our voices had dropped. It was one of the few times in those weeks of talks that he made no effort to cloak his despair, and his hopeless grief allowed a moment of sympathy.

> — *Reprinted from Gitta Sereny, "Colloquy With A Conscience," The [London] Daily Telegraph Magazine, October 8, 1971. © Gitta Sereny, 1971.*

A door to one of the GAS CHAMBERS in the BIRKENAU killing center, photographed after liberation in February 1945. The sign warns, "Poisonous Gas! Entry endangers your life." (Main Commission for the Investigation of Nazi War Crimes, Warsaw, Poland)

"... AND THEN ALL WAS STILL"

The mass murder of Jews at the AUSCHWITZ killing center by poison gas began in January 1942. The first killings took place outside the camp complex in two abandoned farmhouses in a large field that had been sealed and converted into GAS CHAMBERS. Victims were driven or marched through a copse of trees and across the field to the makeshift gas chambers. Due to the farmhouses' inconvenience and their small killing capacity, construction of larger gas chambers located within BIRKENAU began in July 1942.

In an interrogation taken by German prosecutors in 1960, Richard Böck, a truck driver in the SS Drivers Corps, described his experiences at Auschwitz, including selections and gassings. Here he recounts an early farmhouse gassing.

One day, it was in the winter of 1942/43, H. [Karl Hölblinger, a medical van driver] asked me if I felt like going along to a gassing operation. He would say that I was his assistant in the sanitation vehicle, because otherwise it was strictly forbidden for me to be present there.

So I went with him to the garage. We got into the Sanka [*Sani-tätskraftwagen,* a medical van] and drove straight over to Birkenau. During the drive, the Birkenau camp was never mentioned. I cannot even say if I saw any of the camp at all.

The transport train had arrived and was standing in the open space between Auschwitz and Birkenau. The prisoners were being unloaded. It was around 9:00 P.M. The prisoners climbed up wide steps that were placed behind the trucks used to transport the prisoners. All the vehicles were jam-packed full so that no one else could get in. The people were standing on the trucks. I didn't notice any SS doctors or other members of the SS sorting out anybody. They were all loaded up and driven to a former farm about 1.5 km [one mile] from where they were unloaded. Since it was dark, I am unable to say exactly where this place was. In any case, I did not see the crematoria in Birkenau, and I am of the opinion that these were not yet being used at that time. In any case I drove with H. in the Sanka to this farm. We drove behind the trucks. When we arrived, the people had already been unloaded and had to undress in several barracks that stood near the former farm. When they came out of the barracks naked, they were told that they had to go into the building on which the sign "disinfection" was hanging. This building was the old barn that now had been built into a gas chamber. As well as I can remember, it was finished off all around with cement and had large doors on either side which, I think, were out of wood. H. had already told me before that the arriving transport would be gassed in this room. In addition, these gassing operations were common knowledge among us all.

I can still remember that this transport was made up of Dutch Jews: men, women, and children who all had been well dressed. One could tell that they were well-to-do people.

I have to correct something here. The reconstructed barn had only one entrance but with a double door. The "disinfection" sign did not hang on the building but stood a few meters in front of it, like a path marker. The sign was put there to fool the people into thinking that they were only being disinfected.

After the entire transport—it must have been about 1,000 people—was in the building, the doors were shut. Following this, an SS man came up to our Sanka and took out a gas can. He carried this over to a ladder, which looking away from the entrance was on the right side of the barn. While he was climbing up the ladder, I noticed that he had a gas mask on. When he reached the top he opened up a tin trap and shook the contents of the can into the opening. I could clearly hear the clattering of the can as it hit against the wall while the man was shaking out the contents. At the same time I saw a brownish dust rising out of the opening in the wall. Whether this was gas or not, I cannot say. In any case, I clearly saw that he poured in only one can. As he was closing the little door, an indescribable screaming broke out in the room. I simply cannot describe how these people screamed. It lasted about 8–10 minutes, and then all was still. A short time later the door was opened

by prisoners, and one could still see a bluish fog hanging over a huge tangle of bodies. The bodies were all twisted together in such a way that one could not tell to whom individual limbs and body parts belonged. I saw for example that one of the gassed had stuck his index finger several centimeters into the eye socket of another. That shows you how indescribably terrible these people's death must have been. One cannot describe this scene with words. I was so sickened by this sight that I almost threw up.

> — *Reprinted from Henry Friedlander and Sybil Milton, eds.,* Zentrale Stelle der Landesjustizverwaltungen, Ludwigsburg, *vol. 22 of* Archives of the Holocaust *(New York, 1993), 469. Courtesy Garland Publishing, Inc. Translated from the German by Neal Guthrie.*

LABELING DEATH

One poison used by the Germans to gas KILLING CENTER *victims was known by its brand name,* ZYKLON B. *Produced by the insecticide firm* DEGESCH *(acronym for Deutsche Gesellschaft für Schädlingsbekämpfung or German Pest Control Company), Zyklon B was an alcohol-based hydrocyanic acid, or prussic gas. In its crystalline form, the poison looks like small blue chalk beads. Sealed in airtight canisters during storage, the pea-sized pellets produce a lethal gas when exposed to air.*

These labels were used as evidence at the INTERNATIONAL MILITARY TRIBUNAL.

Guaranteed for only a 3-month consumer shelf life!

[flag] Testa/Testa **ZYKLON** [flag] Testa/Testa
[logo] Tesch and Stabenow
International Company for Pest Control, Ltd.
Authorized for use in the territory of the Reich east of the Elbe, the Sudeten district, the General Government, the Reich Commissariat Ostland, and for Denmark, Finland, and Norway.

POISON GAS!
D.R.P. 575 293 D.R.P. 575 293
Cyanide Preparation! [skull and crossbones] to be opened and used only by trained personnel
store cool and dry
protect from sun and open flame
ZYKLON

[emblem] **DEGESCH** [emblem]
ZYKLON
Cyanide Contents 200 grams
Product of the German Company
for Pest Control, Ltd.
Frankfurt am Main

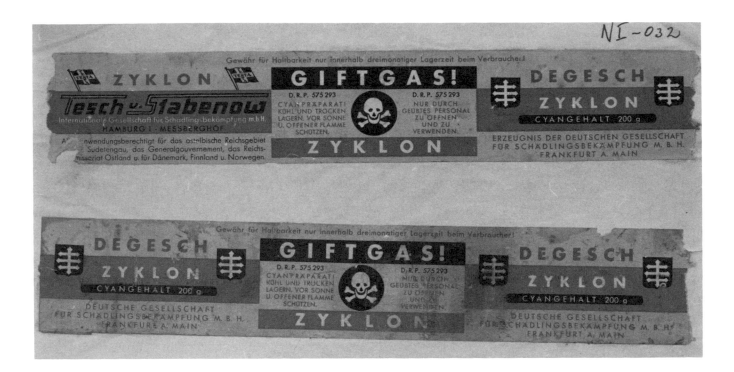

Guaranteed for only a 3-month consumer shelf life!

[emblem] **DEGESCH** [emblem]
ZYKLON
Cyanide Contents 200 grams
Product of the German Company
for Pest Control, Ltd.
Frankfurt am Main

POISON GAS!
D.R.P. 575 293 D.R.P. 575 293
Cyanide Preparation! [skull and crossbones] to be
opened and used only by trained personnel
store cool and dry
protect from sun and open flame
ZYKLON

[emblem] **DEGESCH** [emblem]
ZYKLON
Cyanide Contents 200 grams
Product of the German Company
for Pest Control, Ltd.
Frankfurt am Main

— *Reproduced from the National Archives and Records
Administration, National Archives Collection of World War II
War Crimes Records, Record Group 238, Office of the U.S.
Chief of Counsel for War Crimes, Document NI-032. Trans-
lated from the German by Wendy Lower and Linda Bixby.*

After liberation, two former German guards at the MAJDANEK
killing center pose with ZYKLON B gas canisters used in the camp's
GAS CHAMBER; July 1944. Both men were later tried, convicted,
and executed by a Soviet military court.

(Main Commission for the Investigation of Nazi War Crimes, Warsaw, Poland)

ZYKLON B

ZYKLON B, *hydrocyanic acid (prussic acid), was initially manufactured as an insecticide. Because the gas was colorless and had a weak odor, a tracer was added to give it a distinctive smell as a warning of its presence. When the Germans began to use Zyklon B to gas humans in* KILLING CENTERS, *the* SS *requested that DEGESCH (the German Pest Control Company) produce special shipments of the poison without the tracer. Since the tracer was required by German law, the Germans had to pass regulations that allowed the sale of the "special" Zyklon B.*

The invoice reproduced below was submitted by DEGESCH to Kurt GERSTEIN, *a disinfection expert for the German Hygiene Institute. It was later used as evidence at the* INTERNATIONAL MILITARY TRIBUNAL. *A member of the* CONFESSING CHURCH, *Gerstein was dismissed from state service in 1936 for his religious affiliation and was briefly imprisoned in a* CONCENTRATION CAMP. *After learning that his sister-in-law had been gassed at the* HADAMAR *euthanasia facility, he attempted to learn the truth of such crimes by joining the* WAFFEN-SS. *His attempts to inform the world about the German killing centers met with limited success. Arrested in May 1945 as a suspected war criminal, Gerstein wrote a famous report of his experiences during the war before he was found hanged in his cell. His death was ruled a suicide, but many suspect that he was murdered by fellow SS men confined in the same prison.*

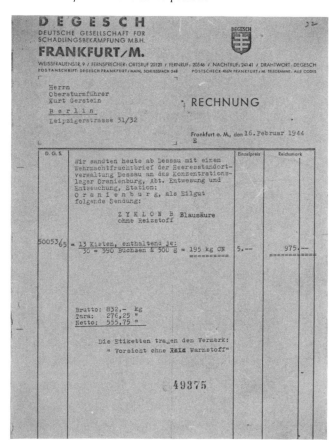

DEGESCH
German Company for
Pest Control, Ltd.
FRANKFURT AM MAIN

[logo] DEGESCH

Weissfrauenstr. 9 / Telephone: Local 20121 / Long distance: 20546 / Night number: 24141 / Wire address: DEGESCH
Postal Address: Degesch Frankfurt am Main, P.O. Box 248
Post Bank Check 48674 Frankfurt am Main Telegram: All Codes

To Mr.
Obersturmführer
[SS 1st Lieutenant]
Kurt Gerstein

Berlin

Leipzig Street 31/32

INVOICE

Frankfurt am Main,
16 February 1944

D.G.S.		Unit Price	Reichsmark
500 53/65	Today we sent from Dessau, with an Army bill of lading from the central Army administration of Dessau, to concentration camp Oranienburg, Delousing and Disinfecting Dept., Station: **Oranienburg**, by express the following shipment: **ZYKLON B** prussic acid without tracing agent =13 cases, each containing: 30=390 cans @500g= 195 kg CN	5.00	975.00
	Gross wt.: 832.00 kg Tara: 276.25 " Net wt.: 555.75 "		
	The labels are marked: "Caution, without tracing agent"		

— *Reproduced from the National Archives and Records Administration, National Archives Collection of World War II Crimes Records, Record Group 238, Office of the U.S. Chief of Counsel for War Crimes, Document 1553-PS. Translated from the German by Wendy Lower.*

CHEMISTS ON TRIAL

In an experiment of killing methods at the AUSCHWITZ killing center, ZYKLON B was first used on humans on September 3, 1941. In this first test of the gas, 600 Soviet prisoners of war were locked into a detention cell whose windows and doors had been sealed with cement. The gas pellets were then thrown in. Based on the "success" of this experiment (all of the victims died within five minutes), Zyklon B became the usual instrument of death in the GAS CHAMBERS at Auschwitz.

Manufactured by DEGESCH, a subsidiary of the chemical conglomerate I.G. FARBEN, the demand for and profits from Zyklon B sales to KILLING CENTERS were so great that distribution of the gas was licensed to a third firm, the Tesch and Stabenow Company. After the war, Dr. Bruno Tesch, chairman of Tesch and Stabenow, and two other officials of the firm were prosecuted for their role in the distribution of this poison gas. Known as the ZYKLON B TRIAL, the prosecution of Bruno Tesch is reported in the news article below.

Poison Gas Trial Opens At Hamburg; Three Are Accused

HAMBURG, March 6 (GNS)—Accused of sharing the guilt for the death of 4½ million human beings by supplying and employing poison gas, three men went on trial Monday at the British court martial for war crimes in Hamburg.

The trial shows up the background of mass-extermination by the cyanide gas "Zyklon."

Witness Tells of Planning

The defendants are: Dr. Bruno Tesch, 46, head of the Hamburg firm of Tesch & Stabenow; Karl Weinbacher, 48, chief clerk; and Dr. Joachim Drosihn, 40, technical head. The three defendants deny knowing that "Zyklon" gas was used to kill human beings.

The first witness, a bookkeeper of the Tesch firm, testified that Tesch had taken notes on a conference which he had with a high ranking army personality. The notes stated the shooting of Jews had increased to such an extent that the burial of the corpses was causing difficulties. It was suggested in the notes that Jews be exterminated by a cyanide gas, and that Tesch was asked to make adequate proposals. The bookkeeper testified that Tesch had accepted an order to train SS men in the use of cyanide gas for extermination purposes.

C. L. Stirling, prosecutor in the Belsen trial, is in charge of the prosecution.

Says SS Ordered Gas

The gas, he said, was produced by a Dessau firm for the IG Farben subsidiary "Degesch," which ceded the exclusive rights of sale for Greater Germany east of the Elbe river to Tesch. The purchasers, including the SS, ordered through him.

The gas caused death within two minutes. The prosecution stated it had been used in large quantities in the concentration camps east of the Elbe river, and that about 4½ million human beings, including civilians of Allied and neutral nations, had been killed by this gas in Auschwitz-Birkenau between 1942 and 1945.

The prosecutor concluded that the defendants participated knowingly in the mass extermination of civilians of Allied nations and that they therefore are to be considered guilty of war crimes, particularly of violating article No. 46 of the Hague Convention of 1907.

— *Reproduced from* News of Germany, *March 7, 1946.*

Jews assigned to a SONDERKOMMANDO (special labor detail) at the BIRKENAU killing center burn corpses in a pit near the CREMATORIA; summer 1944. The killing capacity of the crematoria was overwhelmed by the large numbers of victims killed during the extermination of the Hungarian Jews that summer. This photo was taken surreptitiously and smuggled to the Polish resistance.
(National Museum of Auschwitz-Birkenau, Oswiecim, Poland)

BURNED ALIVE

In fall 1943, the RESISTANCE movement at the AUSCHWITZ concentration camp smuggled information to London regarding mass murder inside the KILLING CENTER. Soon afterwards, the BBC news service began broadcasting reports throughout Europe about the GAS CHAMBERS. In response, the NAZIS replaced key Auschwitz personnel, including the commandant, and tightened security around the camp complex. Such changes actually strengthened the resolve of the resistance movement within the camp. On October 7, 1944, the SONDERKOMMANDO assigned to CREMATORIUM IV at Auschwitz-Birkenau revolted. The extermination of Hungarian Jews was nearly completed and the crematorium workers believed that they too would soon be gassed. Using homemade bombs, the prisoners succeeded in destroying the gas chamber in the crematorium.

In the following testimony taken from the POHL TRIAL, Jerzy Bielski, an Auschwitz survivor, describes measures taken by the SS to disguise camp activities and to compensate for the destruction of one crematorium.

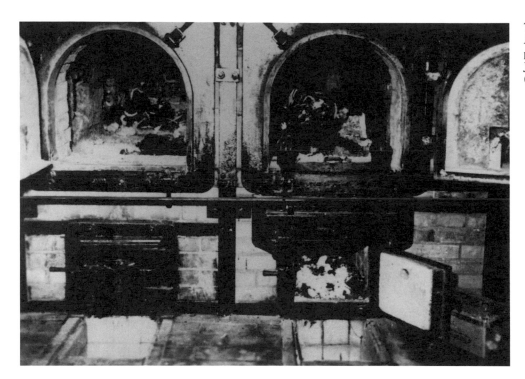

Three CREMATORIA ovens at AUSCHWITZ-BIRKENAU killing center, photographed after liberation; January 1945.
(Yad Vashem, Jerusalem, Israel)

MR. ROBBINS: Would you give us a little more detail on the camouflage phase?

WITNESS BIELSKI: Well, at the time when we worked there, there was no camouflage. Camouflage was used only after the arrival of the Greek transports. That was perhaps towards the end of July or August 1943. That was when the Greek transports arrived from Greece, and at that time the crematoriums worked very often, and it was quite obvious for all the inmates in the camp could see it.

All the people were sent to the crematorium—prior to that time the gas chambers, and that was the reason why camouflage was used at the time. That was the artificial trees I mentioned before. The trees of Babitz were cut off and they were set in there, and there were two rows of those trees right around the crematorium and the gas chamber, and apart from that—I believe that that was later on—a sort of fence was placed around the trees, just small poles, and on that fence one could see small pieces of rags. Later on, when we could no longer enter one could not see how the people were sent to the gas chambers. All we could hear were the screams and we could see the pile of smoke coming out of the chimney of the crematoriums, and we also used some sort of a camouflage—that was in 1944; that was when the Hungarian Jews arrived—we used a music camouflage. At the time the children were burned on big piles of wood. The crematoriums could not work at the time, and therefore, the people were just burned in open fields with those grills, and also children were burned among them. Children were crying helplessly and that is why camp administration ordered that an orchestra be made by a hundred inmates and should play. They played very loud all the time. They played the "Blue

Danube" or "Rosamunde"; so that even the people in the city of Auschwitz could not hear the screams. Without the orchestra they would have heard the screams of horror; they would have been horrible screams. The people two kilometers from there could even hear those screams, namely, that came from the transports of children. The children were separated from their parents, and then they were put to section III camp. Maybe the number of children was several thousand. . . .

When one of the SS people sort of had pity with the children, he took the child and beat the head against a stone first before putting it on the pile of fire and wood, so that the child lost consciousness. However, the regular way they did it was by just throwing the children onto the pile.

They used to put a sheet of wood, then the whole thing was sprinkled with gasoline, then wood again, and gasoline and wood, and gasoline—and then people were placed on there. Thereafter the whole thing was lit.

Q. And what period of time did that continue, Herr Bielski?

A. With the children, you mean?

Q. Yes.

A. That was during those 3 months when most of the Hungarian transports came in; that was June 1944, July, and August; approximately around that period of time. However, what I mentioned about the orchestra was around the end of August. Several thousand children were burned to death alive.

— *Reprinted from* Trials of War Criminals before the Nuernberg Military Tribunals Under Control Council Law No. 10, 14 *vols. (Washington, D.C., 1950), 5: 660–64.*

"THE AUSCHWITZ BUSINESS"

On December 20, 1963, the trial of Robert Karl Ludwig Mulka and other former personnel of the AUSCHWITZ concentration camp began before a German district court in Frankfurt. Better known as the first AUSCHWITZ TRIAL, the proceedings against Mulka et al. *were not a war crimes trial; the twenty-two defendants, all former guards and lower-ranking camp personnel, were charged with murder. In the words of the presiding judge, "political guilt, moral and ethical guilt were not the subject of the [court's] concern." Instead, almost twenty years after the crimes were committed, the court sought to link each defendant with at least one specific act of premeditated murder, the only crime with which the defendants could be charged given the existing German statute of limitations. Although deaths occurred daily within the Auschwitz camp complex, few prisoners survived to recall the specific actions of guards necessary for the trial's successful completion.*

In this selection, Sybille Bedford, an English writer who wrote Faces of Justice, *reports the opening sessions of the trial. The defendants mentioned in the text, Oswald Kaduk and Franz Hofmann, were both convicted. Kaduk received twelve life sentences; Hofmann was sentenced to life in prison.*

'The Auschwitz Business'

Horror and Courtesy in a German Court

The German judge asks "May we have your full name please, Herr Kaduk, and your age?"

The accused pays no attention to the court, grasps the microphone and begins to bark some set farrago about unlawful prosecution and injustice to himself.

He is accused No. 10, an ex-guard at Auschwitz, called in his turn on Monday, the second day of the trial, to be led through his life history.

He is not in a dock, but standing on the floor facing the bench. "I was sentenced to death by the Soviets," he shouts, "criminal proceedings against me here are invalid. . ."

The judge says quietly: "We know all about that, Herr Kaduk, and shall come to it in due course. Meanwhile we want to know something about yourself."

The man's hysteria is momentarily punctured. He admits to being Oswald Kaduk, born in Silesia, primary education, 57 years old, butcher, fireman and male nurse by occupation.

Volunteered for the S.S. in 1940? Yes sir. "What were your reasons?" "No political reasons . . . politics don't interest me . . . . The chess club . . . all the comrades were in the S.S."

Keeping order

After basic training he was put through a special N.C.O.s' course, promoted and presently got to Auschwitz.

"Just like that? to Auschwitz?" asks the Judge. "Had you applied?" Kaduk says he was transferred. An order was an order wasn't it? Then he says he did his best not to go and, in the same breath, that he had no idea where he was going. (The prosecution is expected to call evidence that posting to the concentration camps was highly selective.)

"And what were your functions as block guard at Auschwitz?"

Kaduk bellows: "Quiet, order and cleanliness." He pauses. "And correspondence."

He is asked to enlarge.

"To see there was no sabotage . . . no resistance."

All the accused here are being tried for murder, complicity in mass murder, individual acts of murder.

These men, unlike Eichmann, were no bureaucratic transmitters of orders, no middlemen of death. They were, if the charges against them are true, direct killers and torturers. Generally they killed because they were told to do so, occasionally they killed because they chose to do so.

Throttlings

These men are said to have taken part in acts, and themselves devised acts so abominable that ordinary human consciousness recoils.

The charges against Oswald Kaduk are dreadful. He is alleged to have trampled a young Jewish boy to death because he had overslept. . . .

One night, half-drunk, he throttled some elderly prisoners by laying a walking stick across their necks and standing on the stick, it is alleged. . . .

'Injustice'

Presently, Kaduk is holding forth about his own woes. . . .

"Why did the Russians sentence you to death in 1947?"

Kaduk: "The Auschwitz business. (contemptuously) Ex-prisoners denounced me."

That sentence was commuted to 25 years hard labour. Kaduk served nine years in the East Zone, then was released.

And now he is off again: The inhumanity of the treatment he received—four ozs. [ounces] of bread a day, comrades died like flies, and now we are being reproached.

"After they released me I ought to have stayed in the East. They warned me. They will persecute you in the West, they told me. I chose the West. I bitterly regret it. I never dreamt of such injustice.". . .

One by one through the long day these nightmarish figures take the floor. Each is asked if he would like a chair, all are called Herr before their names, all are treated with careful and detached politeness. . . .

There is the stoker Franz Hofmann who joined [the SS] "for business reasons," his father's beer-house having had a number of SS and SA customers. Moreover, a brother having been in the SS, there was a spare uniform hanging in a cupboard. "So I didn't have any expense, see? I was unemployed."

Hofmann was posted to Dachau in 1933 and, regularly

and rapidly promoted, served in camp after camp for some 12 years.

"Let me tell you something," he says, "when my wife and children joined me at Auschwitz, I applied for a servant and received permission to employ a prisoner. We—my wife and I—had that girl live with us. She was clothed (impressive pause). She was fed (another pause). Why, she was treated like a complete, like a free, human being."

Thug material

This Hofmannn is at present serving a life sentence for murder (West Germany abolished the death penalty after the war). Two murders, we learn, committed at Dachau. "Innocently convicted," says Hofmannn. "There was only one thing they reproached me with, the shooting, and I know nothing about that."

"You were convicted for shooting a man?" asks the judge.

"I can't remember anything about it."

The judge says slowly and gravely: "When there is a question of having shot a human being, one remembers one of two things. One either remembers that one did do it, or one remembers that one did not do it. To say that one remembers nothing about it is not good.". . .

The Third Reich used promising delinquents to construct and service a vast-scale man-made hell.

The present trial here is not—and this is a most important thing for the Germans—a war-crime trial, not a political trial, but an ordinary criminal trial for offenses against the general West German criminal code, heard before an ordinary criminal court. It is the case of the State v. Mulka and others for murder.

It will be a very long trial, a formidable endurance test for bench, jury and counsel. The preliminary inquiry has already been going on for five years. . . .

Eventually 1,300 witnesses, many of them living outside Germany, were questioned and a huge volume of evidence collected. Twenty-three suspected persons, all but two living respectably under their own names, were located and arrested.

All this goes towards answering the frequent questions why this prosecution was brought so late. . . .

After two days out of expected hundreds, the trial, whose moral and technical difficulties will be immense, is still at its earliest stage. After the first shocks and a sense of the utter gap between deeds such as these and human justice, one is led to the slow conviction that the only way in which society can attempt to cope is by conducting, as the scrupulously courteous judges of Frankfurt and the three patient young prosecutors are trying to do, a fair trial according to the law.

— *Reproduced from Sybille Bedford,* The Observer, *January 5, 1964.*

CLOSING STATEMENTS

At the first Auschwitz Trial, *all twenty-two defendants, former members of the* Auschwitz *concentration camp staff, pleaded not guilty to the crimes they were accused of committing at the camp. In their defense, they maintained that they had "only followed orders," that they had been coerced by their superiors, or had been uninvolved with these crimes. When confronted with witness testimony that implicated them, several defendants openly declared that the witnesses lied or that incriminating evidence had been*

A gas chamber in Crematorium I at the Birkenau killing center photographed after the Soviet Army liberated the camp in January 1945. More than 700 people were crowded into the chamber for each gassing before it was shut down in July 1943.
(Dokumentationsarchiv des Österreichischen Widerstandes, Vienna, Austria)

fabricated. At the end of the trial, however, seventeen of the original twenty-two defendants were found guilty.

Under modern German law, a defendant in a criminal trial has the right to make a closing statement in his own words. The following selection reprints the closing statements from a few of the Auschwitz Trial defendants.

HANS STARK, former member of the camp Gestapo, [sentenced to 10 years in prison]: "I took part in the murder of many people. I often asked myself after the war whether I had become a criminal because, being a dedicated National Socialist, I had murdered men, and I found no answer. I believed in the Führer; I wanted to serve my people. Today I know that this idea was false. I regret the mistakes of my past, but I cannot undo them."

DR. WILLI SCHATZ, former member of the dental station, [acquitted]: "I was on the ramp in Auschwitz, but I never selected. I managed not to become involved. I had the good fortune to be able to steer clear of all activities. For the rest I support the presentation of my lawyers."

EMIL BEDNAREK, former prisoner, [sentenced to life at hard labor]: "I killed no one and beat no one to death. If I punished someone or hit someone I had to do it in order to spare him more rigorous measures. I could do nothing else. I consider myself innocent before God and man."

— *Reprinted from Bernd Naumann, Auschwitz: A Report on the Proceedings Against Mulka and Others (New York, 1966), 405, 409–10.*

TESTIMONY

On April 7, 1944, two Jewish prisoners escaped from Auschwitz-Birkenau concentration camp. During their escape preparations, Alfred Wetzler and Walter Rosenberg (who later changed his name to Rudolf Vrba) gathered clandestine notes describing the camp and the extermination operation. These notes, hastily scribbled on dirty scraps of paper, had been prepared by inmates working in the Auschwitz camp offices, on construction crews, and in the Sonderkommandos. Along with this data, Wetzler and Rosenberg also took with them a label from an empty canister of Zyklon B. After their escape, the men wrote a fifty-page report describing the layout and operation of the Auschwitz complex and listed, by country of origin, the number of victims gassed prior to their escape. Later passed on to the Allies, it was one of several reports of Nazi atrocities to be received by the West. It was released to the American press by the War Refugee Board in November 1944.

In his testimony at the Auschwitz Trial, reproduced below, Rudolf Vrba describes how he and Wetzler escaped from the killing center. In German courts, the trial judge may take an active role in questioning witnesses.

Dr. Vrba: I fled from Auschwitz on 7 April 1944 with my friend Wetzler. We had made up our minds to warn the world of what was happening in Auschwitz and especially to prevent the Hungarian Jews from letting themselves be transported to Auschwitz without offering any resistance. At this time we in Auschwitz already knew that large Hungarian transports were already planned. Along with Wetzler I put together complete statistics of the death actions. When we came upon Jewish organizations in Slovakia, we were questioned separately because they did not want to believe our accounts. What we said independently of each other was exactly the same and was recorded in a protocol. I can present the court with a copy of this protocol. I found it in the White House Library.

Presiding Judge: How did you prepare the statistics?

Dr. Vrba: As soon as I was assigned to the clean up commando in the ramp service, I thought about escaping. I have a good head for numbers and tried to remember the number of survivors of every transport. I can still to this day remember the telephone numbers of my friends. I continuously tallied these numbers whenever I talked with acquaintances who came from these transports. So by the end of April 1944, we determined the number of killed inmates to be 1.75 million [historians now estimate the number killed to be 1.2 million.

Prosecuting Attorney Vogel: Is this number of 1.75 million gassed inmates based on your own observations, or is the number of those gassed before your arrival at Auschwitz and your assignment to the clean up commando on the train ramps also included?

Dr. Vrba: The number during the time before mid-1942 was relatively small. I knew that from conversations. But so far as we are able to determine, that is also taken into account.

Representative of the Co-Plaintiff Ormond: When did you consciously start recording these figures? Because you were preparing to escape?

Dr. Vrba: Looking back now it is hard to say. I systematically observed the transports and the numbers.

Ormond: While you were preparing to escape, did you continue to tally the numbers, up until 7 April 1944, or were you so busy with escape preparations that you could no longer do so?

Dr. Vrba: The liquidation of the family camp in March was for me such a monstrous thing. It made a deeper impression on me than all of the others. The number of these victims is certainly there, as well as the victims of the Greek transports that came to Auschwitz in March 1944. The notes go up to this time.

Alternate Judge Hummerich: How did you and Wetzler organize your escape together, and how did you meet with him?

Dr. Vrba: We met in Sector III, the so-called Mexico camp. A bunker was built near the block leader's room. We waited there three days and three nights until the evening of 11 April, because the sentries stood guard in

Hungarian Jewish women selected for SLAVE LABOR at the AUSCHWITZ-BIRKENAU concentration camp after disinfection, during which their heads were shaved; May 1944. (Yad Vashem, Jerusalem, Israel)

chain fashion for three days whenever an escape was noticed. Four prisoners who had escaped before us had used this hiding place. They were caught but did not divulge the place despite torture. At 6:00 P.M., after our escape, the alarm was sounded. They looked for us for three days. We left the following night, when we heard that the sentry chain had been removed.

Ormond: Where did you find refuge after you managed to escape?

Dr. Vrba: We crossed the Polish-Slovakian border on 21 April. A farmer on the other side of the border hid us. We got in contact with the Jewish Community in Zilina, and there we went to Dr. Pollak, a physician. He arranged a meeting for us with the leaders of the Jewish Community in Bratislava. This took place either on 24 or 25 April.

Ormond: What was these people's first reaction?

Dr. Vrba: At first our report seemed unbelievable to them. These were people who had grown up in a civilized world and could not image such atrocities. But when we gave details on the transports that arrived at Auschwitz from Slovakia, they looked at the lists that they had of these transports. Wetzler and I were separated for cross-examination. They soon determined that our information corroborated with their records on the departures of the transports. Finally we were taken to a monastery and introduced to the papal nuncio residing is Bratislava. He had already read the protocol beforehand. He gave us his word of honor that he would pass our report on to the Vatican and the western governments.

— *Reprinted from* Hermann Langbein, Der Auschwitz-Prozess: eine Dokumentation *(Frankfurt am Main, 1995), 122–124. Translated from the German by Neal Guthrie.*

HAIR

Although CONCENTRATION CAMP *prisoners' heads had been shaved since 1939, it was not until 1942 that the idea of utilizing the hair arose. In August 1942, concentration camp commandants received orders from Oswald* POHL, *head of the SS* CENTRAL OFFICE FOR ECONOMY AND ADMINISTRATION (WVHA) *that directed them to begin collecting hair from concentration camp and* KILLING CENTER *victims for possible use by the* REICH. *Soon thereafter, all arriving prisoners were shorn before entering the* GAS CHAMBERS *or beginning work at the camps. After collection, the hair was cleaned and packaged for shipment to felt factories for processing. In exchange, the WVHA received 1 Reichsmark (or $2.18) for 2 kilograms (4.4 pounds) of hair. When Soviet troops liberated the* AUSCHWITZ-BIRKENAU *concentration camp complex on January 27, 1945, they found 15,400 pounds of human hair awaiting shipment.*

This document was introduced as evidence at the INTERNATIONAL MILITARY TRIBUNAL.

Secret
Copy
SS Central Office for Economy and Administration
Office D - Concentration Camps
D II 288 Na/Uag. Tbg. 112 secret.

Oranienburg, 6 August 1942
13th copy

Re: Utilization of Cut Hair

To the
Commandants of Concentration Camps:

Arbeitsdorf, Auschwitz, Buchenwald, Dachau, Flossenbürg, Gross-Rosen, Ludwigsdorf [?], Hartheim/Gusen [?], Natzweiler, Niedernhagen [?],

Neuengamme, Ravensbrück, Sachsenhausen, Stutthof, Moringen [?], SS special camp Hinzert.

The Chief of the SS Central Office for Economy and Administration, *SS-Obergruppenführer* [SS Lieutenant General] Pohl, has given the order that all human hair cut in concentration camps be accordingly utilized. Human hair will be spun into industrial felt and yarn. Yarn stockings for U-boat crews and felt stockings for the Reich Railways will be made from combed and cut women's hair.

It will therefore be ordered that the available hair from female prisoners be stored after disinfection. Hair cut from male prisoners can only be utilized at a length of at least 20 mm [.75 inches].

SS-Obergruppenführer Pohl therefore has given his consent that, for the time being, as a test, the hair of male prisoners will be cut only when it reaches 20 mm. In order to avert escapes eased by increased hair length, the prisoners should be marked in all cases where the commandant finds it necessary in such a way that a strip of hair is cut with a <u>narrow</u> clipper over the middle and top of the head.

It is planned that the hair accumulated in all camps be utilized through the construction of a production unit in a concentration camp. More detailed instructions about the delivery of the collected hair is to follow.

The amount of hair that is collected on a monthly basis, separated according to women's and men's hair, must be reported to this agency on the fifth of each month beginning on 5 September 1942.

> signed Glücks
> *SS-Brigadeführer* and
> *Generalmajor* of the
> *Waffen-SS* [Brigadier General]

Proofread
signed [signature]
SS-Obersturmbannführer
[SS Lieutenant Colonel]

<u>Distribution:</u>
II, III, IV,
<u>Labor deployment</u>
[stamp]
for the certification of the copy
[signature, illegible]
SS-[illegible rank]

> [stamp]–*Waffen-SS*–
> Commandant's Office of
> Concentration Camp
> Sachsenhausen

— Reproduced from the National Archives and Records Administration, National Archives Collection of World War II War Crimes Records, Record Group 238, Office of the U.S. Chief of Counsel for War Crimes, Document USSR-511. Translated from the German by Wendy Lower.

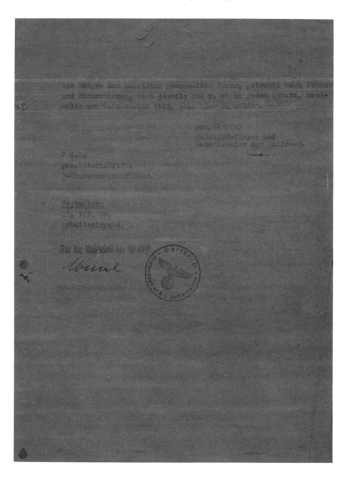

The MAJDANEK concentration camp, located near Lublin, Poland, after its liberation in July 1944. (USHMM)

"THE MARE OF MAJDANEK"

Located on the outskirts of the Polish city of Lublin, MAJDANEK, a LABOR and CONCENTRATION CAMP as well as a KILLING CENTER, held up to 45,000 prisoners from all across Europe. Built during winter 1940–41 by Jewish SLAVE LABOR, Majdanek became known for its sadistic staff of SS guards. Less well-known than other German killing centers, Majdanek was just as deadly. Before the end of the war, more than 200,000 people, including 5,000 Soviet prisoners of war, were killed at this camp by poison gas, starvation, hanging, drowning, exposure, and torture. After the war, 1,100 former members of the Majdanek camp staff were eventually implicated in several WAR CRIMES trials. The largest of these, the MAJDANEK TRIAL, became the longest and most expensive trial ever held in the Federal Republic of Germany. The following newspaper article reports the trial's conclusion on June 30, 1981.

Longest Nazi war crimes trial comes to end in West Germany

By Elizabeth Pond
Staff correspondent of The Christian Science Monitor

Berlin

The last of the big West German trials of Nazi war crimes has come to an end — 5½ years after it began.

The main defendant, Hermine Ryan, was sentenced to lifelong imprisonment June 30.

Spectators in the crowded Düsseldorf courtroom booed the companion verdicts of three to 12 years imprisonment for seven other Majdanek camp officials and the acquittal of the ninth defendant for lack of evidence. Some shouted, "It's a scandal" and "That's an offense against the victims of the Nazis."

This longest and most expensive of all German trials has also been criticized for its protracted nature and for the anguish it has caused some witnesses who were inmates of the Majdanek termination camp.

The extraordinary length of the trial came from the Teutonic thoroughness of the search for evidence; the late West German start in prosecuting Nazi crimes; the difficulty of establishing conclusive proof almost 40 years after mass murders that were designed to have few witnesses; and the delaying tactics of defense attorneys.

Altogether several hundred witnesses were heard, either in the Düsseldorf state court or — in cases where camp survivors were too elderly or too ill to travel — in depositions taken in Poland, Israel, or the United States.

Originally 16 defendants were charged with the shooting, gassing, drowning, or fatal bludgeoning of at least 250,000 people — out of an estimated 1.5 million Jews, Poles, Soviet prisoners of war, political opponents of the Nazis, and others who were killed in the Majdanek camp in Poland between 1941 and 1944.

One defendant died in the interim, one was ruled unfit for trial, and four were acquitted in 1979 for lack of evidence of their specific participation in specific murders.

In the end only former camp overseer Ryan, "the mare," as she was known to inmates because of her alleged fondness for kicking prisoners, could be convicted of having herself committed murder. On two counts. Her sentence was life imprisonment.

The seven others — Maidanek camp overseer Hildegard Lächert, (12 years imprisonment); deputy camp director Hermann Hackmann (10 years); Emil Laurich, (8 years); Heinz Villain (6 years); Fritz Petrick (4 years); Arnold Strippel (3½ years); and Thomas Ellwanger (3 years) — were convicted of aiding and abetting murder.

The Maidanek trial ran the gamut of general and individual proof of Nazi era murders of an estimated 5½ million Jews, half a million Gypsies, and 6 million other civilians. One defense lawyer resurrected the old argument — now discredited by the vast majority of West Germans as well as foreigners — that there is no evidence that more than 100,000 Jews were killed in the Nazi period.

Defense lawyers tried to disqualify one witness — a leading historian — as "prejudiced" because he had studied under a Jew.

In countering the defense, the prosecution presented expert historical evidence that industrial-scale murders were, in fact, committed systematically in Nazi Germany. They proved to the court's satisfaction that it was known at the time that mass murders were being committed at Maidanek; evidence included written orders for tons of deadly Zyklon-B gas that was used only for killing people, and records of the contemporary corruption trial of one Maidanek SS official who had beaten prisoners to death to steal their gold teeth.

On the basis of this evidence the prosecution demanded five life sentences, three prison sentences of 5 to 10 years, and one acquittal.

The West German failure to begin trying Nazi-era murders soon after the war stemmed partly from allied cold war policy and partly from conservative West German government policy. The Western occupation powers originally prosecuted Nazi-era murderers, then subordinated justice to the higher priority of rallying former German elites against the new Soviet threat.

By 1959 virtually all those jailed by the Western powers had been freed; and under allied regulations, neither these persons — nor even those who had been investigated by the occupation but not convicted — could be investigated a second time by West German courts.

When Israel kidnapped Adolf Eichmann and put him on trial in the early 1960s, this finally galvanized world public opinion against the inaction in West Germany. Prosecutions began in earnest and have continued until the present.

"I'M BACK IN THE CAMP"

*The M*ajdanek Trial *tried fifteen members of the Majdanek camp staff. The most notorious defendant at the trial was the camp's former overseer, Austrian-born Hermine Braunsteiner-Ryan. Ryan earned her nickname "Kobyla" (Polish for "mare") for her habit of kicking her victims to death. After the war, Ryan concealed her identity and emigrated to the United States, where she married and became an American citizen. Twenty years later, "Kobyla" was exposed when the Federal Republic of Germany attempted to extradite her. The arrest of this New York housewife and her eventual denaturalization by the U.S. government in the B*raunsteiner Hearing *sparked American interest in the prosecution of war criminals. As a result, the Office of Special Investigations, a branch of the United States Department of Justice, was formed to investigate* war crimes *in 1979.*

In the following excerpt from the Majdanek Trial, witness Hela Rosenbaum identifies the defendant Ryan.

Day 260. 10 May 1978. Following protocol, the presiding judge asks the witness Hela Rosenbaum the question, "Are any of the accused relatives of yours or related to you by marriage?" The woman, fifty-one years old, becomes bright red in the face. "I am a Jew!" The judge explains to her why he must ask this question. The woman pulls nervously on her black velvet jacket. Finally, after she is again asked about any possible relation to the SS guards of Majdanek, she quietly answers, "No. Thank God, no."

Hela Rosenbaum can hardly control the tension that this reunion with the women SS guards has welled up inside her. As she stands in front of the accused Hermine Braunsteiner-Ryan, she is only able to choke out, "Kobyla, that's Kobyla." Then the presiding judge has to interrupt the proceedings. A doctor treats the over-excited woman. Twenty minutes later she is standing in front of Hildegard Lächert. "Bloody Brygida. Never without her whip," she says. Once she received twenty-five lashes from her. She describes that, then pauses. The judge asks her a question. She does not answer. He asks her again. Hela Rosenbaum says, "Excuse me please. I am no longer here, Your Honor. I am back in the camp."

— *Reprinted from Gunther Schwarberg*, Der Juweiler von Majdanek *(Hamburg, 1981), 162. Translated from the German by Neal Guthrie.*

A German defendant, a former official of the M*ajdanek* killing center, stands during the Soviet trial of some of the camp's staff; December 1944.
(Central Armed Forces Museum, Moscow, Russia)

OFFICE OF SPECIAL INVESTIGATIONS

In 1979 the United States Attorney General's Office created the Office of Special Investigations (OSI) as a division within the U.S. Department of Justice. The OSI is responsible for detecting and investigating those individuals suspected of having committed WAR CRIMES in association with the NAZI government during World War II.

The need for such an organization arose after many suspected Nazi COLLABORATORS entered the United States following the war. OSI officials have estimated that as many as 10,000 Nazi perpetrators arrived between 1948 and 1952 under the Displaced Persons Act of 1948. They did this in part by lying about their careers before coming to the United States and by obtaining false identity papers. Others immigrated under the Refugee Relief Act of 1952.

Before OSI's creation, the U.S. Attorney's Office and the U.S. Immigration and Naturalization Service (INS) handled illegal immigration by former Nazis. These agencies, however, lacked the historical and investigative capabilities to deal fully with these cases. Thus, the OSI was set up and given the legal authority to investigate those suspected of inciting, ordering, assisting, or participating in the persecution of any person or group between 1933 and 1945.

Because war crimes occurred in Europe, the OSI lacks the jurisdiction to prosecute these cases directly. However, the OSI can assist in deporting, and in one case extraditing, the suspected individuals to countries legally willing to prosecute them. Cases can be brought to the attention of OSI by countries that make direct charges against citizens of the United States, or they can result from OSI-initiated research of CONCENTRATION CAMP rosters and Nazi staff lists; these lists are then compared with names on U.S. immigration registers.

An accused U.S. citizen is fully protected by the Constitution and can only be deported once he or she has been found guilty of lying in a court of law about material facts affecting one's immigration status. The OSI can then assist in the process of denaturalization and/or deportation. This process can be very protracted; a defense attorney can prolong judicial proceedings with appeals.

War crimes documentation centers, foreign ministries of justice, and Holocaust survivors all assist the OSI in developing cases against suspected criminals. Accusations range from the murder of individuals and mass murder to the responsibility for institutionalizing programs of Nazi GENOCIDE. Most of those individuals listed by the OSI have been low-level functionaries and members of fascist collaborationist armies. The OSI has, nevertheless, handled cases involving high-level officials who were responsible for mass murders, such as Andrija Artukovic.

Artukovic served as the minister of the interior in the Nazi puppet state of CROATIA. He was responsible for dealing with the country's minorities, primarily Serbs. Between 1941 and 1944, hundreds of thousands of Serbs and approximately 20,000 Jews were murdered in concentration camps that Artukovic established. In 1948 Artukovic arrived in New York under an assumed name. After repeated attempts to deport him, the OSI finally succeeded in extraditing him to Yugoslavia in 1986, where he was sentenced to death in Zagreb. He died in prison in 1988. Artukovic had initiated persecutions and was the highest-ranking Nazi war criminal to have entered the United States.

Bohdan Koziy was among the many low-level functionaries that the OSI has helped to expose. As a member of the Ukrainian police, Koziy was accused of personally killing 14 Jews from the town of Lysiec, Ukraine. Koziy entered the U.S. in 1949 under the Displaced Persons Act, claiming he was a tailor and farmhand during the war. Proved in court to have lied on his application for immigration and naturalization, Koziy's citizenship was revoked, and he was sentenced for deportation to the Soviet Union. Before his extradition, however, Koziy fled to Costa Rica, where he enjoyed relative freedom.

The OSI claims both cases to be a success, despite the length of time needed to finalize them. The OSI exposed Artukovic for his wartime crimes and he was finally jailed in his native country for them. While Koziy was not brought to trial, his crimes were exposed and his citizenship revoked.

Since its inception, the OSI has denaturalized 53 persons, and 44 have been removed from the United States. While more than 300 individuals are still under investigation, the Office of Special Investigations may soon be terminated since many of the suspected criminals from Nazi Germany are very old. Nevertheless, with the fall of East European Communism and the opening up of previously closed archives, much more evidence is available to researchers who can assist with investigating war criminals who had previously eluded identification. These archives house a wealth of AXIS documents, which are just now being examined by Western historians and researchers. In effect, the OSI is racing against the clock to bring these cases to justice.

HOLOCAUST CHRONOLOGY

1933

January 30	Adolf HITLER is appointed chancellor of Germany.
March 20	DACHAU concentration camp, the first in a system which came to include thousands of camps and sub-camps by 1944, is established near Munich. Its first prisoners are those arrested for political opposition to the regime.
March 24	The Enabling Act is passed by the German *Reichstag* (parliament); the Act is used by Adolf HITLER to establish his NAZI dictatorship.
April 7	The German "Law for the Restoration of the Professional Civil Service" is promulgated. It excludes most Jewish and "politically unreliable" civil servants and employees from state service.
April 1	An official, nationwide, one-day boycott of Jewish-owned businesses is called by the NAZI PARTY leadership.

1934

June 30	The SS, under Heinrich HIMMLER, purges the SA leadership in the "Night of the Long Knives."

1935

April 1	The REICH and Prussian Ministry of the Interior prohibit JEHOVAH'S WITNESSES from religious activity and publication throughout Germany. By 1939, nearly 7,000 Jehovah's Witnesses are imprisoned in CONCENTRATION CAMPS.
June 28	German officials strengthen Paragraph 175 of the German legal code to introduce more stringent punishment for homosexual behavior; the paragraph is widened to punish all "indecent" acts between men, even those not sexual in nature.
September 15	The so-called NUREMBERG LAWS are promulgated. The "Reich Citizenship Law" and its corollaries exclude Jews and other non-"Aryans" from full REICH citizenship; the "Law for the Protection of German Blood and German Honor" forbids marriage or sexual relations between German Aryans and Jews.

1936

| March 7 | The German Rhineland, demilitarized after World War I, is reoccupied by German troops. |
| August 1–16 | The Summer Olympic Games are held in Berlin, Germany. |

1938

March 12	During the so-called *ANSCHLUSS*, German troops cross the border into Austria; Austria is incorporated into the German REICH.
November 9–10	The *KRISTALLNACHT* pogrom occurs all over Germany following the assassination of German diplomat Ernst vom Rath in Paris by a Jewish youth.
November 12	The confiscation of Jewish property and assets accelerates with the "Decree for the Exclusion of Jews from German Economic Life." The Jews of Germany are fined one billion Reichsmarks as a "punishment" for the assassination of Ernst vom Rath.

1939

January 1	All German Jewish citizens bearing names of "non-Jewish" origin are ordered to add Israel (for men) or Sara (for women) to their given names.
January 30	Adolf HITLER predicts "the annihilation of the Jewish race in Europe" in the event of war in a speech to the German *Reichstag* (parliament).
March 15	Following the annexation of the Sudeten section of Czechoslovakia in October 1938, German troops occupy Prague and the remainder of the Czechoslovak Republic.
September 1	Germany invades Poland; World War II begins. All German Jews are subject to a nightly curfew.
October 9	Adolf EICHMANN organizes the first DEPORTATION of Jews from Vienna, Ostrava, and Katowice to Nisko, near Lublin, in German-occupied Poland. Chaotic conditions in the GENERAL GOVERNMENT cause the RESETTLEMENT project to fail.
October	Adolf HITLER signs a secret decree establishing the "EUTHANASIA" program; the document is ante-dated to September 1, 1939, to make it appear as if the euthanasia program were associated with the war effort.
November 23	Wearing of the JEWISH BADGE becomes mandatory for Jews in the GENERAL GOVERNMENT.

1940

| April 27 | Heinrich HIMMLER orders the first DEPORTATION transport of GYPSIES from Germany to the GENERAL GOVERNMENT. |

May 20	The AUSCHWITZ concentration camp is established.
October 2	German officials issue a decree establishing the WARSAW GHETTO.

1941

March	German physicians begin sterilization experiments on female prisoners at the RAVENSBRÜCK concentration camp.
June 22	The German invasion of the Soviet Union begins; EINSATZGRUPPEN, following closely behind the combat troops, begin the wholesale slaughter of Jews, GYPSIES, and Soviet political functionaries.
July 31	A memorandum signed by Hermann GÖRING requests Reinhard HEYDRICH to prepare a "total solution to the Jewish Question." Historians believe that this directive led directly to the establishment of KILLING CENTERS and the efforts to exterminate the Jews of Europe.
August 24	Adolf HITLER orders an end to OPERATION T4 as public protest concerning the "secret" program grows. Hereafter, the "EUTHANASIA" program continues in a more discreet and decentralized manner.
September 1	A German police ordinance requires German Jews over the age of six to wear the JEWISH BADGE.
September 3	The first gassing of prisoners occurs at the AUSCHWITZ camp complex using ZYKLON B. The victims are 900 Soviet prisoners of war.
September 15	The DEPORTATION of 150,000 Jews from Bessarabia and Bukovina begins, continuing until October 1942.
September 29–30	Members of EINSATZGRUPPEN C murder over 33,000 Jews at Babi Yar near Kiev, Ukraine.
October 15	The systematic DEPORTATION of Jews from Germany begins.
November 24	The THERESIENSTADT Ghetto is established in the PROTECTORATE OF BOHEMIA AND MORAVIA.

1942

January 20	Fifteen NAZI and senior government officials meet at Wannsee in Berlin to plan the fulfillment of the "FINAL SOLUTION," the extermination of Europe's Jews.
February 1	The SS CENTRAL OFFICE FOR ECONOMY AND ADMINISTRATION (WVHA) is established under the leadership of Oswald POHL to manage SLAVE LABOR in German industry and CONCENTRATION CAMPS.
May 4	The first SELECTION of Jews takes place at the AUSCHWITZ-BIRKENAU killing center.
June 9	The Czech town of LIDICE is razed and the population either killed or deported in retaliation for the assassination of Reinhard HEYDRICH by agents of the Czech exile government in England several days earlier.

July 19	Heinrich HIMMLER issues an order to complete the DEPORTATION of all Jews from the GENERAL GOVERNMENT to the KILLING CENTERS.
July 23	The TREBLINKA killing center begins operations as Jews from the WARSAW GHETTO are transported to the camp; most die in the camp's GAS CHAMBERS.
July 31	DEPORTATIONS of Dutch Jews, which began earlier in the month, total 6,000.
December 16	Heinrich HIMMLER issues a decree for the DEPORTATION of "all Roma GYPSIES, all part Gypsies, and all non-German Gypsies of Balkan origin" to the AUSCHWITZ concentration camp.

1943

February 25	A GHETTO is established for the Jews of Salonika, Greece. DEPORTATIONS begin the following month.
April 19	The WARSAW GHETTO Uprising begins as Jewish fighters fiercely resist the German attempt to liquidate the Ghetto; resistance continues for more than a month.
June 11	Heinrich HIMMLER orders the liquidation of all remaining GHETTOS in German-occupied Poland and the Occupied Eastern Territories and the DEPORTATION of their inhabitants to KILLING CENTERS.
June 28	Construction of the last CREMATORIUM in the AUSCHWITZ-BIRKENAU killing center is completed.
July 5	Heinrich HIMMLER orders the closing of the OPERATION REINHARD camps, as most of the Jews in the GENERAL GOVERNMENT have already been killed.
August 2	Jewish prisoners revolt at the TREBLINKA killing center; although more than 150 prisoners escape, most are caught and killed.
October 1	Deportations of Danish Jews begin; however, most escape to Sweden with the help of the Danish RESISTANCE.
November 3	Operation "Harvest Festival" begins as the Germans liquidate the last Jews in the Lublin region of occupied Poland. In this single largest German killing operation, 42,000 Jews are shot to death.

1944

January 4	A conference of high-ranking German officials at the FÜHRER's Headquarters concludes that four million SLAVE and FORCED LABORERS are needed to support the German war effort.
March 8	Over 3,700 Jews transferred from the THERESIENSTADT Ghetto to the AUSCHWITZ-BIRKENAU killing center and held in the so-called family camp are sent to the GAS CHAMBERS.

May 15–July 19	The DEPORTATION of Jews from recently occupied Hungary is carried out; most are sent to the AUSCHWITZ-BIRKENAU killing center where they are immediately gassed.
June 6	D-Day: the ALLIES land on the beaches of Normandy, France.
July 24	The MAJDANEK killing center is liberated by the Soviet Army; it is the first killing center entered by ALLIED troops.
July 28	The first major FORCED EVACUATION begins as prisoners from the Gesia Street CONCENTRATION CAMP in Warsaw are marched to Kutno, occupied Poland.
August 2–3	The GYPSY family camp at the AUSCHWITZ-BIRKENAU concentration camp is liquidated.
September 29	Over 1,800 Italian civilians are massacred by WAFFEN-SS troops in the Marzabatto plateau region of Tuscany in northern Italy.
October 7	Members of a SONDERKOMMANDO destroy a CREMATORIUM during an uprising at the AUSCHWITZ-BIRKENAU killing center.
November 8	The DEPORTATION of Hungarian Jews from Budapest begins as thousands are marched towards the REICH.
November 26	"The Auschwitz Report," detailing the killings at the AUSCHWITZ-BIRKENAU killing center, is released to the public by the WAR REFUGEE BOARD.
November 26	Heinrich HIMMLER orders the dismantling of the CREMATORIA at the AUSCHWITZ-BIRKENAU killing center.
December 11	Gassings end at the Hartheim "EUTHANASIA" facility, where approximately 30,000 people have been killed.

1945

January 17	Massive FORCED EVACUATIONS from the AUSCHWITZ camp complex begin as Soviet forces draw near.
January 27	The AUSCHWITZ camp complex is liberated by Soviet troops.
April 11	The BUCHENWALD concentration camp is liberated by American troops as prisoners start a revolt to forestall the evacuation of the camp.
April 13	More than 1,000 CONCENTRATION CAMP prisoners, part of a FORCED EVACUATION, are burned to death by SS troops in a barn near Gardelegen, Germany.
April 15	BERGEN-BELSEN concentration camp is liberated by British troops.
April 29	The DACHAU concentration camp is liberated by American troops.
April 30	Adolf Hitler commits suicide in Berlin.

May 3   Three German ships carrying prisoners evacuated from NEUENGAMME concentration camp are attacked by ALLIED aircraft in the bay of Lübeck, Germany. Two ships are sunk; approximately 7,300 prisoners are killed.

May 8   V-E Day: Germany surrenders unconditionally to the ALLIES.

WAR CRIMES CHRONOLOGY

1939

September 1

Germany invades Poland; World War II begins.

1940

May 10

Germany invades the Netherlands, Belgium, Luxembourg, and France. The former three countries surrender within the month; France falls on June 22.

1941

June 22

Germany invades the Soviet Union.

October 25

American President Franklin D. ROOSEVELT, referring specifically to the German execution of hostages in France, warns that such acts will "bring fearful retribution." On the same day, British Prime Minister Winston CHURCHILL announces that punishment of WAR CRIMES should be "counted among the major goals of the war."

1942

January 13

Representatives from Belgium, France, Czechoslovakia, Greece, Luxembourg, Norway, the Netherlands, Poland, and Yugoslavia conclude an Inter-Allied conference on the punishment of WAR CRIMES (Saint James Palace Declaration), held in London, with the statement that a primary aim of the war was "the punishment through the channel of organized justice of those guilty of or responsible for these crimes." At this point, "war crimes" are defined as violations of the HAGUE and GENEVA CONVENTIONS.

January 20

The Wannsee Conference convenes in a lakeside suburb of Berlin. Under the chairmanship of CENTRAL OFFICE FOR REICH SECURITY chief Reinhard HEYDRICH, senior German officials coordinate the implementation of the "FINAL SOLUTION," the systematic mass extermination of the Jews in Europe.

May 4

For the first time, a "SELECTION" is carried out at the ramp at the AUSCHWITZ-BIRKENAU killing center, whereby German officers decided who would die in the GAS CHAMBERS and who would live as FORCED LABORERS. This marks the beginning of mass gassing of Jews at the Auschwitz complex.

October 7	The United States and Great Britain issue simultaneous declarations suggesting the creation of a UNITED NATIONS WAR CRIMES COMMISSION to bring war criminals to justice. The Allied governments-in-exile and the French National Committee approve and adopt this concept, and the commission is inaugurated on October 20, 1943. The Soviet Union alone refuses to join, and instead establishes its own war crimes agency, the Soviet Extraordinary State Commission to Investigate War Crimes.

1943

February 2	Surrounded at Stalingrad, the German Sixth Army surrenders to Soviet forces, signalling a turning point in the German war effort.
July 17	In the first adjudication of NAZI WAR CRIMES during World War II, a Soviet military tribunal in the KRASNODAR TRIAL convicts 11 Soviet citizens and 13 Germans (the latter tried *in absentia*) for the murder of 7,000 Soviet civilians, including patients from three hospitals. All the defendants are members of an auxiliary unit attached to the German *EINSATZGRUPPE D*; eight of the Soviets are hanged for their crimes, and three are sentenced to 20 years at hard labor.

1944

January 23	A WAR CRIMES office is established within the office of JUDGE ADVOCATE GENERAL of the U.S. Army to gather evidence on war crimes.
March 16	Herbert Pell, American representative to the UNITED NATIONS WAR CRIMES COMMISSION, presents a resolution that crimes committed against stateless persons or against individuals due to their race or religion be regarded as WAR CRIMES, since such acts are against the "laws of humanity."
April 19	The WARSAW GHETTO Uprising begins. More than 1,300 Jewish resistance fighters defy German forces under the command of *SS-Brigadeführer* [SS Brigadier General] Jürgen STROOP for more than a month.
May 16	Members of the UNITED NATIONS WAR CRIMES COMMISSION agree on measures for the capture of war criminals, including the compilation of lists of such criminals and the need to arrest all members of the SS and GESTAPO on surrender.
June 28	The British War Cabinet approves a memorandum by the Lord Chancellor that states, in part, that Britain will gather evidence of German atrocities against Jews only in occupied countries, since German crimes against German Jews could not be construed as WAR CRIMES.
November 27	Six SS men stand trial before a Polish Special Tribunal, in Lublin, at the first trial of MAJDANEK concentration camp staff. The trial ends several days later with four of the defendants sentenced to death; two men commit suicide before the sentence is carried out.

1945

January 31	Lord Quincy Wright of Australia becomes chairman of the UNITED NATIONS WAR CRIMES COMMISSION.
February 4–12	American President Franklin D. ROOSEVELT, British Prime Minister Winston CHURCHILL, and Soviet Premier Joseph STALIN attend the YALTA CONFERENCE in the Crimea. Among the topics under discussion are the postwar "DENAZIFICATION" of Germany and procedures for the prosecution of AXIS war criminals.
April 22	At the invitation of General Dwight D. EISENHOWER, a bipartisan Congressional delegation begins a tour of the concentration camps of BUCHENWALD, DORA-MITTELBAU, and DACHAU, all liberated by U.S. forces. Senator Alben Barkley (D-Ky.), Senate majority leader, presents the delegation's report to Congress on May 15. Eisenhower also invites 18 American editors and publishers to view the liberated camps. Widespread publication of German atrocities strengthens American resolve to try NAZI war criminals.
May 7	German General Alfred JODL signs terms of unconditional surrender at Rheims, France. War in the European theater officially ends on May 8 (VE-Day).
June 14	The British Government promulgates the Royal Warrant, the basis for jurisdiction for British military courts trying AXIS war criminals.
July 16	United States Forces, European Theater sets up Military Government Tribunals for WAR CRIMES proceedings in the American zone.
July 25	The Darmstadt Trial, the first WAR CRIMES trial tried by the War Crimes Branch of the U.S. Army's JUDGE ADVOCATE GENERAL's Office in the American occupation zone of Germany, begins as eleven German civilians are tried for the beating deaths of six downed American airmen. Prosecutor Colonel Leon JAWORSKI wins ten convictions; seven defendants are sentenced to death and three are given sentences of 15 to 25 years at hard labor.

"Last Chapter of 'Mein Kampf,'" *St. Louis Post-Dispatch,* June 8, 1945.

July 28	The first British WAR CRIMES trial begins with the arraignment of Italian General Bellomo. He is convicted of killing escaped British prisoners of war and is executed on September 11, 1945.
August 8	The LONDON AGREEMENT, establishing the INTERNATIONAL MILITARY TRIBUNAL (IMT) at Nuremberg, is signed by the four major Allied powers: the United States of America, the United Kingdom, the French Republic, and the Soviet Union.
August 15	French Marshal Henri Philippe Pétain is convicted of treason and sentenced to death by the French High Court of Justice for COLLABORATION with German occupation forces. Due to his advanced age and former service, France's Provisional Government under General Charles de Gaulle commutes his sentence to life imprisonment.
August 29	The list of major war criminals to be tried before the INTERNATIONAL MILITARY TRIBUNAL is released.
September 2	Japan signs the instrument of surrender in Tokyo Bay as World War II comes to an end.
October 5	The Berlin Protocol is signed, reconciling discrepancies concerning the interpretation of the concept of CRIMES AGAINST HUMANITY between signatories of the LONDON AGREEMENT (*see* entry for August 8).
October 8–15	At the HADAMAR TRIAL, the first mass atrocity trial in the U.S. zone, seven German civilians are convicted of murdering 476 tubercular Russian and Polish forced laborers at the HADAMAR "EUTHANASIA" facility. Three receive death sentences; four receive sentences ranging from 25 years to life.
October 12	General Anton Doestler is found guilty at the DOESTLER TRIAL of ordering the execution of fifteen U.S. servicemen captured in March 1944. He is sentenced to death by an American military tribunal in Rome and executed on December 1.
October 19	The INTERNATIONAL MILITARY TRIBUNAL formally indicts twenty-four Nuremberg defendants on four counts: CRIMES AGAINST PEACE, WAR CRIMES, CRIMES AGAINST HUMANITY, and CONSPIRACY to commit these crimes.
October 30	The CONTROL COUNCIL FOR GERMANY enacts Control Council Law No. 4, which regulates the reopening of German law courts. The law dissolves the infamous People's Courts (*Volksgerichtshöfe*) and prevents the reopening of the Reich Supreme Court. It also specifically forbids German courts from trying NAZI WAR CRIMES perpetrated against Allied nationals.
November 4	The DACHAU TRIAL begins, as American military officials try forty former members of the DACHAU concentration camp staff at Dachau. Prosecutors win convictions for all defendants on December 15. Thirty-six are sentenced to hang; four receive prison sentences of 10 years to life.
November 17	At the BERGEN-BELSEN TRIAL, the British tribunal trying former camp commandant Josef Kramer and forty-four other defendants for atrocities committed at the BERGEN-BELSEN concentration camp convicts twenty-nine of the defendants. Nine, including Kramer, are sentenced to

hang; twenty defendants receive prison sentences, while fourteen are acquitted. (The original charge sheet accuses thirteen defendants with crimes at Bergen-Belsen and at the AUSCHWITZ concentration camp, a decision that complicates the Bergen-Belsen proceedings.)

November 20

The first public session of the trial of major German war criminals opens before the INTERNATIONAL MILITARY TRIBUNAL at Nuremberg.

December 17

The Central Registry of War Criminals and Security Suspects (CROW-CASS) delivers "Wanted List No. 7" to the U.S. JUDGE ADVOCATE GENERAL's office. It is the first "usable" list to aid in the apprehension of war criminals.

December 20

The CONTROL COUNCIL FOR GERMANY issues CONTROL COUNCIL LAW No. 10, which establishes "a uniform legal basis in Germany for the prosecution of war criminals and similar offenders." The law recognizes four crimes (CRIMES AGAINST PEACE, CRIMES AGAINST HUMANITY, WAR CRIMES, and membership in CRIMINAL ORGANIZATIONS as defined by the INTERNATIONAL MILITARY TRIBUNAL) and regulates the apprehension, extradition, and trial of war criminals in Germany's four occupied zones. It also permits German courts, at the discretion of each zone's military authority, to deal with cases involving crimes committed by German nationals against other German nationals or stateless persons.

"Spectator," *St. Louis Post-Dispatch*, December 3, 1945.

1946

March 8

The ZYKLON B TRIAL, held by a military tribunal in the British zone of occupied Germany, ends with the conviction of two of the three defendants, who are sentenced to death.

May 13

The MAUTHAUSEN TRIAL ends after less than two months with all sixty-one defendants found guilty of violations of the laws of war committed at the MAUTHAUSEN concentration camp. All but three are sentenced to death and executed.

September 5	The former commandant of the PLASZOW labor camp, Amon Goeth, is found guilty of mass murder by Poland's Supreme National Court in Cracow in connection with the liquidation of the Szebnie and Tarnow GHETTOS and with his tenure at Plaszow. Sentenced to death, he is hanged on September 13, 1946.
October 1	The INTERNATIONAL MILITARY TRIBUNAL in Nuremberg convicts nineteen of the twenty-two defendants tried (Martin BORMANN is tried *in absentia*) and acquits three. Ten are hanged later that month; Hermann GÖRING commits suicide before his death sentence can be carried out. Seven are sentenced to prison terms.
October 25	In the DOCTORS TRIAL, U.S. Military Tribunal I tries Adolf HITLER'S chief physician and former Reich Commissioner for Health and Sanitation Karl BRANDT and twenty-two others for WAR CRIMES, CRIMES AGAINST HUMANITY, and CONSPIRACY to commit these crimes. Found guilty in August 1947 of murdering handicapped patients and performing grisly medical experiments on CONCENTRATION CAMP inmates, prisoners of war, and civilians in occupied territories, Brandt and six other defendants are executed; nine receive prison sentences, and seven are acquitted. This is the first of twelve proceedings before U.S. military tribunals known as the Subsequent NUREMBERG MILITARY TRIALS.
November 13	In the MILCH TRIAL, U.S. Military Tribunal II in Nuremberg tries Erhard Milch, German state secretary to the Reich Air Ministry. Milch is convicted in December 1947 of exploiting FORCED LABOR in the development of the German Air Force and is sentenced to life imprisonment. His sentence is later reduced to 15 years.

1947

January 4	In the so-called JURISTS' TRIAL, an American military tribunal tries Josef Altstötter, chief of the Civil Law and Procedure Division in the Reich Ministry of Justice, and fifteen other prominent German jurists with WAR CRIMES, CRIMES AGAINST HUMANITY, and CONSPIRACY to commit these crimes. Convicted on December 4 of supporting the NAZI regime by subverting German law, ten defendants are given prison sentences (four life sentences); four defendants are acquitted; two are not tried.
February 8	The FLICK TRIAL begins as the U.S. Nuremberg Military Tribunal tries prominent industrialist Friedrich Flick and five of his associates for WAR CRIMES and CRIMES AGAINST HUMANITY, including the plunder of conquered territories, utilizing FORCED LABOR, and participating in the "ARYANIZATION" of Jewish property. When the trial ends on December 22, Flick and two others are given sentences ranging from 2 to 7 years; three are acquitted.
March 21	The German HADAMAR TRIAL, held before the district court in Frankfurt am Main, ends with the conviction of eleven of the twenty-five defendants. Dr. Adolf Wahlman and one other are sentenced to death; nine others receive prison sentences of up to 8 years.
May 3	The U.S. Military Tribunal VI in Nuremberg begins the trial of twenty-four officers of the I.G. FARBEN concern, Germany's largest chemical conglomerate, in the I.G. FARBEN TRIAL. Convicted in June of plunder

and spoilation of conquered territories and utilization of FORCED LABOR (most notoriously at their AUSCHWITZ-MONOWITZ installation), thirteen defendants, including Carl Krauch, chairman of Farben's supervisory board, receive prison sentences of one to 8 years.

May 10	The HOSTAGE TRIAL begins as German Field Marshal Wilhelm List and eleven German generals stand accused of WAR CRIMES and CRIMES AGAINST HUMANITY. The trial ends in February 1948, when eight men are given prison sentences ranging from 12 years to life; two are acquitted, while proceedings against an additional defendant are suspended due to ill health. One of the indicted commits suicide before arraignment.
November 3	After a ten-month trial, the POHL TRIAL ends with the conviction of fifteen former members of the SS CENTRAL OFFICE FOR ECONOMY AND ADMINISTRATION. Oswald POHL and three other defendants are sentenced to death, and eleven are given prison terms ranging from 10 years to life; three defendants are acquitted.
November 4	The MINISTRIES TRIAL begins as high-ranking German government officials are tried on eight counts by an American military tribunal. Nineteen defendants are found guilty and given prison sentences when the trial ends in November 1948; of these, former Interior Minister Stuckart, seriously ill, is sentenced to "time served."
November 21	United Nations Resolution 177 adopts the Nuremberg Principles of international law concerning WAR CRIMES and war criminals.

1948

January 12	The United Nations Convention on the Prevention and Punishment of the Crime of GENOCIDE comes into force. The Convention, not immediately ratified by the United States, recognizes various acts that demonstrate the "intent to destroy, in whole or in part, a national, ethnic, racial, or religious group."
March 10	In Nuremberg, the RuSHA TRIAL ends as U.S. Military Tribunal I convicts thirteen of the fourteen defendants, all former members of the SS CENTRAL OFFICE FOR RACE AND RESETTLEMENT, the REICH COMMISSION FOR STRENGTHENING GERMANISM, and various subsidiary organizations, for crimes associated with the "GERMANIZATION" of German-occupied Europe. One defendant is acquitted.
March 29	Rudolf Höss, commandant of the killing center AUSCHWITZ-BIRKENAU, is sentenced to death by the Polish Supreme Court in Warsaw after a trial lasting several weeks. Höss is hanged in Oswiecim on the grounds of the former AUSCHWITZ camp on April 16.
April 10	The EINSATZGRUPPEN TRIAL ends. A U.S. military tribunal convicts twenty-two defendants in connection with *EINSATZGRUPPEN* atrocities in Eastern Europe. Fourteen are sentenced to death; eight receive prison sentences ranging from time served to life.
August 16	The KRUPP TRIAL begins as steel magnate Alfred Krupp and eleven of his associates are tried by an American military tribunal for CRIMES AGAINST PEACE, CONSPIRACY, plunder of occupied territories, and utiliza-

tion of SLAVE LABOR. The following July, eleven are convicted and given prison sentences ranging from 2 to 12 years.

October 28	U.S. Military Tribunal in Nuremberg closes the HIGH COMMAND TRIAL, in which thirteen army generals and one navy admiral had been indicted on four counts: CRIMES AGAINST PEACE, WAR CRIMES against enemy belligerents and civilians, CRIMES AGAINST HUMANITY, and CONSPIRACY. (Counts 1 and 4 were later dropped.) Eleven are convicted and given prison sentences ranging from 3 years to life. Two defendants are acquitted; another commits suicide in his cell during the proceedings.
November 24	Arthur Liebehenschel, briefly the commandant of AUSCHWITZ and later commandant of the MAJDANEK concentration camp, is tried by a Polish court in Cracow along with thirty-nine other defendants, many of whom had held key staff positions at Auschwitz. The following month twenty-three defendants receive the death penalty; sixteen receive prison sentences.

1950

May 8	West Germany issued a fifteen-year statute of limitations on NAZI crimes other than premeditated murder. The statute lists May 8, 1945—the day the European war ended—as the date from which the duration of the statute would be calculated for all Nazi crimes rather than the date on which the crimes were committed, since it was not possible to prosecute these crimes during the Nazi regime (*See* entry for May 8, 1960).

1951

July 18–23	The trial of SS police chief Jürgen STROOP, who presided over the suppression of the 1943 WARSAW GHETTO uprising, begins before the Warsaw District Criminal Court. Accused of the liquidation of the Warsaw Ghetto and the mass murder of Jews and Polish civilians, Stroop is sentenced to death several days later and hanged on March 6, 1952.

1955

May 3	A Transition Agreement, signed by West Germany, the United States, the United Kingdom, and France, stipulates that persons previously tried by Allied occupation authorities will not be tried by German courts for the same offense, regardless of the outcome of the initial trial.

1958

October	The recent trial of German *EINSATZGRUPPEN* members in Ulm, using newly uncovered evidence, convinces German justice officials meeting at Bad Harzburg that many of the most heinous NAZI crimes—especially those committed in the East—have yet to be tried. Justice ministers representing all German federal states (*Länder*) agree to establish the Central Office of State Administrations of Justice for the Investigation of Nazi Crimes (*Zentrale Stelle*) in Ludwigsburg. In its first year it initiates 400 extensive investigations; the most important are those cases involving the actions of the *Einsatzgruppen* and affiliated organizations and mass murder in KILLING CENTERS located in German-occupied Poland.

1960

May 8

Fifteen years after the end of World War II, the statute of limitations expires on the crimes of manslaughter, deliberate physical injury resulting in death, and robbery. In practical terms, West German courts prosecuting NAZI crimes may pursue only those cases involving premeditated murder. Politicians in the German Social Democratic Party (SPD) attempt to introduce a law that would block enforcement of the statute for Nazi WAR CRIMES, but the *Bundestag* (German parliament) votes to retain it.

1961

April 10

Following his dramatic kidnapping from Argentina by the Israeli security service, Adolf EICHMANN is tried in the District Court of Jerusalem. Mastermind of the DEPORTATION scheme that sent at least three million Jews to their deaths, Eichmann is convicted of crimes against the Jewish people, CRIMES AGAINST HUMANITY, and WAR CRIMES, and is sentenced to death. The trial has a profound impact on Holocaust research and documentation and leads to an intensified search for remaining NAZI war criminals.

"The Way of the Crooked Cross," *Los Angeles Times,* **April 11, 1961.**

1964

September 3

The TREBLINKA TRIAL ends with the conviction of nine of the ten defendants who were charged with directly participating in the murder of more than 300,000 people at the TREBLINKA killing center. All are sentenced to prison terms ranging from several years to life.

November 20

Six months before the German twenty-year statute of limitations would block the trial of cases involving NAZI killings, the West German government makes a formal request that foreign governments put at their disposal all available evidence concerning Nazi WAR CRIMES. The request is aimed primarily at Communist bloc countries, where Cold War politics has blocked access to pertinent documents.

1965

March 25	After sharp debate, the West German parliament *(Bundestag)* votes to extend the statute of limitations for NAZI crimes involving murder from May 8, 1965, to December 31, 1969. The statute is extended another ten years in 1969 (*See* entry for July 1979).

1967

January 23	The HARSTER TRIAL begins in Munich, as Wilhelm Harster and two others are tried for aiding and abetting in the murder of Dutch Jews. All three are found guilty on February 17 and sentenced to prison terms.

1968

April 8	Eleven of fourteen former German policemen of Reserve Police Battalion 101 are convicted by a district court in Hamburg of mass shootings of Jews in Lublin, Poland, during summer 1942. Five of the convicted defendants are sentenced to prison terms.

1970

December 22	After seven months, the STANGL TRIAL ends; defendant Franz Stangl is convicted of the murder of over 400,000 victims at the TREBLINKA killing center. He is sentenced to life in prison and incarcerated but dies of heart failure in 1971.

1978

October 30	The U.S. Congress passes the Holtzmann Amendment to the Immigration and Naturalization Act of 1952. The Amendment created a "watch list" of alleged war criminals who are to be denied entry to the United States and permits deportation proceedings against those suspected of committing WAR CRIMES from 1933 to 1945.

1979

June 2	The Office of Special Investigations, U.S. Department of Justice, is founded, with the mission of investigating and taking legal action against individuals who "in association with the NAZI government, ordered, incited, assisted, or otherwise participated in the persecution of any persons because of race, religion, national origin, or political opinion between 1933 and 1945."
July	The German parliament *(Bundestag)* abolishes the existing statute of limitation for crimes of murder under German law. This measure effectively enables German courts to try NAZI war criminals for murder without impediment.

1980

November 26

The ASCHE TRIAL begins in Kiel, Germany; Kurt Asche and two other defendants stand trial for aiding and abetting the DEPORTATION of Belgian Jews. Asche is found guilty and is sentenced to 12 years in prison in June 1981.

1981

June 30

The MAJDANEK TRIAL ends with the conviction of eight of the defendants, including Hermine Braunsteiner-Ryan, the only American citizen extradited from the United States for WAR CRIMES. Braunsteiner-Ryan is sentenced to life in prison. The trial began in November 1975, making it the longest German criminal trial for defendants accused of NAZI war crimes.

1984

December 21

Feodor Fedorenko, a former Ukrainian SS guard at the TREBLINKA killing center, is deported to the Soviet Union to stand trial after he is denaturalized from United States citizenship in the FEDORENKO HEARING. He had concealed his wartime SS activities upon applying for U.S. citizenship.

1987

July 4

Klaus Barbie, "The Butcher of Lyon," is sentenced by a French court to life in prison for CRIMES AGAINST HUMANITY. Barbie was the GESTAPO chief in Lyon and responsible for the DEPORTATION of Jews and the torture and murder of French RESISTANCE fighters.

1993

July 29

Israel's Supreme Court overturns the guilty verdict (death sentence) in the case of John Demjanjuk. He was deported by the U.S. to Israel in February 1986 to stand trial for alleged activities as the SS guard "Ivan the Terrible" at the TREBLINKA killing center.

1994

April 20

Paul Touvier, former Chief of French police in Lyon, France, is sentenced to life in prison for CRIMES AGAINST HUMANITY; he had ordered the shooting of seven Jews near Lyon on June 29, 1944.

1995

December 7

Italy opens what could be the last war crimes proceedings after Argentina extradites SS Captain Erich Priebke at Italy's request. Priebke stands trial for the 1944 massacre of 335 men and boys in the Ardeatine caves south of Rome.

TRIALS APPENDIX

The ALLIES knew of German atrocities almost from the beginning of the Second World War. During the next two years, as evidence of atrocities in occupied Poland and western Europe mounted, the executions of Allied hostages in France during 1941 provided an occasion for strong condemnations from both American President Franklin D. ROOSEVELT and British Prime Minister Winston CHURCHILL. In his statement Churchill resolved that punishment for such war crimes would be "counted among the major goals of the war." As a consequence, the Allied governments established the UNITED NATIONS WAR CRIMES COMMISSION on October 20, 1943, to investigate, record, and assist in the preparation of indictments for NAZI crimes.

The first major implementation of the goals of the Commission occurred during the INTERNATIONAL MILITARY TRIBUNAL. Twenty-four of the most influential and powerful men of the Nazi regime were put on trial on charges of CONSPIRACY, CRIMES AGAINST PEACE, WAR CRIMES, and CRIMES AGAINST HUMANITY.

These men, however, were not the only perpetrators tried by the Allies immediately after the war. The majority of war crimes trials in Allied-occupied and liberated Europe tried "minor" war criminals—civilians or military personnel whose deeds were confined to specific districts, municipalities, or CONCENTRATION CAMPS. The numerous proceedings in the four Allied occupation zones of Germany tried perpetrators who had worked in concentration camps, such as BERGEN-BELSEN in the British occupation zone and DACHAU in the American zone, or in "EUTHANASIA" facilities throughout the former REICH, such as HADAMAR. The manufacturers and suppliers of the poison gas ZYKLON B were prosecuted for their complicity in the murder of thousands at selected killing centers and euthanasia facilities.

After the conclusion of the International Military Tribunal, the Americans established six NUREMBERG MILITARY TRIBUNALS, generally composed of civilian judges, to try the leadership of the Reich ministries, the WEHRMACHT, the German medical and legal establishments, industrial concerns complicit in Nazi crimes, and criminal organizations like the SS. The Holocaust was not included as a separate criminal offense at the International Military Tribunal or at the later American proceedings, but the component parts of the "FINAL SOLUTION"—such as murder, torture, slavery, and plunder—were adjudicated under the charge of crimes against humanity at these subsequent Nuremberg trials.

As part of the Allied effort to DENAZIFY Germany and rebuild democracy, some of the amassed war crimes evidence was turned over to reconstituted German courts. Empowered by Allied Control Council Laws 4 and 10, these courts were authorized to try Nazi crimes committed by Germans against Germans or stateless persons. An early example was the 1947 German HADAMAR TRIAL. Although some of the defendants in this case had already been tried by American authorities in 1945 for the murders of 460 Polish and Soviet FORCED LABORERS, they now faced prosecution for the murders of 15,000 German nationals at the same euthanasia facility.

Two years after the establishment of the Federal Republic of Germany in 1948, the Allies removed postwar restrictions on German courts. This enabled the West Germans to pursue, unencumbered, the investigation and prosecution of Nazi war criminals. Due to insufficient personnel and material resources, the number of war crimes proceedings were minimal. The West Germans focused more on rebuilding their own country, and the western Allies' interest in Nazi war criminals flagged as the Cold War tensions between East and West intensified. In the western occupation zones of Germany, a review of sentences handed down in the early postwar period began in 1949; many were decreased or reduced to time served.

On May 8, 1950, West Germany issued a statute of limitations on Nazi crimes that at once facilitated and hampered the German prosecution of Nazi criminals. The statute identified May 8, 1945—the day the European war ended—as the operative date for all Nazi crimes, since it had not been possible to prosecute these crimes while the THIRD REICH still existed. The new law precluded prosecutions for crimes such as robbery, manslaughter, and deliberate physical injury resulting in death after a period of fifteen years; hence only acts of premeditated murder could be tried in German courts after 1960. Under German law, however, even murder was subject to a statute of limitations of twenty years. In 1965 the German parliament *(Bundestag)* voted to extend the statute of limitations for murder for four more years and extended it yet again for another ten years in 1969. Finally, in July 1979, the parliament abolished all statutes of limitations for crimes of murder under German law. This enabled German courts to try Nazi war criminals for murder without impediment.

In October 1958 the trial in Ulm of German *Einsatz-gruppen* members, using newly uncovered evidence, convinced German justice officials that many of the most heinous Nazi crimes—especially those committed in the East—had not yet been tried. Justice ministers representing all German federal states agreed to establish in Ludwigsburg the Central Office of State Administrations of Justice for the Investigation of Nazi Crimes. In its first year, it initiated 400 extensive investigations; the most important were those cases involving the actions of the *Einsatzgruppen* and affiliated organizations, and mass murder in the KILLING CENTERS located in occupied Poland.

Nazi war crimes trials continued in other countries as well. In April 1961, Adolf EICHMANN, former head of the department of Jewish Affairs of the CENTRAL OFFICE FOR REICH SECURITY was brought before the District Court of Jerusalem, Israel, under the charges of crimes against the Jewish people, war crimes, crimes against humanity, and membership in criminal organizations. Eichmann was convicted and executed. His trial was a catalyst for an intensified search for remaining war criminals worldwide.

Of the thousands of Nazi war crimes trials that have taken place since 1943, the thirty-eight trials listed alphabetically in the Trials Appendix are just a sampling. At these trials, testimony and documents were presented as evidence of the atrocities that occurred during the Nazi regime. At these proceedings, the perpetrators were held accountable for their crimes.

ASCHE TRIAL

Tribunal: *Landgericht* (district court), Kiel, Federal Republic of Germany

Dates: November 26, 1980–June 24, 1981

Charges: Aiding and abetting the mass DEPORTATION and murder of at least 23,000 Belgian Jews to CONCENTRATION CAMPS

Defendants: Kurt Asche, former head of Jewish Affairs for the SD in Belgium, and two other former SS officers

One defendant committed suicide while awaiting trial. Proceedings against a second were dropped when he was deemed too ill to stand trial.

Verdict: Guilty

Sentence: Asche was sentenced to 12 years in prison; this was later reduced to 7 years.

AUSCHWITZ TRIAL

Tribunal: *Schwurgericht* (jury court), Frankfurt am Main, Federal Republic of Germany

Dates: December 20, 1963–August 20, 1965

Charges: Participating and cooperating in the SELECTION and mass murder of prisoners at the AUSCHWITZ concentration camp

Defendants: Robert Mulka, former camp adjutant, twenty-one former camp officials, and one former KAPO

Proceedings against two defendants were dropped: one due to illness, one died.

Verdicts: Guilty: 17
           Not Guilty: 3

Sentences: Robert Mulka and ten other defendants received sentences of 3 to 14 years in prison. Six defendants were sentenced to life in prison.

BERGEN-BELSEN TRIAL

Tribunal: British Military Court, Lüneberg, British Occupation Zone, Germany

Dates: September 17, 1945–November 17, 1945

Charges: Planning and conspiring to torture and murder prisoners and committing acts of murder, torture, and ill-treatment at BERGEN-BELSEN and AUSCHWITZ concentration camps

Defendants: Josef Kramer, former commandant of Bergen-Belsen, and forty-seven other former camp officials and KAPOS of the two camps

Three defendants were not tried, and one not prosecuted because of ill health.

Verdicts: Guilty: 30
          Not Guilty: 14

Sentences: Kramer and ten other defendants were sentenced to death by hanging, one received life imprisonment, and eighteen others received sentences ranging from one to 15 years in prison.

BRAUNSTEINER HEARING

Tribunal: U.S. Immigration and Naturalization Service, New York, New York

Dates: August 22, 1968–April 24, 1973

Charges: Misrepresenting and concealing her 1949 conviction by an Austrian court for the torture and mistreatment of prisoners of the RAVENSBRÜCK concentration camp on a United States citizenship application, and hiding acts of "gross moral turpitude" committed between 1939 and 1945

Defendant: Hermine Braunsteiner-Ryan, a former guard at Ravensbrück and MAJDANEK concentration camps

Verdict: Guilty

Sentence: To avoid deportation, Braunsteiner-Ryan consented to denaturalization from the United States. Braunsteiner was extradited in 1973 to West Germany, where she was tried in the MAJDANEK TRIAL. She was the only German war criminal extradited from the United States.

DACHAU TRIAL

Tribunal: U.S. General Military Government Court, Dachau, American Occupation Zone, Germany

Dates: November 15, 1945–December 13, 1945

Charges: Aiding and abetting murder and cruelties "including tortures, starvation, abuses and indignities" against prisoners of war and civilians between January 1, 1942, and April 29, 1945, at the DACHAU concentration camp

Defendants: Martin Gottfried Weiss, a former commandant of Dachau, and thirty-nine former camp guards and officials

Verdicts: Guilty: 40

Sentences: Martin Gottfried Weiss and thirty-five other defendants received death sentences, one was sentenced to life imprisonment, and three received 10 to 30 years in prison. Eight death sentences were later reduced to prison sentences.

DOCTORS TRIAL

(Case 1 of the American Nuremberg Tribunals)

Tribunal: U.S. Military Tribunal I, Nuremberg, American Occupation Zone, Germany

Dates: October 25, 1946–August 20, 1947

Charges: CONSPIRACY, WAR CRIMES, CRIMES AGAINST HUMANITY, and membership in CRIMINAL ORGANIZATIONS; performing medical experiments on CONCENTRATION CAMP prisoners including high altitude; freezing; malaria; mustard gas; sulfanilamide; bone, muscle, and nerve regeneration and bone transplantation; potable seawater; epidemic jaundice; sterilization; typhus; yellow fever; smallpox; typhoid; paratyphoid A and B; cholera; diphtheria; phosphorus; and poison; murdering 112 Jews for a skeleton collection; murdering thousands of Poles with tuberculosis; and participating in the "EUTHANASIA" program

Defendants: Karl BRANDT (Adolf HITLER'S attending physician and Reich commissioner for sanitation and health), Karl Gebhardt (Heinrich HIMMLER'S attending physician), twenty other physicians, and one medical assistant

The Tribunal determined that it had no competence to try any defendant for the inadequately defined charge of conspiracy, but it could prosecute on the basis of "unlawful participation in formulating and executing plans to commit war crimes and crimes against humanity."

Verdicts: Guilty: 16
          Not Guilty: 7

Sentences: Seven defendants, including Brandt and Gebhardt, were sentenced to death by hanging; five received life imprisonment; and four were sentenced to prison terms of 10 to 20 years. The latter prison terms were later reduced in January 1951.

DOESTLER TRIAL

Tribunal: U.S. Military Commission for Trial of War Criminals, Rome, Italy

Dates: October 8, 1945–October 12, 1945

Charges: Ordering the murder of fifteen American prisoners of war on or about March 24, 1944, near La Spezia, Italy

Defendant: General Anton Doestler, commander of the 75th German Army Corps

Verdict: Guilty

Sentence: Death by firing squad. Doestler was executed several months later.

DORA–MITTELBAU TRIAL

Tribunal: U.S. General Military Government Court, Dachau, American Occupation Zone, Germany

Dates: June 20, 1947–December 30, 1947

Charges: Murder and cruelties against prisoners at the DORA-MITTELBAU concentration camp

Defendants: Hans Moser, former SS lieutenant and head of the PROTECTIVE CUSTODY CAMP within Dora-Mittelbau; thirteen other former staff and guards; four former prisoners; and one former director of a firm with a facility within the camp

Verdicts: Guilty: 15
Not guilty: 4

Sentences: Moser was sentenced to death, seven defendants received life sentences, and the remaining seven were sentenced to between 5 and 25 years.

EICHMANN TRIAL

Tribunal: District Court of Jerusalem, Jerusalem, Israel

Dates: April 10, 1961–December 15, 1961

Charges: Crimes against the Jewish people, WAR CRIMES, CRIMES AGAINST HUMANITY, and membership in CRIMINAL ORGANIZATIONS (the SS, SD, and GESTAPO); specifications included arrest, imprisonment in CONCENTRATION CAMPS, DEPORTATION to KILLING CENTERS, murder, and theft of property

Defendant: Adolf EICHMANN, former head of DEPARTMENT IVb4 of the CENTRAL OFFICE FOR REICH SECURITY

Verdict: Guilty

Sentence: Death; confirmed by Israel's Supreme Court.

Eichmann was executed at midnight, June 1, 1962. His body was cremated and the ashes strewn at sea beyond Israeli territorial waters.

EINSATZGRUPPEN TRIAL

(Case 9 of the American Nuremberg Tribunals)

Tribunal: U.S. Military Tribunal II-A, Nuremberg, American Occupation Zone, Germany

Dates: July 3, 1947–April 10, 1948

Charges: WAR CRIMES, CRIMES AGAINST HUMANITY, and membership in CRIMINAL ORGANIZATIONS (the SS, SD, and GESTAPO); specifications included connection with plans, organizations, or groups linked to atrocities and offenses against civilians (including persecutions on political, racial, and religious grounds; murder; extermination; and imprisonment); participating in a systematic program of GENOCIDE to exterminate foreign nationals and ethnic groups; and atrocities and offenses against persons and property of prisoners of war and civilian populations of countries and territories occupied or controlled by Germany

Defendants: Otto Ohlendorf, commander of EINSATZGRUPPE D, and twenty-three others, all SS officers, who either commanded or were members of the four Einsatzgruppen operating in the Soviet Union

Proceedings against one defendant were dropped after the defendant committed suicide; those against another were dropped because he was too ill to stand trial.

Verdicts: Guilty: 22

Sentences: Ohlendorf and thirteen others were sentenced to death by hanging. Two defendants were given life in prison; and five were sentenced to 10 to 20 years in prison. One defendant was sentenced to time served.

FEDORENKO HEARING

Tribunal: U.S. District Court for the Southern District of Florida, Fort Lauderdale, Florida

Dates: August 16, 1977–July 25, 1978

Charges: Seven counts of misrepresenting and concealing information on a United States citizenship application in violation of the Displaced Persons Act of 1948, which denied admission to the U.S. of refugees suspected of war crimes and collaboration with the NAZIS

Defendant: Feodor Fedorenko, who was suspected of committing WAR CRIMES during his tenure as a guard at the TREBLINKA killing center

Verdict: Acquitted; application for revocation of citizenship rejected

An appeal to the United States Fifth Circuit Court of Appeals reversed the lower court's decision and revoked Fedorenko's citizenship in 1979. In a further appeal, the U.S. Supreme Court upheld the Court of Appeals decision. The Immigration and Naturalization Service (INS) immediately began deportation hearings and ruled for deportation in February 1983. A challenge to the INS Board of Appeals was unsuccessful, and Fedorenko was deported to the Soviet Union on December 21, 1984, where he was tried, convicted, and executed in 1986.

FLICK TRIAL

(Case 5 of the American Nuremberg Tribunals)

Tribunal: U.S. Military Tribunal IV, Nuremberg, American Occupation Zone, Germany

Dates: February 8, 1947–December 22, 1947

Charges: WAR CRIMES, CRIMES AGAINST HUMANITY, and membership in the SS; specifications included involvement with organizations or groups connected with the enslavement and DEPORTATION for SLAVE LABOR of civilian populations of occupied countries; enslavement of CONCENTRATION CAMP prisoners; use of prisoners of war in war industry; use of FORCED LABOR; offenses against property in countries and territories under German occupation; and persecutions on racial, religious, and political grounds, including the "ARYANIZATION" of Jewish properties

Defendants: Friedrich Flick, proprietor of a coal, iron, and steel conglomerate, and five other officials of his companies

Verdicts: Guilty: 3
          Not guilty: 3

Sentences: Count three of the indictment, the "ARYANIZATION" of Jewish property, was dismissed for all defendants; Flick and two other defendants were sentenced to prison for 2 to 7 years.

GOETH TRIAL

Tribunal: Supreme National Tribunal of Poland, Cracow, Poland

Dates: August 27, 1946–September 5, 1946

Charges: Directing the murder of 8,000 inmates of the PLASZOW forced labor camp, liquidating the Cracow GHETTO and the murder of at least 2,000 ghetto residents, liquidating the Tarnow ghetto, murdering several thousand individuals during the liquidation of the Szebnie FORCED LABOR camp, and illegally seizing property

Defendant: Amon Leopold Goeth, commandant of Plaszow forced labor camp (and prominent figure in the 1993 film *Schindler's List*)

Verdict: Guilty

Sentence: Death by hanging, loss of all public and civic rights, and forfeiture of all property. Hanged on September 13, 1946.

HADAMAR TRIAL (AMERICAN)

Tribunal: U.S. Military Commission for the Trial of War Criminals, Wiesbaden, American Occupation Zone, Germany

Dates: October 8, 1945–October 15, 1945

Charges: Murdering and aiding and abetting in the murder of 476 Poles and Soviet prisoners of war by gas, lethal injection, and drug overdose between July 1, 1944, and April 1, 1945, at the HADAMAR "euthanasia" facility

Defendants: Alfons Klein, former superintendent of Hadamar, and six other former staff members of the facility

Verdicts: Guilty: 7

Sentences: Alfons Klein and two other defendants were sentenced to death, one defendant received life imprisonment, and three others 25 to 30 years in prison.

HADAMAR TRIAL (GERMAN)

Tribunal: *Landgericht* (district court), Frankfurt am Main, American Occupation Zone, Germany

Dates: February 24, 1947–March 21, 1947

Charges: Murdering and aiding and abetting in the murder of 15,000 mentally and chronically ill patients at the HADAMAR "euthanasia" facility from 1941 to 1945

Defendants: Adolf Wahlmann, former chief physician, and twenty-four former staff members of the Hadamar mental health facility

Verdicts: Guilty: 11
          Not Guilty: 14

Sentences: Adolf Wahlmann and one other defendant were sentenced to death. Nine others received sentences ranging from 2 to 8 years in prison. In 1949, while the condemned awaited confirmation of their death sentences, the German *Grundgesetz* (constitution), which forbade capital punishment, was promulgated; the death sentences were therefore commuted to life imprisonment.

HARSTER TRIAL

Tribunal: *Landgericht* (district court), Munich, Federal Republic of Germany

Dates: January 23, 1967–February 17, 1967

Charges: Aiding, abetting, and participating in the murder of at least 42,700 Dutch Jews, including Anne Frank, author of the world-famous diary

Defendants: Wilhelm Harster, former chief of the SD in the Netherlands, and two other former SD members

Verdicts: Guilty: 3

Sentences: Harster was sentenced to 15 years in prison, the other two defendants to 9 and 5 years in prison.

HIGH COMMAND TRIAL

(Case 12 of the American Nuremberg Tribunals)

Tribunal: U.S. Military Tribunal V, Nuremberg, American Occupation Zone, Germany

Dates: November 28, 1947–October 28, 1948

Charges: CRIMES AGAINST PEACE, CONSPIRACY, WAR CRIMES and CRIMES AGAINST HUMANITY; specifications included participating in the initiation of invasions of other countries and wars of aggression in violation of international laws and treaties; atrocities and offenses against prisoners of war; issuing unlawful orders that certain captured members of Allied military forces be summarily executed, including Soviet "political commissars" and "commandos" in Europe or Africa; atrocities and offenses against German nationals and the civilian populations of German-occupied countries and territories; deporting and enslaving civilians; plundering public and private property; and wanton destruction and devastation not justified by military necessity

Defendants: Wilhelm von Leeb, former commander of Army Group North, twelve other high-ranking German army generals, and one German navy admiral

One defendant committed suicide before the trial began.

The Tribunal found that none of the defendants occupied policy-making positions, and therefore none were guilty of crimes against peace. The charge of conspiracy was struck down as a separate count since it was included in the other counts.

Verdicts: Guilty: 11
　　　　　Not guilty: 2

Sentences: Two defendants were sentenced to life imprisonment. Von Leeb and eight others were sentenced to 3 to 20 years in prison.

HOSTAGE TRIAL

(Case 7 of the American Nuremberg Tribunals)

Tribunal: U.S. Military Tribunal V, Nuremberg, American Occupation Zone, Germany

Dates: May 10, 1947–February 19, 1948

Charges: WAR CRIMES and CRIMES AGAINST HUMANITY; specifications included murdering hundreds of thousands of civilians by troops under the command and jurisdiction of the defendants (including those arbitrarily designated as "partisans," "Communists," "Communist suspects," "bandits," and "bandit suspects") in retaliation for attacks against German troops and installations; destroying cities, towns, and villages and murdering the inhabitants; illegally ordering that enemy troops be denied the status of prisoners of war and that such captured troops be summarily executed; connection with plans, organizations, or groups linked to the murder, torture, and systematic terrorization, imprisonment in CONCENTRATION CAMPS, arbitrary FORCED LABOR on fortifications, and DEPORTATION to SLAVE LABOR of the civilian populations by troops under their command

Defendants: Wilhelm List, former commander of Army Group A, and eleven other German Army and Air Force generals.

One defendant committed suicide prior to arraignment, and proceedings against another were suspended due to ill health.

Verdicts: Guilty: 8
　　　　　Not guilty: 2

Sentences: List and one other defendant were sentenced to life imprisonment; six received prison sentences of between 7 and 20 years.

I.G. FARBEN TRIAL

(Case 6 of the American Nuremberg Tribunals)

Tribunal: U.S. Military Tribunal VI, Nuremberg, American Occupation Zone, Germany

Dates: May 3, 1947–June 30, 1948

Charges: CONSPIRACY, WAR CRIMES, CRIMES AGAINST HUMANITY, and membership in the SS (three defendants); specifications included planning, preparing, initiating, and waging wars of aggression and invasions of other countries in violation of international laws and treaties; carrying on propaganda, intelligence, and espionage activities; participating in plunder, spoliation, slavery, and mass murder as part of wars of aggression in German-occupied territories; slavery and mass murder; using poison gas and medical experimentation on enslaved persons.

Defendants: Carl Krauch, Chairman, Supervisory Board of Directors of I.G. FARBEN; twenty other officials of I.G. Farben; two officials of other firms; and an SS officer

Proceedings against one defendant were dropped because of ill health.

Verdicts: Guilty: 13
Not Guilty: 10

Sentences: Krauch and twelve other defendants received prison sentences of 1 to 8 years.

INTERNATIONAL MILITARY TRIBUNAL

Tribunal: International Military Tribunal, Nuremberg, American Occupation Zone, Germany

Dates: October 18, 1945 (opening session, Berlin)
November 20, 1945–October 1, 1946 (Nuremberg)

Charges: (1) CONSPIRACY to commit one or more of the following:
(2) CRIMES AGAINST PEACE: planning and waging a war of aggression in violation of international treaties and agreements, or participation in a conspiracy;
(3) WAR CRIMES: violating the laws of war including murder, ill treatment, or DEPORTATION to SLAVE LABOR of civilian populations in occupied territory; murder or ill treatment of prisoners of war; killing of hostages; plunder of public or private property; wanton destruction of cities and towns; and devastation not justified by military necessity;
(4) CRIMES AGAINST HUMANITY: murder, extermination, enslavement, deportation, and other inhumane acts committed against any civilian population before or during the war; persecutions on political, racial, or religious grounds whether or not in violation of the domestic law of the country where perpetrated

Defendants: Hermann GÖRING: commander-in-chief of the LUFTWAFFE, plenipotentiary for the FOUR-YEAR PLAN; Rudolf HESS: deputy to the Führer; Joachim von RIBBENTROP: foreign minister; Robert LEY: head of the German Labor Front; Wilhelm KEITEL: chief of staff, WEHRMACHT High Command; Ernst KALTENBRUNNER: head of the CENTRAL OFFICE FOR REICH SECURITY; Alfred ROSENBERG: minister for Occupied Eastern Territories and Nazi ideologue; Hans FRANK: governor-general of the GENERAL GOVERNMENT in occupied-Poland; Wilhelm FRICK: former minister of the interior and head of the PROTECTORATE OF BOHEMIA AND MORAVIA; Julius STREICHER: publisher of the antisemitic newspaper Der Stürmer; Walther FUNK: president of the Reichsbank; Hjalmar SCHACHT: former minister of economics; Gustav KRUPP VON BOHLEN UND HALBACH: head of the Krupp armaments industries; Karl DÖNITZ: supreme commander of the German Navy; Erich RAEDER: former supreme commander of the German Navy; Baldur von SCHIRACH: leader of the Hitler Youth; Fritz SAUCKEL: plenipotentiary for Labor Mobilization; Alfred JODL: chief of the WEHRMACHT Operations Staff; Martin BORMANN: head of the NAZI PARTY Chancellery (tried in absentia); Franz von PAPEN: first vice-chancellor of the Nazi government; Arthur SEYSS-INQUART: Reich commissioner for the occupied Netherlands; Albert SPEER: minister of armaments and war production; Constantin von NEURATH: former minister of foreign affairs; Hans FRITZSCHE: chief of the Radio Division, Propaganda Ministry

Ley committed suicide in his cell before the trial began. Krupp was found medically unfit to stand trial.

Organizations:
Reich Cabinet
NSDAP Leadership Corps
SS
SD and GESTAPO
SA
General Staff and High Command of the Armed Forces

Verdicts: Guilty: 19
Not Guilty: 3

Sentences: Göring, Ribbentrop, Keitel, Kaltenbrunner, Rosenberg, Frank, Frick, Streicher, Sauckel, Jodl, Seyss-Inquart, and Bormann (in absentia) were sentenced to death by hanging; Göring committed suicide hours before his execution. Hess, Funk, and Raeder received life imprisonment. Schirach and Speer received 20 years, Neurath 15 years, and Dönitz 10 years in prison. Schacht, Papen, and Fritzsche were acquitted.

All death sentences were carried out on October 16, 1946.

The SS, SD and Gestapo, and the NSDAP Leadership Corps were found to be CRIMINAL ORGANIZATIONS.

JURISTS' TRIAL

(Case 3 of the American Nuremberg Tribunals)

Tribunal: U.S. Military Tribunal III, Nuremberg, American Occupation Zone, Germany

Dates: January 4, 1947–December 4, 1947

Charges: CONSPIRACY, WAR CRIMES, CRIMES AGAINST HUMANITY, and membership in CRIMINAL ORGANIZATIONS; specifications included carrying out discriminatory laws and prosecution of Jews and GYPSIES; expanding the definition of "treasonable offenses" to exterminate Jews and others; creating special courts to exterminate Jews and Poles and suppress political opposition; implementing the "Night and Fog" decree (December 1941) against members of the resistance in occupied territories; participating in the Nazi racial program through implementation of sterilization and castration laws for Jews, "ASOCIALS," and other groups in occupied territories; and participating in inciting German civilians to murder Allied airmen downed inside the Reich

Defendants: Josef Altstötter, Chief, Civil Law and Procedure Division, Reich Ministry of Justice, and 15 others who were members of the Reich Justice Ministry; members of the People's Court and Special Courts; and prominent public prosecutors

The Tribunal determined that it had no jurisdiction to try any defendant for the inadequately defined charge of conspiracy, but could prosecute on the basis of "unlawful participation in formulating and executing plans to commit war crimes and crimes against humanity."

One defendant committed suicide before the trial; another was dropped from the proceedings because of ill health.

Verdicts: Guilty: 10
    Not guilty: 4

Sentences: Four defendants were sentenced to life imprisonment; Altstötter and five others received 5 to 10 years in prison.

KRASNODAR TRIAL

Tribunal: Military Tribunal of the North Caucasian Front of the Soviet Army, Krasnodar, Russian Republic, U.S.S.R.

Dates: July 14, 1943–July 17, 1943

Charges: 7,000 acts of torture and murder by GAS VANS of all patients in the Krasnodar municipal hospital, the Berezhanka municipal hospital, and the regional children's hospital

Defendants: 11 Soviet citizens and 13 German members of EINSATZGRUPPE D (the latter tried in absentia)

Verdicts: Guilty: 24

Sentences: Eight Soviet defendants were sentenced to death by hanging, three to 20 years in prison.

KRUPP TRIAL

(Case 10 of the American Nuremberg Tribunals)

Tribunal: U.S. Military Tribunal IIIA, Nuremberg, American Occupation Zone, Germany

Dates: August 16, 1947–July 31,1948

Charges: CONSPIRACY, WAR CRIMES, and CRIMES AGAINST HUMANITY; specifications included CRIMES AGAINST PEACE as participants in the initiation of invasions of other countries; contributing substantially to the ability of the THIRD REICH to wage wars of aggression; plunder and despoliation of public and private property (two defendants excepted); DEPORTATION and exploitation of foreign civilian workers (including women and children) as SLAVE LABOR; exploiting prisoners of war and CONCENTRATION CAMP prisoners under inhumane conditions by subjecting them to atrocities and ill treatment in the iron, steel, and mining industries in Germany and the occupied territories; and persecuting workers brought from occupied countries on political, racial, and religious grounds

Defendants: Alfried F. A. KRUPP VON BOHLEN UND HALBACH, sole owner and director of Friedrich Krupp, Inc., Essen; and eleven other former Krupp officials.

Verdicts: Guilty: 11
    Not Guilty: 1

Sentences: Krupp von Bohlen und Halbach and nine other defendants received prison sentences of 6 to 12 years; one defendant was sentenced to time served.

MAJDANEK TRIAL

Tribunal: *Landgericht* (district court), Düsseldorf, Federal Republic of Germany

Dates: November 26, 1975–June 30, 1981 (the longest war crimes trial to date in the German Federal Republic)

Charges: Murdering and aiding and abetting in the murder of at least 250,000 Jews and 100,000 other victims by gassing, shooting, systematic starvation, drowning, torture, and abuse at the MAJDANEK concentration camp

Defendants: Hermann Hackmann, former head of the PROTECTIVE CUSTODY CAMP within Majdanek, and fifteen other former camp officials, including Hermine Braunsteiner-Ryan (*see* BRAUNSTEINER HEARING)

Proceedings against four defendants were dropped due to deaths of prosecution witnesses, proceedings against two others were postponed indefinitely due to ill health, and proceedings against a seventh were dropped upon her death.

Verdicts: Guilty: 8
        Not Guilty: 1

Sentences: Hermine Braunsteiner-Ryan received two life sentences; Hackmann and six others were sentenced to 3 to 7 years in prison.

MAUTHAUSEN TRIAL

Tribunal: U.S. General Military Government Court, Dachau, American Occupation Zone, Germany

Dates: March 29, 1946–May 13, 1946

Charges: Violating the laws and usages of war; aiding and abetting in the murder of thousands of prisoners at the MAUTHAUSEN concentration camp by gassing, shooting, hanging, exposure, and starvation

Defendants: Hans Altfuldisch, former head of the PROTECTIVE CUSTODY CAMP within Mauthausen, and sixty other former SS staff members of the camp

Verdicts: Guilty: 61

Sentences: Altfuldisch and fifty-seven others were sentenced to death by hanging, three sentenced to life in prison.

MERE TRIAL

Tribunal: College of Criminal Cases of the Supreme Court of the Estonian S.S.R., Tallin, Estonian Republic, U.S.S.R.

Dates: March 6, 1961–March 11, 1961

Charges: Participating in the mass murder of at least 5,000 Soviet citizens at Kalevi-Liiva, Estonia

Defendants: Ain-Ervin Mere, former chief of the collaborationist Estonian Security Police (*in absentia*), and two other former Estonian security policemen.

Verdicts: Guilty: 3

Sentences: Two defendants were sentenced to death and confiscation of all property. They were hanged on March 30, 1961. Ain-Ervin Mere was also sentenced to death *in absentia*, and the confiscation of all his property was ordered. Great Britain refused to extradite Mere for the trial or execution of the sentence on the grounds that the statute of limitations had elapsed since the alleged crimes. There was no extradition treaty between Great Britain and the Estonian Republic of the U.S.S.R. at the time because Great Britain had never recognized the annexation of Estonia by the Soviet Union in 1940.

MILCH TRIAL

(Case 2 of the American Nuremberg Tribunals)

Tribunal: U.S. Military Tribunal II, Nuremberg, American Occupation Zone, Germany

Dates: November 13, 1946–April 17, 1947

Charges: WAR CRIMES and CRIMES AGAINST HUMANITY; specifications included forcibly moving civilian populations from occupied territories and inhumanely subjecting them to SLAVE LABOR, using prisoners of war in war production and murdering those attempting to escape, and performing medical experiments on prisoners of war and nationals of countries at war with Germany

Defendant: Erhard Milch, state secretary, Reich Air Ministry; field marshal, *LUFTWAFFE*; deputy to *Luftwaffe* Commander-in-Chief Hermann GÖRING

Verdict: Guilty

Sentence: Milch was sentenced to life imprisonment.

MINISTRIES TRIAL

(Case 11 of the American Nuremberg Tribunals)

Tribunal: U.S. Military Tribunal IV, Nuremberg, American Occupation Zone Germany

Dates: November 4, 1947–November 18, 1948

Charges: CRIMES AGAINST PEACE, CONSPIRACY, WAR CRIMES, CRIMES AGAINST HUMANITY, and membership in CRIMINAL ORGANIZATIONS; specifications included the planning, financing, and waging of wars of aggression; participating in Hitler's seizure of power; participating in the incorporation and subjugation of conquered territories into Germany; murdering and ill-treating belligerents and prisoners of war; committing atrocities and offenses against German nationals and civilian populations of occupied countries on political, racial, and religious grounds; participating in a systematic program of GENOCIDE and "GERMANIZATION" in Poland and the Occupied Eastern Territories; participating in the program for the extermination of all European Jews; wholesale seizure of cultural and art treasures; planning and committing the DEPORTATION for SLAVE LABOR of the civilian populations of countries and territories under the German occupation; enslaving CONCENTRATION CAMP prisoners including German nationals; and membership in Criminal Organizations (the SS, SD, and the Leadership Corps of the NAZI PARTY).

Defendants: Ernst von Weizsäcker, state secretary, German Foreign Office; six other officials of the German Foreign Office; two SS officers; several officials from other government ministries; and two business and financial leaders (twenty-one defendants)

Verdicts: Guilty: 19
    Not guilty: 2

Sentences: von Weizsäcker and seventeen defendants received prison sentences of 6 to 25 years; one defendant was sentenced to time served.

POHL TRIAL

(Case 4 of the American Nuremberg Tribunals)

Tribunal: U.S. Military Tribunal II, Nuremberg, American Occupation Zone, Germany

Dates: January 13, 1947–November 3, 1947

Charges: CONSPIRACY, WAR CRIMES, CRIMES AGAINST HUMANITY, and membership in CRIMINAL ORGANIZATIONS; specifications included financing the SS; operating CONCENTRATION and LABOR CAMPS in Germany and other countries; supplying labor from concentration camps to industry; furnishing human subjects for medical experiments; carrying out policies to exterminate Jews; carrying out policies of sterilization and castration of certain groups; unlawfully treating prisoners of war; carrying out the "EUTHANASIA" program; deporting citizens of occupied countries and plundering their property and exploiting their labor, especially of Jews, Poles, and Russians; associating with the SS CENTRAL OFFICE FOR ECONOMY AND ADMINISTRATION (WVHA); transporting prisoners in conditions that led to the deaths of thousands

Defendants: Oswald Pohl, chief of the SS Central Office for Economy and Administration, and seventeen other SS officers on its staff.

Verdicts: Guilty: 15
    Not guilty: 3

Sentences: Pohl and three others were sentenced to death by hanging, three defendants received life imprisonment, and eight were sentenced to 10 to 25 years in prison.

RuSHA TRIAL

(Case 8 of the American Nuremberg Tribunals)

Tribunal: U.S. Military Tribunal I, Nuremberg, American Occupation Zone, Germany

Dates: July 1, 1947–March 10, 1948

Charges: WAR CRIMES, CRIMES AGAINST HUMANITY, and membership in a CRIMINAL ORGANIZATION: the SS (all but one defendant); specifications included connection with a systematic program of GENOCIDE to destroy foreign nations and ethnic groups and strengthen the German nation and "ARYAN" race by forcing German language, customs, and education upon selected individuals (GERMANIZATION); plundering property in Germany and in the incorporated and occupied territories; persecuting and exterminating Jews; and participating in the extermination of thousands of German nationals in the "EUTHANASIA" program.

Defendants: Ulrich Greifelt, head, REICH COMMISSION FOR STRENGTHENING GERMANISM (RKFDV), and thirteen other SS officers, most members of the RKFDV or the SS CENTRAL OFFICE FOR RACE AND RESETTLEMENT (RuSHA)

Verdicts: Guilty: 13
    Not Guilty: 1

Sentences: Greifelt was sentenced to life in prison. Seven other defendants received prison sentences of from 10 to 25 years. Five were sentenced to time served.

SCHMID TRIAL

Tribunal: U.S. General Military Government Court, Dachau, American Occupation Zone, Germany

Dates: September 15–18, 1947

Charges: Participating in the murder of Polish prisoners at the DACHAU concentration camp during 1939 and 1940

Defendant: Sebastion Schmid, former SS sergeant, driver, and mechanic at Dachau.

Verdict: Guilty

Sentence: Schmid was sentenced to life imprisonment. The sentence was reduced to 20 years in 1948, then to time served in 1951. Schmid, however, was not released until 1953.

STANGL TRIAL

Tribunal: *Schwurgericht* (jury court), Düsseldorf, Federal Republic of Germany

Dates: May 13, 1970–December 22, 1970

Charges: Murdering 400,000 victims and other CRIMES AGAINST HUMANITY while serving as commandant of the TREBLINKA killing center

Defendants: Franz Stangl, former commandant of the SOBIBOR and Treblinka KILLING CENTERS

Verdict: Guilty

Sentence: Life in prison. Stangl died of heart failure in prison on June 28, 1971.

STROOP TRIAL (AMERICAN)

Tribunal: U.S. General Military Government Court, Dachau, American Occupation Zone, Germany

Dates: January 10, 1947–March 2, 1947

Charges: Murdering nine captured American airmen; membership in a CRIMINAL ORGANIZATION; and aiding and abetting in the killing, beating, and torture of ALLIED prisoners of war

Defendants: Jürgen Stroop, former SS general, and twenty-one former members of the GESTAPO, SD, SS, and NAZI PARTY

One defendant escaped and was dropped from the proceedings.

Verdicts: Guilty: 20
       Not Guilty: 1

Sentences: Jürgen Stroop and twelve other defendants were sentenced to death while seven defendants were sentenced to prison terms ranging from 3 to 15 years. Stroop's sentence was commuted to life imprisonment in March 1947. Stroop was also charged with mass murder in Poland. As the latter charges were of greater magnitude than those tried by the U.S. Military Government Court, he was extradited to Poland where he was tried by a Polish court in 1951; *see* STROOP TRIAL (POLISH).

STROOP TRIAL (POLISH)

Tribunal: Polish Tribunal, Warsaw, Poland

Dates: July 18, 1951–July 23, 1951

Charges: Membership in a CRIMINAL ORGANIZATION (the SS); ordering and leading the liquidation of the WARSAW GHETTO including the murder of at least 56,065 people; ordering the execution by shooting of 100 Poles on July 16, 1943; and participating in mass murders and persecution of the Polish population in the WARTHEGAU.

Defendants: Jürgen Stroop, former SS general

Verdict: Guilty

Sentence: Death by hanging; Stroop was hanged on March 6, 1952.

TREBLINKA TRIAL

Tribunal: *Landgericht* (district court), Düsseldorf, Federal Republic of Germany

Dates: October 12, 1964–September 3, 1965

Charges: Directing, participating, and assisting in the systematic murder of at least 300,000 people by poison gas at the TREBLINKA killing center; executing numerous individuals

Defendants: Kurt Hubert Franz, former deputy, and later commandant of Treblinka, and nine other former SS staff members of the camp

Verdicts: Guilty: 9
       Not Guilty: 1

Sentences: Franz and three other defendants received life imprisonment; five others were sentenced to prison terms of from 3 to 12 years.

TUCHEL TRIAL

Tribunal: *Landgericht* (district court), Hamburg, Federal Republic of Germany

Dates: December 21, 1971–February 23, 1973

Charges: Participating in the EVACUATION and execution of over 25,100 Latvian Jews from the Riga GHETTO on November 30 and December 7–8, 1941, in the forest of Rumbuli, Latvia

Defendants: Otto Tuchel, former German police sergeant, and three other former members of the German police in Riga.

Verdicts: Guilty: 4

Sentences: Otto Tuchel received life imprisonment, another defendant was sentenced to 3 years, and the other two were found guilty but received no sentence.

VENTER TRIAL

Tribunal: *Landgericht* (district court), Berlin, Federal Republic of Germany

Dates: December 9, 1969–April 7, 1971

Charges: Aiding and abetting murder in the DEPORTATION of Jews from Berlin to KILLING CENTERS such as AUSCHWITZ.

Defendants: Kurt Venter, former GESTAPO major, and another former Gestapo officer

Verdicts: Not guilty: 2
Both defendants were acquitted.

ZYKLON B TRIAL

Tribunal: British Military Tribunal, Hamburg, British Occupation Zone, Germany

Dates: March 1, 1946–March 8, 1946

Charges: Supplying the poison gas ZYKLON B with the knowledge that it was to be used in the murder of prisoners in KILLING CENTERS

Defendants: Bruno Tesch, former head of the firm of Tesch and Stabenow, and two other employees of the firm

Verdicts: Guilty: 2
Not Guilty: 1

Sentences: Tesch and one other defendant were sentenced to death; the third defendant was acquitted.

GLOSSARY

Ahnenerbe Society (*Ahnenerbe Forschungs- und Lehrgemeinschaft*, Society for the Research and Teaching of Ancestral Heritage): Founded on July 1, 1935, to establish the genealogical origins and value of "ARYAN" heritage in early German history. Administered by Heinrich HIMMLER's personal staff, the society comprised forty research departments, including those that oversaw the medical experimentation at the DACHAU concentration camp and the development of a Jewish skull collection at the University of Strasbourg.

Allies, Allied: The nations joined in the war against Germany and the other AXIS nations; included the United States, Great Britain, the Soviet Union, as well as the Free Czech, Dutch, French, Norwegian, and Polish, governments-in-exile.

Anschluss (annexation): The incorporation of Austria into the German REICH on March 18, 1938. This annexation was in violation of the 1919 Treaty of St. Germain that established a truncated Austria as an independent state and prohibited it from becoming a part of Germany.

"Aryan": Originally a linguistic term designating peoples speaking Indo-European languages. The NAZIS perverted the term and proclaimed the Aryan "race" superior to all other racial groups. They considered those of Teutonic, that is, Germanic background to be prime examples of Aryan stock. For the Nazis, the ideal Aryan was tall, blond, and blue-eyed.

"Aryanization:: The expropriation of Jewish businesses and property by the German authorities, as well as similar measures by other AXIS nations.

"Asocial": An umbrella social category including the "work-shy," migrants, GYPSIES, homosexuals, pimps, prostitutes, and any person the German police thought unfit for civilian society. Many of those considered "asocial" were arrested by the CRIMINAL POLICE rather than by the GESTAPO. They were sent to CONCENTRATION CAMPS after December 1937 under new laws allowing "protective custody" for prisoners in this category. Some were also sterilized or exterminated under the "EUTHANASIA" program.

Auschwitz: A camp complex in Upper Silesia, German-occupied Poland. *Auschwitz I,* the main camp, was established in 1940 as a CONCENTRATION CAMP. *Auschwitz II* (also known as Auschwitz-Birkenau), a KILLING CENTER built by 1942, was the main site of the GAS CHAMBERS and CREMATORIA. *Auschwitz III* (Auschwitz-Monowitz) was a LABOR CAMP for the I.G. FARBEN industries. Auschwitz ultimately had some 40 subsidiary camps. Auschwitz was liberated by the Soviet Army on January 27, 1945, only after an estimated 1.2 million persons had died there by gassing, exposure, starvation, disease, and brutal medical experiments.

Auschwitz-Birkenau: *See* AUSCHWITZ.

Axis: Alliance of Germany, Italy, and Japan, created by a pact signed in Berlin on September 27, 1940, that divided the world into spheres of political interest. The founding member-states were later joined by Bulgaria, Croatia, Hungary, Romania, and Slovakia.

Belorussia (also Byelorussia or White Russia): A territory divided between Poland and the U.S.S.R. between the two world wars. On the eve of the German occupation in June 1941, the Jewish population was 1,075,000 (670,000 in western and 405,000 in eastern Belorussia). Thousands of Belorussian Jews, GYPSIES, and the disabled were killed by the *EINSATZGRUPPEN* in 1941–42. A second wave of mass murder began in spring 1942 and ended with the virtual annihilation of the Jews of western Belorussia.

Belzec: A KILLING CENTER in German-occupied Poland. Originally a LABOR CAMP, Belzec became a killing center after November 1, 1941, as part of OPERATION REINHARD. Belzec originally had three GAS CHAMBERS that used carbon monoxide from a diesel engine. In June 1942, new gas chambers were built with a capacity of 1,000 to 1,200 people. In December 1942, transports to Belzec ceased, and the camp shut down. Approximately 600,000 people, mostly Jews, were killed in Belzec; their bodies were buried in mass graves. To destroy the evidence of their crimes, the Germans ordered the graves opened, the bodies exhumed and cremated, and the ashes buried. Afterward, the camp was dismantled.

Bergen-Belsen: A CONCENTRATION CAMP complex in modern-day Lower Saxony, in northern Germany. Opened in 1940 as a prisoner-of-war camp for Belgian and French prisoners, in 1941 it was renamed Stalag 311 for about 20,000 Soviet POWs, 16,000 to 18,000 of whom died of epidemics, malnutrition, and exposure by 1942. The camp was renamed Bergen-Belsen in April 1943, and it became a camp for male and female Jews with foreign passports or visas who might be exchanged for German nationals held abroad. Between March 1944 and early 1945, it received incapacitated prisoners for possible exchange, prisoners with foreign visas from other camps, and large numbers of prisoners evacuated from the East. In the last months of the war, rapidly deteriorating conditions led to large-scale epidemics, starvation, and the deaths of thousands.

Birkenau: see AUSCHWITZ.

Blockältester ("block elder"): The senior prisoner functionary within a barracks in a CONCENTRATION CAMP.

Bormann, Martin (1900–1945): Member of the NAZI PARTY and the Storm Detachment (SA) after 1925; chief of the Party Chancellery after 1941. Bormann exercised considerable influence as Adolf HITLER's official secretary and close adviser. As a defendant *in absentia* before the INTERNATIONAL MILITARY TRIBUNAL, Bormann was found guilty of WAR CRIMES and CRIMES AGAINST HUMANITY and sentenced to death. Bormann's skeleton, showing signs of suicide by cyanide poisoning, was found in Berlin in 1972; he was officially declared dead in 1973.

Brandt, Karl (1904–48): Personal physician to Adolf HITLER and his staff from 1934 to 1944, member of the NAZI PARTY after 1932, the SA after 1933, and transferred to the SS in 1934. In 1942 Brandt became the general commissar for health and sanitation and a member of the Reich Research Council. He was also one of the two plenipotentiaries for OPERATION T4. Convicted by the INTERNATIONAL MILITARY TRIBUNAL, he was hanged at Landsberg prison on June 2, 1948.

Buchenwald: A CONCENTRATION CAMP opened in 1937 on the Ettersberg hillside overlooking Weimar, Germany. The first German and Austrian Jewish prisoners arrived in 1938. German and Austrian GYPSY prisoners were deported there after July 1938. During the war, some 65,000 of Buchenwald's quarter-million prisoners perished; others died in its more than 130 satellite LABOR CAMPS. Buchenwald was one of the few major camps whose prisoners rebelled in the days preceding liberation on April 11, 1945, by units of the U.S. Army.

Central Office for Ethnic Germans *(Volksdeutsche Mittelstelle;* VoMi*):* SS welfare and repatriation office for ETHNIC GERMANS. Founded in 1936 by Rudolf HESS and administered by Werner Lorenz for the SS, VoMi assisted the GERMANIZATION of occupied territories through resettlement. Ethnic Germans who had been resettled from their homes throughout eastern Europe were given NAZI ideological training and "reeducation." VoMi also arranged to provide resettlers with clothing, shoes, and furniture confiscated from CONCENTRATION CAMP and KILLING CENTER victims.

Central Office for Jewish Emigration *(Zentralstelle für Jüdische Auswanderung):* Office run by Adolf EICHMANN for the SD and SECURITY POLICE to organize and oversee the emigration and expulsion of Jews from Austria. The office was so successful in developing methods for the mass DEPORTATION of Jews that eventually several branch offices opened in other European cities. After the invasion of Poland, most of the Jewish Emigration Office's staff was shifted to Eichmann's DEPARTMENT IVb4 in the CENTRAL OFFICE FOR REICH SECURITY.

Central Office for Reich Security *(Reichssicherheitshauptamt;* RSHA): NAZI administrative office formed in September 1939 from the union of the SS and the SECURITY POLICE (the latter comprising the GESTAPO and the CRIMINAL POLICE).

Chelmno (in German, Kulmhof): KILLING CENTER in German-annexed western Poland (the *WARTHEGAU*) that operated from December 1941 to March 1943 and again after April 1944 when it reopened during the liquidation of the Lodz GHETTO. At Chelmno, the SS—using special mobile GAS VANS—killed more than 320,000 Jews from the Lodz and Poznan provinces as well as about 5,000 Austrian GYPSIES incarcerated in the Lodz Ghetto.

Churchill, Sir Winston (1874–1965): British prime minister during most of World War II (May 1940–July 1945) and again after the war (1951–55).

Collaboration: Cooperation between citizens of an occupied country and its occupiers. There were NAZI collaborators in all occupied countries.

Concentration camp: Place of imprisonment to which political and religious dissidents and ethnic and racial undesirables were sent, usually without judicial process. Before the end of World War II, the Germans set up more than one hundred major concentration camps with several thousand satellite camps.

Confessing Church: (in German, *Bekennende Kirche*): Protestant church founded by Martin Niemöller, Dietrich Bonhoeffer, Karl Barth, and Eberhard Bethge that confronted the NAZI-organized "German Christian" movement with its declaration that Christianity was incompatible with the Nazi theory of the "total state."

Conspiracy: One of the four charges used by the INTERNATIONAL MILITARY TRIBUNAL and by other war crimes courts in later postwar trials, and defined as a combination of persons for the purpose of committing criminal acts, including WAR CRIMES, CRIMES AGAINST PEACE, and CRIMES AGAINST HUMANITY. Used by the Nuremberg prosecution to indict organizations rather than individuals, conspiracy was not part of the established European legal system or the international laws of war, but was based on the Anglo-American legal tradition. The Tribunal ultimately found conspiracy only applicable to crimes against peace.

Control Council for Germany: Governing body created after the AXIS surrender to deal with matters for the whole of Germany after Germany was divided into zones and its capital city, Berlin, was divided into sectors under the jurisdiction of the four ALLIED powers. In practice, however, each occupying power administered its zone independently. Nevertheless, the Control Council did play a significant role in the DENAZIFICATION of Germany.

Control Council Law No. 10: Promulgated by the CONTROL COUNCIL FOR GERMANY on December 10, 1945, to provide for the apprehension, extradition, and trial of war criminals in all four occupation zones of Germany on charges of CRIMES AGAINST PEACE, WAR CRIMES, CRIMES AGAINST HUMANITY, and membership in CRIMINAL ORGANIZATIONS as defined by the INTERNATIONAL MILITARY TRIBUNAL. The law was based on the LONDON AGREEMENT.

Crematorium (pl. crematoria): Oven used to cremate human bodies. The four crematoria at AUSCHWITZ were individual complexes used for extermination, each consisting of an undressing room, gas chamber, and ovens to cremate the bodies of the victims.

Crimes against humanity: All actions that cause the indiscriminate or systematic destruction of life and liberty, e.g., murder, extermination, enslavement, DEPORTATION, or other inhumane acts carried out on a civilian population. Based on CONTROL COUNCIL LAW NO. 10 and the LONDON AGREEMENT, this charge also included persecution for political, racial, or religious reasons before or during the war. Crimes against humanity was one of the four charges used by the INTERNATIONAL MILITARY TRIBUNAL and by other courts in later postwar trials.

Crimes against peace: Specified in the LONDON AGREEMENT as "planning, preparation, inception, or carrying through an offensive war, or of a war that violates international treaties or agreements." The Nuremberg prosecution argued to expand this definition to include participation in a common plan or CONSPIRACY for carrying out crimes against peace. While the Nuremberg defense objected to the *ex post facto* nature of this crime, the Tribunal upheld its validity based on the "progress of international law and previous treaties on the conduct of war and peace." Victors were not charged with this crime. Crimes against peace was one of the four main charges used by the INTERNATIONAL MILITARY TRIBUNAL and by other courts in later postwar trials.

Criminal organizations: Organizations indicted and found guilty of CONSPIRACY, CRIMES AGAINST HUMANITY, CRIMES AGAINST PEACE, and/or WAR CRIMES by the INTERNATIONAL MILITARY TRIBUNAL. By indicting entire organizations in this manner, the court was able to try hundreds of individuals based on their participation or affiliation with the indicted organizations. The Tribunal identified the NAZI PARTY leadership, the SS, the GESTAPO, and the SA as criminal organizations.

Criminal Police (*Kriminalpolizei; Kripo*): The German detective forces charged with investigating non-political crimes. Together with the GESTAPO, they formed the SECURITY POLICE. In 1939, the Criminal Police became Department V of the CENTRAL OFFICE FOR REICH SECURITY.

Croatia: Fascist puppet state in Yugoslavia established with German encouragement in April 1941 (*see* USTACHI). Among its population of 6.3 million were 700,000 Serbs, 40,000 Jews, and 30,000 Gypsies. During the war, at least 80 percent of the Croatian Jews and the overwhelming majority of the GYPSIES were killed, as were hundreds of thousands of Serbs.

Dachau: The first CONCENTRATION CAMP of the NAZI regime; opened on March 20, 1933, near Munich, Germany. Initially only known political opponents were interned at Dachau; gradually other groups were incarcerated there. Dachau had no mass extermination program, but of the 206,206 registered prisoners, there were 31,591 registered deaths. The total number of deaths at Dachau, including the victims of individual and mass executions and the final DEATH MARCHES, will never be known. Units of the U.S. Army liberated Dachau on April 29, 1945.

Death marches: Forced EVACUATIONS of all able-bodied CONCENTRATION CAMP prisoners from one camp to another, conducted at the approach of ALLIED forces.

Denazification; *also* **Denazify**: The policy of the victorious ALLIES to purge Germany of all NAZI leaders, officials, members, policies, and their influence on German society.

Department IVb4: The Jewish Office created in September 1939 within the CENTRAL OFFICE FOR REICH SECURITY and headed by Adolf EICHMANN to oversee the deportation of most European Jews to KILLING CENTERS as part of the "FINAL SOLUTION."

Deportation: The forced relocation of Jews, GYPSIES, and other "undesirables" from their homes to different localities, usually to GHETTOS, CONCENTRATION CAMPS, LABOR CAMPS, or KILLING CENTERS.

Dönitz, Karl (1891–1980): Supreme commander of the German Navy whom Adolf HITLER named to be his successor. As a defendant at the INTERNATIONAL MILITARY TRIBUNAL, he was found guilty of CRIMES AGAINST PEACE and WAR CRIMES, and sentenced to 10 years in prison. Dönitz was released in 1956.

Dora-Mittelbau: CONCENTRATION CAMP established near Nordhausen in the Harz Mountains of northern Germany in August 1943 as a subsidiary of the BUCHENWALD concentration camp. Originally named Dora, the camp for men provided labor for the production of V-2 rockets in underground factories. Dora became an independent camp in November 1944 and was renamed Mittelbau. Dora-Mittelbau was liberated on April 11, 1945.

Eichmann, Adolf (1906–62): SS lieutenant colonel and head of DEPARTMENT IVb4, the Jewish Affairs department of the CENTRAL OFFICE FOR REICH SECURITY. Eichmann was instrumental in implementing the "FINAL SOLUTION," organizing transports of Jews from all over Europe to the KILLING CENTERS. Arrested at the end of World War II in the American occupation zone of Germany, Eichmann escaped to Latin America, where he went underground and disappeared. In 1960, members of the Israeli Secret Service discovered and kidnapped him in Argentina and covertly took him to Israel for trial. He was tried in Jerusalem (April–December 1961), convicted, sentenced to death, and executed in 1962. *See also* EICHMANN TRIAL.

Einsatzgruppen: Mobile units of the SECURITY POLICE and SECURITY SERVICE that followed the German armies into the Soviet Union in June 1941. The four *Einsatzgruppen* (A, B, C, and D) in the Baltic and the U.S.S.R., subdivided into *Einsatzkommandos,* were to kill all Jews as well as Soviet commissars, the handicapped, institutionalized psychiatric patients, and GYPSIES. They were supported by units of the uniformed German Order Police and often used local auxiliaries (Ukrainian, Latvian, Lithuanian, and Estonian volunteers) and occasionally German army troops. Their victims, including at least one million Jews, were executed by mass shootings and buried in unmarked mass graves; the bodies were often later dug up and burned to disguise all traces of what had occurred.

Einsatzkommando: Subunit of an *EINSATZGRUPPE.*

Eisenhower, Dwight D. (1890–1969): Military leader and 34th president of the United States (1953–61). Eisenhower commanded the ALLIED Forces in Europe that liberated the CONCENTRATION and LABOR CAMPS, several of which he visited as soon as they were opened. After the war, Eisenhower's command of U.S. forces in Europe in part addressed the repatriation of the millions of displaced persons in Germany.

Ethnic Germans *(Volksdeutsche):* Individuals living outside German national borders who had retained their ethnic identity despite their given nationality.

Eugenics: The science to improve the quality of a breed or race, especially of people. The NAZIS' eugenics program aimed to prevent foreign blood and hereditary diseases from polluting the so-called ARYAN race. The primary methods used were genealogy and the registration of physical features: head size, hair and eye color, and physical deformities as well as mental illnesses. In 1936 there were nine institutions that issued "genetic racial reports"; by 1943, there were twenty-two. *(See also LEBENSBORN.)*

"Euthanasia": NAZI euphemism for the deliberate killing of the institutionalized physically, mentally, and emotionally handicapped to "improve" the quality of the "German race." The euthanasia program began in 1939 with German nationals as the first victims; the program was extended to the eastern occupied territories in 1940. *See also* OPERATION T4 AND OPERATION 14F13.

"Evacuation": Nazi euphemism for DEPORTATION.

Extermination camps: *See* KILLING CENTERS.

"Final Solution" (In full, *"die Endlösung der Judenfrage in Europa,"* or "the final solution to the Jewish question in Europe"): NAZI code name for the physical extermination of European Jews.

Flossenbürg: CONCENTRATION CAMP for men opened in May 1938 in northern Bavaria, Germany.

Forced evacuations: *See* DEATH MARCHES.

Forced labor; *also* **Forced laborers:** Workers from German-occupied countries compelled to work in German industry, agriculture, domestic service, and war production. Prisoners of war, ETHNIC GERMANS, and other foreign workers constituted 20 percent of the German workforce by September 1944.

Four-Year Plan: Devised by Adolf HITLER in 1936 for the rearmament of Germany as well as the restructuring of the German economy for war within a period of four years. The goals of the plan were in violation of the Treaty of Versailles. Hermann GÖRING was named commissioner for the implementation of the plan.

Frank, Hans (1900–1946): Member of the NAZI PARTY and SA ("Storm Troops") after 1923, and chief NAZI jurist and founder of the Reich Legal Office of the Nazi Party in 1930. Frank served as administrative head of occupied Poland from 1939 to 1945. As a defendant at the INTERNATIONAL MILITARY TRIBUNAL, he was found guilty of WAR CRIMES and CRIMES AGAINST HUMANITY, and was sentenced to death by hanging.

Frick, Wilhelm (1877–1946): Former minister of the interior and protector of occupied Bohemia and Moravia. As a defendant at the INTERNATIONAL MILITARY TRIBUNAL, Frick was found guilty of CRIMES AGAINST PEACE, WAR CRIMES, and CRIMES AGAINST HUMANITY, and was sentenced to death by hanging.

Fritzsche, Hans (1900–1953): Chief of the German Propaganda Ministry's Radio Division. As a defendant at the INTERNATIONAL MILITARY TRIBUNAL, he was found not guilty of any of the charges and acquitted.

Führer ("leader"): Adolf HITLER'S title as chancellor and head of state in NAZI Germany.

Funk, Walther (1890–1960): President of the Reichsbank. As a defendant at the INTERNATIONAL MILITARY TRIBUNAL, he was found guilty of CRIMES AGAINST PEACE, WAR CRIMES, and CRIMES AGAINST HUMANITY, and was sentenced to life imprisonment. He was released in 1957 due to illness.

Gas chamber: Sealed room at a KILLING CENTER, CONCENTRATION CAMP, or "EUTHANASIA" facility where Jews and other prisoners were murdered by poison gas (ZYKLON B at AUSCHWITZ-BIRKENAU and MAJDANEK) or by carbon monoxide (at the other killing centers).

Gas van: a truck whose engine exhaust was piped into the sealed rear cargo chamber to kill those inside with carbon monoxide gas. The use of gas vans was established by the CENTRAL OFFICE FOR REICH SECURITY to alleviate the "mental anguish" of the EINSATZGRUPPEN caused by shooting unarmed men, women, and children. The first vans were used in September 1941 to gas Soviet prisoners of war in SACHSENHAUSEN. By late June 1942, twenty such vans were in operation: the Daimond with a capacity of 25 to 30 victims, and the Sauer with a capacity of 50 to 60. Approximately 700,000 people died in gas vans, about half of those in German-occupied Soviet territories and half at the CHELMNO killing center.

Gauleiter: NAZI PARTY head of a *Gau*, the principal territorial unit in the REICH during the NAZI period.

General Government *(Generalgouvernement)*: The name for the territories of occupied Poland that were not annexed to the German REICH. Created on October 26, 1939, the General Government comprised five districts: Galicia, Cracow, Lublin, Radom, and Warsaw.

Geneva Convention: A series of international agreements on the conduct of warring nations and the treatment of prisoners of war. Originally drafted in 1864, the convention's 1929 revision stipulated that belligerent powers must treat captured prisoners of war humanely and provide medical care for the sick and wounded. This agreement was ratified and followed by most countries, with the notable exception of the U.S.S.R. It is still in effect.

Genocide: The systematic killing of a nation or race of people. The term was devised and first applied to the goal of the Nazis' "FINAL SOLUTION."

German Peoples' List *(Deutsche Volksliste*; DVL): A central registration program to identify all ETHNIC GERMANS living outside Germany's borders. Begun in October 1939 in occupied Poland, the list also grouped individuals into one of four categories based on their level of ARYAN "racial purity" and willingness to be GERMANIZED.

Germanization; *also* **Germanize**: The process by which the NAZIS sought to restructure Europe's populace along racial lines. Jews, Poles, GYPSIES, and other "undesirable" inhabitants of an area designated for German occupation were systematically deported and replaced by ETHNIC GERMANS, who were to resettle in the area. At the same time, the "racially desirable" settlers underwent ideological indoctrination to "reinforce" their German heritage.

Gestapo (abbreviation from *Geheime Staatspolizei*, "Secret State Police"): Established in Prussia in 1933, by 1936 its authority extended throughout Germany. The Gestapo and the CRIMINAL POLICE together constituted NAZI Germany's SECURITY POLICE.

Ghetto: Compulsory "Jewish Quarter" established mostly in occupied eastern Europe, where all Jews from a city (Lodz, Warsaw, Vilna, Kovno, Riga, Minsk, etc.) and its surrounding area were forced to reside. The NAZIS revived the medieval term "ghetto" to describe these poor sections of a city that were enclosed by barbed wire or walls and sealed so that no one could leave except under strict German supervision. The ghettos were characterized by overcrowding, disease, starvation, and hard labor. Several ghettos (Warsaw, Lodz, and Bialystok) also housed GYPSIES deported from surrounding regions and from western Europe. All the ghettos were eventually dissolved and their inhabitants were deported to KILLING CENTERS and murdered.

Globocnik, Odilo (1904–45): Active in the NAZI movement in Carinthia, Austria, from 1922, Globocnik was appointed deputy GAULEITER of Carinthia in 1933, then *Gauleiter* of Vienna in 1938. Dismissed from the latter post in 1939, he was subsequently designated SS and Police Leader in Lublin, occupied Poland, with the rank of SS major general. Globocnik supervised the KILLING CENTERS of BELZEC, SOBIBOR, and TREBLINKA, as chief of OPERATION REINHARD (1942–43). He also established the San Sabba CONCENTRATION CAMP in Trieste as HIGHER SS AND POLICE LEADER for the Adriatic Coast (1943–45). Arrested by ALLIED troops in Austria, he committed suicide in May 1945.

Glücks, Richard (1889–1945): Member of the SS after 1932 and the NAZI PARTY after 1933; succeeded Theodor Eicke as inspector of CONCENTRATION CAMPS and commander of the Death's Head units in 1939; promoted to SS major general in 1943. As director of the office group in Oswald Pohl's SS CENTRAL OFFICE FOR ECONOMY AND ADMINISTRATION, Glücks supervised the administration of the KILLING CENTERS in German-occupied Poland. Glücks disappeared in 1945; he is believed to have committed suicide.

Goebbels, Josef (1897–1945): Minister of propaganda in NAZI Germany and close associate of Adolf HITLER. On May 1, 1945, Goebbels and his wife took their own lives and those of their six children.

Göring, Hermann (1893–1946): Early associate of Adolf HITLER, responsible for much of the NAZI rearmament program, and the supreme commander of the German *LUFTWAFFE*. As plenipotentiary of the FOUR-YEAR PLAN, Göring was the virtual dictator of the Nazi German economy and was responsible for Germany's air war. He was also responsible for the "ARYANIZATION" of Jewish property. In July 1941, he signed the letter Reinhard HEYDRICH wrote for authorization to organize a "total solution" to the Jewish question; many historians believe this document to be the authorization for a comprehensive "FINAL SOLUTION." As chief defendant at the INTERNATIONAL MILITARY TRIBUNAL, Göring was found guilty of CONSPIRACY to commit and of committing CRIMES AGAINST PEACE, WAR CRIMES, and CRIMES AGAINST HUMANITY. Sentenced to death, he committed suicide hours before his scheduled hanging.

Gross-Rosen: CONCENTRATION CAMP opened in August 1940 for Polish male prisoners in Lower Silesia. Initially a subsidiary of SACHSENHAUSEN, by May 1941 Gross-Rosen became an independent concentration camp. On February 13, 1945, the camp was liberated by the Soviet Army.

Gypsies: A collective term for Roma and Sinti, nomadic peoples believed to have come originally from northwest India, which they left for Persia in the first millennium A.D. They became divided into five main groups that are still extant. Traveling mostly in small caravans, Gypsies first appeared in western Europe in the fifteenth century; during the next century, they spread to every country of Europe. Alternately tolerated and persecuted since that time, they were defined by the NAZIS as "ASOCIALS" or "work shy" because of their race and nomadic life, and thus were considered to be enemies of the state and were relentlessly persecuted. Approximately 500,000 Gypsies are believed to have perished in CONCENTRATION CAMPS and KILLING CENTERS.

Hadamar: City in the German state of Hessen and site of a psychiatric hospital founded in 1906 that was renamed in 1933 as State Psychiatric Hospital and Sanitorium. From 1941 to 1945 the hospital served OPERATION T4 as a "EUTHANASIA" center, where more than 11,000 people were killed (*see* HADAMAR TRIALS).

Hague Convention: A multilateral, international treaty signed in 1899 to create a comprehensive basis for the laws of war and to codify existing international law. The first Hague Convention sought to eliminate unnecessary suffering of prisoners of war and wounded enemy soldiers with rules for humane treatment that provided security to noncombatants and nonmilitary targets, and to establish a permanent court of arbitration between belligerent countries. A second Hague Convention, signed in 1907, modified the rules of the international court.

Hess, Rudolf (1894–1987): Deputy to Adolf HITLER, head of the NAZI PARTY Chancellery until 1941, and member of the Council for Reich Defense. In May 1941, Hess flew to England in an abortive and apparently unauthorized attempt to seek peace with Great Britain. Hitler disavowed the overture and Hess spent the duration of the war in British captivity. As a defendant at the INTERNATIONAL MILITARY TRIBUNAL, he was found guilty of CONSPIRACY to commit and of committing CRIMES AGAINST PEACE, and was sentenced to life imprisonment. He died in prison at age 93, reportedly hanging himself with an electrical cord.

Heydrich, Reinhard (1904–42): Head of the SECURITY SERVICE (SD). In 1939 he combined the SD and SECURITY POLICE into the CENTRAL OFFICE FOR REICH SECURITY. A consummate technocrat, Heydrich was a leading figure in the extermination of the Jews. He organized the *Einsatzgruppen* and the Wannsee Conference, during which definitive plans were laid for the "FINAL SOLUTION." In 1941 Heydrich was also appointed protector of Bohemia and Moravia. Fatally wounded on May 29, 1942, by Czech PARTISANS parachuted in by the British, he died on June 4, 1942. In reprisal, the Germans liquidated the Bohemian village of LIDICE, killing many of its inhabitants.

Higher SS and Police Leader *(Höherer SS- und Polizeiführer)*: Heinrich HIMMLER's personal representatives for the coordination of all SS and police offices and units in a region.

Himmler, Heinrich (1900–1945): Reich Leader of the SS and, after 1936, head of German police forces. Himmler presided over a vast state security empire, including all SS formations, the *WAFFEN-SS*, all police forces, the KILLING CENTERS, all CONCENTRATION and LABOR CAMPS and their Death Head guard units, the SECURITY SERVICE (SD), and the various offices for the resettlement of ETHNIC GERMANS, including the REICH COMMISSION FOR STRENGTHENING GERMANISM. In 1943, he also became minister of the interior. He was the senior SS leader responsible for the implementation of the "FINAL SOLUTION" and told senior SS officers in 1943 that he was implementing Adolf HITLER's orders; in late 1944, however, he ordered an end to the gassings. Early in 1945, with the war turning against Germany, he attempted to negotiate with the ALLIES. Himmler was captured by British troops, but committed suicide before trial and sentencing.

Hitler, Adolf (1889–1945): NAZI PARTY leader, 1919–45, and German chancellor, 1933–45. Hitler committed suicide in a Berlin bunker as the Soviet Army was conquering the city in April 1945.

Höss, Rudolf (1900–1947): Member of the NAZI PARTY since 1922, served a prison sentence for a political murder from 1923–28, joined the SS in 1933 and was promoted in 1942 to SS lieutenant colonel. Höss was commandant of the AUSCHWITZ camp complex (1940–43 and summer 1944) and chief of Department D, the Inspectorate for Concentration Camps, of the SS CENTRAL OFFICE FOR ECONOMY AND ADMINISTRATION (1943–45). Sentenced to death in Poland, Höss was hanged at Auschwitz in 1947.

I.G. Farben: Powerful German industrial conglomerate comprising eight leading German chemical manufacturers that benefitted enormously from Adolf HITLER's FOUR-YEAR PLAN to revitalize Germany's economy for war. Farben established an installation in the AUSCHWITZ camp complex known as Monowitz that took advan-

tage of the SLAVE LABOR there. ZYKLON B gas, which was used in some GAS CHAMBERS, was a product of *DEGESCH*, a firm in which Farben had a major share.

IMT: *See* INTERNATIONAL MILITARY TRIBUNAL.

Jackson, Robert (1892–1954): Pennsylvania-born jurist who became an assistant attorney general (1936), solicitor general (1938), and attorney general (1940) under President Franklin D. ROOSEVELT. In 1941, Roosevelt appointed Jackson to the U.S. Supreme Court. From 1945 to 1946, Jackson served as chief U.S. prosecutor at the INTERNATIONAL MILITARY TRIBUNAL, about which he reported in his book *The Nuremberg Case* (1947).

Jaworski, Leon (1905–82): American jurist and early WAR CRIMES trial prosecutor. A respected corporate lawyer in peacetime, Jaworski served during the war as chief of the Investigations and Examinations Division of the U.S. War Crimes Branch. Following the war, Jaworski became chief of the War Crimes Trial Section in the American zone of occupied Germany and prosecuted a number of early war crimes trials, including the HADAMAR TRIAL (AMERICAN). Jaworski gained fame in the 1970s as a Watergate special prosecutor.

Jehovah's Witnesses: International religious community organized in Germany as the International Bible Students' Association. Although outlawed in several German states beginning in 1933, it was only when the Witnesses refused to use the *Heil Hitler* salute and, after 1935, to serve in the army that they were seen as enemies of the NAZI state. This led to the first wave of arrests and imprisonment in CONCENTRATION CAMPS in 1936 and 1937. At all times, the Witnesses in the concentration camps were a relatively small group of prisoners (not exceeding several hundred per camp), mostly of German nationality; after 1939, Witnesses from Austria, Belgium, Czechoslovakia, the Netherlands, Norway, and Poland were arrested and deported to various concentration camps. About 10,000 Witnesses were imprisoned by the Germans; of these about 2,500 to 5,000 died.

Jewish Badge: Insignia worn by Jews in various countries, on NAZI orders, to distinguish them from the rest of the population. Most commonly it was a badge or arm band imprinted with the Star of David; frequently, the star bore the word "Jew" in the local language.

Jodl, Alfred (1890–1946): Chief of Operations Staff, German Armed Forces *(WEHRMACHT)*. As a defendant at the INTERNATIONAL MILITARY TRIBUNAL, he was found guilty of CONSPIRACY to commit and of committing CRIMES AGAINST PEACE, WAR CRIMES, and CRIMES AGAINST HUMANITY, and sentenced to death by hanging.

Juden: German for "Jews."

Judenrat ("Jewish Council"): Council of Jewish leaders established by the NAZIS in the GHETTOS of Poland and other occupied countries. The *Judenrat* became the ghetto administrative body under Nazi control and, as such, was forced to cooperate in the preparation and management of DEPORTATIONS. In some areas, these councils were also known as the *Ältestenrat* ("Council of Elders").

Judge Advocate General: The senior legal officer and chief legal adviser for the United States Armed Forces.

Kaltenbrunner, Ernst (1903–46): Head of the CENTRAL OFFICE FOR REICH SECURITY after the 1942 death of Reinhard HEYDRICH. Kaltenbrunner played an important role in implementing the "FINAL SOLUTION" as well as the "EUTHANASIA" program. As a defendant at the INTERNATIONAL MILITARY TRIBUNAL, he was found guilty of WAR CRIMES and CRIMES AGAINST HUMANITY, and sentenced to death by hanging.

Kapo: In popular language of the era, a generic term for all prisoner functionaries. Although the origin of the term is not fully known, the word probably came from the Latin *capo*, meaning "head," and was probably introduced to DACHAU by Italian workers in the 1930s.

Keitel, Wilhelm (1882–1946): Chief of the Armed Forces *(WEHRMACHT)* High Command (1938–45) and general field marshal. Keitel signed many orders that affected prisoners of war and civilians in occupied territories, including the infamous "Night and Fog Decree" (1941) under which "enemies" vanished without a trace. On May 8, 1945, Keitel signed Germany's unconditional surrender. As a defendant at the INTERNATIONAL MILITARY TRIBUNAL, he was found guilty of CONSPIRACY to commit and of committing CRIMES AGAINST PEACE, WAR CRIMES, and CRIMES AGAINST HUMANITY, and sentenced to death by hanging.

Killing centers: Camps specifically built to kill Jews and other "enemies of the German nation." The killing centers included BELZEC, CHELMNO, SOBIBOR, and TREBLINKA, as well as sections of the AUSCHWITZ and MAJDANEK concentration camps.

Kristallnacht ("Crystal Night," also called "Night of Broken Glass"): The organized POGROM against synagogues and Jewish stores in Germany and Austria during the night of November 9–10, 1938, ordered by Reinhard HEYDRICH, chief of the SECURITY SERVICE (SD). During *Kristallnacht*, 171 synagogues were burned, 7,500 Jewish businesses were damaged or destroyed, and 91 Jews were killed. The name comes from the smashed window glass that littered the streets.

Krupp von Bolen und Halbach, Alfried: (1907–67) Son of the German industrialist Gustav KRUPP VON BOLEN UND HALBACH who succeeded his father as the chairman of Krupp Works in December 1943. After the war, Alfried Krupp was tried by the NUREMBERG MILITARY TRIBUNAL for CRIMES AGAINST HUMANITY (the use of SLAVE LABOR for armaments production) and WAR CRIMES (the economic plunder and spoilation of German-occupied countries) in the KRUPP TRIAL. He was found guilty and sentenced to 12 years imprisonment. After serving three years, he was released and returned to his position as the head of Krupp Works.

Krupp von Bolen und Halbach, Gustav (1870–1950): Chairman of Krupp Works, a German industrial and armaments conglomerate, from 1909 to 1943; named military and economic leader by Adolf HITLER in 1937. After the war, Gustav Krupp was indicted by the INTERNATIONAL MILITARY TRIBUNAL for his part in Germany's war of aggression and for crimes committed by Krupp Works' SLAVE LABOR program. At both the International Military Tribunal and at the KRUPP TRIAL, these charges were dropped after it was determined that Krupp was too senile to stand trial.

Labor camp: A CONCENTRATION CAMP in which the prisoners were used as SLAVE LABOR.

Lebensborn ("Fount of Life Society"): An SS association established in 1935 to facilitate the adoption of illegitimate children of SS men and "racially" pure women born at *Lebensborn* facilities. During the war *Lebensborn* placed "racially valuable" children, kidnapped from their families in German-occupied countries, with German families to be raised as Germans. After the war, Max SOLLMANN, the head of the *Lebensborn* organization, was tried and convicted by the NUREMBERG MILITARY TRIBUNAL in the RuSHA TRIAL.

Ley, Robert (1890–1945): German politician who, before the NAZIS came to power, co-founded the pro-Nazi and antisemitic Rhineland newspaper *Westdeutscher Beobachter*. As director of the Working Committee for the Protection of German Labor, Ley ordered the arrest of all labor union leaders on May 2, 1933, and founded the German Labor Front, a Nazi organization designed to replace labor unions. Following his indictment by the INTERNATIONAL MILITARY TRIBUNAL on October 20, 1945, Ley committed suicide.

Lidice: A Czech mining village (population 700) liquidated by the NAZIS in 1942 in reprisal for the assassination of Reinhard HEYDRICH. The men and older boys were shot, the women deported to the RAVENSBRÜCK concentration camp, and the children to the WARTHEGAU, where eight were selected for Germanization and adopted by

SS families. The village was razed. After World War II, a new village was built near the site of old Lidice, now a memorial and national park.

London Agreement: The agreement to form the INTERNATIONAL MILITARY TRIBUNAL to try the major war criminals of the European AXIS, signed in London on August 8, 1945, by the United States, the Soviet Union, Great Britain, and France.

Luftwaffe: The German Air Force during World War II, headed by Hermann GÖRING.

Majdanek (also Maidanek): CONCENTRATION CAMP, LABOR CAMP, and KILLING CENTER built in October 1941 near Lublin, in occupied eastern Poland. Majdanek was liberated by the Soviet Army in July 1944.

Mauthausen: A CONCENTRATION CAMP for men opened in August 1938 near Linz, Austria. Established to exploit the nearby stone quarries, it was classified by the SS as a camp of utmost severity. Conditions there were brutal even by concentration camp standards. Many prisoners were killed by being pushed from 300-foot cliffs into the quarries. Mauthausen was liberated on May 5, 1945.

Mengele, Josef (1911–77): Member of the Storm Troopers (SA; 1933–34), the NAZI PARTY and SS (after 1938), and promoted to SS captain in 1943. After being wounded while serving in the *WAFFEN-SS* medical corps, Mengele was transferred to the AUSCHWITZ concentration camp in 1943. As senior SS physician at Auschwitz-Birkenau from 1943 to 1944, Mengele took part in many SELECTIONS of arriving Jews and also conducted many medical experiments, including his notorious experimentation on twins. Mengele eluded capture after the war. In 1985, the corpse of a Wolfgang Gerhard, who had died in Brazil in a swimming accident in 1979, was identified by forensic pathologists as Mengele's.

Mischlinge ("crossbreeds"): NAZI term for persons having one or two Jewish or GYPSY grandparents. In 1943, German policy proposed to deport or sterilize many Germans of mixed Jewish or Gypsy ancestry and to kill or sterilize part-Jewish and part-Gypsy children in Germany. Most *Mischlinge* survived the war because the "FINAL SOLUTION" was applied only to full Jews or those who actively practiced Judaism.

Monowitz: *See* AUSCHWITZ.

National Socialist: *See* NAZI PARTY.

National Socialist Peoples' Welfare Society (*Nationalsozialistische Volkswohlfahrt*; NSV): Organization established by Adolf HITLER on May 3, 1933, to synchronize various independent charity and self-help organizations in order to direct the NAZI PARTY'S social welfare initiatives. Financed in part by contributions from the Winter Relief Agency and contributions from its own members, the NSV provided health care and counseling, pediatric care, and assistance in housing and employment placement.

Natzweiler: A CONCENTRATION CAMP for men opened in May 1941 near Strasbourg in German-occupied France to hold prisoners from western European countries. Natzweiler and its surrounding sub-camps held approximately 19,000 prisoners by the end of the war.

Nazi: abbreviation for the Nazi Party, one of its members, or an adjective used to describe its core philosophies; *see* NAZI PARTY.

Nazi Party (*Nationalsozialistische Deutsche Arbeiterpartei;* NSDAP, "National Socialist German Workers' Party"): The political party that ruled Germany from 1933 to 1945 with Adolf HITLER as its leader. The NSDAP's core philosophies were fascism (militant, nationalistic totalitarianism), antisemitism (prejudice against Jews), and the belief in the superiority of the "ARYAN" or "master" race.

Neuengamme: A CONCENTRATION CAMP opened northwest of Hamburg, Germany, in December 1938 as a SACHSENHAUSEN satellite. Neuengamme became an independent camp in June 1940. British troops liberated Neuengamme on May 4, 1945.

Neurath, Constantin von (1873–1956): Former minister of foreign affairs and protector of occupied Bohemia and Moravia. As a defendant at the INTERNATIONAL MILITARY TRIBUNAL, he was found guilty of CONSPIRACY to commit and of committing CRIMES AGAINST PEACE, WAR CRIMES, and CRIMES AGAINST HUMANITY, and sentenced to 15 years in prison. He was released in 1954.

NSDAP: *See* NAZI PARTY.

NSV: *See* NATIONAL SOCIALIST PEOPLES' WELFARE SOCIETY.

Nuremberg Laws: Legislation promulgated on September 15, 1935, to lay the foundation for further excluding Jews and other non-"ARYANS" from German society. The first law, the "Reich Citizenship Law", stated that only those people of "German blood" could be full citizens of the REICH. The second law, the "Law for the Protection of German Blood and Honor", prohibited marriage or sexual relations between Germans and Jews as well as the employment of German housekeepers under the age of forty-five in Jewish homes. Between November 1935 and July 1943, thirteen ordinances were added to the first law. Ancillary legislation extended all measures to apply to GYPSIES and Blacks.

Nuremberg Military Tribunals: Twelve trials prosecuted by the United States between December 1946 and April 1949 against leaders of THIRD REICH ministries, the military, industrial concerns, German legal and medical professions, and the SS. *See* individual entries in the Trials Appendix.

Nuremberg Trial: For the trial of 1945–46, *see* INTERNATIONAL MILITARY TRIBUNAL; for the "successor" Nuremberg Trials of 1946–49, *see* NUREMBERG MILITARY TRIBUNALS.

Office of Strategic Services (OSS): U.S. agency established June 13, 1942, by President Franklin D. ROOSEVELT for intelligence, sabotage, subversion, and overseas research, with General William J. Donovan as its head. The OSS was the forerunner of the present-day Central Intelligence Agency (CIA).

Operation 14f13: A continuation of OPERATION T4, the NAZI program to exterminate Germany's mentally and physically handicapped. In spring 1941, Heinrich HIMMLER gave orders to extend the so-called EUTHANASIA program to CONCENTRATION CAMP inmates who were sick or unable to work. Selection for this extermination campaign was rarely discriminating; seemingly healthy criminals, political prisoners, and Jewish inmates were also killed by gassing or lethal injection at the Sonnenstein, Bernberg, and Hartheim euthanasia facilities.

Operation Reinhard: German code name (for Reinhard HEYDRICH) for the program to exterminate Jews in the GENERAL GOVERNMENT during 1942 and 1943. Three KILLING CENTERS were set up to carry out the program: BELZEC, SOBIBOR, and TREBLINKA.

Operation T4: NAZI program to exterminate the institutionalized mentally and physically handicapped, named for the address of its Berlin headquarters—Tiergartenstrasse 4. This "EUTHANASIA" program began in October 1939, with German and Austrian mental patients as its first victims. Protests from citizens and church circles halted T4 in August 1941; by then at least 70,000 persons had died by gassing or lethal injection at the program's six euthanasia centers: Bernburg, Brandenburg, Grafeneck, Hartheim, HADAMAR, and Sonnenstein. Many members of the T4 staff subsequently provided the trained force of killers employed at the killing centers in occupied Poland.

Organization Todt: Semi-militarized construction agency established in 1933 and named for its first chief, Dr. Fritz Todt, at his death in 1942. Organization Todt provided FORCED LABOR for building the Atlantic Wall, highways, and other state-funded, military-related construction projects.

Papen, Franz von (1879–1969): Former German chancellor and ambassador to Vienna and Turkey. As a defendant at the INTERNATIONAL MILITARY TRIBUNAL, he was acquitted of all charges.

Partisans: Guerrilla fighters and other combatants not belonging to regular armed forces who singly or in organized groups fought NAZI Germany and its AXIS partners by acts of terrorism, ambush, assassination, or espionage. According to international law, partisans following certain stipulations are to be treated as regular combatants, and as such are entitled to the same rights as prisoners of war under the HAGUE and GENEVA CONVENTIONS. During World War II, most partisan fighters did not meet the stipulations. Partisan activities against German occupation forces throughout Europe resulted in barbaric retaliatory operations by the Germans against local populations.

Plaszow [Plaszów]: LABOR CAMP established in 1942 outside Cracow, occupied Poland. Plaszow held up to 24,000 Poles, Jews, GYPSIES, and German political prisoners. In January 1944, Plaszow was converted to a CONCENTRATION CAMP. At that time, some 8,000 prisoners were massacred in small groups and buried in mass graves. The camp was closed on January 14, 1945, after its prisoners had been deported to AUSCHWITZ. Plaszow's commandant, Amon GOETH, was tried after the war; *see* GOETH TRIAL.

Pogrom: An organized and often officially encouraged persecution or massacre of a minority group, especially of Jews.

Pohl, Oswald (1892–1951): Member of the NAZI PARTY after 1923, chief of the SS CENTRAL OFFICE FOR ECONOMY AND ADMINISTRATION from 1942 to 1945. At Pohl's disposal was a work force of more than 500,000 CONCENTRATION CAMP prisoners, some of whom were also "leased out" to industry. He also ensured that personal and bodily effects from Jews murdered in GAS CHAMBERS were reutilized by the German economy. Pohl was tried by a NUREMBERG MILITARY TRIBUNAL; *see* POHL TRIAL.

Protective custody camp: A section of certain CONCENTRATION CAMPS where individuals, frequently "ASOCIAL" elements, were held in "protective custody" and without recourse to legal procedure.

Protectorate of Bohemia and Moravia: German designation for the territories of Czechoslovakia occupied by the *WEHRMACHT* on March 16, 1939.

Raeder, Erich (1876–1960): Former supreme commander of the German Navy. As a defendant at the INTER-

NATIONAL MILITARY TRIBUNAL, he was found guilty of CRIMES AGAINST PEACE, WAR CRIMES, and CRIMES AGAINST HUMANITY, and sentenced to life in prison. He was released in 1955 due to ill health.

Rascher, Dr. Sigmund (1909–45): Physician who performed formed high altitude and hypothermia experiments on DACHAU prisoners; 190 victims died as a result. Rascher joined the NAZI PARTY in 1933, the SA in 1936, and transferred to the SS in 1939. On orders of Heinrich HIMMLER, Rascher was expelled from the SS in 1945 and shot.

Ravensbrück: CONCENTRATION CAMP for women near Fürstenberg, north of Berlin, built by male inmates from SACHSENHAUSEN during the winter of 1938–39. Designed to hold 15,000 prisoners, Ravensbrück eventually housed more than 120,000 women from 23 nations, including political prisoners, Jews, GYPSIES, and JEHOVAH'S WITNESSES. It later included a separate men's camp and a children's camp at Uckermark. The camp's makeshift GAS CHAMBER was used to kill prisoners in 1945. Ravensbrück was liberated by the Soviet Army in late April 1945.

Red Cross, International Committee of (ICRC): Private humanitarian organization founded in 1863; among its primary roles was the mediation between belligerents in time of war and monitoring the application of humanitarian law. During the war the NAZIS often denied the Red Cross access to CONCENTRATION CAMPS and KILLING CENTERS. It was only near the end of the war that the Red Cross gained this access, when in 1944 the SS allowed visits to THERESIENSTADT.

Reich: "Empire," used from 1871–1945 to describe the unified German state. See THIRD REICH.

Reich Association for Hospitals and Nursing Establishments (*Reicharbeitsgemeinschaft Heil- und Pflegeanstalten*): The agency that arranged the OPERATION T4 killing program. Beginning in October 1939, this organization identified chronic institutionalized adult patients by sending out questionnaires to hospitals and care facilities throughout Germany. All hospitalized individuals incapable of doing simple mechanical work or who had been institutionalized for five or more years were deemed possible candidates for "EUTHANASIA."

Reich Commission for Strengthening Germanism (*Reichskommisariat für die Festigung des Deutschen Volkstums*; RKFDV): SS agency in charge of developing the GERMAN PEOPLES' LIST, selecting candidates for GERMANIZATION, and resettling ETHNIC GERMANS. Administered by Ulrich Greifelt, the RKFDV organized the resettlement of approximately 225,000 ethnic Germans in German-occupied territory.

Reichsführer-SS ("Reich Leader of the SS"): Heinrich HIMMLER's primary title.

Reichssicherheitshauptamt (RSHA): see CENTRAL OFFICE FOR REICH SECURITY.

Resettlement: Wartime German euphemism for deportation to KILLING CENTERS in occupied Poland.

Resistance: Those citizens of occupied countries who actively resisted the Germans through clandestine propaganda, intelligence-gathering, and sabotage. *See also* PARTISANS.

Ribbentrop, Joachim von (1893–1946): German foreign minister. As a defendant at the INTERNATIONAL MILITARY TRIBUNAL, he was found guilty of CONSPIRACY to commit and of committing CRIMES AGAINST PEACE, WAR CRIMES, and CRIMES AGAINST HUMANITY, and sentenced to death by hanging.

RKFDV: *See* REICH COMMISSION FOR STRENGTHENING GERMANISM.

Roosevelt, Franklin Delano (1882–1945): U.S. President from March 1933 until his death in April 1945, almost the entire period of NAZI rule in Germany.

Rosenberg, Alfred (1893–1946): Leading proponent of NAZI ideology and minister for occupied eastern territories. As a defendant at the INTERNATIONAL MILITARY TRIBUNAL, he was found guilty of CONSPIRACY to commit and of committing CRIMES AGAINST PEACE, WAR CRIMES, and CRIMES AGAINST HUMANITY, and sentenced to death by hanging.

RSHA (*Reichssicherheitshauptamt*): *See* CENTRAL OFFICE FOR REICH SECURITY.

RuSHA: *See* SS CENTRAL OFFICE FOR RACE AND RESETTLEMENT.

SA (*Sturmabteilung*; Storm Troopers): Shock paramilitary units of the NAZI PARTY founded on August 3, 1921; also called the Brown Shirts. These troops operated as an instrument of Nazi propaganda and terror. Though the SA leadership was purged and many of its leaders killed in "The Night of the Long Knives" (June 30–July 2, 1934), it was instrumental in many terror campaigns including the *KRISTALLNACHT* pogrom on November 9–10, 1938.

Sachsenhausen: CONCENTRATION CAMP for men, opened in 1936 in Oranienburg, a suburb of Berlin, adjacent to the Inspectorate of the Concentration Camps. It held about 200,000 prisoners, 100,000 of whom perished. It was liberated by the Soviet Army in late April 1945.

Sauckel, Fritz (1894–1946): Plenipotentiary-general for labor mobilization from 1942 to 1945. Sauckel's task was to supply the manpower for the German armaments and munitions production program. His exploitation of Jewish laborers resulted in the deaths of thousands of Jewish workers in Poland. As a defendant at the INTERNATIONAL MILITARY TRIBUNAL, he was found guilty of CRIMES AGAINST PEACE and CRIMES AGAINST HUMANITY, and sentenced to death by hanging.

Schacht, Hjalmar (1877–1970): Former minister of economics and former president of the Reichsbank. As a defendant at the INTERNATIONAL MILITARY TRIBUNAL, he was acquitted of all charges.

Schirach, Baldur von (1907–74): Leader of the Hitler Youth and *GAULEITER* of Vienna. As a defendant at the INTERNATIONAL MILITARY TRIBUNAL, he was found guilty of CRIMES AGAINST HUMANITY, and sentenced to 20 years in prison. He was released in 1966.

SD *(Sicherheitsdienst)*: See SECURITY SERVICE.

Security Police *(Sicherheitspolizei; Sipo)*: NAZI security police, composed of the GESTAPO and the CRIMINAL POLICE.

Security Service *(Sicherheitsdienst, SD)*: The SS security and intelligence service, established in 1932 under Reinhard HEYDRICH and incorporated in 1939 into the CENTRAL OFFICE FOR REICH SECURITY.

Selection: The process of separating Jewish deportees immediately after arrival at a KILLING CENTER into those assigned to SLAVE LABOR and those to be killed. The term also refers to the selection of Jews for DEPORTATION from GHETTOS.

Seyss-Inquart, Arthur (1892–1946): Reich commissioner for the occupied Netherlands. As a defendant at the INTERNATIONAL MILITARY TRIBUNAL, he was found guilty of CRIMES AGAINST PEACE, WAR CRIMES, and CRIMES AGAINST HUMANITY, and sentenced to death by hanging.

Sicherheitspolizei (Sipo): See SECURITY POLICE.

Slave labor; *also* **Slave laborers:** CONCENTRATION CAMP victims and prisoners of war who were forced to perform hard labor for German industry and war production. Brutal treatment, backbreaking work, malnutrition, and disease made "death through work" a murder method in the "FINAL SOLUTION."

Sobibor: One of the KILLING CENTERS of OPERATION REINHARD, located near Lublin, occupied Poland. From May 1942 to October 1943 at least 250,000 Jews were killed in the five carbon monoxide GAS CHAMBERS at the camp. A prisoner revolt in October 1943 hastened the camp's closing, which had been ordered by Heinrich HIMMLER several months earlier.

Sollman, Max (1904–): Member of the NAZI PARTY after 1922, and of the SS after 1937; director of the LEBENSBORN program from 1940 to the end of the war. A defendant in the RuSHA TRIAL, Sollmann was charged with the kidnapping of children in occupied territories, taking away children of Eastern workers, and the plunder of public and private property. He was acquitted of all these charges but found guilty of membership in a CRIMINAL ORGANIZATION, the SS. Time spent in custody during the trial was considered adequate punishment, and Sollmann was released after sentencing.

Sonderkommando ("special squad"): SS or *EINSATZGRUPPE* detachment; also refers to the Jewish SLAVE LABOR units in KILLING CENTERS like AUSCHWITZ-BIRKENAU that moved the bodies of gassed prisoners to facilitate removal of gold fillings and hair to be recycled into the German war economy and for cremation.

Special treatment *(Sonderbehandlung)*: NAZI euphemism for shooting or gassing in GAS VANS or at one of the KILLING CENTERS.

Speer, Albert (1905–81): Adolf HITLER'S architect, Reich minister for armaments (after 1942), and Reich minister for armaments and war production (after 1943). Speer was responsible for the allocation of FORCED LABOR in the German war industry. As a defendant at the INTERNATIONAL MILITARY TRIBUNAL, he was sentenced to 20 years in prison for WAR CRIMES and CRIMES AGAINST HUMANITY. He was released in 1966.

SS *(Schutzstaffel,* "Protection Squad"): Formed in 1925 as Adolf HITLER'S personal bodyguard; became the elite units of the NAZI PARTY after 1929. Heinrich HIMMLER built the SS into a giant organization that, among other roles, provided staff for the police, camp guards, and the fighting units *(WAFFEN-SS)*. These paramilitary, black-shirted troops used as their insignia a symbol copied from Teutonic runes—a parallel jagged double S—that was also used as a warning for high-tension wires or lightning.

SS Central Office for Economy and Administration (*Wirtschafts- und Verwaltungshauptamt*; WVHA): Agency responsible for all SS economic enterprises and, after March 3, 1942, included the Inspectorate of the Concentration Camps that administered the CONCENTRATION CAMPS and KILLING CENTERS.

SS Central Office for Race and Resettlement (*Rasse- und Siedlungshauptamt*; RuSHA): Established in 1931 as a genealogical research service for ss men and eventually involved in multiple aspects of the NAZI plan for the racial restructuring of Europe. RuSHA conducted racial examinations in order to classify individuals based on their "racial purity," helped to kidnap "ARYAN" children for LEBENSBORN, confiscated property belonging to deported Poles and Jews, and disseminated propaganda providing instruction on racial issues. It also screened all SS marriage partners for suitability.

Stalin, Joseph (1879–1953): General secretary of the Communist Party of the Soviet Union and premier of the U.S.S.R. from 1927 to 1953.

Streicher, Julius (1885–1946): Owner and publisher of the antisemitic newspaper *Der Stürmer* and former director of the Central Committee for the Defense against Jewish Atrocity and Boycott Propaganda. As a defendant at the INTERNATIONAL MILITARY TRIBUNAL, he was found guilty of CRIMES AGAINST HUMANITY and sentenced to death by hanging.

Stroop, Jürgen (1895–1952) (SS major general) involved in fighting PARTISANS, in RESETTLEMENTS, and in liquidating Jews in occupied territory. Beginning on April 19, 1943, he led forces that brutally subdued the WARSAW GHETTO uprising. During this action, Stroop reported daily on the military operations in the GHETTO. The "Stroop Report" was later introduced as evidence in several postwar trials. Stroop was sentenced to death by a U.S. military court on March 21, 1947, for shooting captured ALLIED pilots (*see* STROOP TRIAL [U.S.]). Later remanded to Poland for a second trial, which charged him with crimes committed in connection to the Warsaw Ghetto uprising, he was again found guilty and hanged on March 6, 1952 (*see* STROOP TRIAL [POLISH]).

Stutthof: Detention center for Polish men opened near Danzig in September 1939; became a CONCENTRATION CAMP in January 1942. Stutthof received a large number of Jewish women concentration camp prisoners transferred from the Baltic, especially Riga. Soviet troops liberated Stutthof on May 10, 1945.

Taylor, Telford (1908–): U.S. Army brigadier general, member of the prosecution staff at the INTERNATIONAL MILITARY TRIBUNAL, chief counsel for the prosecution at the NUREMBERG MILITARY TRIBUNALS, and author of many books on NAZI Germany and the WAR CRIMES trials.

Terezin: *See* THERESIENSTADT.

Theresienstadt (Terezin): Town in Bohemia near Prague; known as Theresienstadt before 1918, as Terezin after Czechoslovakia's creation, and renamed Theresienstadt under German occupation. The town's "Small Fortress" was a GESTAPO prison that held more than 32,000 political prisoners between 1940 and 1945. Theresienstadt was made into a GHETTO for Jewish deportees from the PROTECTORATE OF BOHEMIA AND MORAVIA, Slovakia, Germany, Austria, the Netherlands, and Denmark. The SS used the ghetto to show various national and international RED CROSS investigators how well Jews were being treated. However, most Jews held there were deported to the KILLING CENTERS in occupied Poland between 1942 and 1944. Barely 1,100 of the 15,000 children incarcerated in the ghetto survived. On May 8, 1945, the Soviet Army liberated Theresienstadt.

Third Reich: Name of the NAZI German state. The first Reich was the Holy Roman Empire; the second was created by Otto von Bismarck and existed from 1871 to 1918. The Third Reich was proclaimed by Adolf Hitler in 1933 and lasted twelve years, until 1945.

Transit camp: Camps, such as WESTERBORK, constructed before the war by the governments of France, the Netherlands, Hungary, and Romania to intern refugees; Belgium, Italy, and Yugoslavia followed suit after the war started. After 1942, under German control, transit camps became collection points for deportations "to the East."

Treblinka: A KILLING CENTER located on the Bug River northeast of Warsaw in the GENERAL GOVERNMENT (occupied Poland); opened in July 1942. The largest of the three OPERATION REINHARD killing centers, the GAS CHAMBERS of Treblinka killed between 700,000 and 860,000 people. The camp was closed in November 1943 after a prisoner revolt that destroyed much of the camp.

United Nations Relief and Rehabilitation Administration (UNRRA): Organization founded in 1943 to aid refugees and the citizens of the ALLIED nations in the liberated countries of Europe and the Far East. The United States held the principle executive post and was responsible for 40 percent of the agency's budget. This organization dealt with financing countries unable to provide basic commodities for their citizens as well as handling and repatriating thousands of displaced persons.

United Nations War Crimes Commission (UNWCC): Founded on December 17, 1942, by a joint declaration to punish NAZI war criminals at the war's end issued by the American, British, and Soviet governments and signed by all other ALLIED governments. The UNWCC investigated, recorded, and assisted in the preparation of indictments of Nazi CRIMES AGAINST PEACE and CRIMES AGAINST HUMANITY, including the crime of GENOCIDE. Between 1944 and 1948, UNWCC compiled 8,178 files relating to more than 36,000 individual criminals and CRIMINAL ORGANIZATIONS. Due to the increasing tensions of the Cold War, various nations refused to extradite persons whom the UNWCC had listed as war criminals. In February 1948, UNWCC operations came to an end.

UNRRA: *See* UNITED NATIONS RELIEF AND REHABILITATION ADMINISTRATION.

UNWCC: *See* UNITED NATIONS WAR CRIMES COMMISSION.

Ustachi (also Ustasha, Ustashi, Ustasi): Croatian fascist organization that came to power in April 1941 with the establishment of a NAZI puppet state in the Croatian region of conquered Yugoslavia. A militia formed under Ustachi auspices set out to rid Croatia of foreign elements, especially its Serbian minority. In collaboration with the Germans, they were responsible for the mass murder of Serbs, Jews, and GYPSIES.

Vichy: Spa town in central France that served as the capital of unoccupied France and headquarters of the pro-NAZI regime headed by Marshal Henri Philippe Pétain. The Germans occupied Vichy, France, in November 1942.

Volksdeutsche: *See* ETHNIC GERMANS.

Volksdeutsche Mittelstelle: *See* CENTRAL OFFICE FOR ETHNIC GERMANS.

VoMi: *See* CENTRAL OFFICE FOR ETHNIC GERMANS.

Waffen-SS: Armed SS military units that served with the German armed forces.

Wallenberg, Raoul (1912–47): Swedish diplomat in Budapest who, in 1944, devoted himself to saving the Jews of occupied Europe. He organized a system of feeding and preserving the lives of Jews in the Budapest GHETTO. He saved thousands by providing them with Swedish "passports of protection." In September 1944 he temporarily concealed himself to avoid the GESTAPO. After the Soviet Army liberated Hungary in January 1945, he made contact with Soviet authorities. On January 15, 1945, Wallenberg was called to the headquarters of Soviet Army Marshal Rodion Malinovski and disappeared without a trace. The Soviets claim he died after the war; in the 1970s, however, rumors that Wallenberg was still alive in a Soviet prison camp awoke an international movement for his release. His disappearance remains a mystery.

War Crimes: Crimes committed against the international laws of war that regulate the relations of belligerent nations with neutral countries, as established by the HAGUE and GENEVA CONVENTIONS. It was one of the four charges used by the INTERNATIONAL MILITARY TRIBUNAL and by other courts in later postwar trials.

War Refugee Board (WRB): U.S. agency for rescuing and assisting World War II victims. The WRB was established by President Franklin D. ROOSEVELT in January 1944, fourteen months after the U.S. had confirmed the systematic destruction of European Jewry. Under its executive director John Pehle, the WRB's major project was the refugee camp at Fort Ontario, New York. The WRB's actions were limited because many U.S. government agencies lacked the desire to act.

Warsaw Ghetto: GHETTO established in the capital of occupied Poland by the NAZIS in November 1940. The Warsaw Ghetto imprisoned almost 500,000 Jews and others at its peak. About 45,000 people died there in 1941 as a result of overcrowding, hard labor, poor sanitation, starvation, malnutrition, and disease. During 1942, most of the ghetto residents were deported to the TREBLINKA killing center. When the Germans, led by Jürgen STROOP, attempted to liquidate the ghetto completely in April 1943, a revolt broke out. After twenty-eight days of bitter fighting, most of the remaining Jewish inhabitants were captured and killed.

Warthegau (Wartheland): District in western Poland annexed by NAZI Germany on October 8, 1939. Containing the administrative districts of Posen, Hohensalza, and Lodz, this area of approximately 17,600 square miles with a population of 4.7 million was one of the first to be GERMANIZED by Nazi authorities and incorporated into the REICH. To this end, the local intelligentsia was murdered, 630,000 indigenous Poles were expelled into the GENERAL GOVERNMENT, and the region's 380,000 Jews were forced into GHETTOS (most of whom were later murdered in the KILLING CENTERS). Following the annexation, ETHNIC GERMANS were resettled in the region.

Wehrmacht: The German armed forces, including the army, navy, and air force.

Westerbork: A TRANSIT CAMP in northeast Holland, built by the Dutch Ministry of Interior in spring 1939. Westerbork initially held 750 German Jews interned by the Dutch after their arrest for illegal border crossings in 1939. From July 1942, when the Germans took command of the camp, to December 1943, more than 90 trains left Westerbork carrying 88,363 Dutch and German Jews and about 500 Dutch GYPSIES to their deaths at AUSCHWITZ, SOBIBOR, BERGEN-BELSEN, and THERESIENSTADT. Westerbork was liberated by units of the 2d Canadian Division on April 12, 1945.

Wirth, Christian (1885–1944): A member of OPERATION T4 who was in charge of setting up the BELZEC killing center. Known as "Christian the Terrible" for his brutality, he became the inspector of OPERATION REINHARD killing centers in August 1942. After the conclusion of Operation Reinhard in January 1943, he was transferred to Trieste to oversee the DEPORTATION of Jews from Italy. Wirth was killed there by PARTISANS on May 26, 1944.

Wirtschafts- und Verwaltungshauptamt (WVHA): *See* SS CENTRAL OFFICE FOR ECONOMY AND ADMINISTRATION.

WVHA *(Wirtschafts- und Verwaltungshauptamt)*: *See* SS CENTRAL OFFICE FOR ECONOMY AND ADMINISTRATION.

Yalta Conference (February 4–12, 1945): A "Big Three" conference in the Soviet Union's Crimea attended by U.S. President Franklin D. ROOSEVELT, British Prime Minister Winston CHURCHILL, and Soviet Premier Josef STALIN. The conference reaffirmed the ALLIES' policy to obtain the unconditional surrender of Germany and planned the postwar occupation of Germany by the four major Allied powers, which now included France. The leaders also discussed the postwar DENAZIFICATION of Germany and procedures for the prosecution of German war criminals. Plans for the San Francisco Conference that would establish the United Nations were made as well.

Yellow Star: *See* JEWISH BADGE.

Zentralstelle für Jüdische Auswanderung: *See* CENTRAL OFFICE FOR JEWISH EMIGRATION.

Ziereis, Franz (1905–45): Commandant of the MAUTHAUSEN concentration camp from August 1939 until its liberation in May 1945. A captain in the German Army when appointed commandant, he was promoted in 1941 to major, in 1943 to lieutenant colonel, and in 1944 to colonel. After the camp was liberated by U.S. troops, Ziereis hid in the camp but was shot and fatally wounded several days later by an American patrol when he tried to escape.

Zyklon B: Hydrogen cyanide (commonly known as prussic acid), a poison commonly used as a pesticide, Zyklon B was employed in crystalline form in the GAS CHAMBERS at the KILLING CENTERS of AUSCHWITZ, MAJDANEK, and, in smaller quantities, at MAUTHAUSEN concentration camp in 1945.

SELECTED READINGS

General

Furst, Francois, ed. *Unanswered Questions and the Genocide of the Jews*. New York: Schocken Books, 1989.

Hilberg, Raul. *The Destruction of the European Jews*. 3 vols., rev. ed. New York: Holmes and Meier, 1985.

Marrus, Michael R. *The Holocaust in History*. New York: New American Library, 1987.

Niewyk, Donald L., ed. *The Holocaust: Problems and Perspectives of Interpretation*. Lexington, MA: D.C. Heath, 1992.

Reitlinger, Gerald. *The Final Solution: The Attempt to Exterminate the Jews of Europe, 1939–1945*. 2d rev. ed. South Brunswick, NJ: Yoseloff, 1968.

Yahil, Leni. *The Holocaust: The Fate of European Jewry 1932-1945*. Oxford and New York: Oxford University Press, 1990.

Discriminatory Laws

Burleigh, Michael, and Wolfgang Wipperman. *The Racial State: Germany 1933–1945*. Cambridge and New York: Cambridge University Press, 1991.

Schleunes, Karl A. *The Twisted Road to Auschwitz*. Urbana, IL: University of Illinois Press, 1970.

Confiscation of Property

Hilberg, Raul, ed. *Documents of Destruction: Germany and Jewry 1933–1945*. London: W. H. Allen, 1972.

Nicholas, Lynn. *The Rape of Europa: The Fate of Europe's Art Treasures in the Third Reich and the Second World War*. New York: Alfred A. Knopf, 1994.

Germanization

Koehl, Robert L. *RKFDV: German Resettlement and Population Policy, 1939–1945*. Cambridge: Harvard University Press, 1957.

Lukas, Richard. *The Forgotten Holocaust: The Poles under German Occupation, 1939–1944*. Lexington: University of Kentucky Press, 1986.

Lumans, Valdis O. *Himmler's Auxiliaries: The Volksdeutsche Mittelstelle and the German National Minorities of Europe, 1933–1945*. Chapel Hill: University of North Carolina Press, 1993.

"Euthanasia"

de Mildt, Dick. *In the Name of the People: Perpetrators of Genocide in the Reflection of Their Post-war Prosecution in West Germany*. The Hague, Netherlands: Martinus Nijhoff Publishers, 1996.

Friedlander, Henry. *The Origins of Nazi Genocide: From Euthanasia to the Final Solution*. Chapel Hill: University of North Carolina Press, 1995.

Lifton, Robert Jay. *The Nazi Doctors: Medical Killing and the Psychology of Genocide*. New York: Basic Books, 1986.

Medical Experiments

Annas, George, and Michael Grodin, eds. *The Nazi Doctors and the Nuremberg Code: Human Rights in Human Experimentation*. Oxford and New York: Oxford University Press, 1992.

Mitscherlich, Alexander, and Frederick Mielke. *Doctors of Infamy: The Story of the Nazi Medical Crimes*. New York: H. Schuman, 1949.

Concentration Camps

Friedlander, Henry. "The Nazi Concentration Camp System." In *Human Responses to the Holocaust: Perpetrators and Victims, Bystanders and Resisters*, edited by Michael A. Ryan, 33–69. New York: E. Mellon Press, 1981.

Kogon, Eugen. *The Theory and Practice of Hell: The German Concentration Camps and the System behind Them*. Translated by Heinz Norden. New York: Berkeley Publishing Corp., 1984.

Krausnick, Helmut. *Anatomy of the SS State*. Translated by Richard Barry *et al*. New York: Walker, 1968.

Slave Labor

Ferencz, Benjamin. *Less than Slaves: Jewish Forced Labor and the Quest for Compensation*. Cambridge: Harvard University Press, 1979.

Homze, Edward. *Foreign Labor in Nazi Germany*. Princeton: Princeton University Press, 1967.

Mass Executions and Reprisals

Arad, Yitzak, Shmuel Krakowski, and Shmuel Spector, eds. *The Einsatzgruppen Reports*. Translated by Stella Schlossberger. New York: Holocaust Library, 1989.

Headland, Ronald. *Messages of Murder: A Study of the Reports of the Einsatzgruppen of the Security Police and the Security Service, 1941–1943*. Rutherford, NJ: Fairleigh Dickinson University Press, 1992.

Klee, Ernst, Willi Dreesen, and Völker Reiss. *The Good Old Days: The Holocaust as Seen by Its Perpetrators and Bystanders*. Translated by Deborah Burnstone. New York: Free Press, 1991.

Deportations

Arendt, Hannah. *Eichmann in Jerusalem: A Report on the Banality of Evil*. New York: Viking Press, 1964.

Marrus, Michael R., ed. *The Nazi Holocaust*, Part 4, *The "Final Solution" Outside Germany*. 2 vols. Westport, CT and London: Meckler Corporation, 1989.

Yahil, Leni. *The Holocaust: The Fate of European Jewry, 1932–1945*. Oxford: Oxford University Press, 1987.

Killing Centers

Arad, Yitzhak. *Belzec, Sobibor, Treblinka: The Operation Reinhard Death Camps*. Bloomington: University of Indiana Press, 1987.

Czech, Danuta. *Auschwitz Chronicles, 1939–1945*. New York: Henry Holt & Co., 1990.

Gutman, Yisrael, and Michael Berenbaum, eds. *Anatomy of the Auschwitz Death Camp*. Bloomington: Indiana University Press, 1994.

Sereny, Gitta. *Into That Darkness: An Examination of Conscience*. New York: Vintage Books, 1983.

Non-Jewish Victims

Berenbaum, Michael, ed. *A Mosaic of Victims: Non-Jews Persecuted and Murdered by the Nazis*. New York: New York University Press, 1990.

Grau, Günter, ed. *Hidden Holocaust? Gay and Lesbian Persecution in Germany, 1933–45*. Translated by Patrick Camiller. Chicago: Fitzroy Dearborn, 1995.

Kenrick, Donald, and Gratton Paxon. *The Destiny of Europe's Gypsies*. New York: Basic Books, 1992.

Collections of Documents

Friedlander, Henry, and Sybil Milton. *Archives of the Holocaust: An International Collection of Selected Documents*. 26 vols. New York: Garland, 1990–1995.

Mendelsohn, John. *The Holocaust*. 18 vols. Garland: New York, 1982.

Noakes, Jeremy, and Geoffrey Pridham. *Documents on Nazism, 1919–1945*. New York: Viking Press, 1975.

International Military Tribunal

Davidson, Eugene. *The Trial of the Germans*. New York: Macmillan, 1966.

International Military Tribunal. *Trial of the Major War Criminals*. 42 vols. Nuremberg: International Military Tribunal, 1947–49.

Smith, Bradley F. *Reaching Judgment at Nuremberg*. New York: Basic Books, 1977.

Taylor, Telford. *The Anatomy of the Nuremberg Trials*. New York: Alfred A. Knopf, 1992.

Tusa, Ann and John. *The Nuremberg Trial*. New York: Atheneum, 1984.

Other War Crimes Trials

Browning, Christopher. *Ordinary Men: Reserve Police Battalion 101 and the Final Solution in Poland*. New York: Harper and Row, 1992.

Ministry of Justice, State of Israel, *Trial of Adolf Eichmann*. 9 vols. Jerusalem: Ministry of Justice, 1992– .

Naumann, Bernd. *Auschwitz: A Report on the Proceedings against Robert Karl Ludwig Mulka and Others before the Court at Frankfurt*. Translated by Jean Steinberg. New York: Praeger, 1966.

Nuremberg Military Tribunals. *Trials of the War Criminals Before the Nuernberg Military Tribunals Under Control Council Law No. 10*. 15 vols. Washington, D.C.: Government Printing Office, 1949–53.

Rückerl, Adalbert. *The Investigation of Nazi Crimes, 1945–1978*. Hamden, CT: Archon Books, 1980.